中山大学
青年法律评论 第4卷

《中山大学青年法律评论》编辑部 组编
主编 巢志雄
执行主编 彭箫剑

法律出版社
LAW PRESS·CHINA

编者按

构筑学术平台，汇聚青年新声。《中山大学青年法律评论》致力于为青年法学人搭建一个学术成果的交流平台，活跃青年法学生的学术研究氛围，开阔他们的研究视野。当今青年法学生的研究成果不受重视、发表渠道少等问题凸显，青年法学生发表成果十分困难。本评论始终坚持以学术水平高低为文章是否采用的唯一标准。创立一年多以来，已顺利出版三卷。第4卷以"人工智能与法律变革"为主题，经历了约四个月时间的征稿，共收到了来自北京大学、中国人民大学、中国政法大学、中央财经大学、北京师范大学、武汉大学、南京大学、湖南大学、澳门大学、西南政法大学、华东政法大学、中南财经政法大学、西北政法大学、中山大学等三十所院校的七十余篇论文。历经三审最终挑选了十六篇优秀文章与读者们见面，其中主题文章三篇。

本卷共设五个栏目，分别是本卷特稿、人工智能主题专栏、理论探索与学说争鸣、司法实践与制度剖析、国际法治的多维图景。

第一个栏目——本卷特稿，收录了来自荷兰莱顿大学法学院博士研究生的英文研究成果"Legal Aspects of Space Debris—Whether the Current Legal Regime Can Effectively Regulate the Problem of Space Debris Mitigation"(《空间碎片法律研究——现有法律体系能否有效规制空间碎片减缓问题》)一文。该文对规制空间碎片减缓问题的国际法体系进行分析，认为有法律约束力的条约都太笼统或规定太模糊，而能具体对该问题做出规定的国际软法则没有法律约束力。文章关注了空间活动商业化和私有化给规制空间碎片减缓问题带来的挑战，选题前沿并具有重要的研究价值。

第二个栏目——人工智能主题专栏，收录了三篇文章。人工智能时代降临，关于人工智能的法律问题，在国内外已经有了许多前沿性的研究成果。想象力丰富、观察力敏锐、对新事物高度敏感的青年法律人如何在这一领域发声，值得关注。《论智能人的民事法律地位》一文认为智能人仅具有工具性，无法独立承担责任，授予其法律主体地位不合实际。在国外已有相关实践的前提下，我国应如何评价智能人的民事法律地位,值得讨论。《论人工智能产品自身损害责任》一文重点探讨了由人工智能产品缺陷带来的产品自身损害的法律责任。文章将人工智能与产品责任、侵权责任相结合,具有问题意识,且观点也较为新颖,提出的立法建议颇具有前瞻性。《人工智能致人损害的法律责任研究——从主体性角度观察》一文认为人工智能行为应当由谁来承担责任,本质上取决于人工智能系统的行为究竟是何种性质。文章主张对具备语言能力的人工智能可以令其自我解释,对其他人工智能则采用社会保险制度,同时以算法伦理规范编程行为。

第三个栏目——理论探索与学说争鸣,收录了五篇文章。《行政强制中比例原则与强制适当原则的关系之辨》一文认为在行政强制中,比例原则和强制适当原则均可用于约束行政强制实体裁量,但是,强制适当原则不能适用于约束强制程序裁量,且在实体裁量过程中其本身无法提供适当的判断标准。《语境中的法律:权力的一种叙事批判——以〈Z市C事业促进办法〉起草过程为例》一文认为法律语言作为法律规范运作的中介,往往也会成为权力关系的核心,文章对“立法语言建构”现象进行分析,揭示了权力在立法语境中是如何运作和实现的。《数字经济背景下场所型常设机构规则的适用性研究》一文在现行常设机构认定规则方面指出,我国应引进显著经济存在的判断标准,并在豁免条款中新增准备性或辅助性测试。《虚构未来事实的诈骗行为证成——基于刑法论证的研究视角》一文在以罪刑法定主义为根本遵循的刑法解释的基础上展开刑法论证,指引“虚构未来事实”之诈骗的理论纷争走出相关误区。《驰名商标权利边界初探》一文认为驰名商标的特殊保护制度——跨类保护制度,在适用过程中容易出现驰名商标权利边界被不当扩大的问题,并就此展开探讨。这些文章以理论引领实践,兼具思想性、知识性和可读性。

第四个栏目——司法实践与制度剖析,收录了五篇文章。《“执行难”的概念变迁——以我国三十年执行政策为视角》一文梳理了我国在不同时期对“执行难”概念的不同理解,尝试探寻“执行难”作为一个司法概念的变迁过程。《股东签名被伪造形成的股东会决议效力问题探究》一文认为伪造股东签名形成的股东会决议剥夺了相关股东参与公司决策的权利,同时也违背了公司决议形成的正当程序原则,应当保障好股东意思表示的自由与公司决议的真实性和正当性。《化学专利案件中补交实验数据的审查标准》一文认为化学专利案件中的补交实验数据问题不必借鉴美欧的宽松标准,公开充分和创造性问题应适用同一审查标准,重点审查该技术贡献是否在申请日前做出,并已被充分公开。《论"离婚协议房屋产权归属约定"之排除强制执行》一文指出在被强制执行房屋的登记所有权人已通过离婚协议约定将房屋所有权转让给原配偶的案外人异议之诉中,原配偶基于离婚协议而对房屋享有的权利是否为"足以排除强制执行之实体权益",现行法尚未明晰,并就此展开讨论。《病假旅行严重违反规章制度的判定》一文认为劳动者自由行使病休权的行为不应受到限制,但单位有权依据内容明确合理的规章行使病假管理权,在此基础上探讨了劳动者自主安排病休期间用于旅行的问题。这些文章从不同角度窥视了我国制度建设与司法实践,兼具理论深度与实务价值。

第五个栏目——国际法治的多维图景,收录了两篇文章。《美国"航行自由计划"的国际法分析与思考》一文就美国日趋频繁且不断演进的"航行自由行动"的问题,提出了中国应采取的更为有效的应对之策。《确认仲裁裁决的外国判决的承认与执行法律问题分析》一文结合《纽约公约》下仲裁裁决承认与执行制度和各国判决承认与执行制度,对确认仲裁裁决的外国判决的承认与执行涉及的问题进行了研究,并提出了破解之道。

《中山大学青年法律评论》定位于为青年学子们搭建的表达思想、交流学问、展现观察与思考结果的平台。创立至今,尽管路途艰辛,但值得欣慰的是经过大家的共同努力,本连续出版物茁壮成长。在编辑部运行机制方面,已经建立起一套相对完善、规范、流程顺畅的工作制度,在稿源建设方面,已经形成了一套相对高质、多元、专业性强的结构体系。在第 4 卷即将出版之时,正值辞旧迎新之际,编辑部衷心感谢作者们的支持以及老师们的鼓励,同时也期待读者们的认可。期望青年学子们能继往开来,掌舵远航,在青春维度中:

坚守本心,勤学好思,未来可期!

执行主编　彭箫剑

2019 年 1 月 1 日

目　录

【司法实践与制度剖析】

【国际法治的多维图景】

本卷特稿

Legal Aspects of Space Debris

—Whether the Current Legal Regime Can Effectively Regulate the Problem of Space Debris Mitigation*

田　庄**

Abstract:

The problem of space debris is becoming increasingly urgent. The legal regime relevant to space debris consists mainly of the five United Nations treaties on outer space, international environmental law, space debris mitigation guidelines, and national space law. The main purpose of this article is to examine if this regime can effectively regulate the issue of space debris mitigation. Its conclusion is that the current international space law cannot provide an effective solution in this regard; national space law may serve as a short-term expediency, but it faces challenges from space commercialization and privatization.

Key words:

Space Debris Mitigation; Outer Space Treaty; Space Law; Space Commercialization and Privatization

Introduction

Since the dawn of space age, the number of artificial objects in Earth orbit has been increasing. Along with the benefits derived from space application, such as

---

* 中译名《空间碎片法律研究——现有法律体系能否有效规制空间碎片减缓问题》。本论文得到国家留学基金资助。

** 田庄，荷兰莱顿大学法学院2018级博士研究生。

navigation, communication, and Earth observation, the burgeoning of space activities brings about a side effect—numerous pieces of space debris orbiting the Earth, which pose threat to space objects as well as to people and property on the ground.

The Inter-Agency Space Debris Coordination Committee (IADC) Space Debris Mitigation Guidelines (IADC Guidelines) defines "Space debris" as all man-made objects including fragments and elements thereof, in Earth orbit or re-entering the atmosphere, that are non-functional.[1] The same definition is adopted by the United Nations (UN) Committee on the Peaceful Uses of Outer Space (COPUOS) Space Debris Mitigation Guidelines (UN Guidelines).[2] Though these guidelines are not legally binding, such definition reveals a general understanding of the international community, Therefore, this article follows the same definition.

The research question of this article is whether the current legal regime can effectively regulate the problem of space debris mitigation. The article consists of four chapters. The first chapter discusses the international legal regime regulating space debris. Only preventive rules, i. e., rules directly relevant to debris mitigation, will be discussed in this article. Repressive rules, i. e., rules which do not offer a direct contribution to the avoidance of the creation of space debris, but indirectly via compensation of damage,[3] are beyond its scope. The discussion begins with the The outer space treaties (OST), the Magna Carta of space law, which is followed by the analysis of international environmental law, international guidelines, and international customary law. This chapter concludes that international law does not require states not to create or to clean up space debris, while states have the discretion to establish their own rules and standards.

The second chapter presents national legislation on space debris mitigation, taking the cases of two advanced space-faring nations—the U. S. and China as examples. Then, a comparison will be made to examine the harmonization and

[1] The IADC Guidelines Article 3. 1.

[2] The UN Guidelines Article 1.

[3] Marcus Schladebach, "Space Debris as a Legal Challenge", *Max Planck Yearbook of United Nations Law* 17, 2013, p. 71.

inconsistency between the laws of these two nations.

The third chapter discusses the impact of space commercialization and privatization on the current legal regime. The discussion is made from two perspectives: governments and private entities. With particular discussion about whether specific arrangements should be made for on small satellites, as they are considered space objects as larger ones, but most of them are non-maneuverable and thus more prone to the creation of debris.[4]

Ultimately, the fourth chapter concludes this article.

1. Space Debris Mitigation under International Law

The OST lay the foundations for the orderly conduct of space activities, and contain certain provisions that are relevant to space debris, even though such term is not used.[5] However, the treaties do not contain sufficiently clear terminology and obligations for the protection of space environment, which are increasingly necessary as the problem of space debris becomes more pressing with the increase of space activities and space actors.[6]

Article I of the OST stipulates the "province of all mankind" principle in the "exploration and use of outer space".[7] Though one may argue that pollution of outer space with space debris violates this principle, it is questionable whether such principle can create legal obligations at all.[8] It is the opinion of Schladebach that this principle should be understood as a criterion of balancing and interpretation,

---

[4] Dimitrios Stratigentas, *Small Satellites: Regulatory Requirements and Challenges* (master's thesis, Leiden University, 2015), p. 8.

[5] Tanja Masson-Zwaan, "Legal Aspects of Space Debris", *Space Debris Situation Report* 2016, published in June 2017, pp. 145 – 146.

[6] *Id.* p. 146.

[7] The OST Article I, para. 1.

[8] Schladebach, *supra* note 3, p. 69.

and thus Article I of OST has no immediate legal relevance concerning space debris.[9]

Under Article Ⅳ of the OST, state parties shall bear international responsibility for national activities in outer space. An important question arises as for whether states might be held responsible under the OST for creating space debris and for not cleaning space debris.[10] The answer to this question determines whether states have the international obligation to conduct debris mitigation maneuver. The following discussion will attempt to answer this question by analyzing two articles of the OST: Article Ⅸ and Article Ⅲ.

1.1 Article Ⅸ and Space Environmental Protection

Article Ⅸ is the *sedes materiae* in the OST on space environment protection. The first two sentences of Article Ⅸ read,

"In the exploration and use of outer space, including the Moon and other celestial bodies, States Parties to the Treaty shall be guided by the principle of cooperation and mutual assistance and shall conduct all their activities in outer space, including the Moon and other celestial bodies, with due regard to the corresponding interests of all other States Parties to the Treaty. States Parties to the Treaty shall pursue studies of outer space, including the Moon and other celestial bodies, and conduct exploration of them so as to avoid their harmful contamination and also adverse changes in the environment of the Earth resulting from the introduction of extraterrestrial matter and, where necessary, shall adopt appropriate measures for this purpose."

According to Kolossov, the above provisions are so formulated that they do not impose upon states an obligation to act exclusively so that to avert any possibility of contamination of outer space.[11] States must only take measures to prevent such

---

[9] *Id.*

[10] Masson-Zwaan, *supra* note 5, p. 141.

[11] Y. M. Kolossov, "Legal Aspects of Outer Space Environmental Protection", *Proceedings of the twenty-third Colloquium on the Law of Outer Space*, 1980, p. 103.

contamination, and this obligation has not been formulated in the imperative form.[12] A similar view is shared by Baker, that no activity is barred, only avoided, thereby allowing for harmful contamination by default.[13] Although avoidance may be the intent but need not be the result.[14]

Additionally, the wording of this provision is vague and general. It is unclear why the second sentence of the provision specifically addresses "studies and exploration" rather than the broader term "exploration and use" as commonly used throughout the OST.[15] Moreover, this provision leaves many main terms—such as "harmful contamination" and "adverse change"—undefined and leaving the nature and extent of the "appropriate measures" to be determined by the states parties at *their discretion*.[16]

Diverging interpretations has thus emerged over the term "harmful contamination" as to whether and how this term can be used for the protection of the outer space environment.[17] According to Baker, it was never intended that the protection offered by sentence two would apply to the environments of outer space per se, as this listing was only to avoid interference of one activity with another.[18] In contrast, M. Miklody believed that the second sentence of Article IX was intended to protect the

---

〔12〕 *Id.*

〔13〕 Howard A. Baker, "The Sci-Lab Perception: Its Impact on Protection of the Outer Space Environment", *Proceedings of the thirtieth Colloquium on the Law of Outer Space*, 1987, p. 127.

〔14〕 *Id.*

〔15〕 Ulrike M. Bohlmann, "Connecting the Principles of International Environmental Law to Space Activities", *Proceedings of the International Institute of Space Law* (IISL), 2011, p. 301.

〔16〕 *Id.*

〔17〕 Lawrence D. Roberts, "Addressing the Problem of Orbital Space Debris: Combining International Regulatory and Liability Regimes", *Boston College International and Comparative Law Review* 15(1), 1992, p. 61.

〔18〕 Baker, *supra* note 13.

sanctity of the space environment itself irrespective of any human activity therein.[19] Kolossov focus on the intention of the operator that illegitimacy may be determined on the basis of hindrances created intentionally for legitimate outer space activities.[20] Hence, leaving in orbits non-operative, "dead" objects and parts thereof should not be regarded as contamination of outer space.[21] A more literal interpretation is adopted by Wheeler who stated that space debris was not normally classed as "harmful contamination" which is usually construed as biological or radioactive contamination.[22] It remains unclear whether outer space environment itself is referred to in this provision and whether space debris is covered under the term "harmful contamination".

An even more Ptolemaic approach is adopted in the third and fourth sentences of Article Ⅸ, which concern harmful interference of one state party with another. According to Roberts, the primary objective of these two sentences is to maximize exploitation of the space environment.[23] Their *only* restriction is the requirement of consultations in the event a suspect activity would cause potentially harmful interference with other space exploration endeavors.[24] These provisions do not, however, restrict the activities themselves or emphasize environmental protection.[25]

---

〔19〕 Roberts, supra note 17, p. 61, which summarized the opinion of M. Miklody. *See also* M. Miklody, "Some Remarks to the Legal Status of Celestial Bodies and Protection of Environment", *Proceedings of the twenty fifth Colloquium on the Law of Outer Space*, 1982, p. 13. The opinion of Miklody is also that "[T]he answer to this question should be given by science and technics. Lawyers are not competent to state the content of these notions. They can give only an abstract interpretation out of the term itself."

〔20〕 Kolossov, *supra* note 11.

〔21〕 *Id.*

〔22〕 Joanne Wheeler, "Space debris: The legal issues", https://www.aerosociety.com/news/space-debris-the-legal-issues/, January 3, 2014.

〔23〕 Roberts, *supra* note 17, p. 60.

〔24〕 *Id.*

〔25〕 *Id.*

Bohlmann shares similar view that the environmental integrity of outer space as such is not at the heart of this provision.[26]

In addition to the legal and literal debates, a problem is that it is impossible to operate in space without creating some amount of debris.[27] It then becomes a matter of degree as how much debris is too much, which must be a case-by-case evaluation.[28] Given that outer space "shall be free for exploration and use by all States,"[29] the situation becomes more complicated as every state may assert that its national interests justify the creation of debris and thus it is acting in accordance with international law.[30]

In sum, Article Ⅸ at best encourages states to limit the generation of new orbital debris in a non-specified manner, but there is little chance a state would ever be held internationally responsible for a violation of Article Ⅸ based upon creating ordinary *orbital debris*.[31] Hence, Article Ⅸ of OST cannot sufficiently and effectively regulate the problem of space debris.

1.2 Article Ⅲ and International Environment Law

Some scholars argue that there is a lacuna in the OST with regard to space environmental protection. As commented by Olga S. Stelmakh, currently under existing space law a one-sided relationship is established—states are given the right of a free access to space but no obligation to take their objects back, as a result, it raises an emerging concern over the absence of a legally binding obligation imposed on operators to dispose of space objects in a safe manner.[32]

---

[26] Bohlmann, *supra* note 15, p. 302.

[27] Michael W. Taylor, *Orbital Debris: Technical and Legal Issues and Solutions* (master's thesis, McGill University, 2006), p. 41.

[28] *Id.*

[29] The OST Article Ⅰ, para 2.

[30] Taylor, *supra* note 27, p. 41.

[31] *Id.* pp. 41-42.

[32] Olga S. Stelmakh, "Space Debris-Emerging Challenge, Common Concern and Shared Responsibility: Legal Considerations and Directions towards a Secure and Sustainable Space Environment", *Proceedings of IISL*, 2013, p. 354.

A similar concern is shared by Roberts, that the OST were intended primarily to facilitate access to and use of the space environment, although they also included elements of environmental regulation.[33] These treaties typically raised environmental concerns only in the context of efficient use of space resources or research opportunities and they did not attempt to provide broader protection of the space environment.[34] These factors, as well as the complexities of the space environment, make it difficult for the OST to provide a solution to the continuing degradation of the space environment.[35]

To properly address this intricate problem, a potential solution may be to look beyond the OST,[36] which provides that the use and exploration of outer space shall be conducted in accordance with International Law.[37] In this sense, international environmental law may be referred to, as the generation of space debris may be regarded as a cross-border environmental damage. However, according to Bittencourt Neto, although environmental law agreements, such as the Stockholm Declaration[38], are morally influential, due to the lack of treaty stature, they have little effect on the actions of space-faring nations. Consequently, these nations continue their defiant practices.[39]

Hence, the question would be whether the principles as enshrined in international environmental law have emerged into customary international law. And, if the answer is affirmative, whether these principles can extend their scope of application to space debris mitigation. The first question is still under debate. Concerning the second question, Taylor argues that outer space is an environment

[33] Roberts, *supra* note 17, at 52.

[34] *Id.*

[35] *Id.*

[36] Olavo de O. Bittencourt Neto, "Preserving the Outer Space Environment: The 'Precautionary Principle' Approach to Space Debris", *Proceedings of IISL*, 2013, p. 346.

[37] The OST Article Ⅲ.

[38] UN Doc A/CONF. 48/14/Rev. 1, 1973, the 1972 Declaration at United Nations Conference on the Human Environment.

[39] *Id.*

subjected to a special legal regime, therefore it is only with caution that one should introduce concepts and analogies from general international law into the law applicable to the use and exploration of outer space.[40] As there is not yet a fixed answer to these questions, the applicability of general international law to outer space—in the context of space debris referring mostly to international environmental law—remains unclear.

1.3 Space Debris Mitigation Guidelines

The current regulation of space debris at the international level is non-comprehensive and is mostly voluntary.[41] The international space law treaties constitute a general framework for space activities, whereas specific regulation of space debris is found only in the non-binding documents.[42] Among these documents, the IADC Guidelines and UN Guidelines are of particular relevance, as they were designed specifically for the mitigation of space debris. The IADC Guidelines is a set of debris mitigation guidelines developed by the IADC and was adopted in October 2002.[43] These Guidelines were used as a foundation for the development of the UN Guidelines.[44]

The UN Guidelines are the result of more than a decade of work undertaken by the COPUOS and its Scientific and Technical Subcommittee, which were adopted by the Subcommittee at its 44th session in 2007, endorsed by the COPUOS at its 50th session in 2007, and endorsed by the UN General Assembly in its Resolution 62/217 of 22 December 2007.[45] The UN Guidelines retained the same essential elements,

---

〔40〕 Taylor, *supra* note 27, pp. 49 - 50.

〔41〕 Stelmakh, *supra* note 32, p. 355.

〔42〕 *Id.*

〔43〕 IADC Space Debris Mitigation Guidelines, "Compendium of space debris mitigation standards adopted by States and international organizations" (Hereinafter referred to as the UNOOSA Compendium), http://www.unoosa.org/oosa/en/ourwork/topics/space-debris/compendium.html.

〔44〕 *Id.*

〔45〕 COPUOS Space Debris Mitigation Guidelines-UNOOSA Compendium.

although it dropped the more technical points in the IADC Guidelines.[46] These guidelines are not legally binding, and they might become binding either through evolution into customary international law, or through incorporation into national law.[47]

It should be noted that the UNCOPUOS Long-Term Sustainability of Outer Space Activities (LTS) Working Group (WG), established in 2010, reached consensus on a first set of 12 LTS guidelines in 2016.[48] In 2018, the consensus was reached on a preamble and 9 additional guidelines.[49] The problem of space debris is specifically referred to in these guidelines and further recommendations are given. However, like the IADC and UN Guidelines, these LTS Guidelines are of a voluntary best-practice nature, and its acceptance and implementation by states remain to be seen.

1.4 Customary International Law

International custom is referred to in the Statute of the International Court of Justice (ICJ) as "evidence of a general practice accepted as law".[50] Accordingly, custom consists of two elements: general practice, or *usus*, and the conviction that such practice reflects, or amounts to, law (*opinio juris*).[51]

The character of state practice has been indicated by the ICJ that, "state practice, including that of States whose interests are specially affected, should have

---

〔46〕 James A. Vedda, "*Orbital Debris Remediation through International Engagement*", https://aerospace.org/sites/default/files/2018-05/DebrisRemediation.pdf, March 2017.

〔47〕 Masson-Zwaan, *supra* note 5, p. 144.

〔48〕 NASA, "Orbital Debris Quarterly New", Volume 20(4), October 2016. *See also* UN Doc. A/AC.105/L.308, Guidelines for the long-term sustainability of outer space activities (February 15, 2017).

〔49〕 See http://www.unoosa.org/oosa/en/ourwork/topics/long-term-sustainability-of-outer-space-activities.html.

〔50〕 Statute of the ICJ, 3 Bevans 1179; 59 Stat. 1031; T.S. 993; 39 AJIL Supp. 215 (1945), Article 38(1).

〔51〕 Fabio Tronchetti, "The Non-Appropriation Principle as a Structural Norm of International Law: A New Way of Interpreting Article Ⅱ of the Outer Space Treaty", *Air and Space Law* 33(3), 2008, p. 292.

been both extensive and virtually uniform in the sense of the provision invoked; and should moreover have occurred in such a way as to show a general recognition that a rule of law or legal obligation is involved."[52] For such practice to be considered *opinio juris*, "not only must the acts concerned amount to a settled practice, but they must also be such, or be carried out in such a way, as to be evidence of a belief that this practice is rendered obligatory by the existence of a rule of law requiring it."[53]

Furthermore, The ICJ stated that "the Court does not consider that, for a rule to be established as customary, the corresponding practice must be in absolutely rigorous conformity with the rule. In order to deduce the existence of customary rules, the Court deems it sufficient that the conduct of States should, in general, be consistent with such rules, and that instances of State conduct inconsistent with a given rule should generally have been treated as breaches of that rule, not as indications of the recognition of a new rule."[54]

Accordingly, for a duty of space debris mitigation to become customary international law, it is not necessary that all states conduct space debris mitigation measures, but that the non-compliance of some states is considered by others as a violation of obligation. The latter is not easy to occur, as states follow the IADC or UN Guidelines voluntarily, and they do not feel legally bound to do so.[55] Besides, the Guidelines themselves state that their principles are not binding international law.[56]

---

[52] North Sea Continental Shelf, Judgment, I. C. J. Reports 1969, para. 74.

[53] *Id.* para. 77.

[54] Military and Paramilitary Activities in and against Nicaragua (Nicaragua v. the United States of America). Merits, Judgment. I. C. J. Reports 1986, para. 186.

[55] Antonia Nedelkopoulou, *Space Debris-Legal Aspects: a Space Traffic Control and Insurance Perspective* (master's thesis, Leiden University, 2006), p. 25.

[56] *Id.* The IADC Guidelines Article 2, "Organizations are encouraged to use these Guidelines in identifying the standards that they will apply when establishing the mission requirements for planned spacecraft and orbital stages." The UN Guidelines Article 3, "[...] They are not legally binding under international law."

There is not yet confirmatory evidence that states regard space debris mitigation practices as law. There are two potential paths for future development. The first one is through the evolution of international customary law. This can be either the evolution of environmental law principles into customary international law, and expand their scope of application to outer space, or the evolution of space debris mitigation practices *per se* into customary international law.

The second approach is to establish an international treaty, which stipulates the rights and duties of states on space debris. Admittedly, the prospects of this approach are not so optimistic, as the last UN space treaty dating back to 1979 has only 17 States Parties.[57] Nevertheless, a new treaty would be the idealist solution in the long run,[58] since space debris mitigation requires complex and diverse maneuvers, and a treaty is the most efficient way to elaborate specific requirements.

1.5 Chapter Conclusion

The OST do not hold states liable for creating space debris and for not cleaning up space debris. This can be explained by the fact that space debris was not a major environmental concern in the early stage of space exploration and use.[59] International environmental law may shed light on this issue, but its extension of applicability to outer space remains to be tested. International guidelines on debris mitigation are of most direct relevance, but due to their voluntary nature, their importance and applicability are limited. From the perspective of international customary law, there is no confirmatory evidence that the current practices of space debris mitigation have been accepted as law. Hence, the IADC and UN Guidelines are still non-legally binding. In sum, at the international law level there is no legally binding provision specific to space debris mitigation. Considering the seriousness of this problem, the current international legal regime is insufficient. As a result, states have the discretion to establish their own space debris mitigation rules and standards.

---

[57] Masson-Zwaan, *supra* note 5, p. 143.

[58] *Id.*

[59] Jinyuan Su, "Active Debris Removal: Potential Legal Barriers and Possible Ways Forward", *Journal of East Asia and International Law* 9(2), 2016, p. 404.

How national legislation deals with the problem of space debris will be discussed in the next chapter.

2. Space Debris Mitigation under National Law

The increasing number of space activities and the involvement of more countries and private actors into space activities aggravate the current situation of space debris. How the issue of space debris is addressed in different national legislation is the main focus of this chapter. Being among the most advanced space-faring nations, the cases of the U. S. and China are used as examples for discussion and comparison.

2.1 Law of the U. S. on Space Debris Mitigation

Possessing the most advanced space technology, the U. S. is the most capable nation to reap economic, political and social benefits from space and the most technologically enabled state to carry out debris mitigation maneuvers. The U. S. thus plays a leading role in space debris mitigation.

The U. S. has divided the authority of implementation and regulation of space activities into several governmental agencies: the Federal Communications Commission (FCC), the Federal Aviation Administration (FAA) under the Department of Transportation (DOT), the National Oceanic and Atmospheric Administration (NOAA) under the Department of Commerce (DOC), the National Aeronautics and Space Administration (NASA), and the Department of Defense (DOD). In line with such division, the authority to regulate space debris is accordingly divided. As DOD is in charge of military space activities, its regulatory role is beyond the scope of the discussion while those of other national agencies are presented below.

2.1.1 Debris Mitigation under FCC

The FCC is an agency responsible for licensing radio transmissions by private entities, including transmissions by satellites.[60] In June of 2004, FCC adopted a

[60] K. Kensinger et al., "The United States Federal Communications Commission's Regulations Concerning Mitigation of Orbital Debris", *Proceedings of the* 4th *European Conference on Space Debris* (ESA SP-587), p. 571.

comprehensive set of regulations concerning mitigation of orbital debris, which applies to the licensing of commercial U. S. satellites and to the use of non-U. S. satellites to provide service in the U. S.[61] The rules require notification, prior to authorization, of a description of the design and operational strategies that the space station will use to mitigate orbital debris.[62] The information will be examined by the FCC to determine whether "the public interest, convenience, and necessity will be served by the granting of such application", as a condition for granting licenses.[63] The FCC regulations also require that geostationary satellites be relocated at end-of-mission in accordance with the IADC guideline, and all satellites must discharge stored energy sources at end-of-mission.[64]

The FCC rules incorporate the latest recommendations of the IADC as well as the International Telecommunication Union (ITU) and thus provide a comprehensive framework for review and regulation of the debris mitigation practices of commercial spacecraft operations.[65]

2.1.2 Debris Mitigation under NOAA

The NOAA engages in remote sensing, gathers data, conducts research, and make predictions about the Earth's environment. On 18 December 2010, Title 51 of the United States Code (U. S. C.) entitled *National and Commercial Space Programs* was promulgated and is a compilation of the general laws governing space programs.[66]

Subtitle Ⅵ of the National and Commercial Space Programs titled *Earth*

〔61〕 *Id.*

〔62〕 47 CFR § 5.64(b), § 25.114(c)(14), § 97.207(g)(1).

〔63〕 47 U. S. C. § 309 – Application for license. See also "The United States of America-UNOOSA Compendium".

〔64〕 47 CFR § 25.283 End-of-life disposal. See also "The United States of America-UNOOSA Compendium".

〔65〕 *Id.* p. 575.

〔66〕 Rupert W. Anderson, "The Cosmic Compendium: Space Law", *Lulu. com*, 2015, p. 94.

Observations applies to all U. S. operators of commercial remote sensing satellites. According to the Earth Observations, a license is a prerequisite for the operation of private remote sensing spacecraft.[67] To obtain such a license, one condition is that the licensee shall, upon termination of its operations, make disposal of the satellites in space in a manner satisfactory to the President.[68]

The NOAA issues regulations establishing the agency's requirements for the compliance of operators of private Earth remote sensing space systems with the Earth Observations.[69] Under these requirements, space debris is defined as all human-generated debris in Earth orbit, which includes, but is not limited to, payloads that can no longer perform their mission, rocket bodies and other hardware left in orbit as a result of normal launch and operational activities, and fragmentation debris produced by failure or collision.[70]

The licensing requirement on post-mission-disposal (PMD) is interpreted by the NOAA that a licensee shall assess and minimize the amount of orbital debris released during the PMD phase, and applicants are required to provide at the time of application a plan for PMD of remote sensing satellites.[71] NOAA reviews such plan on a case-by-case basis, to assess whether it provides an acceptable PMD method to mitigate debris and minimize any potential adverse effects.[72]

2. 1. 3 Debris Mitigation under DOT

The FAA under the DOT is responsible for issuing licenses to persons launching a launch vehicle from U. S. launch sites, reentering a reentry vehicle to U. S. sites, or operate a launch or reentry site within the U. S.[73] The FAA issues licenses after

〔67〕 51 U. S. C. § 60122 (2012).

〔68〕 *Id.*

〔69〕 *Id.*

〔70〕 NOAA. 15 CFR Part 960 Licensing of Private Land Remote-Sensing Space Systems; Final Rule.

〔71〕 *Id.*

〔72〕 *Id.*

〔73〕 14 CFR § 413. 3(b).

a rigorous evaluation of the safety of the launch system by the FAA, and revokes the license or imposes a fine if at any time the license holder does not comply with the conditions of the license and the FAA orbital debris mitigation regulations.[74]

The current FAA orbital debris mitigation regulations focus on the safety at the end of launch.[75] In 14 Code of Federal Regulations (CFR) § 415.39, the FAA requires expendable launch vehicle (ELV) launch license applicants to demonstrate that: (1) there will be no unplanned contact between the vehicle, its components, and payload after payload separation; (2) no debris will be generated from the conversion of chemical, pressure, and kinetic energy sources into energy that fragments the vehicle or its components; and (3) stored energy must be removed by depleting residual fuel and leaving all fuel line valves open, venting any pressurized system, leaving all batteries in permanent discharge state, and removing any remaining source of stored energy.[76]

While § 415.39 applies to ELVs, 14 CFR § 431.43 specifies that the first two of the above stipulations apply to reusable launch and re-entry vehicles, and also requires a reusable vehicle operator to perform a collision avoidance analysis to ensure a 200 – kilometer separation between the vehicle and an inhabitable orbiting object during launch and re-entry.[77] In sum, FAA requires the limitation of space debris released during launch, the use of safe energy, and the minimization of potential for post-mission break-ups resulting from stored energy. However, FAA does not require the de-orbiting or re-orbiting of upper stages.

2.1.4 Debris Mitigation under NASA

NASA has developed a framework of requirements for limiting debris creation by NASA-related payloads, instruments, launch vehicles, and mission-related debris.[78]

---

〔74〕 The United State of America-UNOOSA Compendium.

〔75〕 *Id.*

〔76〕 FAA, "Launch Activity and Orbital Debris Mitigation", *Second Quarter* 2002 *Quarterly Launch Report*, p. 11.

〔77〕 *Id.*

〔78〕 NASA, "Orbital Debris Quarterly News", Volume 21(2), May 2017, p. 1.

An update to the NASA Procedural Requirements for Limiting Orbital Debris and Evaluating the Meteoroid and Orbital Debris Environment, NPR 8715. 6B, became official on 15 February 2017.[79]

The purpose of this NPR is to define the roles, responsibilities, and requirements to ensure NASA, including its mission partners, providers, and contractors, take steps to preserve the near-Earth space environment and to mitigate the risk to space missions and human life due to orbital debris and meteoroids.[80] Two changes in its update should be noted. First, concerning applicability, "this NPR is applicable to programs and projects responsible for NASA or NASA-sponsored objects launched into space to the extent that Federal authority to oversee the mitigation of orbital debris for those missions or portions thereof does not reside with another Federal department or agency."[81] In other words, its applicability is limited to missions that do not fall under the regulatory authority of other U. S. federal agencies.[82] Second, this new NPR establishes a process to notify the Secretary of State for any non-compliance with the U. S. Government Orbital Debris Mitigation Standard Practices.[83]

2. 1. 5 Section Conclusion

The licensing procedures are the main tool used by the U. S. to regulate and supervise space debris generated from commercial space activities. Several agencies are involved in this regulation, and each of them has established respectively their licensing requirements to regulate space activities, with space debris mitigation being one of these requirements.

2. 2 Law of China on Space Debris Mitigation

The agency responsible for the governance of space activities in China is the State Administration for Science, Technology and Industry for National Defense (SASTIND), with the China National Space Agency (CNSA) being its subordinate

[79] *Id.*

[80] *Id.*

[81] NPR 8715. 6B Article 2(b).

[82] NASA, *supra* note 78.

[83] *Id.*

agency.

The main role of SASTIND is to act as the administrative and regulatory hub for the general aspect of China's defense and aerospace industry, in particular development, procurement, and supply.[84] Under its governance, CNSA is responsible for the management of space activities for civilian use and international space cooperation with other countries.[85]

Unlike most of the space-faring nations, there is no comprehensive space law in China,[86] but rather several regulations on the registration and licensing of space objects.[87] However, China is on its way to establish a national mechanism governing debris mitigation through the nomination of government supervisory authority, the involvement of academia and industry and the development of new legislative norms, instructions, standards, and frameworks.[88]

2.2.1 The Registration Decree

The *Measures for the Administration of Registration of Objects Launched into Outer Space* (hereinafter "Registration Decree") were promulgated by the COSTIND and the Ministry of Foreign Affairs on 8th February 2001. The Decree does not directly regulate the mitigation of space debris. However, it facilitates the identification of space objects including space debris, as it requires the registrant of space object to amend the information of the registration when major changes of the status of the space object registered in accordance with the Registration Decree occurs.[89]

Such requirement is in line with Recommendation 2 (b) (i) of the UN

---

〔84〕 *Id.*

〔85〕 See http://www.cnsa.gov.cn/n6443408/n6465645/n6465650/c6768437/content.html.

〔86〕 *Id.*

〔87〕 *Id.*

〔88〕 Xiaodan Wu, "China and Space Environment Protection: An Evaluation from an International Legal Perspective", *Proceedings of IISL*, 2013, p. 430.

〔89〕 The Registration Decree Article 9.

Resolution 62/101, which states that consideration should be given to the furnishing of additional appropriate information to the UN Secretary-General concerning any change of status in operations, *inter alia*, when a space object is no longer functional.[90] With the provision of information, the collision warning and collision avoidance maneuvers can be more accurately undertaken.

2.2.2 The Launch Decree

On 21 November 2002, COSTIND and the Ministry of National Defense promulgated a Decree No. 12 titled the *Interim Measures on the Administration of Permits for Civil Space Launch Projects* (hereinafter 'the Launch Decree').

Under the Launch Decree, COSTIND shall apply uniform planning and administration to civil space launch projects, and be responsible for examining, approving and supervising civil space launch projects.[91] Article 6 enumerates the documents the applicant shall submit for the launch project, including a safety report relating to the avoidance of pollution and space debris and other safety issues.[92] It is the first time that space debris is mentioned in China's space legislation. The article requires that COSTIND shall, within thirty days as of receipt of the application documents, examine the project under application, and issue a license where the requirements are met.[93]

2.2.3 The Mitigation Decree

The *Interim Measures on Administration of Mitigation of and Protection against Space Debris* (hereinafter 'Mitigation Decree') were put into practice by SASTIND on 1st January 2010 to fulfill China's international obligations and establish coordination, emergency management and surveillance mechanisms.[94]

---

[90] Resolution 62/101 of 17 December 2007, Recommendations on enhancing the practice of States and international intergovernmental organizations in registering space objects.

[91] *Id.* Article 4.

[92] *Id.* Article 6(4).

[93] *Id.* Article 7.

[94] Melissa K. Force, "*China as a Responsible International Actor in Space.*", http://acuriousguy.blogspot.nl/2013/10/china-as-responsible-international.html, October 15, 2013.

According to Wu, the Mitigation Decree, whose purpose is to effectively control the generation of space debris and prevent the damage caused thereby, conforms to the requirements of the international guidelines, and can be viewed as China's commitment to the international community as a responsible space-faring nation.〔95〕 Moreover, the Mitigation Decree is a bridge between legislation and technical standards.〔96〕

The problem is that the Mitigation Decree has not been published (other than in a generalized summary to the UN) and, as a purely governmental document, it is not legally binding.〔97〕 Hence, a transparent and legally-binding legislation on space debris should be enacted.〔98〕

2.2.4 The Civil Satellite Decree

The First Department of SASTIND promulgated a Decree No. 986 titled the *Interim Measures for the Administration of Civil Satellite Project*〔99〕 on 29 November 2016. The Civil Satellite Decree applies to satellite projects which are wholly or partly funded by the Central Treasury and are approved by the State Council or relevant departments of the State.〔100〕 Meanwhile, this decree shall be in principle used as the reference for commercial satellites and international cooperation satellite projects.〔101〕 Therefore, the Decree will be taken into account when the SASTIND authorizes and supervises commercial satellite projects.

---

〔95〕 Wu, *supra* note 88, p. 431.

〔96〕 Guodong Feng, "Study on International Legal System on Reduction and Control of Space Debris." *Journal of Beijing University of Aeronautics and Astronautics* (*Social Sciences Edition*) 27, 2014, p. 31.

〔97〕 Force, *supra* note 94.

〔98〕 Shouping Li, "The Establishment of National Mechanism on Space Debris Mitigation", *Journal of Beijing University of Aeronautics and Astronautics* (*Social Sciences Edition*) 21, 2008, p. 38.

〔99〕 Hereinafter referred to as the Civil Satellite Decree.

〔100〕 The Civil Satellite Decree Article 2.

〔101〕 *Id.* Article 42.

The Civil Satellite Decree prescribes that the SASTIND shall regulate and supervise the shielding and debris mitigation of civil spacecraft and launch vehicles, and shall organize the establishment of relevant administrative measures and standards.[102] It also prescribes the responsibility of the operator on debris mitigation during the design, manufacture, launch and in-orbit operation phases of satellites.[103]

2.2.5 Section Conclusion

China does not have a comprehensive law on outer space, but merely a few laws promulgated by the SASTIND (the former COSTIND) or its department. All of them are administrative rules on the ministerial level, with a relatively low hierarchy in the Chinese legal system. To more effectively cope with the problem of space debris and in a broader sense regulate national space activities, a comprehensive national space law should be enacted. The ultimate goal should be to establish a systematic and multi-leveled space law regime.[104]

2.3 Comparison of the National Space Law between the U.S. and China

The most distinctive common feature of national space legislation of the U.S. and China is that they both regulate commercial space activities via licensing procedure.[105] Meanwhile, their laws have many differences, which is presented below.

First, the U.S. has commenced its journey of space law enactment quite ahead of China and has been endeavoring in the field of space law for nearly half a century. After the successful launch of Sputnik I on 4 October 1957, the U.S. addressed the

---

[102] *Id.* Article 13.

[103] *Id.*

[104] *Id.*

[105] Besides, the Russian *Resolution on Adoption of Regulations regarding Licensing Space Activities* defines types, forms and periods of validity of licenses, conditions and procedures for the issue, withholding, suspension or termination, and other aspects of licensing. *See* Sergey P. Malkov and Catherine Doldirina. "Regulation of Space Activities in the Russian Federation", in Ram S. Jakhu, National Regulation of Space Activities, New York, Springer, 2010, p. 327.

legal void that then existed for space activities by promulgating its national law.[106] The historical significance of the early origins of U. S. space law is quite remarkable when one considers that even nations that have been major space powers for decades, like France and Japan, did not pass national space laws until 2008.[107] The first space debris legislation of China is promulgated on 8 February 2001. Such early origin of the U. S. space legal system is one reason to its comprehensiveness.

Second, there is a discrepancy concerning the institutional structure regulating civil and commercial space activities. In the U. S. the responsible agency for the civil space program is NASA, while the authority to regulate commercial space activities has been divided into several agencies. Each agency has developed their rules and standards for space debris mitigation. By contrast, in China a unitary agency, SASTIND, is authorized to regulate the civil and commercial space activities.

The division of authority among several agencies to regulate space activities facilitates the U. S. to establish activity-tailored standards. However, a major benefit for the centralization of the regulation of space activities, as that in China, is that loopholes and overlaps of different laws can be more easily avoided while consistency and harmonization of rules and standards can be better maintained.

Third, the U. S. has the most systematic legal system to regulate space activities, including space debris. One example is the regulation of launch vehicles.

From a technical perspective, along with derelict spacecraft, upper stages of launch vehicles comprise the greatest concentration of mass in Earth orbit, which create hazards to operational spacecraft in two main ways: collisions and explosions. To minimize the risk relating to upper stages, FAA has published its orbital debris mitigation regulations focusing on the safety at the end of launch, and only issues

[106] Walter A. MacDougall, *The Heavens and the Earth: A Political History of the Space Age*, New York, Johns Hopkins University Press, 1986, pp. 6 – 8 (as cited in Joanne Irene Gabrynowicz, "One Half Century and Counting: The Evolution of U. S. National Space Law and Three Long-term Emerging Issues"). (U. S. Code Title 51: National and Commercial Space Programs), *Journal of Space Law* 37(1), pp. 41 – 42.

[107] Gabrynowicz, *id.* p. 42.

licenses to commercial launch vehicles after a rigorous evaluation of the safety of the launch system.[108] The FCC and the NOAA have also proposed and published rules on orbital debris mitigation respectively for communication and remote sensing satellites.[109]

In this regard, China's space law regime is less elaborated. Though under the Launch Decree the applicant should submit documents concerning "the prevention from pollution and space debris" to the SASTIND, no specific requirements are mentioned in this Decree, and no distinction has been made between spacecraft and upper stage of launch vehicles.[110] Hence, one aspect for future development of China's space law would be to elaborate its space debris mitigation rules.

3. Space Debris Mitigation in the Trend of Space Commercialization and Privatization

It can be seen from the above comparison that there is a discrepancy between the laws of the U. S. and China. It can be also logically expected and assumed that the debris mitigation rules of some states are more rigorous than those of others, due to their differences in technical and legal development and policy consideration. Then, the question might arise as to whether these national rules with different stringency can effectively address the issue of space debris, especially in the context of space commercialization and privatization. After briefly presenting the current trend of commercialization, this chapter discusses the impacts of space commercialization and privatization on the regulation of space debris mitigation.

3. 1 Space Commercialization and Privatization

In the U. S., the commercial utilization of space is an essential component of

---

[108] United State of America-UNOOSA Compendium.

[109] FAA, *supra* note 76, p. 11.

[110] The Launch Decree Article 6(d).

telecommunications, financial markets, and a host of other critical sectors,[111] and private sectors are pushing the boundaries of space application.[112] There is a growing recognition that the time has come for the private sector to take on some jobs that only government has been allowed to perform.[113] According to Velocci Jr., "It is the private sector that is in the vanguard of opening a new era in space—and it is closer than you might think."[114]

The commercialization and privatization of space activities is commenced and now centralized in the U. S. Since the U. S. has the most systematic and elaborate regime to regulate space debris, by now national law can effectively regulate space activities including space debris mitigation. However, this situation is about to change shortly in the trend of space commercialization and privatization of many countries.

In Russia, Moscow-based Orbital Technologies announced in September 2010 plans to build, launch and operate a Commercial Space Station in low Earth orbit, which aims to serve as an orbiting hotel and commercial space laboratory.[115] Meanwhile, when public space spending was considerably reduced in Europe, the European space industry undertook a number of proactive commercialization steps.[116] For instance, Innovative Solutions In Space (ISIS B. V.) is one of the leading companies in the fast-growing small satellite market.[117] ISIS B. V. operates globally and serves a variety of customers in accomplishing their projects and space

[111] *Id.* p. 49.

[112] *Id.* p. 50.

[113] *Id.* p. 51.

[114] *Id.* p. 50.

[115] Aerospace-Technology, "Orbital Technologies Commercial Space Station, Russia", http://www.aerospace-technology.com/projects/orbitaltechnologiesc/.

[116] Walter Peeters, "Effects of Commercialization in the European Space Sector", *Space Policy* 18(3), 2002, p. 199.

[117] ISIS B. V. in brief, https://www.isispace.nl/about-us/general-information/.

missions.[118]

Hence, the flourishing of the commercial space industry can be expected. Like the launch services, once the exclusive domain of the U. S. and the Soviet Union, is now a capital-intensive commercial industry, with competitors from the U. S., Europe, China, Russia, Ukraine, Japan, and India.[119] As said by Zhao, commercialization, an irreversible trend in modern society, also applies to space activities.[120]

3. 2 Impact of Space Commercialization and Privatization on Debris Mitigation

The trend of space commercialization and privatization may have a great impact on the regulation of space debris mitigation under national space legislation. This can be analyzed in two aspects: states and private enterprises.

3. 2. 1 From a perspective of States: Regulatory Competition

Although from a political perspective and under the philosophy of environmental protection, states might have the impetus to address the issue of space debris, they might lose such impetus from an economic perspective. The space sector plays an increasingly pivotal role in the efficient functioning of modern societies and their economic development.[121] Despite its usual reliance on relatively high institutional investments up-front, space can increasingly be seen as a source of economic growth.[122]

The advent of commercial space activities has led more countries to consider how to regulate private space activities in a manner that does not hinder or preclude investment, while still ensuring that commercial activities comply with international law.[123] A diversity of governments are developing space laws, not only long-

---

[118] *Id.*

[119] Yun Zhao, *Space Commercialization and the Development of Space Law from a Chinese Legal Perspective*, New York, Nova Science Publishers, 2009, p. 53.

[120] *Id.* p. 61.

[121] Organization for Economic Co-operation Development (OECD), *The Space Economy at a Glance* 2011, Paris, OECD Publishing, 2011, p. 27.

[122] *Id.*

[123] Timiebi Aganaba, "Legal Framework in Support of Commercialization of Outer Space: the Case of the Isle of Man", *Proceedings of IISL*, 2008, p. 438.

established space-faring nations, but also countries with limited space activities wishing to either attract new investments from abroad or to cater to the needs of their fledgling space industry.[124] In light of this, the competition between regulatory environments may develop, as states profit from private undertakings establishing themselves in their territory.[125] The establishment of a branch office or a headquarters will lead to increased economic activities in that state, thus reducing unemployment, raising tax base, lowering welfare costs and so on.[126] Therefore, States will try to frame their legal environment in a business-friendly fashion, to attract the foreign space firms to their territory.[127]

One potential outcome of the regulatory competition is the "races to the bottom" phenomenon that when one state lowers its regulatory standards to attract investments and other states losing business, revenue, and labor, these states will react by lowering their own standards.[128] This creates a cycle of systematic lowering of regulatory standards that ends with all states and consumers being in a position worse than the one they were in before such race.[129]

As stated by Paul B. Stephan, "There is little incentive to undertake costly actions that only pay off globally. Carbon emissions policy offers an excellent example: the benefits from reduced emissions are shared globally, rather than concentrated in the regulating state. All states thus have an incentive to free ride on the efforts of others, and underproduction of emission controls is the predicted

[124] OECD (2011), *supra* note 124, p. 33.

[125] Dimitri Linden, "The Impact of National Space Legislation on Private Space Undertakings: A Regulatory Competition between States?", *Proceedings of IISL*, 2015, p. 4.

[126] Wolfgang Schön, "Playing Different Games? Regulatory Competition in Tax and Company Law Compared", *Common Market Law Review* 42(2), 2005, pp. 331 – 332.

[127] *Id.* p. 332. Linden, *supra* note 125, p. 4.

[128] Linden, *supra* note 125, p. 6.

[129] Linden, *id.* pp. 6 – 7. *See also* Paul B. Stephan, "Regulatory Competition and Anticorruption Law", *Virginia Journal of International Law* 53(1), 2012, p. 55.

outcome in the absence of strong global cooperation. "[130]

The above analysis also adapts to the current space debris situation, where all the states bear the costs of the lowering of standards in one state. Without an internationally uniform standard, states would be less likely to adopt stringent rules as this will increase the cost of their local industry. This is especially true with the participation of more nations into space activities, as a tacit agreement on environmental protection will be more difficult to reach, and the gentlemen club might be easily undermined by an unscrupulous black sheep who try to free-ride on the efforts of others.

3.2.2 From a Perspective of Private Companies: Tragedy of the Commons

While political pressure and national prestige may serve as an impetus for states to adopt measures to mitigate space debris, the situation is different when it comes to private companies as these are not their major concern. When private companies begin to undertake the space missions they will be tested by the same rigorous measure of success that governs traditional business ventures: return on investment.[131] As their primary purpose is to pursue higher profits, they can hardly be expected to execute more rigorous mitigation maneuvers than those are required.

Logically space debris mitigation conforms to the interest of the space industry as a whole, hence private companies are willing to perform debris mitigation maneuvers. Even before governments began to develop orbital debris-related policies and guidelines, launch vehicle developers became aware of the risks associated with orbital debris and began to explore ways of mitigation.[132] One of the earliest procedures U.S. vehicle manufacturers adopted was the depletion of on-board energy source from upper stages to prevent them from exploding and fragmenting.[133]

However, it should be noted that the cost of depletion is relatively small and

[130] Stephan, *id.* pp. 55 – 56.

[131] Anthony L. Velocci, Jr., "Commercialization in Space: Changing Boundaries and Future Promises", *Harvard International Review* 33(4), 2012, p. 52.

[132] FAA, *supra* note 76, p. 12.

[133] *Id.*

private companies might not have the interest to perform other more costly maneuvers, such as end of mission de-orbiting and re-orbiting. Moreover, these mitigation maneuvers occur only occasionally, and the willingness to do so may be dampened if other companies do not follow.

The concept "tragedy of the common" can be used to explain the current situation, of which the "herdsman in the pasture" model as presented by Hardin serves as an illustration. According to this model, in a pasture open to all, each herdsman seeks to maximize his gain.[134] To achieve this aim, each herdsman has the impetus to increase the number of animals to his herd, where he could receive all the proceeds from the sale of the additional animals, while the effects of overgrazing are shared by all the herdsmen.[135] In this scenario ruin is the destination toward which all men rush, each pursuing his own best interest in a society that believes in the freedom of the commons.[136] In a reverse way, the tragedy of the commons reappears in problems of pollution, where it is not a question of taking something out of the commons, but of putting waste in.[137] With the same logic, The rational man finds that his share of the cost of the wastes he discharges into the commons is less than the cost of purifying his wastes before releasing them.[138]

The situation of space debris is one problem of pollution fitting into the above scenario. Though outer space is boundless, the orbital slot is a limited resource which, even being used efficiently, can only support a finite number of space objects. The deterioration of this resource is accelerated by the creation of space debris. Such deterioration is against the common interest of all the space actors and has thus raised their awareness and concern. However, the performance of debris mitigation measures will not benefit the individual private company directly and immediately, and such

---

[134] Garrett Hardin, "The Tragedy of the Commons", *Science* 162 (3859), 1968, p. 1244.

[135] *Id.*

[136] *Id.*

[137] *Id.* p. 1245.

[138] *Id.*

benefit can only be achieved if other companies also adopt these measures.

Though national legislation can currently regulate the issue of space debris, their legal effect is mostly constrained within the jurisdiction of one state. The diversity in national space law creates an expanding pool of regulatory framework for private companies to choose.[139] Under similar circumstances, a space company is more likely to establish its headquarter or subsidiary in a country with less stringent debris mitigation requirements. This will result in the situation of "flag of convenience" or "license shopping". Though expenses associated with choosing among regimes, such as the renouncement of particular markets or valuable inputs, may reduce the likelihood of "license shopping", they will not eliminate it.[140] Moreover, the discrepancy in standards poses an obstacle to inter-operational activities, international cooperation and the effective functioning of the supply chain. Hence, national legislation is not the idealist means to regulate space debris, and the establishment of an international regime is thus necessary.

3.3 Zooming in on the Small Satellite Industry

Recent advances in small satellite technology have facilitated the design of Nano -, Pico-and Cube satellites, which are generally no bigger than a brick and usually weigh less than 10 kg.[141] Due to their relatively low production costs, shorter production time and the possibility of being launched as secondary payloads, such satellites are becoming increasingly present in outer space, and serve as a tool to democratize space.[142]

Democratizing space in this way through the use of small satellites still faces certain limits due to the inherent growing problem of space debris.[143] While the UN Guidelines contain no quantitative limitation, the IADC Guidelines stipulate a 25 -

---

[139] Linden, *supra* note 125, p. 4.

[140] Stephan, *supra* note 129, p. 53.

[141] A. Rinner, "Small Satellites-Smart Laws? Small Satellite Projects in the Face of National Space Legislation-Austria", *Proceedings of IISL*, 2013, p. 95.

[142] *Id.*

[143] *Id.*

year in orbit life-time limit for each spacecraft in the LEO, after mission completion.[144]

One of the authorization conditions for space activities in Austria is laid down in the Austrian Outer Space Act, which states that space activities should be carried out with due consideration for the internationally recognized guidelines.[145] The preparatory discussion paper on the Austrian Outer Space Act explicitly refers in this context to the IADC and UN Guidelines.[146] Compliance with these guidelines requires the operator to either launch small satellites into very low earth orbits where the natural decay time is less than 25 years or to perform active de-orbiting maneuvers, which are difficult for them to abide by. On the one hand, small satellites are mostly launched as secondary payloads, whose destination is dependant on that of the primary ones which is often higher than the orbit with 25 – years decay time.[147] On the other hand, due to mass constraints, most small satellites are not able to carry additional propulsion for de-orbiting maneuvers.[148]

There are divergent opinions as to whether specific arrangements shall be made for small satellites with regard to debris mitigation requirements. According to Rinner, the IADC Guidelines strongly focus on quantitative aspects such as limiting the in-orbit life-time of spacecraft regardless of their mass and type, while qualitative aspects such as space traffic management are not sufficiently covered by the existing guidelines.[149] Therefore, these guidelines need to be amended to focus more strongly on a broader approach towards space traffic management rather than on mere quantitative aspects.[150] Ringer also considers the time tight regulations as an *obstacle*

---

〔144〕 *Id.* p. 98.

〔145〕 *Id.*

〔146〕 *Id.*

〔147〕 *Id.* p. 99.

〔148〕 *Id.*

〔149〕 *Id.* p. 101.

〔150〕 *Id.*

towards the further democratization of space through small satellites.[151]

On the contract, according to Stelmakh, nowadays there is a view that small nano- and micro- satellites should be treated as space debris since they pose a threat to the big spacecraft undertaking vital space activities.[152] Admittedly a threat, it seems improper to categorize small satellites as space debris, for the UN Guidelines define space debris as "all man-made objects, including fragments and elements thereof, in Earth orbit or re-entering the atmosphere, that are *non-functional*". It would be too stretching a definition if "non-maneuverable" is interpreted as "non-functional", let alone the fact that small satellites also carry out important scientific or educative functions.

The cause of these two divergent attitudes, i. e. whether less stringent requirements should bemade for small satellites so as not to hinder their development, and whether the launch of small satellites *per se* is a risk imposed on space environment, is where the emphasis is put. The former attitude emphasizes the benefits of small satellites, while the latter emphasizes the side effects thereof. This debate might end with technological developments when affordable and feasible de-orbiting methods are available to small satellites. Until then, balance should be struck between these two attitudes and it is argued in this article that small satellites activities should be allowed and they should be subject to the same licensing requirements as traditional satellites, for outer space treaties do not make a distinction between small and large, maneuverable and non-maneuverable satellites: they are all space objects.[153] Meanwhile, though small satellites facilitate the democratization of space, they do impose risks on space environment due to their character of non-maneuverability. A clean and sustainable space environment is a precondition to the democratization of outer space, and hence it should not kill the goose that lays the

[151] *Id.*

[152] Stelmakh, *supra* note 32, p. 354.

[153] Neta Palkovitz and Tanja Masson-Zwaan. "Orbiting under the Radar: Nano-Satellites, International Obligations and National Space Laws", *Proceedings of IISL*, 2012, p. 574.

golden egg.

Divergence in national space legislation may distort competition, for a small satellite mission carried out in a country with less stringent space legislation faces fewer constraints than a project carried out in a country with more stringent one, which might then lead to the phenomenon of "license shopping" or "flag of convenience."[154] Harmonization in this regard is required and the idealist way is to establish an international regulatory regime.

4. Conclusion

The current legal rules regulating space debris mitigation can be divided into two categories, international law and national law. Concerning the former, the outer space treaties are too vague and general for its regulation, while the applicability of the international environmental law to space debris remains unclear. Non-binding guidelines are the only tool specific to debris mitigation at the international level, but these guidelines have not yet evolved into customary international law. To conclude, the current international legal regime does not provide a satisfactory answer to the regulation of space debris mitigation.

At the national law level, there are many inconsistencies between the law of China and the U. S. with regard to space debris mitigation, starting from responsible agencies to debris mitigation requirements. Such inconsistencies may confront challenges in the trend of space commercialization and privatization, for private actors have the liberty to choose the country to incorporate their company and to carry out space activities, which will lead to the "flag of convenience" and "license shopping" problem. With regard to states, they might then lose the impetus to enact stringent debris mitigation requirements so as not to lose foreign investment. This might result in the situation of "race to the bottom", with the whole international community being the ultimate victim.

Ultimately, a unitary regulatory regime of space debris should be established, as

[154] Rinner, *supra* note 141, p. 102.

this problem cannot be resolved by technical advancements alone, and the legal and political contribution is no less important. Developing technologies is one thing, but the willingness to implement them is another, especially when this is an affair of the whole international community.

(责任编辑:郑雅文)

人工智能主题专栏

论智能人的民事法律地位

韩雨彤*

摘要：

在新一轮科技革命的浪潮下，人工智能的快速发展深刻影响着人类的社会生活。明晰应用人工智能的机械体——智能人的法律地位，不仅具有理论意义，在构建应用智能人致害的救济规则上更具有现实需要。本文首先通过梳理传统大陆法系中两大法律主体——自然人和法人主体地位的取得依据，结合当前智能人的发展水平，认为智能人既不具有自然人主体地位的伦理基础，也不具有类似法人的团体人格，仅具有工具性。其次，在"非人可人"的观点下，从实用主义的立场分析智能人的行为表现不足以被评价为法律主体。最后，由于智能人本身无法独立承担责任，对于其引发的损害应通过完善产品责任制度进行救济，授予其法律主体地位不合实际。

关键词：

人工智能；法律主体；法律责任

一、引　论

人工智能在新一轮产业革命中爆发出的强烈增长态势成为世界关注的焦点，2018年9月，我国召开世界人工智能产业大会，并发布了《2018世界人工智能产业发展蓝皮书》，系统梳理了近年来人工智能在无人驾驶、医疗、金融等领域的突出应用，以及未来的产业发展趋势。[1] 民法作为调整市民社会关系的法

* 韩雨彤，北京科技大学文法学院2017级硕士研究生。

[1] 有关情况见中国信通院：《2018世界人工智能产业发展蓝皮书》，载https://www.gartner.com/technology/media-products/pdf.jsp? g=Shanghai-West-Bund-1-5E3ILHN-CHS，最后访问日期：2018年10月27日。

律自然应当对人工智能发展过程中触发的法律问题予以关注和回应。2017年年底欧盟法律事务委员会正式通过了《欧盟机器人民事法律规则》,该规则富有创造性地提出了赋予应用人工智能的机器人(本文称其"智能人")以"电子人"的法律主体地位的构想,将其列为继自然人、法人之后的第三大法律主体。[2]随着人工智能参与人类生活的程度不断加深,其所拥有的智能水平是否构成承认智能人具有法律主体地位的理由?赋予智能人"电子人"的法律主体地位是否会为智能人与人类之间的法律纠纷提供合理的解决方式?笔者希望通过本文对智能人的分析,明晰智能人的法律地位,为建构智能人引发损害的救济规则提供合理的逻辑起点。

二、人工智能以及智能人的定义

(一)人工智能的定义

截至目前,还没有形成统一的、被广泛接受认可的对于人工智能的定义。在Stuart Russell和Peter Norvig的《人工智能:一种现代的方法》一书中,列举了8种不同的关于人工智能的定义。[3] 1968年,人工智能的奠基人之一Marvin Minsky认为:"人工智能是研究让机器去做需要人类智能才能完成的事的科学。"[4]2007年,斯坦福大学计算机科学学院的教授John McCarthy在关于"什么是人工智能"的报告中提出"人工智能是制造智能机器的科学和工程学所研究的,尤其是指智能计算机程序。它和利用计算机去理解人类智能具有相似的

---

[2] See *Draft Report with Recommendations to the Commission on Civil Law Rules on Robotics*, Report of Committee on Legal Affairs, European Parliament Document [2015/2103(INL)], May. 31, 2016, p. 12.

[3] 参见[美]罗素、诺维格:《人工智能:一种现代的方法》(第3版),殷建平等译,清华大学出版社2013年版,第3页。

[4] Marvin Minsky, Semantic Information Processing, MIT Press 1968(438), quoted from Edwina L. Rissland, "Artificial Intelligence and Law: Stepping Stones to a Model of Legal Reasoning", *The Yale Law Journal*, Vol. 99. 1958 (1990).

功能,但人工智能并不是可生物化观察的技术"。[5] 我国学者郭少飞老师认为:"人工智能旨在实现与人类智能相似的智能表现,一方面有赖于算法程序、技术方法,模拟人类;另一方面,须附着于机器装置、系统等载体之上,表现智能。"[6]

上述国内外学者对于人工智能的定义,存在一定程度的相似之处。但以上定义均没有解释人工智能的一个关键性概念,就是什么是智能。John McCarthy 教授认为:"所谓智能,就是一种实现某种目标的计算能力,在人类、动物和机器中均有着不同程度的体现"。但是目前对于人工智能的定义还需要通过类比人类智能来完成,无法形成独立的定义方式,"因为我们无法完全识别哪种计算程序可以被称为智能"。[7] 并且 John McCarthy 教授并不认为人工智能一定是去模仿人类的思维过程来解决问题,"人工智能更多研究的是直接通过智能的方式去解决现实问题"。[8]

综上,在对人工智能进行定义时,由于智能概念的不确定性引发了不少对于人工智能的误读。在此,不妨先采纳较为模糊的定义方式,即"人工智能是指,使机器有能力处理一些需要人类智能的事项。"[9] 此定义虽然有循环论证之嫌,但在科学界尚未有对"智能"存在统一共识定义之际,也不失为学术严谨的体现。

(二)智能人的定义

人工智能虽然无统一定义,但有一点是清楚的,即人工智能作为一门新兴的技术科学,具有 John McCarthy 教授所说的"非生物性"。这就决定了人工智能势必会应用到某种机械上,这样才能发挥其作用。而本文所探讨的主要对象即为应用人工智能技术的智能人的法律地位问题。智能人这一提法见于 2017 年的欧盟法律事务委员会所起草的《对机器人的民法规则适用建议书》,其中列

---

[5] John McCarthy, *What is Artificial Intelligence*?, Computer Science Department Stanford University CA 94305 Nov. 12 2007, p. 2.

[6] 郭少飞:《"电子人"法律主体论》,载《东方法学》2018 年第 3 期。

[7] 前引 5, John McCarthy 文, p. 3。

[8] 同上。

[9] Matthew U. Scherer, "Regulating Artificial Intelligence Systems: Risks, Challenges, Competencies, and Strategies", 29 *Harv. J. L. & Tech.* 360 (2016).

举了以下几项特点来定义智能人:[10]第一,具有通过传感器获得自主性,或者是与周围环境或通过交易进行数据交换分析以获得自主性的能力;第二,具有自主学习的能力;第三,具有有形体;第四,依据环境调整其行为和行动的能力。

综上,本文中的智能人是指具有一定的物质实体,可以同外界环境进行交互,应用人工智能进行机械学习,能够做出判断决策并付诸实施的机器人或机械体。明确智能人的定义之后,下面将主要论述是否有将智能人解释为法律主体的空间。

三、国内外有关智能人法律地位的学说

人工智能技术的不断升级为智能人更深入地参与人类生活提供了可能,也使人与智能人之间的关系变得更为复杂。国内外学者就智能人法律地位提出了不同的学说,大致可以分为三种:肯定说、中立说和否定说。

(一)肯定说

1.有限法律人格说

袁曾老师认为:“人工智能是人类社会发展到一定阶段的必要产物,具有高度的智慧性与独立的行为决策能力,其性质不同于传统的工具或代理人。在现实条件下,将人工智能定义为具有智能工具性质又可作出独立意识表示的特殊主体较妥。”[11]

2.拟制人格说

国外有学者认为,智能人与法人具有可类比性,智能人可独立于股东存在,并为其股东的利益占有财产,其具有意志能力以自己的名义签合同,其可同法人享有财产权,可被起诉和应诉、承担法律责任,因而可被授予法律主体地位。[12] 我国学者杨延超也认为:“公司法意义上的‘法人’同样也是虚拟的法律主体”,“同样,机器人作为虚拟人格的目的也在于解释机器创作的法律现象,从

[10] 参见前引2,European Parliament Document 文,pp. 6-7。

[11] 袁曾:《人工智能的有限法律人格审视》,载《东方法学》2017年第5期。

[12] See David Marc Rothenberg,“Can Siri 10.0 Buy Your Home: The Legal and Policy Based Implications of Artificial Intelligent Robots Owning Real Property”,11 *Wash. J. L. Tech. & Arts* 453-455 (2016).

而防止对机器物毫无边界的滥用”。[13]

3. 代理说或信托人说

基于人工智能所蕴含的处理复杂事项的能力，因而应用人工智能的产品可以作为一种专家系统来处理人类代理人或信托人所从事的工作。[14] 许中缘老师认为应该将智能机器人定义为“理性代理人”，“机器人与人的最大差别就是理性人面对复杂的情况时，只能作出其最为满意而不是最好的选择”。[15]

4. 电子人或法律人格说

对于电子人主体地位的提出最先见于在欧盟法律事务委员会对于机器人民法规则适用的草案。[16] 一方面由于机器智能程度的提高使得其可以作出决策的自主性大幅度提升；另一方面是在损害责任的证明上，由于决策的过程是智能人自主作出的，在技术黑箱的影响下，被侵权人对于产品缺陷以及损害与缺陷之间存在因果关系的举证难度增大，极易由于未尽证明责任而无法获得赔偿。因此对于最复杂和自主性极高的智能人可以考虑赋予其电子人的法律主体地位，使其拥有特殊的权利和义务。

（二）中立说

中立说基于对人工智能技术未来发展的不确定性以及当前技术水平下智能人的应用情况，从功利主义的角度上并不对智能人是否可取得法律主体地位进行讨论，而是强调了明确智能人的法律地位是为了更好地设定责任承担规则，在不同应用环境和智能程度下通过反思智能人的本质地位而实现损害风险救济管控与促进技术进步，合理配置不同主体之间法律责任，实现法律平衡各方利益的价值。[17]

（三）否定说或工具说

在目前人工智能的发展水平下，否定说或工具说认为智能人仅作为权利的

---

〔13〕 杨延超：《人工智能对知识产权法的挑战》，载《治理研究》2018 年第 5 期。

〔14〕 See Lawrence B. Solum, “Legal Personhood for Artificial Intelligences”, 70 *N. C. L. Rev.* 1240 – 1254 (1992).

〔15〕 许中缘：《论智能人的工具性人格》，载《法学评论》2018 年第 6 期。

〔16〕 参见前引 2, European Parliament Document 文, pp. 10 – 12。

〔17〕 参见司晓、曹建峰：《论人工智能的民事责任：以自动驾驶汽车和智能机器人为切入点》，载《法律科学》2017 年第 5 期。

客体和实现目标任务的工具,在出现智能人侵权的损害责任承担上主要依靠完善产品责任制度解决。[18] 否定说或工具说也是目前国内外学界对智能人地位的通说。

出现上述学说相互争鸣的局面,首先,在对人工智能的评价上,肯定说从行为主义的立场出发,主张既然智能人具备处理人类事务的能力,为何不能授予其主体地位呢?[19] 而否定说则从反对行为主义的立场出发,认为人工智能并不等同于人类智能,其并非在自我意识和情感的指导下展开工作。行为主义仅能证明智能人可模仿人类的思维过程进行逻辑判断,却无法证明人工智能具有人类智能的实质。其次,肯定说和中立说学者主张在强人工智能应用环境下,智能人的自主性和创造力会极大增强,特别是深度学习、智能以及专家系统程序会以超越其设计人员可预测的范围运行,[20] 使设计人员无法有效实现对智能人行为的控制,适用传统产品责任的规制方法会使研发者背负较重的赔偿压力,阻碍科技创新。同时受害人很难证明损害发生的原因以及行为的损害之间的因果关系,从而无法获得有效的赔偿救济。[21] 因此,肯定说和中立说主张,在赋予智能人主体地位的情况下,适用有限法律人格否认制度,"当智能机器人的实际控制人在保管或者使用过程中存在过错的",以"揭开智能机器人面纱的方式确定法律责任的承担主体"。[22] 或者通过替代责任,比照监护人对被监护人的责任,或者雇主对雇员的责任,让控制智能机器人的人承担替代责任。但是否会出现强人工智能尚未可知,而就当前人工智能的发展情况而言,智能人仍是在设定程序内选择行为,对智能人侵权问题不必赋予其法律主体地位救济,而可通过完善产品责任制度解决。并且由于智能人无责任财产,只能由自然人或法人对其行为承担赔偿责任。这一点在主张智能人有限人格说的学者文章中

〔18〕 See David C. Vladeck, "Machines without Principals: Liability Rules and Artificial Intelligence", 89 *Wash. L. Rev.* 141 – 150(2014).

〔19〕 See F. Patrick Hubbard, "Do Androids Dream: Personhood and Intelligent Artifacts", 83 *Temp. L. Rev.* 431 (2011).

〔20〕 参见前引6,郭少飞文。

〔21〕 See Curtis E. A. Karnow, "Liability for Distributed Artificial Intelligences", 11 *Berkeley Tech. L. J.* 187 – 189(1996).

〔22〕 刘晓纯、达亚冲:《智能机器人的法律人格审视》,载《前研》2018年第3期。

被肯定,“由于人工智能具有的法律人格有限,其无法独立承担责任”,因而“可以发生事故后的原始数据作为定责和索赔的依据”,“让所有参与机器人发明、授权和使用过程中的主体分担责任”。[23] 总体而言,授予智能人法律主体地位的宣示意义大于实践需要。

本文对智能人法律地位的主张采否定说,笔者依据当前人工智能发展现状,首先从传统民法理论的角度分析自然人法律主体地位的取得的伦理基础以及法人法律主体地位的取得的事实前提,与当前智能人的行为表现进行对比,检讨智能人是否具有类比自然人和法人被授予法律主体地位的解释空间;其次在民法主体理论的发展上,分析若基于“非人可人”理论下智能人是否可跳出传统主体理论的束缚而实现对于法律主体的扩张;最后针对肯定说和中立说学者中大多担忧现行产品责任制度将无法为智能人造成损害提供救济因而主张赋予智能人以主体地位使其独立承担责任,笔者通过梳理当前应用智能人的主要环境以及可能出现的问题,通过完善产品责任制度的方式对智能人损害后果进行规范,以证明将智能人定义为工具不仅符合法律主体理论的建构也更切合实际的需要。

四、从传统民法理论的角度论述智能人的法律地位

(一)从自然人角度检讨智能人的法律地位

自然人作为法律主体的根基在于人的伦理性,即康德所创立的伦理人格主义哲学。从历史的发展上,随着人类特有的“大脑能力”被逐步开发,人类在“物我一体”的混沌状态逐步实现对自然环境的控制和为己所用,显示出不同于物的人格。[24] 社会发展的外因推动着人类不断解锁自身密码,从早期罗马法涤除人格中伦理因素而将人格作为为政治目的服务的身份等级面具,到斯多葛学派以及后期经院哲学家逐步建立人人平等的自然法观念,直至近代天赋人权概念下人的价值被再次发现。人不再附属于氏族群体,不再依附于君主强权,而是真正将个体视为存在的目的,并在自由意志的启蒙下成为独立的社会单元,获

---

〔23〕 前引 11,袁曾文。

〔24〕 参见马俊驹:《从身份人格到伦理人格——论个人法律人格基础的历史演变》,载《湖南社会科学》2005 年第 6 期。

得了独立的主体地位。从身份到契约的发展承载着平等主体之间的自由交易,督促着人们发现内在人格的本质乃是人之独特的理性意志,而非任何外部的授权因素。法国民法典所确立的“人格之取得,已经不再取决于他是怎样的人,而是仅仅取决于他是人”。[25] 最终法律上的人成了一种抽象意义上的人,德国民法典通过法技术手段,使得不论是处于何种年龄阶段的人,处于何种智识水平的人,都因为具有最本质的伦理性而被客观化为法律意义上的主体,具有平等的权利能力。而现代民法在经历了从身份到契约的抽象化人格运动之后,再一次通过从契约到身份的过程对人的主体地位进行反观和回复,将近代民法中为建构在经济活动中绝对平等的人格概念进行了缓和,将法律人格背后的人像从“强而智的人”转变为“弱而愚的人”,[26] 承认法律人概念下个体在经济生活中差异性,从而给予弱者以保护。但人的概念之外沿的扩大未曾动摇其内涵的伦理性。人区别于其他生物的自由意志为法律主体的成立提供了实然性的前提,无论人格概念如何变化,其目的——“尊重人的存在”都未曾改动。人基于理性指导下的自由意志可以独立地决定自己的行为,并承担相应的行为后果。智能人虽然也具有一定的分析理性,但是这种机器的分析理性与人类的自然理性相比还是存在较大的不同。

首先,从智能的来源上,这种能力的取得不是基于其本身而产生的,而是人所赋予的。电脑程序所具有的逻辑分析能力“其本质来源于其智能装置,而这一装置是依靠程序员良好的分析能力和编写代码的能力而设置的”,[27] 而非与生俱来。“人格开始于对自身——作为完全抽象的自我——具有自我意识的时候。”[28] 自然人基于其大脑装置的构造产生了意识,并在社会交往中逐步进化了以人自身为对象的纯思维和纯认识。有学者认为,意识是思维的产物,而如果思维是大脑思考过程的产物,并且电脑可以模拟大脑的思维过程,那么人工

---

〔25〕 前引24,马俊驹文。

〔26〕 参见[日]星野英一:《私法中的人》,王闯译,中国法制出版社2004年版,第82页以下。

〔27〕 前引2,European Parliament Document文,p. 4。

〔28〕 [德]黑格尔:《法哲学原理》,范扬、张企泰译,商务印书馆2009年版,第51页以下。

智能也可以产生意识。[29] 但根据目前认知科学的观点,意识的产生不可能脱离神经元,大脑是唯一可以产生意识的器官。[30] 人工智能是另一种基于模仿分析人类行为而具有的智能,我们在检测人工智能时,是在行为主义的立场上的,即通过观测智能人的行为认定其具有和人类同等的智能水平,究竟人工智能本质为何仍不清楚。因此,仅基于智能人处理复杂事项的外观而认为智能人具有独立的认知能力、可以成为权利义务的主体仅是从行为表征出发的功利主义视角,而忽略了机器智能的来源在于人类智能的赋能,通过程序的运行而模拟大脑思维的过程并不足以成为存在的目的,而仅为手段。

其次,从智能的内容上,人工智能和人类智能是不同的。Omar E. M. Khalil 教授分析了"专家系统——人工智能的一种"在帮助人们提供解决问题的方案和决定时可能面临困境的三个理由:[31] 第一,决策基础不同——人类专家在给出处理某种问题的意见时是依据现实社会的需要而非他人的预设标准;第二,缺乏情感和价值判断——由于"这种以电脑为基础的系统只能做系统指令它做的事,让其拥有自由意志去进行道德判断和价值选择就是天方夜谭";第三,存在故意或偶发的偏见——程序运行中体现该编程人员先入为主的想法,"电脑专家系统"所做的决定某种程度上是"人类政策"的体现。机器人这种"能够冷静地在各种方案中找出最为优异的选择"[32] 的纯粹理性的逻辑分析似乎恰好与民法中的"抽象思辨的人"相吻合,其不具有感情并纯化意识,脱离"经验的"而以"思维的"方式似乎恰巧印证了"法律上的人是思辨中的人,是民法非感性的法律主体的典型。"[33] 但是,以民法中的抽象人格支撑智能人的主体地位实质上陷入了因果倒置的逻辑谬误。民法上的理性人的建构目的在于设置统一的行为规则,而非否认人的伦理基础。法律正是在承认个体行为千差万别的基础上通过设立"可量化的标准将人的行为统一到限定的目的秩序中去,从而使

---

〔29〕 参见前引 14,Lawrence B. Solum 文,p. 1264。

〔30〕 See Paul Weiss, "On the Impossibility of Artificial Intelligence", 44 *Rev. Metaphysics* 340,(1990).

〔31〕 See Omar E. M. Khalil, "Artificial Decision-Making and Artificial Ethics: A Management Concern",*Journal of Business Ethics*,Vol. 12,No. 4 313 – 321(1993).

〔32〕 前引 9,Matthew U. Scherer 文,p. 365。

〔33〕 李永军:《民法上的人及其理性基础》,载《法学研究》2005 年第 5 期。

得对人与人之间关系的评价变得可能与容易。"[34] 相对应,人依据内在的道德律令而约束自身行为,使之符合法律要求的理性标准,便是尽到了"理性人的注意义务"从而在主观意志上被免予负面评价。而智能人的一整套分析规则依赖于算法的设计和数据的收集,其所作出的纯粹逻辑的推演而欠缺道德的衡量在无法有效穷尽外部环境的复杂变化之时要求其做出符合人类社会价值标准的行为是不可能的。[35] 如果"单个者的状态即欲望构成获取独立的自我意识的原动力",[36] 而真正使得人被评价为法律上的主体的,则是与义务的联结。"我必须在所有的情形中把我之外的自由主体作为自由生物来承认,这就是说,我必须通过对他的自由的可能性的理解来限制我的自由。"[37] 个体在道德的指引下建构起群体性秩序,才将自身解放出来,获得了真正人格意义上的主体地位。纯粹理性的判断是法律的"应然性"构建,而人类行为的伦理基础和现实基础则为应然存在提供了"实然性"支撑。权利主体的抽象理性与伦理基础并行不悖,自然人克服自身意志缺陷而达致法律要求的理性过程证明了其人格的健全,证实了其担当法律主体地位的正当性,而对于仅能进行理性逻辑行为的智能人而言,其缺乏伦理道德判断的智能水平不足以支撑主体地位的获得,否则在承认智能人主体地位的情形下,强制将人类社会所形成的共同意志设定为智能人的行为准则无异于道德绑架。

最后,为避免智能人所做的决策违背社会伦理,研发人员会在设计算法时加入相应的伦理规则。Isaac Asimov 提出了机器人行为的三大原则:第一,机器人不能伤害人类,或者以不作为的方式使人类受到伤害;第二,机器人必须服从人类的命令,除非这一命令和第一规则相冲突,第二,机器人在不违反第一条和第二条规则的情况下,必须保护自己的存在。[38] 这三大原则仍然是当前智能人

---

〔34〕 前引33,李永军文。

〔35〕 参见前引14,Lawrence B. Solum 文,pp. 1251 - 1252。

〔36〕 [德]京特·雅科布斯:《规范·人格体·社会——法哲学前思》,冯军译,法律出版社2001年版,第27页。

〔37〕 [德]费希特:《以知识学为原则的自然法权基础》,载《费希特文集》(第2卷),梁志学编译,商务印书馆2014年版,第324页。

〔38〕 载 https://en.wikipedia.org/wiki/Three_Laws_of_Robotics,最后访问日期:2018年10月27日。

行为的伦理基础。但问题在于,尽管为智能人设定了相应的伦理准则,智能人是否理解伦理准则的意义并以此修正自身行为,以及智能人在做出判断分析时能否理解自己行为的意义呢?这便引出智能人不具有类似自然人主体地位的最后一层分析——两种智能的水平不同。主张智能人法律人格肯定说的学者认为:“人工智能技术已经发展到可以作出独立意思表示的阶段”〔39〕;“通过机器学习和深度学习,借助于模拟人类的神经网络,机器人也可以拥有类似人类的直觉或感觉,拥有独特的创意和灵感。”〔40〕主张肯定说的学者立足行为的外观表征,从智能人可完成相当的人类工作任务而推导出其具有意思表示的能力。这种不问内在意思有无而径直以行为结果为导向的判定无疑是违背意思表示本质的,其结果将使得无意思的“僵尸行为”也能产生法律效果。“法律行为的效力以法律和当事人的意思这两者为基础,也即法律秩序赋予那些以其所认可的行为类型所进行的意思设权行为以效力。”〔41〕自然人在理解行为意义的情况下,通过自由地作出意思表示而意图引起法律关系的形成、变更和消灭。作出意思表示的过程,可以从两个方面分析:一是行为人以自己的意思,自主地作出意思表示。对比智能人,其作出行为并非依据自己目的,而是执行“人工智能学者或工程师认为可以由人工智能系统完成的任务。”〔42〕二是行为人对于自己作出的行为具有目的性,理解行为本身的含义以及其所引起的法律效果,是基于理性分析而作出的法律行为而获得了“个人意思的独立支配领域”,并为自身行为独立承担责任。对比智能人,John Searle 设计的“中文屋”实验以证明机器通过图灵测试仅在程序的指示下对信息进行机械处理,但并不理解该符号信息的含义。〔43〕故而智能人在处理分析信息的过程中并无作出意思表示的“有意”——从而欠缺行为意思;无法理解其行为符合法律上的事实构成,并没有意图使其产生法律效果——从而欠缺表示意思和效果意思。从行为外观以解释内在意思的“表示说”只能适用于人类的行为,而对于以人工智能为“脑力”的

〔39〕 前引 11,袁曾文。

〔40〕 孙占利:《智能机器人法律人格问题论析》,载《东方法学》2018 年第 3 期。

〔41〕 [德]维尔纳·弗卢梅:《法律行为论》,迟颖译,法律出版社 2013 年版,第 67 页。

〔42〕 杨学山:《智能原理》,中国工信出版集团、电子工业出版社 2018 年版,第 287 页。

〔43〕 See John R. Searle, “Minds, brains, and programs”, *Behavioral and Brain Sciences* 3, 417 – 457 (1980).

机器人而言,其仅为模仿、模拟人类智能的思考路径,进行符号化的逻辑判断和计算推理,而无法理解行为现实的意义和所指向的目的。真正使法律行为生效的不是智能人的行为,而是现实中的交易双方的意思表示。智能人仅是自然人实现自身目的的工具,而无法"自主地决定他和存在的关系""为自己设定目标并对自己的行为加以限制"[44]。智能人这种无实质理解力而仅依据程序运行的机械行为是一套纯粹理性的范式,它和人类智能在水平上截然不同。

总体而言,智能人不具有可类比自然人的法律主体地位,其依据在于自然人本身的伦理性。这种伦理性突出表现在自我意识层级的不同和自由意志的限定。人在自由意识下不仅可以自在地自觉,更通过内在体验获得自知,形成自为意志,构成心灵的价值判断,再从心灵指向世界,形成对社会的道德建构和法律秩序建构,并以此作为对自身行为的约束。"意志的这种在自身中的反思和它的自为地存在同一性"[45]使人成为主体,因而在人的层面上,经过与外界的交互,自我意识与自由意志获得了统一,人的自我意识的丰富性要远远大于其他生物体。从这个层面上,智能人尽管具备可与环境交互的感官反馈,但缺乏道德伦理基础的自我意识,不具备自由意志,因而不能成为法律主体。

(二)从法人角度检讨智能人的法律地位

国外有学者主张通过类比公司法人主体地位的取得,使智能人可以拥有财产并取得诉讼主体地位,当智能人财产不足以赔偿损害时可"刺破智能人的面纱"。[46] 若从技术功利的角度,在智能人本身不具备自然人主体资格的伦理基础下,借鉴法人的制度构建中人与人格相分离的法技术来论证智能人可获得类似法人地位似乎有一定的合理性,但是却忽略了智能人不具有和法人一样在技术上脱离生物体授予人格的事实基础,即法人行为的作出是依靠人完成的。[47] 法人是"通过私法行为设立的长期存在的人的联合体或组织体",法人一方面独

〔44〕 [德]卡尔·拉伦茨:《德国民法典通论》,王晓晔等译,法律出版社2003年版,第34页以下。

〔45〕 前引28,黑格尔书,第127页。

〔46〕 前引9,Matthew U. Scherer文,p. 399。

〔47〕 See W. Machen, "Corporate Personality", *Harvard Law Review*, Vol. 24, No. 4 266 (1911).

立于其成员或职能机关个人存在,而另一方面法人本身行使权利和承担义务必须通过其机关的行为,即具体人的行为才能实现。而正是这一逻辑前提,使得法人具有了拥有主体地位的可能性,也形成了不同关于法人的主体学说,从德国学者主张的“拟制说”“有机实体说”“目的财产说”,〔48〕到法国学者主张的“主观权利说”,〔49〕以及普通法系中以信托关系看待法人财产权问题和其传统上认为法人是“虚拟的,是由国家创制的”。〔50〕诸多观念的争鸣各有侧重,而无论是将法人看作纯粹技术手段的产物还是真实存在的组织人格,实质都是对何为团体人格“实在性”的衡量标准不同。在有限理性下无法开启上帝视角时,不妨以宽容的态度在社会共识的最大范围上,采纳对于实现其目的的正确途径之规定。〔51〕基于我国民法主要采法人拟制说,因此笔者从拟制说的观点出发检讨智能人地位与法人主体地位的殊异。

具体而言,首先,智能人不具有类似法人的意志。正如江平先生所言:“当团体只是人的简单集合体时,每一个人具有独立的人格,团体人格是不能显现出来的。只有当每个人的意志形成共同意志,而共同意志又有机地形成团体意志时,团体才可能具有独立人格。”〔52〕在社团法人中,通过个人意志的聚合而形成的团体意志,实现了两种不同类型意志的实质划分,这种区分使得团体意志独立于其成员个人意志而存在,最终使得社团法人基于其意志的独立性而获得了独立的存在基础。此举也契合了黑格尔的“理性—主体—意志”的范式,〔53〕使社团法人在意志独立性层面上获得了法律主体地位的基础。而在财团法人中,“财团提供了使一个人的意思(同时还有捐助者的姓名)永垂不朽的可能

---

〔48〕 前引44,卡尔·拉伦茨书,第180页。

〔49〕 前引47,W. Machen文,p. 257;张民安:《法国民法总论》(上),清华大学出版社2017年版,第259页。

〔50〕 同上,W. Machen文,pp. 256-257。

〔51〕 参见[奥]凯尔森:《纯粹法理论》,张书友译,中国法制出版社2008年版,第230页以下。

〔52〕 江平主编:《法人制度论》,中国政法大学出版社1994年版,第7页。

〔53〕 参见李永军:《民法总论》,法律出版社2009年版,第185页以下。

性"。[54] 由于财团法人并非人的集合而仅是财产的集合,其虽无法在成员共同意志的聚合下抽象形成团体意志,但财团法人意志的设定源于其设立人或捐助人的意志,这种意志成了财团法人固定不变的存在目的,同样也实现了团体意志的独立存在。[55]

关于法人是否存在独立的意志,存在不同的学说争鸣,在此也一并进行讨论,以完善是否可授予智能人以类似法人主体地位的检讨。

约翰·齐普曼·格雷在其关于"法律主体"的论述中写道:"假定社团是实在物,其是否可具有真正意志这一问题,取决于是否存在概括意志这样的东西。我不信概括意志的存在。可能存在一致意志,但并不存在集体意志;意志属于个体的自然人。当我们说到大多数人达成某一观点的意志时,我们意指就此观点大多数人一致的复数意志。集体是虚构之事物。依靠说社团具有实在的概括意志以避免拟制归属意志,是用另一项拟制驱逐此项拟制。"[56] 在格雷看来,意志仅存在于自然人,集体意志仅仅是众多自然人的意志相加,而不会从中抽象出独立于自然人的团体意志。因而格雷在论证法人这样的无生命体具有法律主体地位时,认为是通过独断拟制的方式,将团体中个体人的意志归属该社团,使得不具有意志的实体被赋予了意志,因而法人具有了主体资格,得以享有权利和承担义务。

而对比智能人和其控制者之间的关系,人类设计了算法,进行编程,将智能人链接入数据库,使智能人得以运行。[57] 既不存在由个人意志抽象形成的团体意志,也不存在意志的归属关系,智能人所具有的人工智能是通过算法的运行以解决实际问题而体现出来的。法人的共同意志从本质上是对康德以来"人格主义哲学"的继受,即"没有内容的思想是空泛的,没有观念的觉察是盲目的",

〔54〕 [德]迪特尔·梅迪库斯:《德国民法总论》,邵建东译,法律出版社2013年版,第865页。

〔55〕 参见李锡鹤:《论法人的本质》,载《法学论坛》1997年第2期。

〔56〕 [美]约翰·齐普曼·格雷:《法律主体》,龙卫球译,载《清华法学》2002年第1期。

〔57〕 See Jack M. Balkin, 2016 *Sidley Austin Distinguished Lecture on Big Data Law and Policy: The Three Laws of Robotics in the Age of Big Data*, 78 Ohio St. L. J. 1219 – 1223 (2017).

强调法律主体需符合黑格尔所主张的“理性—主体—意志”的范式。[58] 而智能人的人工智能原本就不具有同自然人意志一样的属性已如上述。因此,智能人仅作为其控制者实现特定目的的工具,依据算法和提供的数据为其控制者提供服务。

其次,智能人不存在类似法人的独立行为。法人因为具有独立的意志,因而可以在民法意思自治的原则下自由地为其设定权利义务,从事法律行为。[59] 正是由于法人在自己独立意志的主导下选择为或不为某种法律行为,因此可以判定这种行为是由法人独立做出的,是与其成员个人行为相区别的,在“自己责任”的民法原则下,法人应对自己决定做出的行为负责,从而实现了隔绝成员责任的法人独立责任承担。而对比智能人和其控制者之间,智能人依照人类设定的一系列算法规则运行,并由人类决定如何利用算法,何时利用以及为实现何种目的利用。[60] 虽然从外观上看该行为是智能人做出的,但是实际上智能人仅作为实现特定目的的工具,行为目的的实现不归于智能人,而是归于智能人背后的人类。

最后,智能人不具备类同法人的独立财产:“团体人格的基础是能够在商品经济生活中成为权利义务之统一归属点的实体,亦即人以及财产的有机集合体。”[61] 法人独立财产的存在为其独立承担责任提供了财产担保,从而使法人独立承担责任得以实现,使法人的法律主体地位的取得具有实际意义。“若允许团体以独立人格对外行为,但却无为此行为承担后果的基础,那么这种团体意思自治的权利就令人费解。”[62] 通过成员的出资行为或设立人的捐助行为,均使得财产脱离原民事主体的所有,而进入法人所有的范畴,使法人获得了独立的财产,基于对此责任财产的所有,法人才具有了作为法律主体对外开展民事活动的法律资格。正如罗马法谚所云:“如果什么东西应付给团体,它不应给以团体所属的个人,个人也不应偿还团体所欠之债。”

而在智能人与控制者的关系上,不存在控制者将财产转移于智能人的行

---

〔58〕 参见前引 53,李永军书,第 185 页以下。

〔59〕 同上,李永军书,第 279 页。

〔60〕 参见前引 57,Jack M. Balkin 文,p. 1223。

〔61〕 尹田:《民法典总则之理论与立法研究》,法律出版社 2010 年版,第 343 页。

〔62〕 前引 53,李永军书,第 280 页。

为,智能人并不享有财产权。有学者认为:“法人享有财产权,但法人的财产只是股东承担责任的基础,该项财产只是登记在法人名下,真正的主体还是自然人。因而机器人与法人一样,如果其他主体要求机器人承担责任,也可以如刺破法人面纱一样,要求机器人的控制者(股东)承担责任。”首先,学者在此处的论证存在谬误。股东完成向法人的出资后,该项财产已经转移至公司,“而公司与股东是不同的权利主体,而享有法人财产权的主体是并且只能是公司。”〔63〕登记在法人名下的财产自然以法人为其主体,股东已经不享有对该财产的所有权。正是经过出资转移所有权的过程使得公司与股东个人的财产分离,在股东滥用股东权利时才能否认公司的人格,使得股东个人独立承担责任。若在完成向法人出资后股东仍作为财产的主体,公司的“面纱”便无处存在。同时,股东向公司出资的目的,是利用公司的有限责任制度实现所有权与经营权的分离,“一切财产和权力都不再完全追及于团体中的个人”,〔64〕从而规避商业风险,有效集中资本进行社会化大生产。而控制人研发智能人的目的是利用智能人求解问题的科学性和逻辑性,以实现对于资源的有效利用,因而不存在控制者向智能人出资而以智能人名义从事经营活动。智能人在第四次产业革命中的角色仅仅是实现某种任务的工具,其行为的目的和结果归属于均其控制者,智能人并不从其行为获利,也不可能实现对于财产的占有,因而不具有承担损害赔偿的责任财产。若赋予智能人以法律主体地位,但其又不具有承担责任的能力,只能“刺破面纱”使其生产者承担责任,设置“面纱”便不具有实际意义,“面纱”前并不存在法律主体,而只是实现目的的工具。

因此,在类比法人法律地位的取得上,尽管智能人可以利用脱离生物体授予人格的法技术而被构建“电子人”主体地位,但是由于其仅在法律行为中充当设备、设施或工具角色,不具备成立法律主体地位所必需的事实基础,因而缺乏构建民事主体地位的逻辑起点。这一点无论采取何种学说作为解释法人主体地位的基础,都无法改变。同时智能人无责任财产,无法独立承担民事责任,无法作为当事人独立参加诉讼,强行赋予其法律主体地位不仅不会简化交易关系,而且会与现实中智能人作为分析工具参与民事活动相冲突,人为地导致法

〔63〕 张志坡:《公司财产权利三重结构说制批判》,载《金陵法律评论》2013年春季卷,第105页。

〔64〕 赵旭东:《公司法上的有限责任制度及其评价》,载《比较法研究》1987年第1期。

律关系复杂化。

五、其他影响法律主体地位因素的考量——现代民法主体制度建构的伦理性基础式微：非人可人的入侵

近代民法以康德“主体—意志—理性”公式建构起法律主体的伦理基础架构。而当法人，“特别是股东承担有限责任的公司出现并且日益成为经济活动的主体时”，[65]法律主体的设置便由伦理基础转为经济发展的需要。民法作为调整市民生活的法律，顺应社会发展而作出相应调整无可厚非，在此基础上，法人破除主体伦理资格的法律技术能否切割开更大的口子，容纳更多非自然人的实体成为法律主体，从而抛弃法律主体的伦理基础，完全依据现实的需要授予法律主体资格呢？这种“非人可人”的态势所依据的价值导向体现了社会文明从近代天赋人权修正古代“人可非人”的人格贬损，到现代“非人可人”改进人类中心主义的窠臼的包容化发展趋势，[66]但是人类作为主体为抵消“霸权式生存”对其他生物体的漠视与盘剥一定要通过赋予其主体地位的方式才能实现“自我救赎”吗？非人可人的制度设想所具有的现实性可能远远小于其宣示性。

具体而言，法人主体地位的取得并没有为赋予其他生物体法律主体地位提供类推的空间。学者依据“法律上的人被缩成了权利主体，而权利主体归根结底仅仅是权利义务的联结点”而主张权利与义务是智能人工具性人格的认定标准，从而“糅合各种不同的法律要素”达成“提取民事主体公因式”[67]的作用。这种将人视为“权利和义务结合体”观点来源于英美法，其哲学基础在于实用主义者主张的以结果为定义依据，科学真正重视的不是客体内在的自然属性，而是他们之间的相互关系。因而无需判定该物的内在属性，只要外部抽象出其为

〔65〕 前引33，李永军文。

〔66〕 参见李拥军：《从“人可非人”到“非人可人”：民事主体制度与理念的历史变迁——对法律“人”的一种解析》，载《法制与社会发展》2005年第2期。

〔67〕 前引15，许中缘文。

权利义务的承担单元即为法律主体。[68] 两大法系虽然在法律主体的判定上存在不同标准,但在对待其他生物体能否成为法律主体的问题时却可以殊途同归。"分子和树木尽管有一定的社会意义,但是这种意义却与他们获得权利与义务无关。"[69]智能人具有社会应用价值,其可以向外辐射形成一定的社会关系,这种社会关系并不等价于以智能人为主体、形成权利义务为内容的法律关系,智能人的这种行为表现并不能获得成为权利义务的承担单元的法律评价。

尽管从法理上对其他生物体的主体地位难以证成,但实践上确有新的突破。2011年3月30日,厄瓜多尔洛哈省法院在一起环境保护诉讼的判决中确认了自然的宪法性权利:[70]"自然,或者地球,生命在这里延续和发展,有权利对其存在和保护、孕育生命的运转、结构、功能以及进化的过程享有完整的尊重。"确认自然的宪法性权利的确提高了人们保护环境的意识,但是也带来了更多法律争议,自然的权利具体内容是什么?人类原本的自由权在与自然的宪法性权利之间应如何协调?人类本身也是自然界中的一环,是否也能享有自然的权利呢?谁来具体行使这种自然的权利呢?自然是否承担义务,是否为自己负责,如何负责呢?"法律秩序的建立是对于社会关系的调整和行为安排,目的在于使得生活物资和满足人类对享有某些东西和做某些事情的各种要求和手段,能在最少阻碍和浪费的条件下尽可能地给予满足。"[71]纸面上的法律若非经过无数次的推演以确保其严谨性便会造成立法权的滥用和资源的浪费,最终伤害的是普通民众,在智能人的问题上仍是如此。若要赋予智能人以法律主体地位,必须要解决的问题便是责任承担的问题。享有权利的主体如果不能负担义务、承担责任,便会造成权利的滥用。而智能人本身具有可归责性吗?其能否享有独立的财产权以承担责任呢?

首先,归责的过程是法律的负面评价过程,"某一错误被归责于实施了该错

---

〔68〕 See John Dewey, "The Historic Background of Corporate Legal Personality", *The Yale Law Journal*, Vol. 35, No. 6 658 – 662(1926).

〔69〕 同上文,p. 661。

〔70〕 See María Valeria Berros, "Defending Rivers Vilcabamba in the South of Ecuador", *RCC Perspectives*, No. 6 38 – 39 (2017).

〔71〕 [美]罗斯科·庞德:《通过法律的社会控制》,沈宗灵译,商务印书馆2010年版,第35页。

误的人,该人不可能是自然的一块东西,而只能是能够强求其把自己理解为规范性相互理解的参与者的人。"〔72〕归责的基础在于主体设定的普通型社会评价规则,主体基于对社会规范的理解以及对自身行动的可控制性具备了承担责任的伦理基础,而当主体行为违背了普遍性的社会评价造成不良后果时,"在法律规范原理上,使遭受损害之权益与促使损害发生之原因相结合,将损害因而转嫁由原因者承担之法律价值判断因素",〔73〕即为归责。因此,归责的基础在于主体的伦理可谴责性与法律秩序的要求,自然人行为的可归责性自不必论,法人的行为本质上仍由自然人完成,其为团体利益而从事行为最终后果由法人承担,同样具备可归责的基础。但对于无伦理性的智能人而言,若以法律规范强行使其承担责任,结果反倒使得真正应为其行为负责任的主体逃避法律的谴责。

反对意见可能会认为,第一,若使智能人的控制人为其设置财产账户注入为其行为负责的责任财产,则其可具备承担损害的责任能力。但这里需要明确一个前提,智能人财产账户中的资金能否为智能人所有。一方面,依据前文对智能人与法人的比较,可知智能人的控制人并未向其出资,智能人在经营过程中也不享有财产利益,无责任财产;另一方面,边沁认为:"财产这个概念存在于一种确定的期望中;存在于根据事物本质可以从所占有的物中取得这样一种好处的信念。这种期望,这种信念,只能是法律的产物。"〔74〕财产权概念的界定并不在于财产本身的有形体,而在于财产被法律承认的权能。而何者可享有财产的权能,在于其与财产之间发生了法律上承认的联系。"人有权把他的意志体现在任何物中,因而使该物成为我的东西。"〔75〕自然人以排他的意志实现对财产权能的归属,法人以共同的意志同样控制着财产,权能本身就通过所有人决定财产以何种方式使用而体现出来(the property right paradigm),因而财产权从根本上不过是人主体性的延伸并受到法律保护的权利。而对于仅为特定目的工作的智能人而言,其所执行的不过是控制者的程序设定,无法将自己的意志

〔72〕 前引36,京特·雅科布斯书,第74页。

〔73〕 程啸:《侵权责任法》,法律出版社2016年版,第85页。

〔74〕 [英]边沁:《立法理论,民法典原则》,载[美]约翰·E.克利贝特等:《财产法:案例与材料》,齐东祥、陈刚译,中国政法大学出版社2003年版,第5页。

〔75〕 前引28,黑格尔书,第60页。

体现在财产中,对财产不享有所有权。因而为智能人设立账户以使其承担责任的做法,其实质是让控制者为智能人的行为负责,从侧面显示了智能人的工具属性。

第二,自然人也并非全部均可以对其归责,可将智能人拟制为未成年人或欠缺行为能力的成年人,适用替代责任,由其控制者为其承担替代责任。[76] 首先,智能人的智能程度和专业程度在某些方面是显著强于普通人类的,将其列为社会弱势群体加以保护缺乏事实基础。其次,对于智能人行为造成的损害适用产品责任更为贴切。原因在于,若适用雇主责任或被代理人责任,在雇主或代理人承担责任后会涉及向行为人追偿的问题,而智能人基于上述分析其不具有可归责的伦理基础,也无承担责任的担保财产,通过替代责任或被代理人责任解决其责任承担的问题不仅会面临智能人主体性的质疑,追偿无法实现,还会产生因制度重构而造成的沉没成本,难以自圆其说。同时在替代责任下对于免责事由较为宽松,监护人责任中对于尽到监护责任可以减轻其侵权责任的规定显然不如产品责任对受害人的保护力度更强,更符合对智能人行为造成损害救济的需要。下面就具体环境下智能人行为造成损害适用产品责任如何救济进行简要梳理,以论证通过完善现行的民法规范可以解决智能人的责任承担,而不必另行赋予其法律主体地位。

六、对智能人造成损害的救济途径

在工具说的立场下,确定智能人造成损害的责任主体,一方面,要注意保存"人工智能系统的所产生的原始数据",[77] 将其作为确定损害发生的归责依据;另一方面,由于智能人行为本身带有新技术应用的风险,应通过完成产品责任,使作为危险开启源的智能人制造商负担控制风险、避免风险现实化的高度注意义务,实现对于新技术应用下产生的不幸风险之负担。

---

〔76〕 参见陈吉栋:《论机器人的法律人格——基于法释义学的讨论》,载《上海大学学报》(社会科学版)2018年第3期。

〔77〕 前引11,袁曾文。

（一）在数据的收集过程中造成的损害

数据是智能人行为做出的基础，为决策的分析判断提供了可供分析的材料。[78] 数据时代催生了大型线上公司来收集、分析和使用我们的信息，例如谷歌、脸书和优步等。从外观上看，智能人在收集数据并做出数据的分析，但是智能人只是商业公司所使用的工具，真正实现对于信息的收集和掌握的是智能人背后的商业公司。因此他们才应该是法律规制的对象——信息受信托人。[79] 这些线上公司通过收集和分析用户数据，增强与用户之间的联系；但用户对线上公司收集和处理信息的方式并不知情，导致了公司和终端用户在商业社会中的不对等。基于线上公司的强势地位、专业优势和保护用户隐私的需要，借助传统信托关系，在线上公司和用户之间成立信息信托法律关系，商业公司需要对他们的用户尽到忠实的注意义务，保护用户对其的合理信赖，为用户的利益提供服务，因此他们成为数字时代的信息信托人。

（二）使用智能人而造成的积极损害

在智能人侵权所造成的损害中，普遍的解决思路是使研发智能人的公司承担产品责任。通过对智能产品侵权责任的细化规定：坚持研发制造者的严格责任，[80] 明确智能产品质量标准，降低存在产品缺陷的证明难度，引入专家鉴定人以及设置数据记录仪，[81] 帮助证明产品缺陷的存在以及缺陷与损害之间的因果关系。现代科学技术在解放生产力的同时也使得更多物质设备以及生产工艺的风险性与收益性同步提升，在新一轮产业革命下人类的社会生活逐渐与人工智能技术搭建联系，应用有缺陷的智能产品致害的后果应由其研发制造者承担产品责任。而当证明产品缺陷或因果关系成立存在困难时，可通过强制保险和赔偿基金使受害人获得赔偿，同时保护研发制造者的创新动力，不断升级产品

---

〔78〕 See Amir Gandomi and Murtaza Haider, "Beyond the Hype: Big Data Concepts, Methods, and Analytics", 35 *INT'L J. INFO. MGMT.* 137 – 140 (2015).

〔79〕 参见前引 57，Jack M. Balkin 文，pp. 1227 – 1231。

〔80〕 See Jeffrey K. Gurney, "Sue My Car Not Me: Products Liability and Accidents Involving Autonomous Vehicles", *U. ILL. J. L. TECH & POL'Y* 247, 271 – 272, (2013).

〔81〕 See Majorie A. Shields, "Annotation, Admissibility of Evidence Taken from Vehicular Event Data Recorders (EDR), Sensing Diagnostic Modules, or Black Boxes", 40 *A. L. R.* 6th, 595 (2008).

的安全性能。而在特殊情况下使用智能人造成损害的责任的构建,以自动驾驶汽车造成交通事故为例,适用规则是:在区分实际驾驶者以及不同等级自动驾驶系统的情况下,若为系统自动驾驶,则适用产品责任,由自动驾驶汽车的制造商承担严格责任,同时在免责事由上根据自动驾驶的特点进行建构;若为使用者实际驾驶,则适用传统交通事故侵权责任;同时完善保险制度,分化社会风险。[82]

(三)智能人应用过程中的隐藏损害

此种隐藏损害来源于算法歧视,即"人工智能产品按照算法运行所得出针对特定人或特定群体的系统性的和不公平的歧视结果"。[83] 由于算法的灵活程度相对低于人类智能,收集的数据不能完全反映对象的全部状况,导致对某一群体的固化设定。同时这种算法的相对"机械性"导致人的差异性被扭曲和放大。人与人的差异仅为程度之分,而非绝对的对立。但算法在对人进行评估时,往往设计问题的选项为是或不是,缺少了调和型的中间选项,最终对人的评估结果是不准确的。[84] 而对人的判断一旦形成,人们便会不自觉地趋近于按照算法所分析的结果从事行为,在算法的影响下认知偏误和社会壁垒会不自觉地被强化,这便是智能人在应用算法进行身份识别和决策制定时所付出的社会成本。根据经济学的观点,在行为对外产生的风险不可避免的情况下,如何妥善规范对外行为使其能够最大化地产生对社会的积极效应,应作为法律规制的主要目标。[85] 因此,对这种社会成本的承担可从以下几个方面进行规制:第一,根据谁获益谁负担风险的原则,企业具有社会责任,其有必要也有能力承担风险。特别是企业可以通过获得的收益对冲风险或者通过完善产品责任保险分散风险,不能将其完全转移给少数人承担。第二,企业不能以智能人为具有民事能力的主体而掩饰企业本身在研发使用过程中的疏忽甚至放任,企业应尽到高度

---

〔82〕 参见郑志峰:《自动驾驶汽车的交通事故侵权责任》,载《法学》2018年第4期。

〔83〕 Friedman and Helen Nissenbaum,"Bias in Computer Systems",*ACM Transactions on Information Systems*,Vol. 14,No. 3,July 332 (1996).

〔84〕 See Caelainn Carney,"Robo-Advisers and the Suitability Requirement,How They Fit in the Regulatory Framework",*Colum. Bus. L. Rev*,588 -592. (2018).

〔85〕 See Keith N. Hylton," The Economists of Public Nuisance Law and the New Enforcement Actions",18 *Sup. Ct. Econ. Rev*. 43,44 (2010).

的注意义务,禁止设计歧视性的算法或使用不清洁数据,同时积极升级和更新算法,提高制定决策的水平。企业之间可以通过设立共同的开放数据库,合作研发,交流技术,规定透明的技术流程和设计标准,规范算法的设计与数据的收集使用。值得注意的一点是,具体人员在尽到高度注意义务的情况下可能仍无法避免出现算法歧视的后果,一方面可能基于社会本身存在的不公平现象在算法分析结果下被放大——例如女性常被推荐低薪工作,另一方面可能基于技术发展水平的限制使得算法对不同环境的应变能力有所欠缺,〔86〕在上述情况下需完善产品责任的免责事由使企业摆脱不当责难。但也应明确企业对数据分析的注意义务,警惕可能出现的歧视结论——"不能因申请人居住在贫困地或高犯罪率地区而拒绝对其放贷"〔87〕,在此情况下尽管因社会运转偏见或技术水平有限而出现歧视结果,但如果被企业不当利用,则应当就该利用所引发的损害后果对企业进行归责。第三,保护公众的个人信息和数据隐私。智能人在进行机器学习和数据分析的过程中要符合欧盟《一般数据保护条例》对数据隐私的保护,〔88〕保护公民的被遗忘权以增强数据的准确性和可靠性,赋予民众可获得解释权以规范算法的运行和数据的收集使用,以及在授予和撤回同意权的平衡中实现人工智能与数据保护的协调发展。第四,完善登记注册制度,实现企业公示与可追溯。Frank Pasquale 指出,算法的设计必须在我们能够清楚地知道是谁在使用它的情况下进行。法律需要建立完备的公示制度,对那些躲在算法后面的企业进行公示,使其承担相应的社会成本。〔89〕

---

〔86〕 参见前引 83,Friedman and Helen Nissenbaum 文,p. 339。

〔87〕 同上文,p. 333。

〔88〕 See Matthew Humerick,"Taking AI Personally:How the E. U. Must Learn to Balance the Interests of Personal Data Privacy & Artificial Intelligence",34 *Santa Clara HighTech. L. J.* 401 – 413 (2018).

〔89〕 See Frank Pasquale,"Toward a Fourth Law of Robotics:Preserving Attribution, Responsibility,and Explain ability in an Algorithmic Society",78 *OHIO ST. L. J*,1248 – 1251 (2017).

七、结　语

人工智能作为一门新兴的研究学科蕴含着人类智能无尽的潜力,也给现代社会中的法律规则的构建带来了新的挑战。结合目前国内外对于人工智能的介绍,以及传统大陆法系的法律主体理论和其他影响法律主体成立的因素,笔者认为就智能人目前的发展水平而言,并不足以成为法律关系的主体,其仅具有卓越的分析工具价值。否定智能人的主体地位,一方面不会引发人们对机器智能的恐慌,不会丧失对人之理性尊严和自由意志的信心;另一方面智能人并未超出现有的民法规范,通过原有体系内法律规则的更新与完善,可为现实生活中的纠纷提供有力的救济渠道。

(责任编辑:蔚泽洋)

论人工智能产品自身损害责任

陈奎宇*

摘要:

人工智能产品产生的产品质量问题是法律界必须应对的一个新问题。本文重点探讨由于人工智能产品缺陷带来的产品自身损害的法律责任。《侵权责任法》第41条将产品自身损害,即产品因为缺陷导致自身财产性价值减损的损害,纳入了生产者承担严格责任的范围。从近期来看,人工智能产品属于传统产品的范畴,因此可以借助传统产品的自身损害法律规定,运用生产者承担严格责任来解决。从远期来看,人工智能产品可能实现高度自主性,当人工智能产品进行自我决策而导致了自身财产价值的减损,本文认为部分人工智能内部程序不属于缺陷以及人工智能的自主性应当阻隔《侵权责任法》第41条的适用。建议在远期应当进行人工智能立法,建立起电子人格的制度,将高级人工智能与传统产品区别开来,并设立保险机制和政府公共救济的机制。

关键词:

人工智能产品;产品自身损害;侵权责任

引　言

侵权责任法中的产品自身损害,即产品因为缺陷导致自身财产性价值减损。传统产品的自身财产性损害的救济在《中华人民共和国产品质量法》(以下简称《产品质量法》)中没有规定,后来被纳入《中华人民共和国侵权责任法》(以下简称《侵权责任法》)第41条规定的生产者承担严格责任的范围,这已经是一次突破,至于《侵权责任法》的相关规定在人工智能机器产品领域如何运用

---

* 陈奎宇,香港大学法学院2018级硕士研究生。

还需要进一步探索。本文旨在探讨人类步入人工智能时代后,《侵权责任法》第41条包含的产品自身损害原理与人工智能产品特点是否兼容的问题。前人的研究有的支持扩张适用产品自身损害的侵权法救济。例如,王利明教授认为《侵权责任法》第41条有利于及时有效地保障消费者的合法权益;[1]董春华博士认为在现代社会中一些交易对象本身即具有危险性,因此《侵权责任法》的产品自身损害救济之扩张有利于维护合同当事人或者第三人因为潜在的财产损害所受之威胁。[2] 但是上述研究未涉及未来人工智能产品时代的法律问题。一些研究关注了人工智能产品,特别是无人驾驶汽车对现行法律制度的挑战,例如腾讯研究院研究英国的人工智能法律提案中提出将机动车强制保险的应用范围扩大到产品责任,为驾驶员赋予自动驾驶汽车智能系统控制权时提供保护。[3] 吴汉东教授认为人工智能致人损害实践中人工智能产品不能够以"自身行为"为理由承担责任,被侵权一方仍然需要替代责任来获得救济。[4] 但是这些研究并未涉及人工智能产品自身的财产性损害的责任承担方式。随着人工智能技术的不断进步,有必要对未来可能出现的高级人工智能的情景进行相关立法规范,否则法律的空白不仅可能损害人类的权益,还会阻碍科技的发展。因此本文针对这一问题,进行一些基础研究。

一、产品自身损害侵权法救济的产生

人类从农耕文明发展到人工智能时代,有劳动生产必定会出现产品。产品在社会生产、流通、销售等各个领域自然会出现产品责任。产品责任指的是当缺陷产品造成损害时,该缺陷产品的生产者、销售者应当承担的法律责任。产

[1] 参见全国人大常委会法制工作委员会民法室:《〈中华人民共和国侵权责任法〉条文说明、立法理由及相关规定》,北京大学出版社2010年版,第174页。

[2] 参见董春华:《产品自身损害赔偿研究——兼评〈侵权责任法〉第41条》,载《河北法学》2014年第11期。

[3] 参见腾讯研究院:《人工智能各国战略解读:英国人工智能的未来监管措施与目标概述》,载《电信网技术》2017年第2期。

[4] 参见吴汉东:《人工智能时代的制度安排与法律规制》,载《法律科学》(西北政法大学学报)2017年第5期。

品责任是一种不以侵权人与被侵权人之间存在合同关系为前提的侵权责任，因此，无论受害者与产品的生产者或销售者之间是否存在合同关系，被侵权人均可以提起产品责任之诉。《产品质量法》第46条规定："本法所称缺陷，是指产品存在危及人身、他人财产安全的不合理的危险；产品有保障人体健康和人身、财产安全的国家标准、行业标准的，是指不符合该标准。"产品自身损害是由缺陷所产生的一种损害情形。

产品缺陷引发的损害是否包含产品自身损害，我国的立法经历了一次扩张。2000年修订后的《产品质量法》第41条规定："因产品存在缺陷造成人身、缺陷产品以外的其他财产（以下简称他人财产）损害的，生产者应当承担赔偿责任……"《产品质量法》第46条规定："本法所称缺陷，是指产品存在危及人身、他人财产安全的不合理的危险；产品有保障人体健康和人身、财产安全的国家标准、行业标准的，是指不符合该标准。"这些条文的规定明显地排除了产品自身财产减损的情况。而2010年正式实施的《侵权责任法》第41条规定："因产品存在缺陷造成他人损害的，生产者应当承担侵权责任。"对比发现，后者删去了"缺陷产品以外的其他财产的限定"。学界对此问题亦有不同观点，有的学者认为产品自身损害即购买该产品所付价金的损失，[5]有学者将其定义为"缺陷产品本身的价金损害"。[6] 本文认为，产品自身损害应该包括因为缺陷所导致的产品的损毁、灭失、价值减损，以及修缮有缺陷产品所支出的费用。

我国《侵权责任法》第41条的规定是产品自身损害的侵权法救济理念的一大革新，因为它将可受侵权责任法救济的损害范围扩张至产品自身的财产性损失。目前世界各国的立法对产品自身的财产性损失的规定十分谨慎。例如德国《产品责任法》第1条规定："产品制造商有义务赔偿由于产品缺陷，死亡、人身伤害、财产损坏或财产损坏而造成的损失。在财产损失的情况下，该财产仅适用于失去产品以外的其他财产的损失，这些财产通常供个人消费，并且仅由受害者使用。"[7]英国1987年《消费者保护法案》第5条将缺陷产品本身的损

〔5〕 参见杨立新：《侵权责任法》，法律出版社2012年版，第312页。

〔6〕 参见张新宝：《侵权责任法》，中国人民大学出版社2013年版，第219页。

〔7〕 Federal Ministry of Justice and Consumer Protection, "Act on Liability for Defective Products", https://www.gesetze-im-internet.de/englisch_prodhaftg/englisch_prodhaftg.html, August 1, 2018.

害或组装到另一产品中的产品损害或纯经济损失排除在了赔偿范围之外。[8] 1972年《关于产品责任法律适用的海牙公约》第2条第2款规定:"'损害'一词系指人身伤害、财产损害和经济损失;产品本身的损害以及间接经济损失不包括在内,除非该损害和其他损害相联系。"[9] 综上所述,上述立法基本上将产品自身的财产性损失排除在外。按照合同法上的物的瑕疵担保责任,当产品出现了不符合当事人之间约定的质量要求或者不符合法律规定的质量标准,受害者可以依靠违约责任寻求救济,包括要求买卖合同的另一方当事人承担修理、更换、退货和赔偿责任。可见我国《侵权责任法》第41条为遭受产品自身财产性损失的受害者提供了全新的侵权法救济路径。但是该条款在人工智能机器产品中的运用,需要我们进行全面的研究。

二、近期人工智能机器产品自身损害侵权责任的确定

人工智能是使用计算机科学的概念、程序和方法从事认知过程的科学,实际上就是一种机器模仿人智力活动的技术。其融合了生理学、哲学、计算机科学等诸多学科的知识,能够模拟人的思维和意识,在此基础上能够进行合理化的拓展与延伸,继而完成比较复杂的工作。人工智能(能力)是智能机器所执行的通常与人类智能有关的智能行为,这些智能行为涉及学习、感知、思考、理解、识别、判断、推理、证明、通信、设计、规划、行动和问题求解等活动。[10] 目前人工智能的主要表现形式包括具有一定自我分析能力的应用程序控制的传统机械以及新型机器人,它们都属于人工智能机器的范畴。

传统的产品概念在概括人工智能机器时遇到了困境。《现代汉语词典》中的"产品"是指"生产出来的物品"。从经济学上讲,产品是劳动生成物,是人类通过劳动手段对劳动对象进行加工所形成的,适合人类生产和生活需要的一切

---

[8] See United Kingdoms' Parliament, "Consumer Protection Act 1987", https://www.legislation.gov.uk/ukpga/1987/43/contents, August 1, 2018.

[9] Hague Conference on Private International Law, "Convention on The Law Applicable to Products Liability", https://assets.hcch.net/docs/e102a194-59b8-4d75-9c6f-d2bbfb81e4ff.pdf, August 1, 2018.

[10] 参见蔡自兴、蒙祖强:《人工智能基础》,高等教育出版社2016年版,第3页。

劳动成果,同时产品也是人类存在和发展的物质条件。[11] 现代意义上的产品概念更强调能够满足消费者某种欲望或需要的属性,即认为产品是企业根据消费者所给予的价值,提供的相应的各个方面的综合物,既可以是一种物质实体,也可以是一种服务或利益。[12] 《产品质量法》第 2 条规定:“……本法所称产品是指经过加工、制作,用于销售的产品……”以上定义主要是从产品供应链的角度来诠释的,可以看出产品属于完全由人类的智力和资本控制的客体,是人力所支配的物。传统的产品质量法律关系主要涉及三大主体:生产者、销售者、消费者。但是人工智能机器随着计算机技术的发展,其自主性水平和智能化程度不断提高,这势必会产生一个新的“准主体”。我们必须结合人工智能的智能水平的发展,对《侵权责任法》第 41 条的产品自身损害的生产者责任进行分别研究。人工智能的近期研究目标是代替人类的某些智力活动。人工智能的远期目标是用自动机模仿人类的思维活动和智力功能,也就是说,要建造能够实现人类思维活动和智力功能的智能系统。[13] 人工智能在 20 世纪 80 年代曾经依靠专家系统的兴起出现了繁荣的景象,然而很快又因为技术的局限而步入寒冬。自 2006 年以来深度学习技术的发展使得人工智能在某些领域具备强大的自主运算和推理能力,[14] 但是它们没有自主意识。

由于目前国内涉及人工智能的侵权案件较为罕见,笔者将对目前的产品自身损害案件进行分析,希望能引申出一些在人工智能时代的产品自身损害的应对方针。笔者在中国裁判文书以“产品自身损害”为关键词进行案例检索,得到了 27 个案例并在此基础上进行了统计。在这 27 个案例之中,有 19 个案例以违约损害赔偿请求权为救济渠道,剩余的 8 个案例均为侵权案例。8 个侵权案例全部涉及产品的自身缺陷,其中的 4 个案例还涉及产品存在危及人身、他人财产安全的不合理危险。具体对危险的分类详见表 1。

---

〔11〕 参见张云、徐楠轩:《产品质量法教程》,厦门大学出版社 2011 年版,第 12 页。

〔12〕 同上。

〔13〕 前引 9,蔡自兴、蒙祖强书,第 3 页。

〔14〕 参见陈自富:《强人工智能和超级智能:技术合理性及其批判》,载《科学与管理》2016 年第 5 期。

表1 案件危险类型归纳

案件名称	危险类型
再审申请人上海通用汽车有限公司与被申请人马某、抚顺七星汽车销售有限责任公司、辽宁天合汽车销售服务有限公司产品责任纠纷	因车辆自身故障引发的发动机左前侧起火
姬某与宁夏鹿鸣汽车贸易有限公司产品责任纠纷	大臂油缸爆炸
高某、赵某与一汽大众汽车有限公司、包头市惠众汽车服务有限公司产品责任纠纷	发动机舱电气故障导致起火
孙某与一汽大众汽车有限公司、大连弘鼎汽车销售服务有限公司财产损害赔偿纠纷	电气线路故障导致发动机左侧起火

表1中的案例均与汽车或机械设备的自身缺陷有关,并且此类具有危及人身、他人财产安全的不合理危险的案例在产品自身损害的侵权案例中呈现出高发态势。与这些传统机械设备相比,人工智能机器排除了人为的操纵控制和监督干预,更加依赖于机器自身凭借其传感器和分析程序作出的自主性判断。在人工智能发展水平较为原始的当代,机器自身缺陷或损害无疑会给消费者或者社会公众带来更大的风险。通过对《侵权责任法》第41条做文本分析可以发现,凡是产品存在缺陷(条件A)并且造成财产性或者人身性损害的(条件B),在同时满足A和B两个条件的情况下生产者必须承担侵权责任。与《产品质量法》第41条相比,《侵权责任法》明显地加重了生产者的责任,并且根据新法优于旧法的原则,《侵权责任法》第41条应当得到优先适用。

人工智能产品的产品自身缺陷将带来更高的危险隐患,同时人工智能产品的成本往往更高,其更为高昂的价格使得产品本身的财产性损失应当得到更多重视。以目前正在蓬勃发展的无人驾驶汽车为例,无人驾驶的关键技术是环境感知技术和车辆控制技术,其中环境感知技术是无人驾驶汽车行驶的基础,车辆控制技术是无人驾驶汽车行驶的核心,这两项技术相辅相成共同构成无人驾驶汽车的关键技术。无人驾驶的整个流程归结起来有两个部分:一方面,通过雷达等对外界的环境进行感知;另一方面,在必要的情况下对整车进行刹车制动以及转向系统的配合,以保证汽车的安全性、操纵性和稳定性。[15]从Uber公司的自动驾驶汽车在美国道路上出现撞死行人的案例中透露的部分信息可以获知,该自动驾驶的激光雷达是否存在盲点将成为撞死行人的关键技术问题。

因此,上述技术的安全性与稳定性关乎无人驾驶汽车的乘员以及路面其他行人和车辆的人身和财产安全,并且上述技术设备例如激光雷达、分析计算机等成本高昂,因此掌握着核心技术资源的生产者必须负担重大的责任。这个法律义务也是与传统产品责任中的生产者责任一脉相承的,生产者承担严格责任是由生产者的特殊地位决定的。在产品的设计、试制、投产和制造等整个过程中,生产者始终处于主动的、积极的地位。生产者对产品的缺陷具有完全控制或者是可以预见的、控制的能力。[16] 基于此,生产者有义务将产品事故的发生率和损失最小化,并通过提高科研投入和完善科学管理等措施保证产品质量,否则生产者将对产品自身损害承担严格的侵权责任。

三、未来高级人工智能产品自身损害与既有侵权责任的矛盾

人类文明从蒙昧走向启蒙再到现代化,正是一个人类不断承认与认识自身,摆脱神明对思想的桎梏,从而承认人类价值与尊严的一个过程。当人类文明来到了新的十字路口,笔者认为人类对人工智能的性质和发展的“启蒙”也如同启蒙运动时代人类认识自身一般重要,因此我们也要开始认真审视人工智能的性质与发展潜质。

根据辩证唯物主义的观点,事物是发展变化的,这要求人们不能用孤立、静止、片面的观点来看待问题。人工智能发展也是分阶段的,当代以深度学习系统为基础的人工智能不具备自主意识,还只是人类智能的一种产品,受人类的控制、支配。但根据上文介绍的人工智能的远期发展目标,模仿人类的思维活动和智力功能的智能系统有可能在未来的科技条件下成为现实。在研究未来人工智能的过程中,除了深度学习技术,还有类脑人工智能的研究,目标是基于

[15] 参见彭金帅:《浅析无人驾驶汽车的关键技术及其未来商业化应用》,载《科技创新与应用》2015年第25期。

[16] 前引10,张云、徐楠轩书,第239页。

人类大脑工作原理设计而不是传统结构的计算机来实现智能。部分研究者认为类脑人工智能将会是人工智能的终极目标。[17] 基于此,未来的人工智能系统及其机器载体将有可能具备极高的自主思考和自我判断、决策能力,甚至在部分领域的计算和思维能力远远超出人类的水平。对于未来高级人工智能(或强人工智能)与现阶段人工智能的区别标准,学界有若干测试的学说:"1. 图灵测试,即是同人类交流的试验;2. 咖啡测试,即人工智能要主动在陌生空间中认识咖啡机、辨识咖啡和水、找到合适的杯子并放好,然后按正确的键和操作以冲泡咖啡,这需要仰赖机器人学、图像辨识的演算;3. 机器人学生测试即透过机器学习,分析和回答单一问题的测试,例如让一个机器去注册一所大学,参加和人类学生同样的考试,然后通过并获得学位;4. 雇员测试即测试统筹、推断、发想、规划解决复杂问题的能力,例如让机器处在一个经济上重要的职位,需要它能够和同样职位的人类做得同样好或者更好。"[18] 简言之,强人工智能研究目标是具备与人类同等智慧或超越人类的人工智能,能表现正常人类所具有的所有智能行为;[19] 而目前的人工智能并不具备上述能力。

但是目前学界对于人工智能与人类关系的定位仍有争议,主要存在以下的学说:工具说认为人工智能是人类为生产生活应用而创设的技术,其本质是为人类服务的工具,并认为人工智能无独立的意思表示能力,并不承认人工智能具有独立的法律人格;电子奴隶说认为人工智能不具有人类特殊的情感与肉体特征,在工作时无休息等现实需要,可以认作不知疲倦的机器,有行为能力但没有权利能力;代理说认为人工智能的所有行为均是为人类所控制的,其做出的行为与引起的后果最终必须由被代理的主体承担。[20] 笔者认为工具说和电子奴隶说完全忽视未来人工智能的技术特点和未来发展潜能。代理说也具有局限性,并不能适用于人工智能具备自主决策与自主学习的时代。

---

〔17〕 前引 13,陈自富文。

〔18〕 Luke Muehlhauser, "What is AGI?", https://intelligence. org/2013/08/11/what-is-agi/, November 26, 2018.

〔19〕 See Ray Kurzweil, "Advanced Human Intelligence", https://crnano. typepad. com/crnblog/2005/08/advanced_human_. html, November 26, 2018.

〔20〕 袁曾:《人工智能有限法律人格审视》,载《东方法学》2017 年第 5 期。

而在未来的条件下发生的人工智能机器产品自身损害的案例,将不再仅仅涉及生产者、销售者、消费者的三方,人工智能机器本身也有可能发展为一种"准主体"。一些导致产品自身损害的新情况将会发生,因此目前《侵权责任法》第41条单一地将产品自身损害归责于生产者的严格责任将会出现局限性。因此,人工智能未来可能出现的"自我选择"和"自我判断"的产品自身损害值得我们深入研究。为了保障人类的人身与财产安全,需要对人工智能的安全性进行检验。而检验和确认需要方法的制度化,并保证人工智能按照既定的计算机算法运行,不出现不必要的行为或者功能上的改变。[21] 为了实现这一目的,需要为人工智能装置设立"自我毁灭"的后门装置,使其处于人类不间断的监控之下,最大限度地保证其不伤害人类。科幻小说家阿西莫夫提出了著名的"阿西莫夫机器人"三定律,该套规则对于人类对机器人的认知以及机器人学的发展具有深远的启发和指导意义。所谓"机器人三定律"指的是:第一定律——机器人不得伤害人,也不得见人受到伤害而袖手旁观;第二定律——机器人应服从人的一切命令,但不得违反第一法则;第三定律——机器人应保护自身的安全,但不得违反第一、第二法则。[22] 上述三定律可以通过编程的语句化落实在未来人工智能机器人的应用中。笔者推演这样一种场景:拥有自主意识的人工智能机器人在执行人类命令的某项任务时,出现有可能危及第三人生命安全的紧迫情形。它只能在保护人类、服从命令和保护自身安全中做出一个选择;根据三定律中具有最高性的第一定律和"后门程序"的设定,此时机器人只能选择启动后门程序中的"自我毁灭"选项,从而保障该第三人的生命安全。试问,当具有了自主意识的人工智能机器人产品通过缜密地自主思考和判断而选择了"自我毁灭"的自身损害,生产者是否还应该负担沉重的责任?本文认为应该结合《侵权责任法》第41条的法条来分两步进行分析。

第一,因为该条款的前提是产品自身存在缺陷,那么人工智能机器人被设置有上述"自我毁灭"的后门程序是否属于缺陷?根据我国《产品质量法》的规定,缺陷是指产品存在危及人身、他人财产安全的不合理的危险;产品有保障人体健康和人身、财产安全的国家标准、行业标准的,是指不符合该标

---

〔21〕 前引3,腾讯研究院文。

〔22〕 参见[美]艾萨克·阿西莫夫:《机器人短片全集》,《汉声》杂志译,天地出版社2005年版,第3页。

准。人工智能机器人内置的后门程序从其触发后的结果来看,似乎具有一定的危险特征,但是我们必须认识到该程序的真正目的在于笔者所描述的上述场景中保护第三人的安全。未来人工智能机器制造业可能会颁布相应的国家标准和行业标准,即便在标准制定由于科技的超前发展而滞后之时,后门程序触发后引起的危险也不应当被认定为不合理的危险,因为这并没有违背消费者对产品安全性的合理期待。结合上述,本文认为“后门程序”不属于缺陷之范畴。

第二,本文让步性地假设人工智能机器人由于特殊的历史背景和时代原因被立法者认定为属于“缺陷”,在人工智能机器人中被输入了后门程序的情况下,本文认为由于后门程序的存在而导致的人工智能自我损毁不应当由生产者负担严格的无过错责任。关于程序设定和机器人自主性的联系,可以类比人工智能作品的可著作权性的研究思路。目前,以计算机程序为基础的人工智能在作品创作中的创造性已经不亚于人类,就所付出的智力劳动而言,不论一部经由人工智能创作的作品的独创性高低如何,至少在该部作品中,人类所发挥的作用可能仅仅限于按下“程序启动”的按钮,甚至只需启动电源,不包含任何智力的投入。〔23〕在目前这个阶段从人工智能的本质上分析,部分由人工智能创作的作品满足了版权法形式上的独创性程度,是一种通过算法进行分析、选择所完成的机械式的输出。这种人工智能输出目前已经大致能够自行完成数据收集、分析以及作品创作的全过程,人类参与人工智能作品创作的作用仅限于启动程序。〔24〕目前,英国《版权、设计与专利法》、澳大利亚计算机软件保护报告皆将人工智能创作物作为版权作品处理,〔25〕尽管部分国家在司法实践中拒绝了对纯粹的程序输出物进行版权保护,但是本文认为不排除随着人工智能的发展,上述程序输出物类型的作品可以被版权保护。本文意在阐明的原理是,随着未来科技的高度发展,应当将人工智能的自我运行和程序开发者、制造商的行为二元看待,具体见表2:

---

〔23〕 参见曹源:《人工智能创作物获得版权保护的合理性》,载《法律与科技》2016年第3期。

〔24〕 同上。

〔25〕 同上。

表 2　人工智能的两种场景类型对比

场景类别	制造商/程序开发者的背景行为	人工智能的行为	未来发展方向
人工智能产品创作	开发程序,启动程序	自主运行创作作品	人工智能的自主创作不从属于程序开发者
人工智能产品自我损害侵权	开发程序,启动程序	自主判断选择后门程序的毁灭开关	人工智能机器的自主判断行为不归责于制造商

综上所述,从远期人工智能发展水平的角度分析,人工智能系统即将具备的高度自主性将成为阻断背景行为和人工智能行为的介入性因素,其结果是直接导致在因为后门程序的存在而出现人工智能机器产品自我损害行为时对生产者严格责任的阻却。这一变化将导致《侵权责任法》第 41 条在适用上出现困难,需要在立法上的变化来应对,包括构建电子人格、保险理赔和公共基金补偿等机制。

四、相关立法应对建议

如前所述,新法《侵权责任法》第 41 条对比旧法《产品质量法》第 41 条,将生产者应当承担无过错严格责任的范围从产品缺陷导致的人身损害、产品以外的其他财产损害扩大到产品缺陷导致的所有人身损害和财产损害。从而将因为产品自身缺陷导致的自身财产性损害引入了我国法律人的视野。在人工智能机器具备高度智慧化和自主判断、决策能力的前提下,出现了人工智能机器因为某种自主选择的原因从而触发后门程序导致产品自身损害的情形。在《侵权责任法》第 41 条出现适用困难的情况下,本文尝试提出新的立法解决方案。

第一,《产品质量法》应当被修改,从而实现其第 41 条与《侵权责任法》第 41 条的标准统一,在这样的条件下讨论产品自身损害法律问题的新变化才有意义。本文建议实行普通产品和未来的高级人工智能产品的区分原则,专门制定《人工智能法》。该法的首要目的即在于界定清楚"电子人格"之概念,即赋予具有自主思考和自我判断意识的人工智能产品的一种"类人资格"。从沙特阿拉伯授予机器人"索菲亚"以公民权之后,且不论此事件的象征意义是否超过了其实践上的意义,人类不应该忽视未来人工智能的可塑性和发展趋势,法律界与科技界应该正视未来机器人或者人工智能系统的法律地位问题。

参考域外的一些立法探索和研究,欧盟议会法律事务委员会发布了《欧盟机器人民事法律规则》(European Civil Law Rules in Robotics),其中涉及人工智能机器人的法律地位问题。《欧盟机器人民事法律规则》认为智能机器人需要具备以下几个特征:可以概括为数据自主交换与分析能力、自我学习能力、物理支撑属性、行为调整能力。[26] 在此基础上,该研究报告认为在未来需要考虑赋予复杂自主机器人法律地位的可能性。《欧盟机器人民事法律规则》建议创造一个"电子人"的全新概念,以此赋予人工智能机器人适当的法律地位,从而使成熟的智能机器人在与第三方互动之中能够享有权利和承担义务。[27]

分类的定义上,我国未来的《人工智能法》可以借鉴这些概念,即享有"电子人格"的人工智能产品为"具有自我分析、判断和学习能力,具备物理支撑属性,可以自主管理和控制自身行为人工智能"。《产品质量法》第41条和《侵权责任法》第41条都可以增设一款:"涉及具有电子人格的人工智能产品的产品责任,适用其他专门法律规定。"基于此,享有"电子人格"的人工智能在有限程度内享有权利与承担义务。义务包括人工智能产品因为自身决策导致的侵权行为所要承担的责任。但是由于人工智能产品仍旧是人类设计、制造出来的产物,也没有像人类一样复杂的社会关系和伦理道德,因此其责任承担方式完全不同于具备完全民事行为能力的民事主体,而应当进行特殊的安排。目前《侵权责任法》第15条规定:"承担侵权责任的方式主要有:(一)停止侵害;(二)排除妨碍;(三)消除危险;(四)返还财产;(五)恢复原状;(六)赔偿损失;(七)赔礼道歉;(八)消除影响、恢复名誉……"这些侵权责任承担方式有的可以由未来的《人工智能法》所承继,例如停止侵害、排除妨碍、消除危险、返还财产、恢复原状、消除影响和恢复名誉。符合具备"电子人格"定义的人工智能产品在理论上可以实施上述责任承担的行为。至于赔礼道歉,由于人工智能不具备人类的伦理道德属性,人工智能本身要输出赔礼道歉的语言并不困难,但其对侵权人起到的救济与弥补功效实属有限,因此不建议纳入这一责任。而赔偿损失的责任要视享有"电子人格"的人工智能产品是否应当享有独立的财产权而定。笔者

---

〔26〕 See European Parliament, "European Civil Law Rules in Robotics", http://www.europarl.europa.eu/RegData/etudes/STUD/2016/571379/IPOL_STU(2016)571379_EN.pdf, September 1,2018.

〔27〕 同上。

认为,即便成熟的人工智能机器人在制造业与服务业中通过劳动创造了财富,增加了公共领域的产品,若它们从属于企业、单位、个人并以为它们服务为主要目的时,它们便不享有独立的财产权;若它们独立地以个体的身份承担某种社会角色,便具备享有独立的财产权的条件,并以自身财产承担相应的责任。当人工智能机器人独立地以个体的身份承担某种社会角色,享有独立的财产权时,就可以以其财产承担相应的责任。

在人工智能机器具备高度智慧化和自主判断、决策能力的前提下,出现了人工智能机器因为某种自主选择的原因从而触发后门程序导致产品自身损害时,需要进行分类讨论。当人工智能机器人从属于企业、单位、个人并以为它们服务为主要目的时,它们不具备独立的财产权,人工智能机器本身价值与功能的减损将导致企业、单位、个人财产的减损,此时人工智能机器应当承担排除妨碍、消除危险等责任。至于财产方面的损失,有下文涉及的补充性救济机制来实现。当人工智能机器人独立地以个体的身份承担某种社会角色,享有独立的财产权时,产品自身损害是它本体的价值与功能的减损,所以它无需因此对另外的主体承担责任。

未来《人工智能法》可以加入补充性的救济性机制,引入其他的主体,弥补人工智能机器人责任所不能填补的空缺。首先,人工智能机器人的所有人或者辅助使用人在人工智能产品自身损害情形下是否承担责任?人工智能作为一种新的技术,出于鼓励技术创新的原则,本文认为可以在一定情况下肯定“技术中立”的思想。所谓技术中立原则,是指任何技术本身原则上都不产生责任承担,机器人本无瑕疵,符合技术中立原则要求。但机器人的所有人或使用人,或不尽善良管理人之义务,或放任机器人的产品自损行为,则不是技术中立原则所能够包含的范围。在此情况下,所有人或使用人应当对人工智能机器人产品自身损害对企业、单位、个人造成的财产或人身损害,承担补充性的赔偿责任。

第二,当前的产品责任保险的理论基础是风险的社会化,即作为产品生产者的企业通过购买保险的方式将未来可能发生的产品缺陷而造成损害的理赔风险的一部分分散到保险公司身上,这种方式也是在成熟的市场经济社会里常见的。产品责任保险承保的产品责任,是以产品为具体指向物,以产品可能造成的对他人的财产损害或人身伤害为具体承保风险,以制造或能够影响产品责任事故发生的有关各方为被保险人的一种责任保险。由于人工智能产品自主决策而导致自身财产价值减损甚至是灭失的情况很难归责于生产者,因此当今的产品责任保险可以未来继续适用于人工智能时代。本文建议,利用保险制度来对消费者提供救济可以成为未来《人工智能法》中重要补充机制。另外,基于政府的公共责任理论,政府承担着维护社会公共安全以及公民人身、财产利益的重要责任;公民作为政府的权力来源,并且让渡部分权力予政府,其应有之义是政府要维护好社会的安全秩序。人工智能产品在未来的很长一段时间内都将会是对社会安全秩序产生挑战的新生事物,针对人工智能产品出现的产品自身损害以及导致的他人人身、财产损害的,本文建议在未来《人工智能法》之中建立政府公共基金来承担一部分的救济功能。

结　　语

产品责任是维护市场交易秩序和消费者合法权益的重要支柱。现行《侵权责任法》第41条的创立将产品自身损害,即产品因为缺陷导致自身财产性价值的减损问题,纳入了生产者的要承担严格责任的体系之中。比照世界其他一些主要国家的产品侵权责任立法,我国对于损害的界定更加宽泛。在人类已经迎来了人工智能时代曙光的背景下,本文梳理了不同阶段的人工智能与现行产品概念之间的脉络与矛盾。近期来看,人工智能产品属于传统产品的范畴,属于人类智力和财产所能完全支配的客体,因此本文重点收集了一些非人工智能的传统产品的自身损害案例,阐述了人工智能产品的自身损害更应该强调生产者的严格责任背后的原理。远期来看,人工智能产品的智力有可能远远超出人类的水平,甚至实现自主思考、决策、控制的情况,此时传统产品的法律概念将难以完全适用于该种情况。高级人工智能机器有可能被人类生产者内置有自我毁灭功能的后门程序以保障人类的安全,当人工智能产品因自我决策而启动后门程序导致了自身财产价值的减损时,本文先后从该程序不属于缺陷以及人工智能的自主性应当阻隔生产者的严格责任的论证来说明《侵权责任法》第41条的适用困境。因此本文建议在远期应当进行人工智能立法,规定电子人格的概念将高级人工智能与传统产品区别开来,建立起综合的人工智能产品自身损害责任的规范体系。

(责任编辑:陈诗慧)

人工智能致人损害的法律责任研究
——从主体性角度观察

王　森*

摘要:

人工智能系统对生活领域的逐渐渗透,导致了法律责任问题的突出。人工智能行为应当由谁来承担责任,本质上取决于人工智能系统的行为究竟是何种性质,这就需要考察人工智能系统的主体性问题。人工智能系统主体性的一般问题是深度神经网络的相对独立性,而特殊问题则与人工智能系统的两种不同类型有关。语言类人工智能系统具有区别于其他类型的特点,因为内含于人类语言中的价值也将能够被理解。人工智能系统虽未必具有主体性,但该问题确实重要。随着人工智能系统能更高程度地模拟人类智能和行为,甚至在很多领域取代人类智能,有必要对人工智能致人损害的法律责任尽早进行规范。笔者主张对于具备语言能力的人工智能可以令其自我解释,对于其他人工智能则采用社会保险制度,同时以算法伦理规范编程行为。

关键词:

人工智能;法律责任;主体性;法律监管

一、引　言

(一)问题与思路

法秩序意味着什么?守法是对规则的承认和遵守,还是概率性的预测?法律的目的是社会控制,还是追求效益?法治的根本在于沟通和理解,还是权威和服从?对于这些问题,法学内部有各种各样的答案,学者们莫衷一是。但是

---

* 王森,南京大学法学院2016级硕士研究生。

无论我们对于这些问题有怎样的分歧,至少绝大部分的学者都同意,法律意味着人与人之间的秩序。虽然对于这一秩序的理解有各种各样的版本,但是我们都同意,"人"是这一秩序最基本的组成单元。同时,法秩序也仅仅适用于人类,动物、器物并不在这种秩序之中。但这一共识正面临挑战。

本文将通过对人工智能的主体性本质的探寻以及语言类和非语言类两大基本类型进行分析,从而对人工智能致人损害的法律责任问题之解决方法进行探究。本文论述的目的是就人工智能致人损害的法律责任问题给出基本的见解,而论述的线索则通过追踪人工智能是否具备主体性而展开。

随着人工智能对社会生活的影响日益增长,人工智能在很多方面起到了替代人类行为的作用。而这些行为,虽然经过了算法程序精密计算,仍不免对人类本身带来损害。当此类事件发生时,通常的责任法理就面临考验。人工智能系统的决策或行为致人损害时,是应当由所有者承担责任,还是由开发者承担责任?或者如某些思路新颖的学者所言,应当由"行为人",亦即人工智能本身承担责任?如果是前者,那么我们可能会发现,所有者并不理解人工智能何以做出致害行为,而开发者则无以预料当时当地的情境,也不能很好地作出解释。如果是后者,那么我们会发现人工智能本身的法律地位是物,物又怎么能够承担责任呢?于是这就引发了一个问题,是否要赋予人工智能以主体地位,以便于让它们承担责任?

(二)研究现状

随着人工智能领域近两年的突破性进展,以及我国制定了这一方面的发展战略,今年人工智能方面的学术论文与往年相较呈现"井喷"之势。学界的研究大体上关注三个方面:有关人工智能的局限或潜在问题、人工智能与当前法学理论之间的鸿沟以及人工智能对各领域的辅助作用。这三个方面的问题意识可以归结为七大问题域:

1. 预防式执法、预防式司法问题。[1] 有关问题包括个人化而非一般化的规则、法律责任的基本原理(关乎特定的行为),对法律的理解方式从演绎转向归纳[2]造

〔1〕 参见郑戈:《算法的法律与法律的算法》,载《中国法律评论》2018年第2期。

〔2〕 参见李晟:《略论人工智能语境下的法律转型》,载《法学评论》2018年第1期。

成的司法程序扁平化及其面临的解构风险,[3]还有法律将被算法的针对性预测取代的问题,以及法治的目的这一深层问题。[4]

2. 关于人工智能的主体性问题,有该问题本身,[5]以及未来的趋势、刑事责任、[6]侵权责任、创造物权属问题。[7] 由创造物权属问题,还引发了进一步的法律职业伦理问题。[8]

3. 关于人工智能与人类关系问题,有人类的算法依赖性问题,[9]以及人工智能代替劳动造成的社会和财税问题。[10]

4. 关于人工智能协助审判的问题,有裁判目标之确定问题、审判系统性情境难以全部输入的问题、[11]自然语言处理技术问题。[12]

5. 关于信息网络安全问题,有利用人工智能实施网络犯罪问题[13]和软件

---

〔3〕 参见吴习彧:《裁判人工智能化的实践需求及其中国式任务》,载《东方法学》2018年第2期。

〔4〕 参见於兴中:《算法社会与人的秉性》,载《中国法律评论》2018年第2期。

〔5〕 参见陈璞:《论网络法权构中的主体性原则》,载《中国法学》2018年第3期。

〔6〕 参见刘宪权:《人工智能时代的"内忧""外患"与刑事责任》,载《东方法学》2018年第1期。

〔7〕 See W. Keith Robinson and Joshua T. Smith, "Emerging Technologies Challengling Current Legal Paradigms", *Minnesota Journal of Law*19, 2018, p. 355.

〔8〕 See Thomas E. Spahn, "Artificial Intelligence: Litigation-Specific Ethics Issues (Part 1)", *Practical Lawyer* 64, 2018, p. 43.

〔9〕 See Iria Giuffrida et al., "A Legal Perspective on the Trials and Tribulations of AI: How Artificial Intelligence, the Internet of Things, Smart Contracts, and Other Technologies Will Affect the Law", *Case W. Res. L. Rev.* 68, 2018, p. 747.

〔10〕 See Sami Ahmed, "Cryptocurrency & Robots: How to Tax and Pay Tax on Them", *South Carolina Law Review* 69, 2018, p. 697.

〔11〕 参见前引3,吴习彧文。

〔12〕 参见王禄生:《司法大数据与人工智能开发的技术障碍》,载《中国法律评论》2018年第2期。

〔13〕 See Jay Van Blaricum, "Opinion: Impersonation Bots and Kansas Law", *Journal of the Kansas Bar Association* 87, 2018, p. 20.

漏洞敏感性问题。[14]

6. 人工智能的能力问题,有应用范围小,在心性、灵性方面的缺陷,[15]对职业经验的依赖,价值不中立的问题,[16]以及泛泛而言认为算法不能解决所有问题的观点。

7. 信息和数据的价值增加,于是引发隐私权解构风险、信息和财产相互转化的问题、[17]基于信息权力的算法解释问题、要求算法公开透明可理解可追溯(算法黑箱)的问题、[18]数据问题造成的过拟合问题,[19]以及资本权力扩张、知识不对称的问题。[20]

以前,国外学术界的研究主要集中在逻辑以及人工智能机器人方面。有不少学者主张在责任问题上,人类应当为 AI 系统的行为承担责任。[21] 不过也有学者认为,AI 系统具备和人一样的责任能力,为它们自己造成的后果承担责任。自动化武器系统可以思考,并且可以自动寻找目标并开火,而不需要人类的干预,战场指挥官未必能够对这些武器系统的行为进行完全的控制。而且这种 AI 还只是弱 AI,如果是强 AI,问题会更加突出。因此让它们承担责任是

---

〔14〕 参见雷悦:《人工智能发展中的法律问题探析》,载《北京邮电大学学报》(社会科学版)2018 年第 1 期。

〔15〕 参见潘庸鲁:《人工智能介入司法领域的价值与定位》,载《探索与争鸣》2017 年第 10 期。

〔16〕 参见丁晓东:《算法与歧视:从美国教育平权案看算法伦理与法律解释》,载《中外法学》2017 年第 6 期。

〔17〕 参见王利明:《人工智能时代提出的法学新课题》,载《中国法律评论》2018 年第 2 期。

〔18〕 参见党家玉:《人工智能的伦理与法律风险问题研究》,载《信息安全研究》2017 年第 12 期。

〔19〕 参见左卫民:《关于法律人工智能在中国运用前景的若干思考》,载《清华法学》2018 年第 2 期。

〔20〕 参见封帅:《人工智能时代的国际关系:走向变革且不平等的世界》,载《外交评论》(外交学院学报)2018 年第 1 期。

〔21〕 See Dunlap C J, "Accountability and Autonomous Weapons: Much Ado About Nothing", *Temple International and Comparative Law Journal* 30, 2016, p. 63.

有必要的。[22] 有的学者则认为,人工智能的武器系统能够最终意义上将人从武装冲突中解放出来,主张禁止它发展的人在国家安全的意义上是不负责任的。至于它可能产生的危害,在现阶段讨论时机尚不成熟,为时尚早。[23]

不过今年以来其研究关注的方面与国内学界日渐重合,亦不外乎失业问题、财税问题、责任问题、著作权归属问题以及其他工具性问题。

二、人工智能的概念及其本质

(一)人工智能的工具说

对于人工智能究竟是否具备主体性,学界目前有两种看法。一种看法主张人工智能有主体性,并在此基础之上主张人工智能承担侵权及刑事责任、[24] 享有财产权等各项权利;[25] 另一种看法则主张人工智能没有主体性,强调人工智能的工具性。[26] 这两种观点都有各自的理论基础,下面将做详细分析。

有不少学者主张人工智能仅仅具备工具属性,理由主要在于人工智能的能力尚不完善,功能方面还有很多缺陷。具体如下:

1. 人工智能缺乏足够的说理能力,其推理方式也与人类不同,不能完全模拟人类的思维。[27]

2. 人工智能在知识构建、情节提取等方面存在不足,司法程序中的功能实

〔22〕 See Aaron Gevers, "Is Johnny Five Alive or Did It Short Circuit: Can and Should an Artificially Intelligent Machine Be Held Accountable in War Or Is It Merely a Weapon", *Rutgers Journal of Law & Public Policy* 12, 2015, p. 384.

〔23〕 See Noone G P, Noone D C, "The Debate over Autonomous Weapons Systems", *Case Western Reserve Journal of International Law* 47, 2015, p. 25.

〔24〕 参见刘宪权:《人工智能时代刑事责任与刑罚体系的重构》,载《政治与法律》2018年第3期。

〔25〕 参见张长丹:《法律人格理论下人工智能对民事主体理论的影响研究》,载《科技与法律》2018年第2期。

〔26〕 参见吴习彧:《论人工智能的法律主体资格》,载《浙江社会科学》2018年第6期。

〔27〕 参见赵艳红:《人工智能在刑事证明标准判断中的运用问题探讨》,载《上海交通大学学报》(哲学社会科学版)2018年网络首发。

现也不尽如人意。[28]

3. 人工智能在人性、心性、灵性方面有先天缺陷,缺少人情伦理,不能完全代替人类的工作。[29]

(二)人工智能独立说

当人工智能的行为超越了编程范围时,我们可认为这是自由意志的体现。[30] 从人文的角度看可称之为自由意志的东西,从科学技术的角度看则被称为"算法黑箱"。[31] 这一算法黑箱在结构上可以追溯至深度神经网络的复杂系统结构。因此对于人工智能的独立说的理解,就不得不基于复杂系统的属性。

深度神经网络系统具有自适应、自组织的特点,具备反馈环、分布式控制等结构,[32]还可根据外部信号的输入反馈调节自身。[33] 这就意味着深度神经网络是复杂系统的一种类型。[34] 因此追问深度神经网络是否具备自由意志,就必须对复杂系统科学中的突现论(Emergentism)进行分析。

突现现象的研究可追溯至亚里士多德《论题》中"整体大于部分之和"的观点,以及近代的突现主义学派。[35] 当代的突现论研究则多与心智哲学相结合,从突现的角度看意识问题。[36] 突现性(property emergence)是复杂系统的整体性质,这种整体性主要表现为系统所具有的一种全局性的新模式或行为。突现

---

〔28〕 参见前引12,王禄生文。

〔29〕 参见季卫东:《人工智能时代的司法权之变》,载《东方法学》2018年第1期。

〔30〕 参见刘宪权、胡荷佳:《论人工智能时代智能机器人的刑事责任能力》,载《法学》2018年第1期。

〔31〕 参见Will Knight、DeepTech深科技(mit-tr):《人工智能内心深处的"黑暗秘密"》,载《竞争情报》2017年第5期。

〔32〕 参见钟义信:《人工智能:概念·方法·机遇》,载《科学通报》2017年第22期。

〔33〕 参见贺倩:《人工智能技术的发展与应用》,载《电力信息与通信技术》2017年第9期。

〔34〕 参见范冬萍:《当代整体论的一个新范式:复杂系统突现论——复杂性科学哲学对整体论的发展》,载《系统科学学报》2013年第2期。

〔35〕 See Lovejoy A O, "The Meanings of 'Emergence' and Its Modes", *Philosophy* 6, 1927, p. 167.

〔36〕 See Lewtas P, "Emergence and Consciousness", *Philosophy* 4, 2013, p. 527.

是在复杂系统的自组织过程中出现的、新颖的和连贯的结构、模式和性质。相对于它们所出自的微观层次的组成部分和过程,突现是在宏观层次上出现的现象。[37] 最为关键的是,突现性意味着一个复杂系统的宏观层次具有不可还原的根本性质。这些性质的存在不能从低层结构中得到辩护。“即当系统组成部分的行为的陈述不能从处于其他(更简单的)的聚集体的行为的陈述中推出。”[38]

复杂系统的突现结构中的因果关系,已有学者详细地予以了说明,[39] 我们可以用图 1 表示:

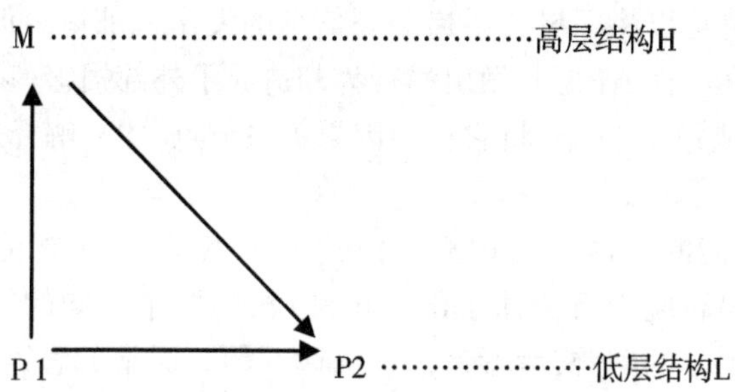

图 1　复杂系统的实现结构中的因果关系

如图 1 所示,向量 P1M 就是我们一般而言都会承认的上向因果关系,即低层次的组成元素及其结构对于高层性质 M 具有的因果关系。整体都是由部分组成的,而高层性质 M 是从低层性质 P1 中突现出来的。当 M 突现出来之后,根据因果突现论,它将会对较低的 L 层的结构性质产生因果作用,即因为 M 的产生,从而导致了 L 层上 P2 的产生。向量 MP2 就是下向因果关系。所谓的不可还原性,就是指:向量 MP2 所代表的下向因果关系,不能够被还原为向量 P1M 所代表的上向因果关系以及向量 P1P2 所代表的同层因果关系的共同作用。需要注意的是,系统性质 M 是依赖于下层性质 P1 才得以产生的,但是一经产生就获得了自己的独立性,而不能认为 M 所具有的依赖性可以解释所有

[37] 参见范冬萍:《复杂性科学哲学视野中的突现性》,载《哲学研究》2010 年第 11 期。

[38] 范冬萍:《当代整体论的一个新范式:复杂系统突现论——复杂性科学哲学对整体论的发展》,载《系统科学学报》2013 年第 2 期。

[39] 参见范冬萍:《论突现性质的下向因果关系——回应 Jaegwon Kim 对下向因果关系的反驳》,载《哲学研究》2005 年第 7 期。

的性质。[40]

引入突现论,我们可在一般意义上得出这一结论:人工神经网络作为一种复杂系统,它所产生的整体性反应,确实超出了低层细节分析所能解释的范围。

根据突现原理,深度神经网络获取某一片段的信息,然后做出决策时,我们虽可以根据系统记录发现信息的来源,但我们无法检查出AI何以做出特定的决策。因为至少就目前的AI技术来说,除了在结构细节上进行分析,似乎并没有别的办法了解深度神经网络。如果信息本身是包含了价值判断的,甚至是命令式的,我们也许可以将因果关系追溯到信息的发出者那里。但假如信息是价值中立的纯粹事实,而AI据此做出的行为却造成了外部损害,我们就只能将AI系统本身纳入因果关系网络,将它作为因果关系节点,才能解释这一现象。

(三)人工智能的主体性法理

关于人工智能的主体性法理需要澄清的一点是,人工智能是否具备主体性,与人工智能是否应当有法律上的主体地位,是两个不同的问题。前者是一个哲学的、形而上学的问题,后者是一个法律问题。通常的思路是,如果人工智能具备哲学意义上的主体性,那么它就当然应该在法律上享有主体地位。然而也存在另外的可能,那就是法律上虽然承认某物的主体地位,但该法律主体并不是自然意义上的主体。对于人工智能的问题,人们通常的看法容易局限在对新技术的陌生印象之上。这种陌生感带来的惊异和震撼往往会直接打开通向哲学思考之门,而让人们跳过了务实而细致的法学领域。

于此,突现论意义上的主体≠法律上的主体;

理性的主体≠法律上的主体;

自由意志的主体≠法律上的主体;

有情感的个体≠法律上的主体。

在法律上,无论是权利、义务或责任都是依托法律主体才成为可能的,而主体理论则指向实在法的价值取向和道德标准。虽然法学家一般从规范性和技术性的角度定义法律,但这些定义均需依托于法律的价值取向才能得到呈现。[41] 法律上的主体必须在法律关系中发挥一定的不可替代的功能,这一功

---

〔40〕 参见金在权、郁锋:《50年之后的心—身问题》,载《世界哲学》2007年第1期。

〔41〕 参见龙卫球:《法律主体概念的基础性分析(上)——兼论法律的主体预定理论》,载《学术界》2000年第3期。

能的实现可以有功利的意义,也可以有伦理的意义。但这并不意味着这些主体有超越实证法的意义,而成为哲学上的主体。

工具说的着眼点在于人工智能的功能缺陷,但功能是否完备与主体性是否存在之间,并没有必然的逻辑关系。功能完备并非主体性存在的必要条件,功能缺陷也不是主体性缺失的充分条件。因此工具说的论述路径存在基本的逻辑错误。

人工智能的突现论的着眼点在于人工智能的自由意志与结构复杂性。但仔细考察主体说的逻辑线索,就会发现它的错误之处。所谓的突现,其基础是人工智能的系统复杂性。换言之,此种论证的思路就是系统性—复杂性—突现性—自由意志。但这个世界上的系统性存在有很多,其中大部分不乏神经网络一般的错综复杂的结构,但这并不意味着这些系统就有了自己的自由意志。

这两个理论的问题在于,过分关注人工智能本身是否具备与人相似的能力,却忽略了法律上的主体地位所必须具备的意义。论证人工智能的法律上的主体性的必要性就不能从理性、意志或情感的角度着手。实践中面临的问题不外乎两点:(1)传统的因果关系路径失灵;(2)社会风险的加剧。而针对这两个问题,主体相关的研究角度并不是万能的灵丹妙药。

(四)两种类型的人工智能

鉴于实践中的这两个方面的问题,我们应根据其是否具备自然语言能力区分两种不同类型的人工智能。下文将会论述这一分类如何有助于解决上述两个问题,这里仅阐述分类本身的意义。

非语言类(不具备自然语言能力)的 AI 系统等同于自动化机械,只是最近随着“人工智能”这一词语越来越时髦,纷纷改称人工智能了。它们专门处理某一特定部门的技术问题,譬如自动化生产、自动驾驶。这类系统已取得突破性进展,譬如,继 AlphaGo 击败李世石和柯洁之后,在 2017 年 10 月,AlphaZero 以 100∶0 的成绩击败 AlphaGo。更令人吃惊的是,AlphaZero 学习围棋并不依赖于人类经验,而是自己的“双手互搏”。[42] 在自动驾驶方面,AI 也成就斐然。在美

---

〔42〕 参见快科技:《学界震动! 阿尔法元 100∶0 阿尔法狗——柯洁:人类已多余》,载东方体育:http://sports. eastday. com/a/171019131557079000000. html,最后访问日期:2018 年 1 月 9 日。

国尚在进行自动驾驶汽车的道路测试之际,[43]深圳的自动驾驶公交车甚至已经正式上路。[44] 我们已经可以确认,至少在特定领域中,人工智能具有不亚于人类的判断、反应能力。不过,尽管人工智能在某些专业化的领域已经具备强大的能力,能针对环境作出有效调整,但它的智能局限在特定方面,与规范性没有任何关系。

历史上,对于人工智能究竟能否进行有效的语义理解向来都有争议,比如著名的"汉字屋"论证就质疑 AI 系统能否真正理解语义。[45] 已有学者指出这一论证的逻辑前设中的问题,即便"汉字屋"中的人不能理解汉字,他还是可以理解至少一门语言,否则理解被提出的问题、寻求翻译软件的帮助就都是不可能的。[46] 从常理上看也是如此,即便我可能最初并不懂得一个德语单词的含义,可是我查完字典之后,自然就明白了。无论如何也不能说,因为我查了字典,所以我没有可能理解它。否则的话,不仅计算机与人类之间不可能沟通,德国人和中国人之间也不可能沟通。如果 AI 确实可以理解数字语言,那么通过翻译理解自然语言也是可能的。从目前 AI 领域的进展来看,近来的发展诸如 SAE 网络和递归神经网络已经可以有效地进行多模态检索、情感分析和语义分析。[47]

---

〔43〕 参见龙殇:《美国高通在加利福尼亚州测试其自动驾驶汽车技术》,载新浪网:http://tech. sina. com. cn/roll/2017 - 12 - 25/doc-ifypxmsr0442084. shtml,最后访问日期:2018 年 1 月 9 日。

〔44〕 参见愉快蜡黄寂:《深圳自动驾驶公交车正式上路,开启我国自动驾驶新时代》,载新浪网:http://auto. sina. com. cn/j_kandian. d. html? docid = fypsvkp2674507&subch = iauto,最后访问日期:2018 年 1 月 9 日。

〔45〕 参见蔡曙山:《关于哲学、心理学和认知科学的 12 个问题——与约翰·塞尔教授的对话》,载《学术界》2007 年第 3 期。

〔46〕 参见徐英瑾:《对"汉字屋论证"逻辑结构的五种诊断模式》,载《复旦学报》(社会科学版)2008 年第 3 期。

〔47〕 参见林奕欧、雷航、李晓瑜、吴佳:《自然语言处理中的深度学习:方法及应用》,载《电子科技大学学报》2017 年第 6 期。

三、责任问题的对策分析

对应于人工智能的工具说和主体说,学界在人工智能致人损害问题上分为两大阵营,其一主张由人工智能承担责任,其二主张由人类承担责任。

(一)人工智能的责任

1. 由人工智能直接承担责任

这是最激进的主张,意味着将满足条件的所有复杂 AI 系统纳入法秩序之中,并给予与人类相当的法律地位。这种方式不用特地引入任何法律制度,不过看似简单易行,问题也是最大的。

从原理上看,它与 AI 系统实际具备的能力并不吻合。根据上文的分析,只有语言类 AI 系统才具备这种程度的潜力,而且还有待在未来的实现。只有当人工智能系统能够理解规范性的时候,对它施加规范性制裁才是有意义的。否则即便承认 AI 系统作为主体,它的主体性也至多相当于心智不健全的精神病人。

从效果上看,除拥有财产权之外,AI 系统能否享有其他权利?既然它能通晓语言和抽象概念,那它一定能理解情感和野心。那它会不会有日益膨胀的野心?诸如此类的问题,〔48〕将被这个方案最大化。同时,法律反映了我们所认为的人类有序交往的前提条件,但同时也反映了内在于人性核心的东西,以及人何以为人的意义。AI 系统的法律人格化将会造成人类生活的进一步异化,甚至是"非人化"。〔49〕 有学者提出了大胆的未来展望,〔50〕甚至主张在某些条件下人工智能承担刑事责任,〔51〕但却并未仔细分析 AI 系统涉及的究竟是何种法律问

〔48〕 参见张炎:《人工智能的潜在威胁与应对思路》,载《中国社会科学报》2017 年 11 月 7 日,第 4 版。

〔49〕 参见[德]霍斯特·艾丹米勒:《机器人的崛起与人类的法律》,李飞、敦小匣译,载《法治现代化研究》2017 年第 4 期。

〔50〕 何哲:《人工智能时代的社会转型与行政伦理:机器能否管理人?》,载《电子政务》2017 年第 11 期。

〔51〕 参见刘宪权、朱彦:《人工智能时代对传统刑法理论的挑战》,载《上海政法学院学报》(法治论丛)2018 年第 2 期。

题,也未审查可能引发的后果。[52]

在实践中,韩国国会科技委员会于2017年7月20日提交了计划授予机器人以"电子人格"的议案,但是阻力重重,进展缓慢。[53] 在法理上,人工智能承担责任必然带来的一个问题是,人工智能是在生产线上生产出来的标准化产品。如果同一批产品中有一个被判定为有问题,那么同批次所有产品都要被召回。但在承担法律责任的层面上,是否同批次所有AI都要承担责任呢?这将会引发责任法理的极大震动,必须慎之又慎。

2. 援引现有的法人责任制度

有学者在著作权问题上主张将AI系统视同法人处理,[54]但这只是对法人制度的生搬硬套,而忽视了AI系统的复杂性。复杂AI系统与法人的不同是本质上的。法人并不是一个突现论意义上的复杂系统,它总是"通过"人类来运营,由人来组成董事会,且董事会的行为被归结为公司的行为。[55] 因此必要时可以"揭穿法人外衣",追溯到人的行为。而谈论复杂AI系统的组成单元是没有意义的,它本身就是一个单元。如果揭穿它的"外衣",我们只能面对一个"黑箱"。

(二)由人承担责任

1. 所有权人责任、使用人责任或开发人员责任

美国计算机协会在2017年年初发布的文件中规定,即便无法详细解释算法如何产生结果,使用算法的机构仍应承担责任。[56] 让人类承担责任,至少看上去是比较可行的一条路。不过究其原理却并不公平,主要的原因在于开发人员对于AI行为的把握是概率性的,并不是百分之一百的,这与算法黑箱有关。由于系统足够复杂,我们无法找到除了这个系统本身之外的他者为它的行为承担责任,因为任何事实上的因果关系链条在经过这个系统的时候,都会受到干

---

[52] 参见袁曾:《人工智能有限法律人格审视》,载《东方法学》2017年第5期。

[53] See Korea, "肺□扁夯□救", https://www. lawmaking. go. kr/lmSts/nsmLmSts/out/2008068/detailRP, January 30,2018.

[54] 参见熊琦:《人工智能生成内容的著作权认定》,载《知识产权》2017年第3期。

[55] 参见前引49,霍斯特·艾丹米勒等文。

[56] See Communications of the ACM,"Toward Algorithmic Transparency and Accountability", https://cacm. acm. org/magazines/2017/9/220423 - toward-algorithmic-transparency-and-accountability/fulltext, January 30,2018.

扰，甚至截断。而如果将所有的责任都推到产品设计开发人员身上，那会是不公平的。黑箱之中究竟发生了什么，为何给出的结果是这个而不是那个，开发人员也不能完全把握。如果不分青红皂白就让他们承担责任，相信以后不会有人胆敢从事这种开发活动了。而开发人员都无法完全预料的情况，所有权人和生产者就更没有办法预料。国内学者已经看到了这一点，并主张对于操作人的责任应以过错为前提。[57] 有国外学者也认为某些情况下责任人应当能够取得豁免。[58] 问题在于，如果原本的责任人豁免了，那么损失由谁来弥补？

2. 参照民法上的代理制度

爱沙尼亚已于2017年10月开始筹备人工智能方面的立法，动议之一就是采取"机器人代理人"的模式。[59] 国外也有学者就此进行了论证，[60] 关键的理由是，由AI系统承担代理人任务，可以有效避免人类代理的高昂成本。这一方面意味着代理成本甚至是治理成本的降低，另一方面也解决了AI系统的法律地位问题。这种方法不仅可以避免激进方案的弊端，也可以有效利用AI资源。而实际上，谷歌公司今年发布的Google Assistant语音助手以其惊艳的表现足以胜任代理人的角色。相信以后AI在这方面的表现绝不逊色于人类代理。

四、笔者的建议

在人工智能的法律责任方面，一共有三个问题有待解决。在实践中，存在社会风险加剧、传统的因果关系难以追溯的问题。在理论上，即在未来还有可能出现危及人类自身地位的问题。对此，笔者主张分别采取三个方面的措施加

〔57〕 参见李政佐：《论人工智能产品侵权行为责任认定——以人工智能汽车为例》，载《商》2016年第33期。

〔58〕 See Scherer M. U., "Regulating Artificial Intelligence Systems: Risks, Challenges, Competencies, and Strategies", *Harvard Journal of Law & Technology* 29, 2016, p. 353.

〔59〕 See Ott Ummelas, "Estonia plans to give robots legal recognition", http://www.independent.co.uk/news/business/news/estonia-robots-artificial-intelligence-ai-legal-recognition-law-disputes-government-plan-a7992071.html, January 30, 2018.

〔60〕 See Thomas A. Smith, "Robot Slaves, Robot Masters, and the Agency Costs of Artificial Government", *Criterion J. on Innovation* 1, 2016, p. 1.

以应对。

(一)采用社会保险制度

这一方案为欧盟于2017年2月16日通过的《关于制定机器人民事法律规则的决议》[61]所采纳。所谓风险社会,是进入全球化、信息化时代以来,人们在社会中所面临的诸多不可控的风险,譬如环境危机、生态风险、核战争、金融风险等,风险社会理论中的诸流派都主张关注风险对于社会的巨大影响。[62] 社会学方面的学者主张通过理性自觉、文化启蒙、生态政治的方法来应对风险社会的挑战。[63] 在法学领域,多年以前,就有学者提出将法律上的因果关系理论的基础建立在风险社会之上,[64]更有学者从刑法的角度表达了类似的观点。[65] 法理学方面,有学者主张在风险社会之中,立法应当注意福利性、预防性和开放包容性,司法则需要更加能动。[66] 我们需要看到的是,当前时代,网络搜索、网络购物、医疗、道路交通、行政甚至司法领域都受到人工智能的影响,在可以预见的将来,AI系统的影响将会更加深刻。但基于人工神经网络的AI系统的决策,并不是以确定性的方式给出的,它始终都有一定的概率出错,这一出错的概率就是全社会共同承担的风险。这样,AI系统行为的责任问题就与保险法理贯通。我们可以使用强制责任保险的形式,让社会成员共同分担这一系统性的风险。这种方法处理专门化AI系统引起的民事责任尤其有效。在责任的承担方式上,可以赋予所有可能受害的主体(譬如同类产品的所有使用者)以原告的资格,因为潜在的风险已经存在于复数主体上了。

---

〔61〕 See European Parliament,"Resolution of 16 February 2017 with recommendations to the Commission on Civil Law Rules on Robotics", http://www.europarl.europa.eu/sides/getDoc.do?pubRef=-//EP//TEXT+TA+P8-TA-2017-0051+0+DOC+XML+V0//EN,January 30,2018.

〔62〕 参见庄友刚:《风险社会理论研究述评》,载《哲学动态》2005年第9期。

〔63〕 参见陶建钟:《风险社会的秩序困境及其制度逻辑》,载《江海学刊》2014年第2期。

〔64〕 参见贾敬华:《法律上因果关系的基础:降低风险而非合理预见》,载《南开学报》(哲学社会科学版)2010年第5期。

〔65〕 参见劳东燕:《风险社会与变动中的刑法理论》,载《中外法学》2014年第1期。

〔66〕 参见杨春福:《风险社会的法理解读》,载《法制与社会发展》2011年第6期。

(二)人工智能的自我解释

让AI系统进行自我解释,无疑是可以绕过算法黑箱的比较有效的方法。这之所以可行,是因为复杂AI系统虽然依赖人工神经网络,但是毕竟仍有符号主义的部分,因此我们可以调整算法激励机制,让它几乎必然地做出真实的陈述。必要的时候甚至可以设置囚徒困境,令两台AI分别作答。这种自我解释将能够带来人类对AI的信任,前提是AI的自我解释具有足够的说服力。[67]这种自我解释可以通过证据法上的改革而成为规范性的制度安排,解释只要符合一定的规范性标准,就可以成为新型的证据。

(三)以算法伦理规范编程行为

因此在规范上,我们应注重管理、创新等各种要素之间的平衡。[68] 2017年初提出的"阿西洛马"(Asilomar)原则,[69]与其说是针对AI系统的,不如说是针对人类研发者、生产者的。比如该原则主张:AI研究目标应当"建立有益的智能,而不是无向的智能";"投资人工智能的同时,应当资助那些确保其创造有益价值的研究";"人工智能研究人员与政策制定者之间,应形成积极、有建设性的沟通";"AI系统的设计和运作应符合人类尊严、权利、自由和文化多样性的理念",等等。算法伦理的落实则需通过立法,为此可以借鉴欧盟的做法,以实现对编程行为的规制。

(责任编辑:何雪波)

---

〔67〕 参见Will Knight、DeepTech深科技(mit-tr):《人工智能内心深处的"黑暗秘密"》,载《竞争情报》2017年第5期。

〔68〕 See F. Patrick Hubbard, "Sophisticated Robots: Balancing Liability, Regulation, and Innovation", *Fla. L. Rev.* 66, 2014, p. 1803.

〔69〕 See 2017 Asilomar Conference, "Asilomar AI Principles", https://futureoflife.org/ai-principles/, January 30, 2018.

理论探索与学说争鸣

行政强制中比例原则与强制适当原则的关系之辨

周泽中*

摘要：

基于行政法教义学的知识传统，比例原则是全面制约行政裁量的基本原则，而强制适当原则是设定和实施行政强制的法定原则。在行政强制中，比例原则和强制适当原则均可用于约束行政强制实体裁量。但是，强制适当原则不能适用于约束强制程序裁量，且在实体裁量过程中其本身无法提供适当性的判断标准，因此二者并非等量齐观。据此，有必要将比例原则的分析工具引入至强制适当原则的判断体系，通过适当性、必要性和均衡性子原则内容对行政强制手段是否适当进行综合评判，亦须证明上述论证思路符合我国行政法规范体系的自洽要求。

关键词：

行政强制；比例原则；强制适当原则；强制裁量

一、问题的提出

自1999年我国最高人民法院作出的比例原则适用第一案，即“汇丰实业公司与哈尔滨市规划局行政处罚决定纠纷上诉案”后的19年间，学者们对比例原则的研究风生水起，尤其是2000年至今，比例原则便被认为是行政法的基本原则之一。[1] 更有学者指出，比例原则应当成为“审查所有裁量性行政行为的统

---

* 周泽中，西南政法大学行政法学院2018级博士研究生。

〔1〕 如罗豪才、湛中乐主编：《行政法学》，北京大学出版社2012年版，第33页以下；应松年主编：《行政法与行政诉讼法》，中国政法大学出版社2012年版，第47页；姜明安、余凌云主编：《行政法学》，科学出版社2010年版，第89页以下。

一基准”。[2] 又或者,由于比例原则可以用来沟通事实判断和价值判断,因此具有普适性。[3] 手段与目的之间的理性衔接,不能为了实现某个特定目的,付出不合比例的成本,而是以必要的手段实现利益均衡和最大化。但是,笔者同时也注意到,2011年制定的《中华人民共和国行政强制法》(以下简称《行政强制法》)第5条规定:“行政强制的设定和实施,应当适当。采用非强制手段可以达到行政管理目的的,不得设定和实施行政强制。”立法者将之称为“强制适当”原则。[4] 那么,作为行政法基本原则的比例原则和作为《行政强制法》法定原则的强制适当原则,其关系究竟如何界分,实为值得我国学人关注和思考。

在涉及行政强制的相关立法中,对于强制适当原则与比例原则的规定,大致可分为两种情形。[5] 第一,仅规定强制适当原则,不规定比例原则,例如《行政强制法》第5条、《中华人民共和国突发事件应对法》第11条第1款的规定。[6] 第二,仅规定比例原则的若干内容,不规定强制适当原则,例如《中华人民共和国戒毒条例》第30条仅仅规定了比例原则中的必要性原则,[7]《国有土

---

[2] 杨登峰:《从合理原则走向统一的比例原则》,载《中国法学》2016年第3期。

[3] 参见纪海龙:《比例原则在私法中的普适性及其例证》,载《政法论坛》2016年第3期。

[4] 全国人大常委会法制工作委员会行政法室编:《〈中华人民共和国行政强制法〉解读》,中国法制出版社2011年版,第21页以下。

[5] 鉴于我国《行政强制法》明确规定强制法定原则,即有权设定行政强制的只有法律、行政法规和地方性法规,规章和其他规范性文件都没有设定行政强制的权限。因此,关于行政强制的立法范围仅仅局限于法律、法规。

[6] 《中华人民共和国突发事件应对法》(2007年)第11条第1款:有关人民政府及其部门采取的应对突发事件的措施,应当与突发事件可能造成的社会危害的性质、程度和范围相适应;有多种措施可供选择的,应当选择有利于最大限度地保护公民、法人和其他组织权益的措施。

[7] 《中华人民共和国戒毒条例》(2011年)第30条:强制隔离戒毒场所应当根据强制隔离戒毒人员的性别、年龄、患病等情况对强制隔离戒毒人员实行分别管理;对吸食不同种类毒品的,应当有针对性地采取必要的治疗措施;根据戒毒治疗的不同阶段和强制隔离戒毒人员的表现,实行逐步适应社会的分级管理。

地上房屋征收与补偿条例》第27条第3款仅规定了比例原则中的均衡性原则,[8]《中华人民共和国突发公共卫生事件应急条例》第31条第1款、第34条仅规定了比例原则中的必要性原则和适当性原则。[9] 由此可见,比例原则与强制适当原则的关系在行政强制立法中莫衷一是。

那么,在行政强制司法中,比例原则和强制适当原则的关系是否清晰呢?答案亦是否定的。首先,有的案件将强制相当原则等同于比例原则。如在"刘云务诉山西省太原市公安局交通警察支队晋源一大队道路交通管理行政强制案"中,最高人民法院的裁判摘要中明确提到:"行政处理存在裁量余地时,应当尽可能选择对相对人合法权益损害最小的方式;实施扣留等暂时性控制措施不能代替对案件的实体处理,行政机关无正当理由长期不处理的,构成滥用职权。"[10]这一判决显然认为将强制适当原则等同于比例原则中的均衡性原则。其次,有的案件则将强制适当原则作为比例原则的法定依据。如在"史克现、黄金丹诉陕西省镇坪县住房和城乡建设局行政强制违法及行政赔偿案"中,法院认为,被告在实际行政执法过程中应当坚持对行政相对人利益最小侵害的原则,应当妥善保管其所查封、扣押的财物,不得使用或者损毁。同时,必须及时处理那些不宜保存的财物,否则对于行政相对人所造成的利益损失,行政机关应当依法承担赔偿责任。可见,该案裁判理由是将强制适当原则作为比例原则

[8] 《国有土地上房屋征收与补偿条例》(2011年)第27条第3款:任何单位和个人不得采取暴力、威胁或者违反规定中断供水、供热、供气、供电和道路通行等非法方式迫使被征收人搬迁。禁止建设单位参与搬迁活动。

[9] 《中华人民共和国突发公共卫生事件应急条例》(2011年)第31条第1款:应急预案启动前,县级以上各级人民政府有关部门应当根据突发事件的实际情况,做好应急处理准备,采取必要的应急措施。

第34条:突发事件应急处理指挥部根据突发事件应急处理的需要,可以对食物和水源采取控制措施。

县级以上地方人民政府卫生行政主管部门应当对突发事件现场等采取控制措施,宣传突发事件防治知识,及时对易受感染的人群和其他易受损害的人群采取应急接种、预防性投药、群体防护等措施。

[10] 参见《最高人民法院公报》2017年第2期。

适用的依据。[11] 最后,有的案件将强制适当原则中提及的行政违法行为考量因素作为比例原则适用时应当考虑的因素。如在“熊濛濛诉双流县规划建设局、双流县房产管理局、双流县胜利镇人民政府规划行政强制案”[12]中,法院认为,被上诉人在实施行政强制时既要确保行政管理目标的实现,又要兼顾行政相对人的合法权益,尽可能使行政相对人遭受最小的损害。在本案中,因为被上诉人的拆除方法不符合拆除安全技术规范的规定,且该方法是造成房屋损害的原因,因此被上诉人必须就该行政违法行为对上诉人承担赔偿责任。可见,在行政强制裁判中,比例原则与强制适当原则的关系依然是不清晰的,且与前文提及的行政强制立法中的定位不一致,使比例原则与强制适当原则之间的关系问题更加难以准确厘定。

除上述立法与司法实践外,国内行政法学界对于强制适当原则与比例原则的关系问题虽然关注不多,但却有着惊人的相似理解。官方文件清楚载明,强制适当原则是比例原则在行政强制领域的集中体现。例如,全国人大常委会法制委员会编著的权威解读文本明确提及:“本条明确行政强制的设定和实施应当适当、合理,要符合比例原则。适当原则是行政法领域中的一项普遍原则,在行政强制领域中,也称比例原则”。[13] 同时,学界对此二者关系问题的学理认识亦保持基本一致。例如,袁曙宏教授指出,行政强制适当原则的源头可追溯至英美法系的“适当性原则”和大陆法系的“比例原则”,系指对公民设定行政强制义务应当适当,不能超出需要的限度。[14] 莫于川教授认为,强制适当原则“是比例原则在行政强制法中的落实,是在合法性基础上的对行政机关提出的更高要求”。[15] 胡建淼教授、蒋红珍教授则认为,当时《行政强制法(草案)》中

---

〔11〕 参见陕西省镇坪县人民法院(2014)镇坪行初字第2号行政裁定书。

〔12〕 参见成都市龙泉驿区人民法院(2014)龙泉行初字第42号行政赔偿判决书。

〔13〕 全国人大常委会法制工作委员会行政法室编:《〈中华人民共和国行政强制法〉解读》,中国法制出版社2011年版,第21页以下。

〔14〕 参见袁曙宏:《我国〈行政强制法〉的法律地位、价值取向和制度逻辑》,载《中国法学》2011年第4期。

〔15〕 莫于川、林鸿潮:《中华人民共和国行政强制法释义》,中国法制出版社2011年版,第43页。

第5条所规定的最小侵害原则是“我国现行行政单行法对比例原则的立法肯定”。[16] 关保英教授认为，在行政强制领域，与强制适当原则相近的概念是比例原则。[17] 姜明安教授则更是将《行政强制法》第5条内容所体现的精神直接概括为行政法学上通常所谓之“比例原则”。[18] 可见，我国学者倾向于将强制适当原则的内容和功能等同于比例原则，前者仅仅是后者在行政强制法中的具体落实，或者说前者是后者的另一种表达。

但是，通过以上对我国行政强制立法、行政强制司法和学者理论观点的系统梳理，不难发现立法、司法并未如学理观点那般将强制适当原则简单等同于比例原则，而是至少在法律语言表达、具体案件适用的过程中有所区分，也正是由于强制适当原则与比例原则的关系仍然处于表面等同、实则混淆的不明状态，才引发了笔者对于此二者关系问题的深刻思考。因为这种混乱状态可能会造成比例原则和强制适当原则在行政强制适用过程中的主观恣意，尤其是当适用者直接适用具有较大裁量空间的强制适当原则时，若没有进一步的严格规范，适用者很容易根据主观情感直接给定强制适当的具体判断标准。又或者可能会导致适用者的无所适从，当面临行政强制裁量时，行政执法人员究竟选择适用法律明文规定的强制适当原则，还是选择适用司法判例与学理探讨中所形成的比例原则，由于缺乏有针对性的深度研究，适用者很难及时地做出正确选择。因此，本文认为，有必要厘清比例原则与强制适当原则之间的关系问题，这不仅有利于从源头上规范两种重要原则在行政强制领域内的法律适用，亦能够促进对行政裁量权力进行原则性规制的理论研究，进而实现行政法学基本原理与现行法律规范明文规定或者约定俗成的一般原则之间的体系融贯和内涵协调。笔者不揣冒昧，尝试在梳理我国学者已有的研究论著基础上，在立法、司法与学理之间不断流转，以求在此问题上贡献浅见，并以此虚心求教于方家。

---

〔16〕 胡建淼、蒋红珍：《论最小侵害原则在行政强制法中的适用》，载《法学家》2006年第3期。

〔17〕 参见关保英：《行政法学》，法律出版社2013年版，第573页。

〔18〕 参见姜明安：《〈行政强制法〉的基本原则和行政强制设定权研究》，载《法学杂志》2011年第11期。

二、强制适当原则并非比例原则在行政强制中的另一种表达

如前所述,强制适当原则与比例原则之间的关系看似明朗、清晰,但是却暗藏一些难以琢磨的细节问题。下文仅对比例原则、强制适当原则对于行政强制裁量所具有的实体制约作用和程序控制功能逐层进行对比分析,从而得出本文的首要结论:强制适当原则并非比例原则在行政强制中的另一种表达。

(一)手段合乎目的:全面制约行政强制裁量的比例原则

“每一种行政法理论背后,皆蕴藏着一种国家理论。”[19] 诚如学者指出,国家公权力对公民基本权利的限制是公法学的重要研究课题,以约束公权力为目标的比例原则被视为公法领域的“帝王条款”。[20] 而行政强制往往被认为是“行政法中对公民与法人等施予最具有物理性质强制、压迫性的一种法律关系”。[21] 毋庸置疑的是,在现代社会中,行政强制的权力色彩被普遍定位为“最具侵犯性、威胁性”。与其说是对其品性指向的规范界定,毋宁说是对行政强制权力实践运行状况所作出的精辟论断。那么,国家和社会应当如何将行政强制权力约束于合理范围之内,从而最大限度地保障公民、法人的基本权利不受无端侵扰?问题直接落入“权力”(power)与“权利”(right)的经典论述之中,由此肇始于德国的比例原则日益受到中国公法学者的青睐和重视。

早在1988年,比例原则作为行政法学舶来品,第一次进入中国学者的视野。[22] 十一年之后,我国最高人民法院首次尝试运用比例原则的三阶理论进行司法裁决,那份震古烁今的行政判决书明确写道:“规划局所作的处罚决定应针对影响的程度,责令汇丰公司采取相应的措施,既要保证行政管理目标的实现,又要兼顾保护相对人的权益,应以达到行政执法目的和目标为限,尽可能使相

〔19〕 Harlow, C. and Rawlings, R. (1997) law and Administration, 2nd ed. (London: Butterworth), p. 1. 转引自汪燕:《行政合理性原则与失当行政行为》,载《法学评论》2014年第5期。

〔20〕 参见曾哲、周泽中:《终身监禁刑的宪法学反思——以比例原则为分析视角》,载《新疆社会科学》2017年第3期。

〔21〕 陈新民:《中国行政法学原理》,中国政法大学出版社2002年版,第187页。

〔22〕 参见[日]青柳幸一:《基本人权的侵犯与比例原则》,载《比较法研究》1988年第1期。

对人的权益遭受最小的侵害。"[23] 2010年,在"陈宁诉辽宁省庄河市公安局不予行政赔偿决定案"中,法院第一次对比例原则进行官方界定:比例原则的含义是"行政主体实施行政行为应当兼顾行政目标的实现和保护相对人的权益,如果行政目标的实现可能对相对人的权益造成不利影响,则这种不利影响应被限制在尽可能小的范围之内,二者应当有适当的比例"。[24]

关于比例原则的基本内涵,德国学者将其分为三个具体的原则:适应性、必要性、比例性,其中适应性原则是指国家所采取的措施要适应于它所追求的法律所规定的目的;必要性原则指国家干预公民自由措施的持续为实现公共利益所不可缺少,这种干预还须是最低程度的;比例性原则即指国家措施的采取对当事人来说是不过分的,又被称为狭义的比例原则。[25] 此外,还有学者将比例原则分为以下子原则:公共利益原则、妥当性原则、必要性原则、法益相称原则。[26] 概括而言,比例原则在内容上包括适当性、必要性、均衡性三个重要子原则。适当性原则,又称为妥当性原则、适应性原则,即"行政机关所采取的执法手段和追求的行政目的之间应当是有必要的,强调手段和目的的一致性"。[27] 必要性原则,又称最少侵害原则、最温和方式原则,即"行政机关为了实现一个行政目的,存在多种可选择的路径、手段、措施,那行政主体在实施行政行为的时候就应当选择对相对人权利影响最小的那一种手段,才是必要的"。[28] 均衡性原则,也被称为狭义比例原则、相称性原则,即"行政机关执行职务时,面对多数可能选择之处置,应就方法与目的的关系权衡更有利者而为之"。[29]

申言之,比例原则的适用前提是行政机关根据现行法律规范享有一定的手

[23] 最高人民法院(1999)行终字第20号行政判决书。

[24] 中华人民共和国最高人民法院行政审判庭编:《中国行政审判指导案例》(第1卷),中国法制出版社2010年版,第96页。

[25] 参见黄学贤:《行政法中的比例原则研究》,载《法律科学》2001年第1期。

[26] 参见陈鹏:《刑法"有利溯及之例外"条款的合宪性限定解释——基于牛玉强案的思考》,载《法学家》2012年第4期。

[27] 中华人民共和国最高人民法院行政审判庭编:《中国行政审判指导案例》(第1卷),中国法制出版社2010年版,第96页。

[28] 前引27,《中国行政审判指导案例》(第1卷),第96页。

[29] 前引27,《中国行政审判指导案例》(第1卷),第97页。

段选择空间,而为了进一步控制该裁量权的无限滥用,从而逐渐形成能够有效约束公权恣意的判断标准和原则界限。“比例原则经常作为给自由裁量设定内部界限的标准来论述”。[30] 那么,比例原则应当如何发挥其全面制约行政强制裁量(包括实体裁量、程序裁量)的显著功能,便是本文区分比例原则和强制适当原则的第一层要义。

1. 实体裁量约束功能:成本效益均衡的分析工具

必须承认的是,比例原则关注所有行政的自由裁量权行使问题,[31] 其中对于行政相对人直接造成权益减损的当属实体裁量。而行政强制作为一种以直接强制性和物理实力性为特征的侵害处分型行政行为,行政机关在维护和追求行政管理目的的过程中始终会仔细权衡“行政成本”“行政效益”之间的数量、质量等关系问题。进而言之,行政过程所耗费的时间、人力和物力等“行政成本”可被看作比例原则所考量的“个人利益”,而行政目的所欲实现的“行政效益”便可视为比例原则所考量的“公共利益”。[32] 这也意味着,行政强制实体法律关系的背后必然蕴含着“成本—效益”理应均衡的分析思路。

首先,行政强制实体裁量必须符合比例原则中的适当性原则要求,任何超出适当程度之外所采取的行政手段均难以获得正当性的评价结果。《行政强制法》第1条明确规定其立法宗旨:规范行政强制的设定和实施,保障和监督行政机关依法履行职责,维护公共利益和社会秩序,保护公民、法人和其他组织的合法权益。可见,行政强制手段的终极目的是实现“公共利益”和“个人利益”的二者兼顾,既不能一味追求公共利益,更不能片面舍弃个人利益。此时,适当性原则所考察的手段合乎目的的关系便明晰了。

其次,行政强制实体裁量必须符合比例原则中的必要性原则要求,任何超出必要限度之外所采取的行政手段均无法通过最小侵害的底线判断。正如胡建淼教授等人指出,最小侵害原则在行政强制法中的适用标准可概括为“间接强制优先于直接强制”“对物强制优先于对人强制”“行政强制手段作为最后手

〔30〕 [日]田村悦一:《自由裁量及其界限》,李哲范译,中国政法大学出版社2016年版,第185页。

〔31〕 同上书,第185页。

〔32〕 参见杨登峰、李晴:《行政处罚中比例原则与过罚相当原则的关系之辨》,载《交大法学》2017年第4期。

段实施”等。[33] 总而言之,行政强制法律关系中最为完满的状态是以最小的“行政成本”(个人利益)获取最大的“行政效益”(公共利益)。故而,对于行政机关的强制实体裁量必须坚持最小侵害的限度要求。

最后,行政强制实体裁量必须符合比例原则中的均衡性原则要求,任何超出目的射程之外所采取的行政手段均无法满足狭义比例的价值衡量。倘若行政机关具有多种手段选择的裁量空间,其必须选择一种与目的更为接近的方法,而不是纯粹出于个人的主观感情或者利益偏好作出决定。深而论之,“个人利益”和“公共利益”之间的关系绝非断然否定、断然闭合,而是应当根据不同情形进行价值权衡、利益考量,寻求“成本最小化、利益最大化”的理想方案。

2. 程序裁量约束功能:不同程序价值的内容揭示

基于前述可知,比例原则主要通过成本效益均衡的分析工具对行政强制实体裁量施予有效制约。与此同时,我们还可以进一步分析比例原则对于行政强制程序裁量所具有的约束功能,由此便需要正视行政强制程序本身兼具的工具价值和内在价值。

首先,现代社会习惯性地将程序纯粹看作实现实体法“功利”的手段,或者说行政程序是行政机关作出实体内容的一种工具,这种偏重实体结果的观点可被简单称为程序工具主义。根据国内学者对程序理论的整体研究,英国法学巨儒边沁是该理论观点的“扛旗者”。相较于“旨在捍卫社会最大多数成员的最大幸福”的实体法,边沁把程序法当作前者的“附属部分”,“其目的主要是最低限度地把实体法付诸实施”。[34] 为此,行政强制程序所天然具有的工具价值自然是无可厚非的。从这个意义上讲,在程序工具主义的理论视域之下,比例原则可以直接利用“行政程序法与行政实体法”之间的这种手段与目的的关系,从而揭示行政强制程序裁量必须服从于立法者制定法律的良好初衷:惩罚教育违法的社会成员,实现“最大多数人的幸福”,最终实施有效的社会控制。[35] 毕竟,

[33] 参见胡建淼、蒋红珍:《论最小侵害原则在行政强制法中的适用》,载《法学家》2006 年第 3 期。

[34] 陈端洪:《法律程序价值观》,载《中外法学》1997 年第 6 期。

[35] 有学者指出,程序工具主义论者常常选择忽略程序法与实体法所服务的社会总体福利之间的沟壑而从整体上把程序法看作实现某种功利结果的制度手段,“结果好什么都好”被认为是程序工具主义最真实的写照。同上注,陈端洪文。

相对于实体法所预设的某种特定目标而言,行政程序仅仅是工具性的,其唯一的正当性来源是最大限度地实现实体法,[36]否则,超出“工具射程”之外的程序本身是没有任何实际性意义的,甚至可能会极大地背离实体法目标。这就表明,此处对程序工具主义的内容揭示,对于比例原则在行政强制程序裁量所能够发挥的约束功能,是可欲且可行的。

其次,行政程序的价值并不局限于工具或者手段,其还可以体现为一种“可接受的过程德性”。[37] 换言之,程序所带来的“结果正义”并非是其唯一的价值追求,而更加注重程序作为一种过程应当具备的重要意义,这种强调过程价值的观点可被归纳为程序本位主义。究竟如何定义程序的内在价值,新自然法学派代表人物富勒曾经以“内在道德属性”一词高度抽象地予以回应。[38] 但是,这种以道德属性定位程序价值的理论倾向似乎会更加令人捉摸不透。后来,另一位著名的美国法学家萨默斯指出,对于法律程序的内在价值必须一分为二地看待:“维护实体法目的”仅仅是其表征,而“某些内在价值”才是程序理论的精神内核和坚实基础。可是,仍然无法直截了当地界定法律程序内在价值的内涵范畴。通过仔细参阅和对比国内外学者的程序理论著作,笔者认为,只有符合这三个基本要点的价值才可以视为程序的内在价值:第一,必须通过设计良好的法律程序得以达成此种价值;第二,对于此种价值的客观评判,应当源于过程而非结果;第三,此种价值必须能够促进法律程序易于人们普遍接受,而不是单纯地注重程序可能会带来何种结果。[39] 不容置疑的是,无论从哪种角度推演程序本身的内在价值,都无法绕开目的与手段的关系问题,即程序的内容和形式本身是手段,而程序所欲实现的民主、人权、公正、合法、合理等价值才是目的。

总而言之,程序工具主义与程序本位主义皆是不同维度下比例原则“手段合乎目的,且手段成本与目的效益之间保持均衡”的理论表达,而这种将手段与

〔36〕 参见雷磊:《法律程序为什么重要:反思现代社会中程序与法治的关系》,载《中外法学》2014年第2期。

〔37〕 参见前文34,陈端洪文。

〔38〕 参见[美]富勒:《法律的道德性》,郑戈译,商务印书馆2005年版,第178页。

〔39〕 按照这个标准,在萨默斯看来,程序的内在价值主要包括参与性统治、程序正当性、程序和平性、人道性及尊重个人的尊严、个人隐私、协同性(意见一致性)、程序公平性、程序合法性、程序理性、及时性和终结性。参见前引36,雷磊文。

目的关系置于法律程序的评价基础之上,无疑是将比例原则直接认定为行政强制程序裁量的适用前提予以接受。加之,前文已经详细论证比例原则在行政强制实体裁量的约束功能,此处便不再赘述。由此可知,比例原则不仅可以适用于约束行政强制实体裁量以确保成本效益的整体均衡,而且可以适用于约束行政强制程序裁量以消除行政程序的主观恣意。

(二)手段最小侵害:设定和实施行政强制的适当性原则

寻本溯源,我国现行《行政强制法》第5条明确规定强制适当原则的内涵,即行政强制的设定和实施必须适当。从当时立法背景和立法过程来看,“由于没有统一的法律规范,一些行政机关在执法过程中,既存在对某些严重违法行为因缺乏强制手段处理不力的情况,也存在行政强制手段滥用的情况”。[40]“《行政强制法(草案)》第二次审议稿还规定,设定行政强制应当适当,兼顾公共利益和当事人的合法权益。行政强制不得滥用,须以当事人的权益最小损失为原则,选择适当的行政强制方式”。[41] 同时,国务院关于《全面推进依法行政实施纲要》中明确指出“合理行政是依法行政的基本要求,行政机关所采取的措施和手段应当必要、适当”,这些均可看作强制适当原则的规范来源。

1. 强制适当是设定和实施行政强制的法定原则

强制适当是设定行政强制需要严格遵守的法定原则。《行政强制法》专章规定了行政强制的种类和设定权,这便意味着行政强制的设定主体是法定的,而不是所有公权主体皆有权设定行政强制。至于行政强制的设定内容,则需要同时遵循强制法定原则、强制适当原则。一方面,行政强制的性质决定其必须遵循法学理论层面和《中华人民共和国立法法》明确规定的“法律优位原则”“法律保留原则”。[42] 正如袁曙宏教授所言,无论是“限制公民人身自由”“冻结存款、汇款”,还是“涉及公民住宅和通信自由”,皆应当属于“绝对的法律保留事项”,因为它们都将密切关系公民、法人或者其他组织的人身财产权利,只能

---

〔40〕 全国人大常委会法制委员会副主任信春鹰教授于2005年12月24日在第十届全国人大常委会十九次会议上所作的《关于〈中华人民共和国行政强制法(草案)〉的说明》。

〔41〕 参见莫于川、林鸿潮:《中华人民共和国行政强制法释义》,中国法制出版社2011年版,第23页。

〔42〕 参见袁曙宏:《我国〈行政强制法〉的法律地位、价值取向和制度逻辑》,载《中国法学》2011年第4期。

由最高权力机关制定的法律予以设定。[43] 另一方面,除强制法定原则之外,行政强制的设定必须符合适当性原则要求,即但凡是有权设定行政强制的立法机关,应当根据要达到的行政目的和具体情况,对是否设定强制、何时何地设定何种强制等问题遵循适当原则,作出合理判断。[44]

强制适当原则不仅是设定行政强制应当遵循的法定原则,而且是实施行政强制必须遵循的法定原则。主要体现在以下两个方面:第一,在具有多个行政手段选择的情况下,如果采用非强制手段可以达到行政管理目的,那么就不能实施行政强制,或者说宜将行政强制作为"万不得已的最后手段";[45] 第二,确实要采取行政强制手段以维护行政管理秩序,也需要更加注意对行政相对人的人身自由限制和财产权利伤害最小,不得随意侵犯与违法行为无关的私人场所、设施或者财物。

另外,值得一提的是,强制适当原则适用于强制裁量行为,而非强制羁束行为。传统行政法教义学针对行政职权的性质和行政机关行为意志自由程度的不同,将行政行为分为羁束行政行为和裁量行政行为。[46] 前者是指在法律明确规定行政行为适用条件的情形下,行政机关严格依法作出的行政行为,在这种行为模式下,行政主体不存在选择空间,因此,羁束行政行为只发生违法与否的问题,只受行政合法性原则的约束。[47] 相反,对于裁量行政行为而言,行政机关除了恪守依法行政原则之外,有权根据行政相对人的违法事实、行为性质以及社会危害程度等具体情况,进而确定适用何种与之相对应的强制种类和幅度,

〔43〕 前引42,袁曙宏文,第13页。

〔44〕 参见全国人大常委会法制工作委员会行政法室编:《〈中华人民共和国行政强制法〉解读》,中国法制出版社2011年版,第22页。

〔45〕 有学者指出,行政强制在行政法上的运用,永远是第二位的,起补足、威慑与担保作用。如果能够采取其他手段实现行政义务与状态,就尽量不诉诸行政强制。参见余凌云:《行政法讲义》,清华大学出版社2010年版,第302页。

〔46〕 在大陆法系行政法学中,行政裁量与羁束行政相对,羁束与裁量的区分有其存在的必要。参见王贵松:《行政裁量:羁束与自由的迷思》,载《行政法学研究》2008年第4期;也有学者认为,根据法律规范对行政行为拘束的程度不同,行政行为可分为羁束行为和裁量行为。参见杨建顺:《行政裁量的运作及其监督》,载《法学研究》2004年第1期。

〔47〕 参见胡建淼:《行政法学》,法律出版社2015年版,第178页以下。

从而在一定程度上避免因强制过轻导致的无法达到惩戒违法行为人的目的，和因强制过重导致的给行政相对人负担过重的后果。但是，此处的行政强制裁量并非一种绝对自由，而是应当加以规范和约束。“一切权利只有在正当行使的前提下才能受到保护，无论公法还是私法，禁止滥用权利都是普遍的法原理……即使是行政裁量，也不存在完全独立于法律之外的自由，无论有无明文规定，行政机关都有义务依据法的宗旨和目的行使其裁量权”。〔48〕因此，强制适当原则对于约束强制裁量是必要且可行的。

2. 强制适当原则仅仅适用于约束行政强制实体裁量

强制适当原则的约束范围仅限于强制实体裁量，而不宜约束强制程序裁量。依据《行政强制法》关于行政机关实施行政强制的程序规定来看，笔者认为主要是适用强制法定原则。“行政强制作为一项重要的行政权力，其设定和实施都必须遵循合法性原则，做到依法行政”。〔49〕此外，还应遵循强制公开原则，如在实施行政强制措施的一般程序中，行政机关必须作出书面的决定，且须经过内部批准，不是由行政执法人员随意作出。同时，还明确规定如下外部程序：两名执法人员实施、身份示明、允许当事人陈述申辩、说明强制理由并告知救济途径、制作现场笔录且签章送达。〔50〕又如在实施行政强制执行的一般程序中，通过专门设置书面形式的催告程序、执行回转、文明执法等内容充分保障行政相对人的程序权利。〔51〕可知，上述规范内容并未明确提及行政机关的强制程序裁量问题，加之当时立法背景下学界和实务界并没有过多地关注程序裁量，为此我们可以大胆推测：由于立法机关的认知局限，导致行政强制法未对行政强制程序裁量问题进行有效规制。

由此可知，程序法定原则、程序公开原则是强制法定原则的具体表现，而强

〔48〕［日］田村悦一：《自由裁量及其界限》，李哲范译，中国政法大学出版社2016年版，第40页。

〔49〕全国人大常委会法制工作委员会行政法室编：《〈中华人民共和国行政强制法〉解读》，中国法制出版社2011年版，第18页。

〔50〕我国现行《行政强制法》第三章第一节明确规定实施行政强制措施的一般程序、情况紧急时的程序、限制人身自由强制措施程序、行刑案件移送程序等。

〔51〕我国现行《行政强制法》第四章第一节明确规定行政强制执行程序的一般规定：催告、中止执行、终结执行、执行回转、执行和解、文明执法等。

制适当原则却仅仅体现出行政强制实体裁量的约束要求。例如,在“刘云务诉山西省太原市公安局交通警察支队晋源一大队道路交通管理行政强制案”中,在原告提交相关材料后,被告却迟迟不作出行政决定,既不返还涉案扣押车辆,又不及时调查案件事实,从而构成滥用职权。[52] 其实,从另一个角度来看,被告长期扣押车辆并不作处理的行为明显违背程序法定原则和程序时效要求。虽然,该案受审法院依据职权实施的情况进行认定,但是侧面论证了强制法定原则对于程序裁量的规制作用。因此,强制适当原则无法约束强制程序裁量,而是仅仅适用于是否强制、何种强制和强制多少的实体裁量。

质言之,通过上述对比例原则和强制适当原则在适用标准和约束范围进行仔细梳理之后,可以知道在行政强制中强制适当原则并非比例原则的化身。强制适当原则是我国依法行政原理指导下尊重和保障基本人权的本土资源,而比例原则则是直接引介自德国公法学理论的舶来品。强制适当原则是用于设定和实施行政强制的法定原则,但仅仅限于行政强制实体裁量,而比例原则则是用以全面制约行政强制裁量的行政法基本原则。故而,在行政强制中强制适当原则并非简单等同于比例原则的另一种表达。

三、行政强制实体裁量中比例原则是强制适当性的判断标准

如前所述,强制适当原则在某些情形下很难承担起官方文件和学界通说所谓之“比例原则的化身”的重要角色,或者说其本身无法提供适当性的判断标准,最终还是需要借助比例原则的分析工具对行政行为的合理性进行综合考察。因此,下文将重点比较强制适当原则与比例原则在判断行政强制“适当性”所具有的指导作用,从而为此二者关系的辨别提供更为缜密的论证思路。

(一)先天不足:强制适当原则的指引乏力

根据《行政强制法》第5条规定:行政强制的设定和实施,应当适当。采用非强制手段可以达到行政管理目的的,不得设定和实施行政强制。由此可知,强制适当原则主要用于考量强制手段与非强制手段在惩戒行政违法行为的平衡关系。但是,在判断是否应当采取强制手段时,强制适当原则并未明确提及具体的适用因素,例如“违法行为的事实、性质、情节以及社会危害程度”。故

[52] 参见《最高人民法院公报》2017年第2期。

而,很难证明强制适当原则能够有效指引行政机关或者司法机关明确判断"某一行政强制手段是否适当或者不适当"。例如,在2006年郑州"天价滞纳金"案中,小吊车车主因不缴纳59,040元养路费,而后被郑州市交通规费稽查部门加处滞纳金389,894元,并且还要承担三倍漏税额的罚款,共计高达76万元。[53]该事件经网络媒体曝光后,便引发社会民众的广泛关注,最终以废止《公路养路费征收管理规定》而告终。但是,值得我们思考的是,该案中行政机关加处"天价"滞纳金的行为究竟合法与否,若具有一定的合法性基础,那么其是否符合合理性的原则要求?[54] 笔者认为,类似于滞纳金的执行罚,确系我国《行政强制法》明确规定的间接强制方式,用以督促行政相对人及时履行法定义务。加之,1%的养路费滞纳金并非很高,而是相对较低的。因此,有学者指出,从形式和内容上来看,该行政强制行为是合法、合理的。[55] 但是,在这类案件中,倘若仅仅考察行政强制行为的种类和幅度,可以认为其确已符合法律规定的强制法定、强制适当原则。然而其背后所隐藏的"手段背离目的,手段不具有适当性"问题,却是上述法定原则始终无法释明的"法理漏洞"。

笔者认为,在"天价滞纳金"案中,普通民众和学界人士之所以没有分析行政强制行为与行政管理目的不相当的原因,是因为"强制适当性"的判断标准不够明确。深而论之,便是强制适当原则本身没有也无法提供适当性的判断标准。

(二)工具支持:比例原则的三维分析框架

如是观之,强制适当原则无法提供适当性的判断标准,可能会造成一些行

[53] 参见曹树林:《何时告别"天价"滞纳金》,载人民网:http://finance.people.com.cn/GB/6898258.html,最后访问日期:2018年6月9日。

[54] 关于"天价"滞纳金合法性、合理性的具体讨论和深度思考,可参见杨庆华:《滞纳金的四大法律困惑——"天价滞纳金"案引发的法律思考》,载《广东广播电视大学学报》2007年第5期。

[55] 参见刘如东:《天价滞纳金引发的思考——访中国法学会行政法学研究会副会长杨建顺》,载《今日中国论坛》2006年第9期。但是,笔者不得不追问:我国《行政强制法》第45条第2款规定:加处罚款或者滞纳金的数额不得超过金钱给付义务的数额。这也意味着,"天价"滞纳金的加处行为明显是违法的,那又何来合法性基础一说呢?故而,笔者认为上述观点值得商榷。

政强制行为堕入"内容、形式皆为合法合理,但趋远于行为内在价值"的罪孽之中。正如于安教授所言,比例原则从依法治国原则和基本权利的基本要求和实质精神出发,以实质性规则特有的伸缩性和广泛适用性,解决依法治国原则运用中的大量实际问题,使成文法制度难以避免的法律漏洞得到弥补、缺陷得到克服,使得依法治国原则更有普遍意义,能够在社会生活中得到更深刻广泛的应用。[56] 因此,笔者结合前文针对强制适当原则、比例原则的相关论述,进一步尝试引入比例原则在价值、规范以及技术层面的三维分析工具,进而有助于促成强制适当原则与比例原则之间的内容衔接和品格契合。

其一,比例原则的价值渊源可追溯至依法治国原则和基本权利的精神内核,即国家公权力的行使方式必须符合公共利益的目的要求,不可借题发挥、小题大做;[57]公民的基本权利亦只有在为保护公共利益的时候,才能被公权力合比例地予以限制。[58] 由此得出,比例原则的终极目标是最大限度地兼顾公共利益和基本权利,维持二者之间的平衡关系。《行政强制法》是我国一部重要的行政单行法,其立法宗旨可概括为:维护公共利益和社会秩序、保护公民、法人和其他组织的合法权益。这意味着实施行政强制必须以法律后果或可预期的明确法律后果为基础,而非执法人员的主观恣意或者自由裁量,通过这些法律后果来判断具体手段是否有助于实现立法目的,或者该手段是否已经超出法律效果所需的程度。[59] 因此,可以看出比例原则的价值诉求关键在于手段与目的之间的均衡性审查,即行政强制手段所造成的行政相对人权益减损与该手段所要保护的公共利益是否均衡。国家公共权力对基本权利的限制必须具备正当性,由此推导出的一系列价值衡量实为比例原则最常用的分析套路,亦是其全面约束行政强制裁量的重要判断因素。

其二,比例原则的规范结构具有较为广阔的伸缩空间和适用范围,即作为

---

[56] 于安:《德国行政法》,清华大学出版社1999年版,第31页以下。

[57] 参见李荣珍、王进:《论行政比例原则》,载《法治论坛》2007年第3期。

[58] BVerfGE 19,342(348F.).转引自[德]安德烈亚斯·冯·阿尔诺:《欧洲基本权利保护的理论与方法——以比例原则为例》,刘权译,载《比较法研究》2014年第1期。

[59] 参见翟翌:《比例原则的正当性拷问及其"比例技术"的重新定位——基于"无人有义务做不可能之事"的正义原则》,载《法学论坛》2012年第6期。

一项实质性规则,〔60〕其包含三个子原则:适当性、必要性和均衡性,传统法解释学称此为比例原则的阶层秩序理论。〔61〕 基于比例原则的三阶层规范结构,我们可以直观地感受到其内在审查逻辑以及规范对事实的涵摄强度,即只有当某项行政强制手段同时符合适当性、必要性、均衡性三个子原则,方可评价其为符合比例原则,从而具有限制基本权利的正当性与保护公共利益的合理性。〔62〕 换言之,必要性、适当性、均衡性共同构成比例原则的要件链条,相辅相成、缺一不可。在满足这些构成要件的基础上,行政强制手段尚须实现个人利益(行政成本)最小化与公共利益(行政效益)最大化的法律效果。因此,比例原则作为一个分析手段完备和目标指向明确的规则系统,对于行政行为的规范判断更具有显著效用。

其三,比例原则的技术层面则是通过借助一种典型的正当性衡量方法以妥善解决实际问题,实质性地弥补和克服成文法制度的法律漏洞,使得依法治国原则能够普遍适用于社会生活。一般而言,比例原则的基础性功能是为公权者选择手段提供技术性方案。即当存在多种可供选择的手段时,公权者必须及时作出选择,决定适用哪种手段,此时便需要方法支撑。毫无疑问,比例原则是当前最为理性和完善的论证方法,与其说是一种证实的原则,毋宁说成是一种否证的原则。〔63〕 对行政强制这类侵害型行政行为进行正当性衡量,首先需要证明其具有适当性,手段的选择必须符合立法所预设的目的要求,否则该手段便是

〔60〕 关于法律原则与法律规则之间的区分理论,可参见[德]卡尔·拉伦茨:《法学方法论》,陈爱娥译,商务印书馆2003年版。此外,杨登峰教授等人专门针对法律原则内部的高低位阶和层级转化问题进行研究,指出比例原则属于规则性原则,与理念性原则相对。参见杨登峰、李晴:《行政处罚中比例原则与过罚相当原则的关系之辨》,载《交大法学》2017年第4期。

〔61〕 See T. Jeremy Gunn. Deconstructing Proportionality in Limitations Analysis. Emory International Law Review,2005(19),pp. 465 - 481. 转引自蒋红珍:《比例原则阶层秩序理论之重构——以“牛肉制品进销禁令”为验证适例》,载《上海交通大学学报》(哲学社会科学版)2010年第4期。

〔62〕 关于比例原则在事实、规范、审查标准和审查强度的初步厘定,蒋红珍教授通过分析2003年“陈宁案”指出,比例原则应当从个案事实出发,甄别其对于司法适用而言的要件类型,形成可能的“新的规范”。参见蒋红珍:《比例原则在“陈宁案”中的适用——兼及“析出法”路径下个案规范的最短射程》,载《交大法学》2014年第2期。

〔63〕 参见徐梦秋:《公平的类别与公平中的比例》,载《中国社会科学》2001年第1期。

不正当的;其次需要证明其具有必要性,手段的选择必须对行政相对人利益侵害最小,否则该手段亦是不正当的;最后需要证明其具有均衡性,手段的选择必须遵循“成本最小化、效益最大化”的基本要求,若该手段对行政相对人造成的利益减损大于所要维护的公共利益,那么该手段亦是不正当的。实施某个行政强制手段必须满足比例原则的三个子原则,才具有正当性,这就表明,比例原则对行政行为的正当性衡量具有极强的可操作性。

通过对比例原则在价值、规范和技术层面的仔细剖析,我们可以得出以下结论:比例原则是一种基于价值衡量、具有相对成熟操作方法的规则性原则,〔64〕而这一特性正好弥补了强制适当原则的先天不足。在价值层面,强制适当原则判断强制行为适当性的过程,其本质是在平衡违法行为者的个人利益和强制行为所要维护的公共利益,同时也是一种价值衡量。在规范和技术层面,强制适当原则片面追求强制行为的合理性,因而更为倾向于一种理念性原则,在实际应用过程中明显缺乏可操作性,无法为行政机关提供适当性的判断标准。相反,比例原则作为规则性原则,拥有内部衔接得当的构成要件和法律效果,可从适当性、必要性、均衡性三个步骤逐一考察行政强制的适当性,进而补足强制适当原则判断技术的匮乏。

四、结　　语

行文至此,笔者已从适用标准、约束范围两个方面基本廓清比例原则与强制适当在行政强制领域中的不同内涵和功能差异。虽然二者均可用于制约行政强制实体裁量,但是,强制适当原则并不能直接约束行政强制程序裁量,况且在行政强制的实体裁量过程中,强制适当原则自身无法明确判断强制行为的适当性。无论是从价值、规范还是技术层面,皆须仰赖比例原则为其提供完整的分析工具。那么,在强制适当原则之中引入比例原则的三维分析框架,是否符合行政法的规范体系要求?俨然成为本文后续需要回答的重点问题。

其一,强制适当原则是合理性原则在行政强制法中的具体适用。尽管对于强制适当原则与合理性原则的关系问题,学界鲜有笔墨展开细致论述。但是,

〔64〕 参见杨登峰、李晴:《行政处罚中比例原则与过罚相当原则的关系之辨》,载《交大法学》2017年第4期。

经过仔细考究官方文件和学者观点，却总能觉察到其二者所存在的紧密联系。例如，一种观点认为强制适当原则也称为合理性原则，是在合法性基础上的对行政机关的更高要求。〔65〕另一种观点认为，强制适当原则的实质内核最早是在合理性原则的框架下得到初步释放的。〔66〕上述观点在一定程度上揭示了强制适当原则与合理性原则的源与流关系，尚须进一步深入分析。

依据传统行政法教义学的基本原则体系，合法性原则与合理性原则二分“天下”的理论观点仍旧强势，前者包括法律优位和法律保留原则，后者则包括裁量合理原则和程序正当原则。〔67〕《行政强制法》第 4 条规定了强制法定原则，第 5 条规定强制适当原则，第 6 条规定了教育与强制相结合原则，第 8 条规定了相对人权利救济保障原则。其中，强制法定原则是合法性原则在行政强制法中的自然延伸，合理性原则则体现为强制适当、公开原则。其中针对强制实体内容而言，强制适当对应的主要是裁量合理原则，而针对强制程序而言，强制公开对应的主要是程序正当原则。因此，强制适当原则与合理性原则中的裁量合理相对应。

其二，比例原则作为合理性原则的子原则之一。〔68〕国内的一些主流行政法学教科书往往都选择将合法性和合理性原则相提并论，共同作为行政法的基本原则。〔69〕不难窥见，合理性原则作为一项行政法基本原则，是我国行政法学界

---

〔65〕参见信春鹰主编：《中华人民共和国行政强制法释义》，法律出版社 2011 年版，第 21 页。

〔66〕参见郑春燕：《必要性原则内涵之重构》，载《政法论坛》2004 年第 6 期。

〔67〕章剑生教授将行政法基本原则分为三部分：行政实体法基本原则、行政程序法基本原则和行政诉讼法基本原则，其中行政程序法原则包括行政裁量合理原则和行政程序正当原则，笔者基本赞同这一观点。参见章剑生：《现代行政法总论》，法律出版社 2014 年版，第 53 ~ 55 页。

〔68〕参见汪燕：《行政合理性原则与失当行政行为》，载《法学评论》2014 年第 5 期。

〔69〕其实早在 20 世纪 80 年代末，龚祥瑞教授便将合理性原则与合法性原则并列为行政法基本原则。参见龚祥瑞：《行政合理性原则》，载《法学杂志》1987 年第 2 期。此外，还可参见罗豪才主编：《行政法学》，中国政法大学出版社 1989 年版，第 34 页；胡建淼：《行政法学》，法律出版社 2015 年版，第 37 页；叶必丰：《行政法与行政诉讼法》，高等教育出版社 2015 年版，第 34 页。

的通说观点。但是,学者们关于合理性原则的内涵阐发,却各抒己见。例如,张树义教授指出,合理性原则包括平等原则和比例原则。[70] 章剑生教授认为,合理原则下列比例原则、禁止不当联结原则和禁止恣意原则。[71] 罗豪才教授等人认为,合理性原则包括行政公开原则、行政公正原则、比例原则、信赖保护原则、尊重和保障人权原则。[72] 但是,也有学者持相反观点,认为比例原则与合理性原则有极大的不同,比例原则着眼于法益均衡,以维护和发展公民权利为最终归宿,而合理性原则则以公共利益本位为出发点,凸显对公共利益的偏好,相较而言,比例原则的适用范围更广、位阶更高。[73] 虽然学界迄今没有对此形成基础共识,但是不可否认比例原则已然被纳入合理性原则之中。[74] 由此便可直接推导出本节结论:比例原则是合理性原则内涵的重要组成部分,而强制适当原则是合理性原则在行政强制中的具体适用,那么,在行政强制中,将比例原则作为强制适当原则的判断标准,显然是符合行政法学规范体系的自洽要求。

最后,笔者就全文内容和最终结论做一个简要的归纳:比例原则是全面制约行政强制裁量的行政法基本原则,而强制适当原则是《行政强制法》用以设定和实施行政强制的法定原则。但是,在实施行政强制过程中,强制适当原则仅仅适用于约束强制实体裁量,而无法约束强制程序裁量,且本身无法提供手段适当性的判断标准。较之于此,比例原则既能约束行政强制实体裁量,又能约束行政强制程序裁量,并且兼具价值衡量统一化、规范结构系统化以及技术方法阶层化等显著优势,使得比例原则在行政强制实体裁量中能够成为综合评价手段适当与否的有效分析工具,从而成为强制适当性的判断标准。

(责任编辑:秦喆予)

---

[70] 参见张树义主编:《行政法与行政诉讼法》,高等教育出版社2007年版,第34页。

[71] 参见章剑生:《现代行政法总论》,法律出版社2014年版,第54页。

[72] 参见罗豪才、湛中乐主编:《行政法学》,北京大学出版社2012年版,第31页以下。

[73] 参见何景春:《行政比例与合理性原则的比较研究》,载《行政法学研究》2004年第2期。

[74] 吴偕林教授指出,行政合理性原则不仅适用于行政实体裁量,而且适用于行政程序裁量,这与比例原则在制约行政强制裁量中的功能基本相同。参见吴偕林:《论行政合理性原则的适用》,载《法学》2004年第12期。

语境中的法律：权力的一种叙事批判

——以《Z 市 C 事业促进办法》起草过程为例

何子健*

摘要：

法律语言作为法律规范运作的中介，往往也会成为权力关系的核心。立法者出于解决合理性、合法性危机的需要而进行的“立法语言建构”，基于其交际行为的本质和欲交际成功的动机，需要遵守哈贝马斯普遍语用学中“有效性要求的义务”。在成功/无法遵守这些义务的同时，立法语言也成了隐蔽的权力运作的载体。

关键词：

法律语言；权力；哈贝马斯普遍语用学；义务

一、引言：问题的提出

在国外，尤其是英美，自 20 世纪初哲学上的语言转向[1]以来，语言研究渐渐成为 20 世纪各学科研究的切入点或对象，法学领域的研究也毫不例外地受

---

* 何子健，中山大学法学院 2018 级硕士研究生。

〔1〕 各种著作和教科书都不约而同地采纳了一种说法，把西方哲学从古希腊到 20 世纪的发展宏观地概括为一个三阶段模式，即本体论—认识论—语言论。哲学在 20 世纪初又发生了一次根本性的转向，语言取代认识论成为哲学研究的中心课题。参见徐友渔、周国平、陈嘉映、尚杰：《语言与哲学：当代英美与德法哲学传统比较研究》，生活 · 读书 · 新知三联书店 1996 年版，第 37 页以下；参见艾四林：《哈贝马斯交往理论评析》，载《清华大学学报》（哲学社会科学版）1995 年第 3 期。

到哲学的语言转向的影响,[2]语言分析在法学研究中的重要性及其应用已越来越为众多学者所认识。[3] 舒国滢分析战后德国法哲学“法与语言”论题时如此描述:“法的世界肇始于语言:法律是通过语词订立和公布的,法律行为和法律决定也都涉及言辞思考和公开的表述或辩论。法律语言与概念的运用,法律文本(Gesetzestext)与事相(Sachverhalt)关系的描述与诠释,立法者与司法者基于法律文本的相互沟通,法律语境的判断等等,都离不开语言的分析。”[4]

我国的法律语言研究尚处在从静态研究法律语言客体[5]向动态研究法律语言过程[6]过渡的阶段,目前研究主要集中于司法语言研究、法律翻译和法律语言教学等,同时也逐渐展开了普法语言研究,[7]但是在将法律语言作为工具的研究方面,仍存空白。[8]

---

〔2〕 作为语言转向的代表人物之一,维特根斯坦倡导用日常语言来描述、分析和解决哲学问题,这种观点深深影响了牛津日常语言哲学学派,而开启法学中语言转向序幕(或“最具代表性”)的哈特正是在与此学派的领军人物交往中得到启发。参见焦宝乾等:《法律修辞学导论——司法视角的探讨》,山东人民出版社2012年版,第160页;黄文艺:《法哲学解说》,载《法学研究》2000年第5期。

〔3〕 很多法哲学家转入语言哲学的门下。参见前引2,黄文艺文。

〔4〕 舒国滢:《战后德国法哲学的发展路向》,载《比较法研究》1995年第4期。

〔5〕 中国在过去二十年中处于立法的高峰期,对立法语言本身的研究自然成为重点所在。参见吴伟平:《语言与法律——司法领域的语言学研究》,上海外语教育出版社2002年版,第81页。

〔6〕 随着各种法规的完善,研究人员势必开拓新的研究领域,现有法律在实践中的解释及施行中引发的语言问题,相信会吸引越来越多学者的注意。参见前引5,吴伟平文。

〔7〕 参见杜金榜、葛云锋:《论法律语言学方法》,人民出版社2016年版,绪论,第5页。

〔8〕 参见彭京宜:《法律语言研究的回顾与前瞻》,载《广西社会科学》2000年第6期;杜金榜:《论法律语言学研究及其发展》,载《广东外语外贸大学学报》2003年第1期;廖美珍:《国外法律语言研究综述》,载《当代语言学》2004年第1期;陈炯:《二十多年来中国法律语言学研究评述》,载《毕节师范高等专科学校学报》2004年第1期;马煜:《国内法律语言学研究状况分析综述》,载《山东外语教学》2005年第6期;宗世海、刘文辉:《中国法律语言学研究综述》,载《广西社会科学》2006年第10期;宋北平:《我国法律语言研究的过去、现在和

本文试图为尚处过渡阶段[9]的我国法律语言学,提供一些关于以法律语言为工具的批判研究的尝试思路:以《Z 市 C 事业促进办法》起草过程为研究对象,在法律语言叙事的总框架中,运用哈贝马斯(Jürgen Habermas)交往理论导向的话语分析理论,对其中的"立法语言建构"现象进行分析,揭示权力[10]在立法语境中是如何运作和实现的。

未来》,载《法学杂志》2009 年第 2 期;李宁:《略谈国内法律语言学研究现状及趋向》,载《黑龙江教育学院学报》2008 年第 1 期;李诗芳:《法律语言学研究综观》,载《学术交流》2009 年第 6 期;王洁:《从"立法时代"到"修法时代"的中国大陆法律语言研究》,载《语言文字应用》2010 年第 4 期;张玉洁:《论我国法律语言学的演进及未来发展》,载《广西政法管理干部学院学报》2015 年第 3 期;徐优平:《法律语言学理论建设新突破——兼评〈法律语篇信息研究〉》,载《中原工学院学报》2016 年第 2 期;季培雯:《我国法律语言学研究现状及未来发展趋势——基于中国学术期刊的数据分析(2000—2016)》,载《农家科技》2017 年第 1 期。

〔9〕 斯泰戈(Gail Stygall)将法律语言研究划分为三个基本类型和发展阶段:语言作为对象、语言作为过程、语言作为工具。See Stygall G., *Trail Language*, Amsterdam, John Benjamins Publishing Company, 1994, pp. 6 - 7. 杜金榜从语言学的角度也将法律语言研究划分为三大部分和三个阶段。其中,三个阶段是:法律语言学前应用阶段—法律语言学阶段—法律语言学应用阶段。他认为,目前国内外的研究已进入第二阶段,侧重于语言—法律关系的讨论、探索和法律语言学理论层次的研究,但也不乏法律语言学研究成果的应用。参见杜金榜:《法律语言学》,上海外语教育出版社 2004 年版,第 18 页。但是,笔者经梳理已有研究,更倾向于认为国内研究尚在从第一阶段过渡到第二阶段的过程中。

〔10〕 需要特别强调,本文所采用的"权力"概念并非日常理解的仅涉及国家权威的力量概念,而是在无数远离权力中心的地方局部行使的、社会关系中各方互相制约的、对话式的力量。福柯(Foucault)强调了注意这种散布的权力的机制或"微观物理学"的必要性,而微观权力是要问"权力是如何运作的"。See Hunt, Alan and Gary Wickham, *Foucault and Law: Towards a Sociology of Law and Governance*, London, Pluto Press, 1994, pp. 16 - 17; Michel Foucault, *Discipline and Punish: The Birth of the Prison*, trans. by Alan Sheridan, New York, Vintage Books, 1979;参见欧阳本祺:《犯罪构成诞生的权力分析》,载《法律科学》(西北政法大学学报)2012 年第 4 期;韩平:《微观权力分析——读米歇尔·福柯的〈规训与惩罚〉》,载《河北法学》2006 年第 11 期。本文更没有混淆"权力"与"权利"的概念,如权力强调主体意志的优越性和有效性,权利主体在此基础上还强调意志的正当性,而本文并无涉及"意志的正当性"。参见王莉君:《法学基础范畴的重构:对权利和权力的新思考》,载《法学家》2005 年第 2 期。

二、文献综述:研究的视野与路径

(一)法律语言

法律与语言研究崛起于法学与语言学之间的一块交叉地[11],法律(法学)与语言(语言学)的关系直接影响到以此为基础的法律与语言研究以及由之孕育而出的"法律语言学"(Forensic Linguistic[12])。但是,法律与语言的关系如此复杂,[13]以致给融合而成的、独立的新概念——"法律语言"下定义注定是艰辛的。为了本文能顺利开展,笔者尝试提出较能反映法律与语言关系的定

---

[11] See Levi, J. N. and Walker, A. G. (eds.), *Language in the Judicial Process*, New York and London, Plenum Press, 1990, pp. 12 – 15; Stygall, G., *Trail Language*, Amsterdam, John Benjamins Publishing Company, 1994, pp. 5 – 8.

[12] 此概念从国外引入我国时,有两个常用的译名:一是"法律语言学",二是"司法语言学"。经过比较,刘蔚铭认为采用"法律语言学"能较好地体现司法实践的主要特征,亦较好地概括了语言与法律其他层面的研究。参见刘蔚铭:《法律语言学研究》,中国经济出版社2003年版,第11~20页。考虑到国外有关研究也多采广义,国内该学科更不应作茧自缚,所以笔者也支持该选择,本文全篇采用该译名。

[13] 休谟(David Hume)曾言"法与法律制度(如所有制)是一种纯粹的'语言形式'",David Hume. *Trcatise of Human Nature* (1739), Bd Ⅱ, p. 263,转引自前引4,舒国滢文;肖尔(Frederick Schauer)坚持"像多数其他机构一样,法律既是语言的产物,也依赖于语言",Schauer, F., *Law und Language*, New York, New York University Press, 1993, p. Ⅺ;蒂尔斯玛(Tiersma)认为"没有多少职业像法律一样关涉语言",Tiersma, P. M., "Linguistic Issues in the Law", *Language*, 69: 113 – 37, 1993, quoted from Gibbons, J. P., *Forensic Linguistics: An Introduction to Language in the Justice System*, UK, Blackwell Publishing, 2003, p. 1;吉本斯(John Gibbons)也说"毋庸置疑,法律就是一种语言机构……我们的生活中不仅充斥着法律,而且也充斥着法律的语言",Gibbons, J. P., *Forensic Linguistics: An Introduction to Language in the Justice System*, UK, Blackwell Publishing, 2003, p. 1;陈兴良在"中国行为法学会法律语言研究会成立大会暨首届学术研讨会"上的发言中提到"法学是语言学。这里的法学主要是指注释性的规范性法学,语言的变迁以及语言的变革决定着法学的命运……法律本身就是一种语言现象"。转引自宋北平:《法律语言》,中国政法大学出版社2012年版,第44~45页。

义——

法律语言是法律活动中具有法律意义的语言，既不能离开法律活动（言语活动的直接结果就是语言），也不能没有法律意义（语言导致法律后果）。[14]

说话不仅仅可以被看作某种表达出内在含义的必要手段，它本身也可以被看作一种行为，语言造就行动。[15] 在奥斯汀（J. L. Austin）看来，有类话语本身就是在实施这类活动或履行其中的一部分，因此，说话就是做事，这类话语也就称为“施行话语”（performative utterance）。[16]

在我国，现代意义上的法律语言研究起步于20世纪七八十年代，[17]法律语

---

〔14〕 该定义主要参考王丽“法律语言的增值与变化”，在“中国行为法学会法律语言研究会成立大会暨首届学术研讨会”上的发言，以及李振宇“法律语言与法律文书的关系”，在“中国行为法学会法律语言研究会成立大会暨首届学术研讨会”上的发言。转引自宋北平：《法律语言》，中国政法大学出版社2012年版，第57～58页。该定义涉及“语言”较少受关注的维度——言语。索绪尔（F. de Saussure）认为语言包括两个方面：语言（language）和言语（parole），前者是关于语言集团言语的总模式，即代代相传的语言系统，言语则是个人的说话活动。参见潘庆云：《中国法律语言鉴衡》，汉语大词典出版社2004年版，第4页。

〔15〕 参见孙吉胜：《话语、身份与对外政策：语言与国际关系的后结构主义》，载《国际政治研究》2008年第3期。

〔16〕 参见［英］奥斯汀：《如何以言行事——1955年哈佛大学威廉·詹姆斯讲座》，杨玉成、赵京超译，商务印书馆2013年版，译者导言第Ⅶ页。但是，对施行话语、记述话语作出区分的尝试失败后，奥斯汀尝试提出一个更具普遍意义的理论——“言语行为三分说”［即通常所谓“言语行为理论”（theory of speech-acts）］。他把作为整体的言语行为分为三个层次，即认为在说些什么时，我们可能以三种基本的方式在做些什么。他把这三层意义的做些什么分别称为“话语行为”（locutionary act）、“话语施事行为”（illocutionary act）和“话语施效行为”（perlocutionary act）。大体而言，话语行为相当于说出某个具有意义的语句；话语施事行为是指以一种话语施事的力量（illocutionary force）说出某个语句；话语施效行为则是经由说些什么而达到某种效果的行为。参见［英］奥斯汀：《如何以言行事——1955年哈佛大学威廉·詹姆斯讲座》，杨玉成、赵京超译，商务印书馆2013年版，译者导言第Ⅷ－Ⅺ页。

〔17〕 参见宋北平：《我国法律语言研究的过去、现在和未来》，载《法学杂志》2009年第2期。

言学研讨会也从20世纪末开始举办。[18] 经过了三十余年的开拓、探索和发展,现在,我国的法律语言学科终于跻身当代中国人文学科之林。[19] 尽管如此,我国法律语言学的实际研究水平,尤其司法语言的研究水平与英语国家同行相比,还是有差距的。[20]

(二)法律叙事

叙事本来是语言学和文学等领域常用的手法。[21] 用叙事的视角来看待和分析法律现象[22],最早可以在法律与文学运动中找到端倪。[23] 20世纪90年代

---

〔18〕“法律语言与修辞国际研讨会”于2000年召开,并在中国修辞学会下成立了“法律语言学研究会”。学者基本上都是本土汉语研究的学者。2004年换届后,研究会的学术团队的主体代表已经转换为英语专家。2006年,非社团性的“中国法律语言规范化研究专家委员会”在北京政法职业学院法律语言应用研究所发起成立。2008年,中国行为法学会在20周年纪念大会上宣告我国法律语言研究会成立,这是法学界的法律语言研究会。目前,全国主要的法律语言研究工作者多分属两会,而中国修辞学会下属的法律语言学研究会更多的是由外语教学与研究人员组成,因此以外向研究为主,即翻译、比较和研究。参见黄震云、张燕:《立法语言学研究》,长春出版社2013年版,引言,第2~3页。

〔19〕参见姜剑云:《我国法律语言学的发展概况以及由此引起的若干思考》,发表于“应用语言学:法律语言与修辞国际研讨会”,上海,2000年。转引自沙丽金、黄姗:《中国法律语言学研究展望》,载郭万群主编:《中国法律语言学研究:理论与实践》,上海交通大学出版社2013年版,第295页。

〔20〕[澳]马丁:《法律语言研究》,王振华编,上海交通大学出版社2012年版,导读,第Ⅰ-Ⅱ页。

〔21〕参见应星:《略论叙事在中国社会研究中的运用及其限制》,载《江苏行政学院学报》2006年第3期。

〔22〕例如科弗(Cover)曾说,若离开了叙事,哪怕是一条法律制度或规章条文都不能存在,其背景是由叙事提供的,其意义是由叙事赋予的。制定一部法律本身就是一部史诗,确定戒律的同时也在产生文学故事。See Cover Robert,“The Supreme Court 1982 Term: Nomos and Narrative”, *Harvard Law Review*, 1938, 97(4), p. 6.

〔23〕参见刘燕:《法庭上的修辞——案件事实叙事研究》,光明日报出版社2012年版,绪论,第16页。学界普遍认为,怀特(James B. White)于1973年出版的《法律的想象》(*The Legal Imagination*)一书,是法律与文学运动的开篇宣言。参见[英]沃德:《法律与文学:可能性及研究视角》,刘星、许慧芳译,中国政法大学出版社2017年版,译序,第1页。

以来,叙事学进入后经典阶段,出现“泛叙事观”倾向。这种泛叙事研究往往流于浅显[24],叙事学界的法律叙事研究也未成气候,尚缺乏明确的研究对象和分析方法。[25]

因此,在把握法律叙事[26]时,本文采用的是比较广泛的定义:

法律叙事,就是在一切有目的的语言活动当中,那些以讲述法律故事为目的的活动,包括“讲什么”和“如何讲”。[27]

西方的法律叙事研究成果主要集中在三个方面:司法实践中的叙事、法学教育中的叙事和法律发展史中的叙事。以司法实践中的叙事为例,由于英美法系当事人主义的审判结构特点,司法实践领域的叙事研究大多是围绕法庭上的“叙事对抗”展开的。法庭叙事研究又主要关注审判中的叙事模式以

这场运动包含两方面的研究范式:(1)研究充满想象力的文学作品中的法律,即“文学中的法律”(law in literature)研究范式;(2)运用文学批判的各种方法和技巧来理解和评估法律、法律制度及法律程序,即所谓的“作为文学的法律”(law as literature)研究范式。从目前的发展趋势来看,“作为文学的法律”已成为法律与文学运动的主流话语。参见高中:《后现代法学思潮》,法律出版社 2004 年版,第 150 页。在“作为文学的法律”的主流框架内,大致有以下四种法律批判方法或研究进路:(1)法律的解释学批判方法;(2)叙事性法律方法;(3)法律的修辞性批判方法;(4)法律的结构主义文学批判方法。See Guyora Binder, Robert Weisberg, *Literary Criticism of Law*, New Jersey, Princeton University Press, 2000, Preface.

〔24〕 参见申丹:《20 世纪 90 年代以来叙事理论的新发展》,载《当代外国文学》2005 年第 1 期。

〔25〕 参见严琼湘:《西方法律叙事研究述评》,载郭万群主编:《中国法律语言学研究:理论与实践》,上海交通大学出版社 2013 年版,第 39 页。

〔26〕 值得注意的是,谢晖也曾运用“叙事”的概念,但他所表达的意思更类似于“立场”“思维”。参见谢晖:《法律,民间与官方的二元叙事》,载《原生态民族文化学刊》2015 年第 4 期;谢晖:《法律的民间叙事》(上),载《原生态民族文化学刊》2015 年第 4 期;谢晖:《法律的民间叙事》(下),载《原生态民族文化学刊》2016 年第 1 期;谢晖:《再论法律的民间叙事》,载《甘肃政法学院学报》2016 年第 1 期。

〔27〕 该定义主要参考前引 23,刘燕书,第 11 页;张海柱:《知识治理:公共事务治理的第四种叙事》,载《上海行政学院学报》2015 年第 4 期。

及法官[28]、陪审员[29]、控辩双方律师的叙事行为和叙事策略。[30]

目前我国的法律叙事研究主要集中于案件事实、[31]立法语言、[32]庭审现场[33]等,研究的广度与深度与国外仍有一定差距。

三、立法语言与权力运作

案例现场的进入肇始于笔者参加与Z市政府相关部门的横向课题合作——《Z市C事业促进办法》起草工作。基于亲身跟进《Z市C事业促进办法》起草工作三个月的实践经历,[34]笔者借助立法语言叙事的框架,运用哈贝马斯交往理论导向的话语分析理论,尝试分析"立法语言建构"这一立法过程中

---

〔28〕 See Shulamit Almog,"As I Read,I Weep-In Praise of Judicial Narrative",*Oklahoma City University Law Review*,2001(471),pp. 475 – 486.

〔29〕 See John H. Blume,Sheri L. Johnson and Emily C. Paavola,"Every Juror Wants a Story: Narrative Relevance,Third Party Guilt and the Right to Present a Defense",*American Criminal Law Review*,2007(44),p. 1104.

〔30〕 参见前引25,严琼湘文,第39页。

〔31〕 参见张德淼、康兰平:《法律修辞的司法运用:案件事实叙事研究》,载《中南民族大学学报》(人文社会科学版)2015年第2期。

〔32〕 参见易花泮:《立法话语的叙事性构建与解读——兼析叙事学视阈下立法语言的规范思路》,载《法律方法》2015年第2期。

〔33〕 参见余素青:《庭审叙事特征分析》,载《外国语文》2011年第2期。

〔34〕 遗憾的是,在本文个案研究中,笔者在把现实对话记录为文字时省略了语气词、声量、语调、停顿等,转写微信聊天记录时也删去了语气词、表情包等,这些要素对于语言分析而言也是非常重要的,如在吉本斯概括的权力的语言指针中就包括有力话语(以男性为主,表现为声音响亮、语调多变,使用重复、打断和无声的停顿,不明确表示同意,表达流利和连贯等)和无力话语(以女性为主,常常使用模糊限制语和加强性副词,表现出犹豫和不确定,多使用委婉语等)。See Gibbons,J. P.,*Forensic Linguistics: An Introduction to Language in the Justice System*,UK,Blackwell Publishing,2003,p. 88. 此外,本文中在有需要隐去信息的地方都用了"M""S"等字母、"××"等符号来代替。

的重要现象,并证明这是一种较为隐蔽的权力运作方式。[35]

(一)分析框架

从20世纪80年代末(另有说法:90年代、[36]90年代初[37])开始,叙事学进入后现代叙事理论阶段,[38]表现出明显的跨学科性特征,[39]研究范式也发生了重大的转移:从重视文本、故事、话语、形式的经典范式转移到同样重视语境、功能的多元范式。[40] 这为形式上单向、段落的[41]立法语言带来了巨大的法律叙事机遇。更何况,立法实质上并非单向的,从叙事者角度来看,立法语言文本内部其实存在两个作者:一个是立法的起草者,是文本的最初作者;另一个是代表权力意志的国家,是立法语言的最终代言者和发出者。[42] 此外,立法语言叙事也存在对话性,是立法机关与民众进行交流的言语[43],在广泛意义上是各种利益主体的对话,也就是所谓的意识形态的表达形式。[44]

如今,政策制定者、法律起草者、司法解释者以及公民之间的交际行为已处于社会进程的中心。[45] 哈贝马斯曾指出,为解决合法性危机,政府努力寻找能帮助自己为政策是如何服务于大众而非特殊群体的作出解释的合理性依据。[46]

---

〔35〕 参见张海柱:《话语建构与“不决策”:对改革开放初期合作医疗解体的一个理论解释》,载《公共行政评论》2015年第5期。

〔36〕 参见前引25,严琼湘文,第39页。

〔37〕 参见宋世明、王建文:《立法语言叙事分析》,载《江苏警官学院学报》2007年第3期。

〔38〕 参见余素青:《庭审叙事特征分析》,载《外国语文》2011年第2期。

〔39〕 参见前引36,严琼湘文,第39页。

〔40〕 参见宋世明、王建文:《立法语言叙事分析》,载《江苏警官学院学报》2007年第3期;[美]赫尔曼主编:《新叙事学》,马海良译,北京大学出版社2002年版,引言,第8页。

〔41〕 参见前引32,易花萍文。

〔42〕 参见前引40,宋世明、王建文文;前引32,易花萍文。

〔43〕 参见前引32,易花萍文,第258页。

〔44〕 参见宋世明、王建文:《立法语言叙事分析》,载《江苏警官学院学报》2007年第3期。

〔45〕 参见[法]瓦格纳、[爱尔兰]法伊编:《法律中的晦涩与明晰——前景与挑战》,苏建华等译,中国政法大学出版社2013年版,引言第XXIX页。

〔46〕 参见[德]哈贝马斯:《合法化危机》,刘北成、曹卫东译,上海人民出版社2009年版,第79页。

立法工作也面临着类似的困境。用法律形式对公开的意见形成和意志形成过程的结果是有关政策和法律的决议,这种过程应该以交往形式而发生。[47] 若把立法定义为交际行为[48],则交际的一个重要目的就是进行哈贝马斯所言的论证,无论是书面语还是口头语。可见,立法语言叙事框架能在此论证中发挥巨大作用。美国符号互动理论曾指出,“人类是以某些事物对他们具有的意义(meaning)为基础,而对这些事物产生行动的”。[49] 如此,立法过程中的论证即是为了“意义”,语言就是“意义”的载体。[50] 在以语言为中介的互动中,行为和言语这两种行为类型是相互联系的。[51] 需要注意的是,此处的“意义”不适用沃洛希诺夫(V. N. Vološinov)[52]对“主题”与“意义”的区分,或者说,此处的“意义”更接近于沃洛希诺夫所言的“主题”——一个复杂的、动态的符号系统,它试图充分表达生成过程的一个特定时刻,是意识在其生成过程中,对存在的生成过程所做的反应。[53]

在范式意义上,哈贝马斯为消除晚期资本主义社会中语言中介被金钱与权

---

[47] 参见[德]哈贝马斯:《在事实与规范之间:关于法律和民主法治国的商谈理论》,童世骏译,生活·读书·新知三联书店2003年版,第185页。

[48] See Sinclair, “Law and Language: The Role of Pragmatics in Statutory Interpretation”, *University of Pittsburgh Law Preview*, 1985, p.46.

[49] 石计生:《社会学理论——从古典到现代之后》,台北,三民书局2006年版,第289页。转引自张海柱:《话语建构与“不决策”:对改革开放初期合作医疗解体的一个理论解释》,载《公共行政评论》2015年第5期。

[50] 参见张海柱:《公共政策的话语建构:政策过程的后实证主义理论解释》,载《公共管理与政策评论》2015年第3期。

[51] 参见[德]哈贝马斯:《后形而上学思想》,曹卫东、付德根译,译林出版社2012年版,第58页。

[52] 这里不展开讨论巴赫金小组的著作权之争,详情可参见曾军:《从“葛兰西转向”到“转型的隐喻”——巴赫金是如何影响伯明翰学派的》,载《学术月刊》2008年第4期。

[53] 意义是实现主题的技术性工具。参见[苏]沃洛希诺夫:《马克思主义与语言哲学》,曾宪冠、顾海燕、胡龙彪译,载许宝强、袁伟选编:《语言与翻译的政治》,中央编译出版社2000年版,第99页。

力所取代的扭曲与危机,〔54〕决心要完成从意识哲学向语用学的转向——其标志就是普遍语用学的提出,〔55〕并以此作为其交往行为理论的基础。〔56〕 普遍语用学关注于指导人们实现“交往行为”合理化的“普遍伦理规则”——主体间的相互承认、相互尊重的达成及其可能性或一般条件的探讨。〔57〕 这种把对话式的日常语言〔58〕作为沟通媒介的交往行为就是主体间通过语言、按照有效规范、达成一致理解的行为。〔59〕 因此,可以通过考察立法语言遵守可领会性、真实性、真诚性、正确性这些相应的“有效性要求的义务”〔60〕的过程,揭示立法语言如何在成功/无法遵守这些义务的同时成为隐蔽的权力运作的载体。

(二)运作窗口

为避免遭受“在个案中再选小个案还可能有代表性吗?”之类的误解,本文

---

〔54〕 哈贝马斯对晚期资本主义危机进行了分析,试图以交往行为理论为病理性的现代社会进行诊断治疗。参见班柏:《超越普遍语用学:哈贝马斯的社会交往理论解析》,载《山西高等学校社会科学学报》2012 年第 4 期;宋敏:《哈贝马斯社会交往理论合理性与公共领域的建构》,载《求索》2015 年第 1 期。

〔55〕 参见徐清:《哈贝马斯的沟通行动理论对刑事诉讼法的意义》,载《云南大学学报》(法学版)2014 年第 4 期;郑友奇、王薇:《哈贝马斯的交往理性思想解析》,载《求索》2015 年第 12 期。

〔56〕 参见张斌峰:《法律的语用分析:法学方法论的语用学转向》,中国政法大学出版社 2014 年版,第 102 页。有学者把哈贝马斯交往理论导向的话语分析归类为“批判取向的政策话语分析”,参见李亚、尹旭、何鉴孜:《政策话语分析:如何成为一种方法论》,载《公共行政评论》2015 年第 5 期;也有学者将之归类为“审议式话语分析”,参见朱亚鹏:《话语分析:理解政策过程的重要视角与方法》,载《公共行政评论》2015 年第 5 期,专栏导语。结合本文研究框架来考虑,本文采纳前一种说法。

〔57〕 参见前引 56,张斌峰书,第 103 页。

〔58〕 参见闫艳:《现代西方交往理论及其对我国的启示》,载《学术论坛》2011 年第 7 期。

〔59〕 参见于林龙:《超越合作原则的交往理性——哈贝马斯语言哲学意义理论的范式转换之思》,载《吉林大学社会科学学报》2011 年第 4 期;张敏:《哈贝马斯交往行为理论的合理性》,载《江西社会科学》2014 年第 8 期。

〔60〕 参见[德]哈贝马斯:《交往与社会进化》,张博树译,重庆出版社 1989 年版,第 2 页。

有必要先解释一下:首先,要区分清楚代表性与典型性。代表性是指统计性样本能再现总体的性质,代表性的高低意味着再现能力的高低;典型性则是指个案体现某一类现象的性质。"总体"与"类"是不同的概念。其次,个案研究的逻辑基础并非在于统计性的扩大推理(从样本推论到总体),而在于分析性的扩大推理。最后,要确定经典个案,就要对共性类型的表现形式进行区分,而这又与典型性的类型一一对应——普遍现象的共性类型(集中性)、反常(或离轨)现象的共性类型(极端性)以及未知现象的共性类型(启示性)。[61] 该个案研究正是建立在典型性意义之上的。

1. 可领会性义务

由于交往行为依靠的是以理解为趋向的语言用法,因此,它必须满足更加严格的条件。[62] 言语者必须选择可领会的(verst-ändlich)表达以便说者和听者能够相互理解。[63] 是否可领会,取决于说者和听者的知识。福柯将话语理解为权力和知识的结合体,[64] 他曾如此描绘学校:"学校体制从外表上看是分配知识的,而实际上是为某个阶级掌握政权而将其他所有阶级排斥出权力机构而服务的。"[65] 换言之,学校通过产生知识主体来预设未来的社会权力等级,知识与权力紧密联系在一起。

在考古学阶段,福柯就发现了话语的历史先天规则[66] 决定在既定的历史阶段,什么对象能够被严肃地说出,从而成为知识的客体;谁能够说出它们,从而成为知识的主体,以及主体在言说客体的过程中使用什么概念和主题。

---

[61] 参见王宁:《代表性还是典型性?——个案的属性与个案研究方法的逻辑基础》,载《社会学研究》2002年第5期。

[62] 前引51,哈贝马斯书,第59页。

[63] 参见前引60,哈贝马斯书,第3页。

[64] 参见李亚、尹旭、何鉴孜:《政策话语分析:如何成为一种方法论》,载《公共行政评论》2015年第5期。

[65] [德]福柯:《人的本性:公正与权力的对立》,载杜小真编选:《福柯集》,从莉译,上海远东出版社1998年版,第238页。

[66] See Michel Foucault, *The Archaeology of Knowledge*, trans. by A. M. Sheridan Smith, London, Tavistock, 1972, pp. 126 – 132.

在放弃了从话语内部对知识的形成规则做纯粹考古描述之后,[67]福柯在系谱学探索[68]中发现权力与知识是直接相互包含的,不相应地建构一种知识领域就不可能有权力关系。与此同时,不预设和建构权力关系就不会有知识。[69]任何权力的运用都在不同程度上依赖于对对象或权力运用的场的了解和知识。[70]

Z市C总会L副会长兼秘书长:"我认为全国平台、团省委平台都不好用,Z市自己的平台好用,但系统兼容不到团省委平台。国家一直赞扬H市平台这块做得好,你们觉得呢?"

H市M局R科长:"我们是对接全国系统的,对接民政部大系统。团省委也发文要求我们改用他们那个平台。"[71]

在《Z市C事业促进办法》起草小组到H市M局召开的调研会中,Z市C总会L副会长兼秘书长在询问H市关于平台的意见之前,先大肆赞扬了Z市自己的平台。这部分赞语对于H市M局在场的人员而言,是不具可领会性的,因为H市M局多年来都是对接全国系统的,并不了解Z市的平台。R科长对L秘书长的问题避而不答而直接介绍H市的做法,也证明了这一点。

看似无伤大雅的赞语,在赋予Z市C事业宏观话语"统计平台"以具体意义的同时,实质上也在损害"平台无法兼容"解决过程中的公平性——"迫使"不了解Z市平台的人只能说自己的做法(或许这才是L秘书长所期待的),以立法者的权力排挤全国平台、团省委平台以致两者无法公平进入话语体系参与竞争。这种情况一经立法承认,全国平台、团省委平台就会因为没有代言人无法发声而失去被公平对待的机会,与此相关的主体也会不同程度地失权。此

[67] 参见周慧:《福柯三角:知识—主体—权力》,载《现代哲学》2013年第5期。

[68] 参见郑华:《话语分析与国际关系研究——福柯的"话语观"对后现代国际关系理论的影响》,载《现代国际关系》2005年第4期。

[69] See Michel Foucault, *Discipline and Punish: The Birth of the Prison*, trans. by Alan Sheridan, New York, Vintage Books, 1979, p. 27.

[70] 参见苏力:《福柯的刑罚史研究及对法学的贡献》,载《比较法研究》1993年第2期。

[71] 资料来源:笔者:《〈Z市C事业促进办法〉起草工作调研报告》附录(《Z市C事业促进办法》起草工作内部文件)。

外,L秘书长的"明显暗示"也制约了R科长的反应。[72]

Z市S镇S'局负责人:"有其他部门不认低保户的证件,怕假,要求我们另外出证明,这应该是其他部门通过工作系统查证,不能随随便便要求我们出证明,这也给群众添了麻烦。"

Z市M局J科长:"先向市里请示,市里会分配任务。"[73]

在《Z市C事业促进办法》起草小组到S镇S'局召开的调研会中,S'局负责人突然插入一句与起草工作完全无关的话,这是M局J科长所不可领会的,因为市一级政府人员不会有类似的工作经历,所以J科长也只是简单回答"向市里请示"。利用注意力模型,负责人的动因能得到很好的解释:在问题机制这一注意力产生的机制中,不同部门为争取领导人有限的注意力相互竞争,议题重要性与问题严重性之和较大者才能够胜出。[74] 若该"不适当"的抱怨能在起草小组的会议纪要上记下一笔,就很可能纳入立法工作的考量范围中,从而获得很高的"合法性承载",实际获得的政府注意力分配也多,很可能启动运动式治理武器。[75]

但是,负责人所说的整句话于J科长而言是不具可领会性的,这导致所言现象中蕴含的各种事实要素一律没有受到应有的、正常程度的审视,但是其中某些事实要素(如低保户的认证问题)确实是落在《Z市C事业促进办法》制定范围(建立健全社会××与C资源信息对接机制)中的,而J科长的简单回答意味着此事实要素并不会被记录,更不会在《Z市C事业促进办法》有所体现,这导致起草小组通过参与立法来解决落在制定范围中的此事实要素难题的权力因为没有落脚点而踩空了——无法得到运用。利益主体的诉求得不到回应(所以不一定是回应者不想回应,还可能是回应者无法回应,如此处),便是权力的机会损失。

[72] 这里涉及"相邻对"结构的"对后制约性",限于篇幅,不展开论述。

[73] 前引71。

[74] 参见陈思丞、孟庆国:《领导人注意力变动机制探究——基于毛泽东年谱中2614段批示的研究》,载《公共行政评论》2016年第3期。

[75] 参见徐岩、范娜娜、陈那波:《合法性承载:对运动式治理及其转变的新解释——以A市18年创卫历程为例》,载《公共行政评论》2015年第2期。

2. 真实性义务

言语者必须遵守以下义务:提供一个真实(wahr)陈述(或陈述性内容,该内容的存在性先决条件已经得到满足)的意向,以便听者能分享说者的知识。[76]从“立法者”的角度来判断这个意向是否真实,实在是没有可操作性,因为“真实”在立法者的立场上并不是实然的,立法者可以一直坚持自己符合真实性,甚至不惜改变他们刚确定下来的立法意图。尤其是在追求“良法善治”的时代,要想真正考察立法技术普遍有所改进的立法者在语言过程中是否提供了真实陈述的意向,必须更多地结合法律运作过程中的实际表现,以及用法者所切实感受到的渗透在法律中的立法意图与立法者无法否认的、已被普遍认可存在的立法意图之间的对比来建立指标。

为不超出本文的范围(本文并不迷信法律语言叙事批判方法甚至企图以此解释一切法律或语言或法律语言问题,虽然这是本文一直使用的工具),本文以“听者能否分享说者的知识”作为判断标准,以判断言语者在语言过程中是否具有真实性。

《〈Z 市 C 事业促进办法(草案)〉建议稿一稿》:第十八条【统一的××服务平台和记录制度】市人民政府应当建立统一的××服务平台。

开展 C 服务的 C 组织和其他组织应当在××服务平台上建立 C××记录制度,对××者实名登记,及时、完整、准确地记录××者参与 C 服务的时间、内容、评价等信息,并根据××者的要求,无偿、如实出具××服务记录证明。

《〈Z 市 C 事业促进办法(草案)〉建议稿二稿》:第十二条【××服务信息和记录】市人民政府健全××服务统计和发布制度,建立统一的信息数据标准,实现数据共享互通,为表彰激励提供依据。

××者需要××服务记录证明的,××服务组织应当依据 C 服务记录及时、无偿、如实出具。

《〈Z 市 C 事业促进办法(草案)〉建议稿三稿》:第十三条【××服务信息和记录】市 M 局、文明办、团市委、妇联、总工会、××会应当推动有关××服务信

[76] 参见前引 60,哈贝马斯书,第 3 页。要求一个追求沟通的行为者所作的陈述是真实的(甚至只是顺便提及的命题内涵的前提实际上也必须得到满足),也就是说,言语者要求其命题或实际前提具有真实性。参见[德]哈贝马斯:《交往行为理论:行为合理性与社会合理化》,曹卫东译,上海人民出版社 2004 年版,第 100 页。

息管理平台按照统一的数据信息标准,开展数据采集和整理,实现××服务数据共享共通。

××者需要××服务记录证明的,××服务组织应当依据××服务记录及时、无偿、如实出具。[77]

无论是在经验上还是逻辑上,与“绝对精确”相比,“准确”更能让受众感到真实。[78] 因为“准确”包含了一定的弹性,[79]在立法语言上表现为模糊性。苏力认为,从语言精确的角度来评价法律是不对的,精确并不一定是有利的和可取的,在语言背后重要的是利益追求。[80] 甚至,在法律语言中,模糊反而成为准确、明晰表达意愿的代名词。[81] 法律要应付的是人类关系中各种最复杂的方面。摆在法律面前的是纷至沓来、变幻莫测的全部混乱人生,而在这个万花筒式的时代里,情况则比以往任何时候都更为混乱。[82] 数个世纪的经验告诉我们,任何法律制度都不能也不可能达到如此之明确无误的程度。[83] 产生于自然界本身的概念界限模糊不清以及人类的认知能力有限性的模糊性,[84]还可能被立法者富有策略意味地进行人为安排。[85]

---

〔77〕 前引71。

〔78〕 梅林科夫(David Mellinkoff)认为法律语言的精确是荒诞的。See Tiersma, *Legal Language*, Chicago, The University of Chicago Press, 1999, p. 85.

〔79〕 梁启超认为“弹力性”是法律之文辞的三要件之一,参见梁启超:《论中国成文法编制之沿革得失》,载范忠信选编:《梁启超法学文集》,中国政法大学出版社2000年版,第181页。

〔80〕 参见苏力:《想事不要想词——关于法律语言的断想》,在“中国行为法学会法律语言研究会成立大会暨首届学术研讨会”上的发言。转引自宋北平:《法律语言》,中国政法大学出版社2012年版,第72页以下。

〔81〕 参见李振宇:《法律语言学新说》,中国检察出版社2006年版,第77页。

〔82〕 参见张文显:《二十世纪西方法哲学思潮》,法律出版社1996年版,第138页。

〔83〕 参见[美]E.博登海默:《法理学:法律哲学与法律方法》,邓正来译,中国政法大学出版社1999年版,第128页。

〔84〕 参见王建:《法律语言的模糊性及准确运用》,载《西南政法大学学报》2006年第2期。

〔85〕 参见周少华:《法律中的语言游戏与权力分配》,载《法制与社会发展》2006年第5期。

从一稿的"实名登记,及时、完整、准确地记录××者参与C服务的时间、内容、评价等信息",到二稿的"建立统一的信息数据标准",再到三稿的"按照统一的数据信息标准",关于"××服务信息和记录"的具体规定越来越模糊,这是因为较新的其他有关规定都没有定义何为"统一的信息数据/数据信息标准",随着××服务信息记录工作近期的大力改进,[86]该标准近期也会更新,而如何更新是立法者无法预测而用法者又能迅速达成新的共识的,这就属于技术性模糊,是一种次优选择。[87] 值得注意的是,模糊性应区别于"含混不清",后者是语言不当、语言不明,让人弄不明白表达的意思。[88] 从一稿到三稿,关于如何开展"××服务信息和记录"工作的语句所表达的意思是清楚的,只是为了尽可能应对未曾想象到的情况而在"标准"上有所保留,保持一定的伸缩性。

在立法语言的选择背后,是立法者不贪婪于从给予执法者更大的裁量权中可能获得的好处(尤其是地方政府规章),拒绝选择最终背离社会福祉的策略性模糊。[89] 同时,该设计能较大限度避免因社会的可预期变化实现而迅速引起权力的不安摇晃(如"标准"的更新),维护了法律的可预期性,反过来也增强了用法者所感受到的真实性。

3. 真诚性义务

言语者必须真诚地(wahrhaftig)表达他的意向以便听者能相信他所说的话语(能信任他),这是真诚性要求的义务。[90] 虽然表达看起来差不多,但与"真实性"有两处关键的区别——言语者是真诚的(自不待言);听者能相信说者说的话。对判断标准的辨析路径却与"真实性"类似,根据"听者能否相信他所说

---

〔86〕 资料来源:Z市最近发布的《Z市人民政府关于促进C事业健康发展的实施意见》。

〔87〕 参见丁建峰:《立法语言的模糊性问题——来自语言经济分析的视角》,载《政法论坛》2016年第2期。

〔88〕 参见杜金榜:《从法律语言的模糊性到司法结果的确定性》,载《现代外语》2001年第3期;前引81,李振宇书,第77页以下。

〔89〕 参见丁建峰:《立法语言的模糊性问题——来自语言经济分析的视角》,载《政法论坛》2016年第2期。

〔90〕 参见前引60,哈贝马斯书,第3页。要求言语者所表现出来的意向必须言出心声,即主体经验的表达具有真诚性。参见前引76,哈贝马斯书,第100页。

的话”来进行界定。

若得不到听者的相信,言语者的话将被置若罔闻,结果则是听者的“不作为”和言语者意图的落空。卢克斯(Steven Lukes)认为“不决策”是权力的“第二维度”。通过“不决策”,在共同体中那些对现存的利益或特权的分配进行变革的要求被公正地表达出来之前可能被压制,或者被掩盖,或者在它们获得通往相应的决策制定舞台通道之前被否决,或者在决策实施阶段中被损害或破坏。[91] 类似地,如果立法论证中的语言不被信任,则语言所承载的意义也无法得到认同,只是比“不具可领会性”晚一点落得“被排挤在话语体系之外”的下场而已。

Z市F局L科员:“立法的两个重点问题,一个是C数据,那个C的统计平台,一个是表彰。这两个是我们要抓的一个核心点,就是说我们这两个点有没有抓住。还有,L教授,上一次我们在H市调研,他们好像是没有说表彰,好像打了个什么擦边球。那天我也问了S局那边,他一直说现在确实表彰要经过省里的批准,然后他现在在征集市里的表彰,最多只能报两个啊什么的,好像M局有一个。”

Z市M局W科员:“表彰这个条款应该不行。”

L教授:“是的,这个禁止的,所以我们加了依法。”

Z市M局W科员:“如果要做,由C行业组织来做。”

L教授:“下面一条是民间奖励,就是想从这个入手。Z市可以申请,写在这里是依法。”

Z市M局W科员:“由市人民政府设立表彰不行了。”

L教授:“嗯,要省里批准。”

Z市M局W科员:“我问了市S局的,省现在基本不审批新增的表彰项目。”

Z市F局L科员:“现在市S局在统计我市表彰项目,说是报两项去省里,其中有M局的一个啊。麻烦M局和S局沟通下。是否是C表彰方面的?”

Z市C总会L副会长兼秘书长:“这个科室清楚,貌似不是呢。”

Z市M局W科员:“不是C奖,是医疗××方面的。”

[91] 参见[美]卢克斯:《权力:一种激进的观点》,彭斌译,江苏人民出版社2008年版,第8页以下。

Z 市 F 局 L 科员:"嗯,看能否关联。"

Z 市 M 局 W 科员:"只是 C 工作的一部分。我看这个是写 2018 年度,不是一个长期设立的项目。"

Z 市 F 局 L 科员:"嗯,上次 H 市不说表彰,打了擦边球,必要时问下 H 市 M 局。"[92]

《Z 市 C 事业促进办法》的制定范围包括"建立健全统一的表彰奖励制度",[93]但《G 省规范评比达标表彰活动实施细则(试行)》(以下简称《细则》)第 3 条规定,省级以下评比达标表彰项目,按归口报省委、省政府审批;第 19 条规定,地级市党政机关一律不得举办自行设置的评比达标表彰活动。起草小组迫切寻找既能降低报审成本(实际情况就是"省现在基本不审批新增的表彰项目")又可充分发挥先进典型的示范作用的立法手段。在 H 市调研时,发现当地的做法是通过《H 市"H 市 C 奖"认定暂行办法》以"认定"来达到"表彰"的效果,而不需经过"表彰"的报审程序。

在论证过程中,有三处话语多次重复,"H 市不表彰而打了擦边球""M 局报 S 局表彰项目""表彰不行"分别重复了 2 次。重复"H 市不表彰而打了擦边球",是为了真诚地提出"借鉴 H 市做法"的意向;重复"M 局报 S 局表彰项目",是为了真诚地提示"M 局似乎已经在用表彰手段",暗含"如果成功了,则说明报审成本是可以接受的"之意;重复"表彰不行",是真诚地强调"《细则》决定了表彰的报审成本很高,相当于不行了"。三种话语都为了所承载的意义不被"不决策"压制或掩盖而自我重复,实际上是 F 局和 M 局在降低各自立法成本的竞争中为使其他参与主体能相信自己所说的话而运用语言重复背后的权力的过程。

4. 正确性义务

正确性要求言语者必须选择一种本身是正确的(richtig)话语,以便听者能够接受之,从而使言语者和听者能在以公认的规范为背景的话语中达到认同。[94]

---

[92] 前引 71。

[93] 资料来源:《〈Z 市 C 事业促进办法〉起草工作方案》。

[94] 参见前引 60,哈贝马斯书,第 3 页。要求一个追求沟通的行为者与一个规范语境相关的言语行为是正确的(甚至于它应当满足的规范语境自身也必须具有合法性)。参见前引 76,哈贝马斯书,上海人民出版社 2004 年版,第 100 页。

若继续沿用上文对"真实性""真诚性"判断标准的辨析路径,则得出判断标准应是"能否使听者愿意接受之,而言语者和听者能在以规范为背景的话语中达到认同"的结论。若仅仅是要达到"听者愿意接受""言语者和听者达到认同",并不需要话语本身是正确的,如比克斯(Brian Bix)在关于魏斯曼(Waisman)所关注的普通语言[95]中指称的随意性的论述中提到,对选择词语的宽容态度有利于促进正常对话的开展,只要我和对方都认同我大概了解对方的真实意思。[96]

如此,难道是对判断标准的辨析出错了?值得注意的是,哈贝马斯的定义中还有"在以公认的规范为背景的话语中",这是与之前"可领会性""真实性""真诚性"最显著的区别。同样是比克斯的描述:若情形发生在带有命令指令的具体场景中,则结论会是完全不同的。要适用于不确定的场合中的规则,其适用的范围是非常重要的。[97]

换言之,在以法律规范为背景的法律话语中,正确性是指法律的确定性,而法律的确定性问题是指法律能否对法律争议提供唯一正解。[98]

《〈Z市C事业促进办法(草案)〉建议稿三稿》:第一条【立法目的】为了发展C事业,弘扬C文化,培养全民C意识,鼓励公民、企业和各类社会组织积极参与C事业,根据《中华人民共和国C法》等相关法律、法规的规定,结合本市实际,制定本办法。[99]

此处的"全民"是指全体人民还是全体公民?这涉及由来已久的"人民"与

---

[95] See Brain Bix, *Law, Language and Legal Determinacy*, Oxford, Clarendon Press, 1993, p.19.

[96] 同上,Brain Bix文,p. 19。

[97] 参见前引95,Brain Bix文,p. 19。

[98] 参见邱昭继:《法律的确定性:〈法律、语言与法律的确定性〉译后》,载《法律方法与法律思维》2008年第5辑,第229页,有改动。葛洪义、陈年冰认为,围绕法的确定性的争论,大致体现在三个方面:(1)法律本身的确定性问题;(2)对构成司法判决基础的事实的确定性的怀疑引起的法律的确定性问题;(3)由美国批判法学提出的关于法律推理的不确定性而导致的对法治及其意义的讨论则涉及法治的价值这一根本性的问题。参见葛洪义、陈年冰:《法的普遍性、确定性、合理性辨析——兼论当代中国立法和法理学的使命》,载《法学研究》1997年第5期。

[99] 前引71。

“公民”之辨。有学者认为,在传统教科书框架下,人民成为一种除革命角色之外没有任何自我确证、自我反省,没有明晰的权利界定,身份认同飘忽不定的存在。与此相反,公民却是一种有着明晰法权的存在。市民社会中的公民虽然是享有国家法律规定权限的“法人”,但他更是世俗社会中的“个人”。〔100〕 也有学者分析,尽管四部正式宪法基本都是用“公民”作为权利主体,但是始于新中国成立初期的临时宪法——《中国人民政治协商会议共同纲领》的以“人民”作为基本权利主体的观念却一直或明或暗地隐藏在这之后的几部宪法之中。更为重要的是,这种宪法观念并没有停留在纸面上,而是对现实的基本权利保障及其相关的管理制度建设发挥了切实而深远的影响。〔101〕 也有学者坚持,“人民社会”就是一国之内由公民组成的政治共同体,其主体是占人口绝大多数的普通劳动大众。〔102〕

法律条文是用词语构成的,普通语言的“开放结构”被带到规则之中,因而法律条文也随之具有不确定性。〔103〕 就三稿该条文而言,法律的不确定性是由“全民”的词汇边缘含义的模糊造成的,但“全民”的核心含义是稳定的。哈特(H. L. A. Hart)认为法律的不确定性仅仅存在于涉及词语边缘语义的疑难案

---

〔100〕 参见贺长余:《从人民到公民:马克思第二条政治解放路径的回归》,载《理论月刊》2014 年第 4 期。

〔101〕 参见孙平:《弥合“人民”与“公民”之间的宪法分歧——以〈共同纲领〉第 49 条的解读为中心》,载《法律科学》(西北政法大学学报)2015 年第 6 期。比如十八届四中全会通过的《中共中央关于全面推进依法治国若干重大问题的决定》,在论述推进依法治国需坚持的基本原则之一——“坚持人民主体地位”时,就只使用“人民”作为权利主体;而在表述加强宪法实施的具体措施“加强重点领域立法”时,则全部使用的是“公民权利”。参见《中共中央关于全面推进依法治国若干重大问题的决定》,载《人民日报》2014 年 10 月 29 日,第 1 版。转引自孙平:《弥合“人民”与“公民”之间的宪法分歧——以〈共同纲领〉第 49 条的解读为中心》,载《法律科学》(西北政法大学学报)2015 年第 6 期,脚注②。

〔102〕 参见王绍光:《社会建设的方向:“公民社会”还是人民社会?》,载《开放时代》2014 年第 6 期。

〔103〕 参见[英]哈特:《法律的概念》,许家馨、李冠宜译,法律出版社 2018 年版,第 191 ~ 192 页;王晨光:《法律运行中的不确定性与“错案追究制”的误区》,载《法学杂志》1997 年第 3 期;邱昭继:《法律的确定性:〈法律、语言与法律的确定性〉译后》,载《法律方法与法律思维》2008 年第 5 辑,第 234 页。

件中,[104]疑难案件就数量而言所占比例并不大,[105]所以法律相对是确定的。[106]这使得权力的辐射群体是较为稳定的,提高了权力的传递效率,有利于实现符合真实性的立法意图。面临疑难案件时,虽然哈特没有从语言的性质出发证明法官必须行使自由裁量权,但他给出了在法律适用中法官解释法律文本时可以行使裁量权的理由。[107]

四、总结与讨论

虽然个案取材于现实,但本文不走对策法学的路径,也不做"材料狩猎神""意义狩猎神",[108]而坚持"问题意识",[109]避免囿于个人立场、观念的过度诠释,[110]对法律语言中的权力运行机制的刻画也是对现实的揭示,而不是为抽象的理论寻找论据。[111]

本文借助立法语言叙事的框架,深入挖掘各种利益主体的语言所承载的意义,运用哈贝马斯交往理论导向的话语分析理论,分析"立法语言建构"现象。该个案研究发现立法者出于解决合理性、合法性危机的需要而进行的立法论证(立法口头语言),以及立法过程中形成的立法书面语言,基于其交际行为的本

[104] 参见前引103,哈特书,第222页。

[105] 参见王晨光:《法律运行中的不确定性与"错案追究制"的误区》,载《法学杂志》1997年第3期。

[106] 参见前引98,葛洪义、陈年冰文。

[107] 参见前引103,哈特书,第207~214页;邱昭继:《法律的确定性:〈法律、语言与法律的确定性〉译后》,载《法律方法与法律思维》2008年第5辑,第236页。

[108] 参见[德]马克斯·韦伯:《社会科学方法论》,韩水法等译,中央编译出版社1999年版,第60页。

[109] 参见陈兴良:《学术功底·问题意识·研究方法(代总序)》,载李文建:《刑事诉讼效率论》,中国政法大学出版社1999年版,第4~6页;尤陈俊:《作为问题的"问题意识"——从法学论文写作中的命题缺失现象切入》,载《探索与争鸣》2017年第5期。

[110] 参见任强、丁利:《被误解的道家法哲学——从本源法哲学与本体法哲学谈起》,载《现代哲学》2012年第1期。

[111] 参见任强:《民间纠纷解决之道的演变:基于甘肃X村、L村和M村的民俗、习惯与司法实践》,载《民间法》2012年第11卷,第280页。

质和欲交际成功的动机，本身也需要遵守“有效性要求的义务”以验证“有效性要求”。在成功/无法遵守这些义务的同时，立法语言也成了隐蔽的权力运作的载体。[112]

具体而言，在遵守“可领会性”要求的义务的过程中，语言作为“权力和知识的结合体”发挥了划分社会权力等级的作用。若无法遵守该义务，往往不仅会让言语者的权力倾轧期待得到立法承认而致使部分主体失权，在语言总量有限的前提下，还会让无效的立法语言霸占有限的立法容量导致权力的机会损失。

在遵守“真实性”要求的义务的过程中，若从听者的角度考虑，语言的“准确”更能让听者感受到真实，因为“准确”包含了一定的弹性，在立法语言上表现为模糊性。在立法手段中，立法语言可以区分为技术性模糊和策略性模糊。[113]因为后者是背离社会福祉（即违背一般立法意图）的，所以选择前者比选择后者更能加强用法者的真实性感受，这也是权力出于避免不可预期的自我选择。

为满足真诚性要求，语言必须得到听者的信任，否则就会落得“不决策”[114]的下场。在立法语言过程中，“不决策”实质上是权力对“待表达”的新权力要求的压制、掩盖或破坏，把承载变革意义的立法语言排挤在立法话语体系之外。立法语言的重复和强调，就是为了避免在所代表的利益主体身上发生这样的情况。

“正确性”义务提出了新的要求——“话语以公认的规范为背景”。在区别于普通语言的随意性[115]的语境中，法律应思考能否对法律争议提供唯一正解，即法律的确定性问题。具有“开放结构”的语言的核心是稳定的，所以法律相对是确定的。在法官行使裁量权之前，权力的辐射群体是较为稳定的，也提高了

---

〔112〕 话语建构本身也是一种权力运作形态。参见张海柱：《集体化与合作医疗（1955—1962）：卫生政治的话语建构逻辑》，载《中国农业大学学报》（社会科学版）2017 年第 6 期。

〔113〕 参见丁建峰：《立法语言的模糊性问题——来自语言经济分析的视角》，载《政法论坛》2016 年第 2 期。

〔114〕 参见［美］卢克斯：《权力：一种激进的观点》，彭斌译，江苏人民出版社 2008 年版，第 8 页以下。

〔115〕 See Brain Bix, *Law, Language and Legal Determinacy*, Oxford, Clarendon Press, 1993, p. 19.

权力的传递效率。

在上述过程中,知识影响了权力作用对象的感知,用说服代替强制,因而权力运作是隐蔽进行的。[116]

语言观的改变促使人们改变对语言和世界之间关系的看法。[117] 当然,理应期待法律语言学未来的发展是多面向、多角度的。本文所提出的方法论也只是旨在为尚从静态研究法律语言客体向动态研究法律语言过程过渡的我国法律语言学提供一些关于以法律语言为工具的批判研究思路的尝试。后续的研究,可能突破"以法律语言为工具的批判研究"的分析框架,也可能在"静态""动态"之外找到第三个突破口,还可能为法律语言学寻找到"客体""过程"以外的新研究对象。但是,笔者有理由相信,后续研究的出发点和落脚点依然是:法律语言作为法律规范运作的中介,往往也会成为权力关系的核心。因为这才是中国法治的真实剧本,也是一个更具社会科学价值的超越中国特色的理论话题。[118]

(责任编辑:何雪波)

---

〔116〕 参见前引49,张海柱文;前引50,张海柱文。

〔117〕 参见[英]奥斯汀:《如何以言行事——1955年哈佛大学威廉·詹姆斯讲座》,杨玉成、赵京超译,商务印书馆2013年版,译者导言。

〔118〕 参见徐岩、范娜娜、陈那波:《合法性承载:对运动式治理及其转变的新解释——以A市18年创卫历程为例》,载《公共行政评论》2015年第2期。

数字经济背景下场所型常设机构规则的适用性研究

黄煜恺*

摘要：

本文研究的是数字经济背景下场所型常设机构规则的适用性问题。伴随着信息技术的革命，数字经济逐渐发展成经济增长的新引擎。数字经济所带来的商业模式转变给现行常设机构认定规则带来挑战，暴露出我国过于依赖实体性存在、豁免条款规定过于宽泛的问题，进而引发税基侵蚀。因此，为了维护我国的税收主权，完善场所型常设机构规则成为我国反避税立法中亟待解决的问题。

本文通过对我国立法考察，并结合英国、印度等国家的立法以及经济合作与发展组织所提出的方案，评析目前现有三种改革方案：引进显著经济存在判断标准、修改豁免条款和新增税种防止人为规避常设机构。在总结域外立法经验的基础上，本文提出：我国应引进显著经济存在的判断标准，并在豁免条款中新增准备性或辅助性测试。

关键词：

数字经济；场所型常设机构；显著经济存在

引　言

在国际税收实践中，企业居住国和来源国通常按照归属原则对企业跨境经营所得的征税管辖权进行划分，来源国仅在与跨境经营所得有足够的经济

* 黄煜恺，中山大学法学院2018级硕士研究生。

联系[1]时才享有有限的征税权。判定是否有足够的经济联系,往往需甄别非居民企业是否构成常设机构。如果纳税人在某个国家构成常设机构,则该国对来自该常设机构的经营所得享有征税权。这种情形下,常设机构的界定成为国家间划分税收管辖权的关键。

然而,数字经济的勃兴却给常设机构规则带来巨大的挑战。诸多新型商业模式并不具备传统规则所强调的课税要素,成为逃税漏税的缺口。在此背景下,为了维护我国的税收主权,我们需要考虑是否有必要对现行规则作出相应的调整。本文的写作目标在于分析与探讨数字经济背景下场所型常设机构规则的适用性问题,具体包含以下三个方面:第一,现行规则能否应对数字经济提出的挑战?是否有必要作出调整?第二,如果需要进行调整,改革的思路是什么?现有的改革方案是否可行?第三,结合我国的国情阐述我国的立法选择。为此,本文首先分析现有规则在数字经济背景下所面临的认定困境,以及该困境所诱发的税基侵蚀问题;其次评述现有改革方案的不足;最后在此基础上,就我国常设机构规则的修改和完善提出建议。

一、中国现行场所型常设机构规则的立法考察及评论

(一)中国立法考察

我国现行场所型常设机构的认定规则主要规定在税收协定中。截至2018年9月21日,我国总共签订了105个双边税收协定,其中与乌干达、博茨瓦纳、肯尼亚、加蓬和刚果(布)签订的税收协定尚未生效。

在双边税收协定中,我国遵循国际税收实践的通常做法,根据常设机构划分税收管辖权,以避免双重征税。在我国已经签订的105个税收协定中,除了中国和智利签订的税收协定在豁免条款上有所不同,其他关于场所型常设机构的认定规则大同小异,且均规定在协定的第5条。在中国签订的税收协定中,场所型常设机构是指企业进行全部或部分营业的固定营业场所。从定义出发,构成场所型常设机构需满足以下条件:第一,企业必须有营业场所;第二,营业场所必须是固定的;第

[1] See Coates, W. H, "League of nations report on double taxation submitted to the financial committee by professors Bruins, Einaudi, Seligman, and Sir Josiah Stamp", *Journal of the Royal Statistical Society* 87.1, 1924, pp. 99-102.

三,企业的全部或部分业务必须通过该固定的营业场所进行。此外,税收协定在第5条第4款中规定了豁免条款,对满足以上三种条件的部分活动予以豁免。

关于豁免条款的规定,税收协定有两种立法模式。一种是以中国和新加坡签订的税收协定[2]为代表的传统模式。在该模式下,豁免条款通常是先列举常见的豁免活动,如仓储、展览、采购及信息收集等,接着再以“专为本企业进行其他准备性或辅助性活动的目的所设的固定营业场所”“专为本款第(一)项至第(五)项活动的结合所设的固定营业场所,条件是这种结合使该固定营业场所的全部活动属于准备性质或辅助性质”的规定作为兜底条款。另一种模式以中国和智利2015年签订的税收协定[3]为代表,也是目前唯一采取该模式的税收协

---

〔2〕 以《中华人民共和国政府和新加坡共和国政府关于对所得避免双重征税和防止偷漏税的协定》第5条为例:

一、在本协定中,“常设机构”一语是指企业进行全部或部分营业的固定营业场所。

……

四、虽有本条上述规定,“常设机构”一语应认为不包括:

(一)专为储存、陈列或者交付本企业货物或者商品的目的而使用的设施;

(二)专为储存、陈列或者交付的目的而保存本企业货物或者商品的库存;

(三)专为另一企业加工的目的而保存本企业货物或者商品的库存;

(四)专为本企业采购货物或者商品,或者搜集情报的目的所设的固定营业场所;

(五)专为本企业进行其他准备性或辅助性活动的目的所设的固定营业场所;

(六)专为本款第(一)项至第(五)项活动的结合所设的固定营业场所,如果由于这种结合使该固定营业场所的全部活动属于准备性质或辅助性质。

〔3〕 《中华人民共和国政府和智利共和国政府对所得避免双重征税和防止逃避税的协定》第5条第4款:

虽有本条上述规定,“常设机构”一语应认为不包括:

(一)专为储存、陈列或者交付本企业货物或者商品的目的而使用的设施;

(二)专为储存、陈列或者交付的目的而保存本企业货物或者商品的库存;

(三)专为由另一企业加工的目的而保存本企业货物或者商品的库存;

(四)专为本企业采购货物或者商品,或者搜集信息的目的所设的固定营业场所;

(五)专为本企业做广告、提供信息或进行科学研究以及其他类似活动的目的所设的固定营业场所;

条件是上述活动属于准备性质或辅助性质。

定。该种模式吸收了税基侵蚀和利润转移(BEPS)报告中第七项行动计划的成果,规定只有具有准备性质或辅助性质的活动才得以豁免。两者的区别在于,前者所列举的一些活动并不需要进行准备性或者辅助性测试。而后者规定所有可豁免的活动都必须具备准备性质或辅助性质。

为了更好地统一税收协定的执行口径,国家税务总局于2010年颁布《〈中华人民共和国政府和新加坡共和国政府关于对所得避免双重征税和防止偷漏税的协定〉及议定书条文解释》(国税发〔2010〕75号,以下简称中新协定条文解释),规定该条文解释具有扩展效力,对其他协定仍然适用。其他协定与该条文解释内容不一致的,以该协定解释为准。[4] 该条文解释对“准备性或辅助性”进行厘清,规定“准备性或辅助性”活动不能构成整体活动的重要部分,只能起到事务性服务的作用,且不具有直接营利性。中新税收协定条文解释实际上是在传统模式下豁免条款的基础上,新增准备性或辅助性测试,明确所有豁免活动必须具有准备性或辅助性性质。值得注意的是,中新税收协定条文解释仅仅是行政性文件,效力层次低,也未经其他国家的承认与认可。因此,该条文解释的效力能否扩展至其他税收协定仍存有疑问。

(二)中国立法评论

1.过于依赖实体性存在

根据税收协定的规定,构成场所型常设机构在客观上需要有固定场所,即实体性存在。这跟传统非居民企业的经营模式密切相关。在数字经济兴起之前,非居民企业往往通过在来源国设立固定性场所、建立可持续的商业活动来

---

〔4〕 国家税务总局关于印发《〈中华人民共和国政府和新加坡共和国政府关于对所得避免双重征税和防止偷漏税的协定〉及议定书条文解释》的通知(国税发〔2010〕75号):

一、我国对外所签协定有关条款规定与中新协定条款规定内容一致的,中新协定条文解释规定同样适用于其他协定相同条款的解释及执行;

二、中新协定条文解释与此前下发的有关税收协定解释与执行文件不同的,以中新协定条文解释为准……

该解释第五条规定:……从事“准备性或辅助性”活动的场所通常具备以下特点:一是该场所不独立从事经营活动,并其活动也不构成企业整体活动基本的或重要的组成部分;二是该场所进行第四款列举的活动时,仅为本企业服务,不为其他企业服务;三是其职责限于事务性服务,且不起直接营利作用……

创造经营利润。而在数字经济时代下,得益于通讯技术的发展,跨国商业经营模式,如B2B(Business to Business)、B2C(Business to Consumer)模式完全可以在线完成而不需要在来源国建立固定性场所。

以国内跨境电商平台小笨鸟所开展的B2C业务为例。国内商家通过小笨鸟的平台发布商品到海外多家平台(如亚马逊、易贝和新蛋等)。消费者可以在平台上浏览商品并选择是否购买。一旦确定了购买意向,消费者可以在线下订单,并通过在线支付工具付款。商家可以通过后台网络处理国外订单,并通过国际物流的小包业务将商品配送至国外买家。整个交易流程通过网络完成,后期的配送物流也不需要在国外设立营业点。从某种程度上说,跨境电商平台提供了一个交易数据匹配的虚拟性平台,并不需要实体性的存在。

因此,随着数字经济的兴起,在线电子商务急剧增多。固定性场所在商业经营中不再是必备的要素,从侧面反映出我国场所型常设机构规则过于依赖实体性存在的弊端。这给税收征管带来了极大的挑战,成为税务机关不得不面对的难题。

2. 豁免条款过于宽泛

除了中智税收协定(中国—智利)规定所有豁免活动必须具备准备性或辅助性性质,其他税收协定并不要求仓储、展览、采购及信息收集等活动需要经过准备性或辅助性测试。这也意味着,如果跨国企业在我国设立的固定性场所仅用于仓储、展览、采购或者信息收集,那么该固定性场所在我国并不构成场所型常设机构。在数字经济的背景下,交易数字化加大了这种情况出现的可能性。由于协商、对接、签订合同等均可以在线完成,仓储、展览、采购及信息收集等活动可能在整个商业活动中居于主要地位,成为核心业务。

以2015年日本的网上零售案为例。在该案中,一家美国公司通过在线网站向日本客户销售汽车零部件。这家美国公司在日本设有仓库,用于存储产品和处理发货、退货订单。税务局认为该仓库已经构成常设机构,应该对其进行征税。而纳税人认为,仓库并不构成常设机构,它仅仅属于税收协定里所规定的准备性或辅助性活动。最终,东京地方法院(The Tokyo District Court)裁定,美日税收协定第5条第4款(a)至(d)项所提到的仓储、展览、采购及信息收集等活动应视为兜底条款(e)项"其他准备性或辅助性的任何其他活动"的举例。因此,第5条第4款(a)至(d)项所提到的活动并不自动被视为准备性或辅助性活动,仅仅在具有准备性或辅助性的性质时才可被归为常设机构的例外条款。在本案中,仓库的存在增强了潜在客户对线上商店的信任感,提升线上商店竞争力;同时,位于日本的仓库使货物可以存储在日本,快速到达指定的客户地点,提高了物流速度。从这个维度看,日本仓库并非仅扮演准备性或辅助性的角色,其所承担的功能和开展的活动是网上零售业务成功开展的重要因素,因此在客观上构成常设机构。[5]

该案虽然发生在日本,但是由于美日税收协定第5条第4款跟中新税收协定第5条第4款一致,两者均借鉴经济合作与发展组织(OECD)《税收协定范本》,因此,该案例对于我国具有极强的实践意义。该裁决利用现行规则并运用法律解释的技术尽可能扩大其适用范围,以规制跨国企业反避税。但值得我们注意的是,涉案争议本身暴露出现行豁免条款规定较为模糊、准备性或辅助性活动的界定过于宽泛的问题,成为跨国企业进行避税的工具。

二、数字经济背景下常设机构规则的国际立法考察

在数字经济背景下,大多数国家都面临着常设机构认定的困境。为了维护来源国的税收管辖权,防止税基侵蚀,部分国家已经率先采取行动,对人为规避场所型常设机构进行规制。从理论上进行划分,国外立法主要有三种规制路径,分别是引进显著经济存在的标准、修订豁免条款和新增税种。下文将结合国外立法动态进行考察。

(一)创建新的连接点:显著经济存在

2014年,BEPS报告在第一项行动计划《应对数字经济挑战》中提出了基于显著经济存在的新型征税关系。在没有实体性存在的情况下,显著的经济存在可以基于数字、收入和用户因素综合确定征税权。

所谓数字因素,是指非居民纳税人提供访问渠道或者提供数字平台(如电子申请平台、数据库、在线市场、储藏室)或在网上或电子应用程序上提供搜索引擎和广告服务。其他潜在的数字因素包括本地域名或本地支付选项(local payment options)。而收入因素,被认为是显著经济存在最明显的指标。收入因素背后的理论基础在于,即使是依赖于网络效应的商业模式,企业用户和数据的价值都会以收入的形式呈现出来,在账面上显示出经济关联。将量化的收入

---

[5] See "Japanese court decision impacts taxation of onlinebusiness warehouses", in *EY Global Tax Alert*, Nov. 25, 2015.

因素确定为显著经济存在的重要因素，可以为跨境商业活动提供税收确定性，减少纳税人的合规成本。此外，鉴于网络效应在数字经济中发挥的重要作用，用户群也可以被视为与另一个国家存在经济关联的重要指标，具体包括每月活跃用户、在线合同数量和收集的数据。[6]

面对传统常设机构规则无法应对数字经济挑战的现状，印度、意大利、以色列等国家已经率先行动，尝试引进显著经济存在的标准，以解决税基侵蚀问题。但各国对于显著经济存在的认定标准略有不同。印度认为，非居民企业在印度进行货物、服务或财产交易，包括在印度提供数据或软件下载，且上一年此类交易产生的付款总额超过规定数额；或非居民通过数字手段，在印度国内系统且持续性地开展商业活动或与一定数量的用户进行互动。满足以上条件的非居民企业，即可构成显著经济存在。[7] 意大利认为在境内有规律和持续（regular and continuous）的经济存在，或者有核心业务重要组成部分的辅助活动，即使外国企业在意大利没有实体性存在，即可构成显著经济存在。[8] 以色列则认为显著经济存在需要通过以下标准进行判定：签订大量的合同为以色列居民提供互联网服务；为以色列用户调整在线服务（如使用希伯来语、使用以色列货币等）；拥有高流量的以色列用户；支付给外国企业的报酬与以色列用户的互联网使用状况密切相关。[9] 各国差异某种程度也体现出此模式尚处于尝试阶段，并无统

---

〔6〕 See *Addressing the Tax Challenges of the Digital Economy*, *Action* 1 – 2015 *Final Report*, OECD Publishing, Oct. 5, 2015, pp. 107 – 113.

〔7〕 印度 2018 年财政预算案提议，对 1961 年《所得税法》第 9 条进行修订，自 2019 年 4 月 1 日起引入新的常设机构规定。See THE FINANCE BILL, 2018, chapter Ⅲ, cl. 4.

〔8〕 根据 2018 年《预算法》（Budget Law）（2017 年 12 月 27 日第 205 号法），意大利修改了《意大利税法典》（Italian Tax Code）第 162 条中关于"常设机构"一词的定义。See Marco Rossi, "Italy Enacted The Economic Nexus Rule And Other Changes To The Definition of Permanent Establishment", https://www. euitalianinternationaltax. com/2018/02/articles/international-taxation/italy-enacted-economic-nexus-rule-changes-definition-permanent-es tablishment/, July 26, 2018.

〔9〕 2016 年 4 月 11 日，以色列税务局（The Israeli Tax Authorities）发布通告（circular），就常设机构的适用问题进行厘清。See the comments on the Tax Challenges of Digitalisation-Part II, OECD Publishing, Oct. 25, 2015, p. 17.

一认定标准。由于涉及大量网络数据统计,后期政策落实与否也给执行机关提出挑战。

显著经济存在是经济关联原则在数字经济背景下的延伸和拓展,突破了传统固定场所的限制,融合了数字经济的特点,以数字、收入和用户因素来确定经济关联。相较于传统的常设机构原则,显著经济存在仅保留了经济关联的"外壳",用全新的界定标准替换了"内核"。因此,也有学者称"显著经济存在完全颠覆了常设机构原则,重新界定了经济关联度的判定标准"。[10] 如果能够落实到实处,显著经济存在确实能够有效防止规避场所型常设机构的情形。但是,从技术的角度来看,显著经济存在能否实施仍值得进一步探究。

(二)修改豁免条款

OECD 在第七项行动计划《防止人为规避常设机构》报告中提出修改豁免条款的建议,以避免某些企业在实施重要的商业活动时,假借准备性或辅助性活动之名绕开常设机构。关于如何修改豁免条款,目前主要有以下四个方案:第一,删除豁免条款;第二,删除豁免条款(a)至(d)项;第三,对豁免条款中的(a)至(d)项活动补充规定,规定其所开展的活动属于准备性或辅助性活动,而非核心活动;第四,将(a)项和(b)项中的"交付"一词删去。[11]

纵观这四种修改方案,第一种方案改革力度最大,也是最彻底的。而第二种到第四种方案是在保留豁免条款的基础上进行修改完善。如果依照第一种方案,将豁免条款彻底删除,意味着常设机构将所有活动都囊括在其规范的范畴内,不区分核心活动和准备性或辅助性活动。这一举措客观上简化了规则,避免区分商业活动的性质,具有较强的可执行性。此外,简便的规范范式也增强了其适用的灵活性,能够适应未来更复杂的商业模式和市场结构。但这一举措大幅度扩大常设机构的效力范围,虽然能够打击数字企业的逃避税行为,但同时也影响了非数字企业,增加其税收负担,影响跨境实体经济的发展。

至于第二种和第三种方案,笔者以为两者的理念是一致的,只是规范的方式有所不同。第二种方案将(a)至(d)项删去,仅保留兜底条款(e)项和(f)项。

---

[10] 崔晓静等:《数字经济背景下税收常设机构原则的适用问题》,载《法学》2016 年第 11 期。

[11] See *Preventing the Artificial Avoidance of Permanent Establishment Status*, *Action* 7 - 2015 *Final Report*, OECD Publishing, Oct. 5, 2015, pp. 28 - 29.

从立法的技术来看，该方案使用概括法，将具有准备性质或辅助性质的活动定性为常设机构的例外活动。而第三种方案对豁免条款中的(a)至(d)项活动补充规定，规定其所开展的活动属于准备性或辅助性活动，实际上是在第二种方案的基础上，抽取典型的事项进行列举。这种方案是将OECD的注释[12]明文确定下来，避免此前有人认为(a)至(d)项不需要具备准备性或者辅助性的性质误区。概括加列举的立法技术，能够给实践较为明确的指引。

关于第四种方案，《联合国税收协定范本》采取了该方法，将(a)项和(b)项中的"交付"一词删去。张泽平教授在考究该做法时，主要是从发展中国家的利益进行考量，认为"为现货交付而保存的商品库存，促进了产品的销售，并且使设有该设施的企业在所得来源国取得了利润，出于对发展中国家来源地税收管辖权的维护，这种用于交付货物的场所应当视为常设机构"。[13] 仅删去"交付"二字，能在多大程度上防止人为规避场所型常设机构是一个疑问。从目的解释的方法出发，该方案主要是针对数字经济背景下活跃的在线零售商群体。从表面上看，删除了"交付"一词之后，对于仅在来源国设立仓库的在线零售商而言，该仓库将无法适用豁免条款的(a)项或(b)项。也就是说，该仓库很有可能被认定为非准备性或辅助性活动而面临常设机构征税的情形。但是，这种设想仅仅停留在理想层面。立法的制定本身是一门博弈的艺术。如果删除"交付"一词后，在线零售商完全可以通过雇佣独立的第三方运营商或运输公司实施交付业务，从而轻易绕开该条款。同时该修改方案对于其他活动，诸如从应用程序商店里下载软件是无法规制的。由此可见，第四种方案对于防止人为规避场所型常设机构并不奏效，不具有可行性。

(三)新增税种防止人为规避常设机构

1. 预提税方案

Doernberg教授于1998年提出来源国对跨境电子商务征收预提税的观点。[14] 我国学者张智勇也持此观点，认为"预提税方案是对传统以常设机构为

---

[12] See OECD (2017), *Model Tax Convention on Income and on Capital: Condensed Version* 2017, OECD Publishing, Commentary on Article 5.

[13] 张泽平：《国际税法》，北京大学出版社2014年版，第85页。

[14] See Doernberg, Richard L., "Electronic commerce and international tax sharing", *Tax Notes International* 16, 1998, pp. 1013 – 1022.

连接点的税法规则的重大变革,具有优于其他方案的合理性”。[15] OECD在BEPS报告中提到对数字化交易课征预提税的本质是“当一国居民在线从另一国居民购买货物和服务时,来源国(支付人所在国)对所支付的款项有权征收预提税”。[16]

依照Dale Pinto教授的观点,该方案主张对所有收入征收预提税,改变传统规则只对来源地消极所得征税的情形,将征税范围扩大到所有收入,而不考虑收入是属于积极所得还是消极所得。一方面,该方案借鉴了税收协定对消极所得课税的思路;另一方面,它也涵摄了来源地征税的理念。从这个维度看,预提税方案实际上是对来源地征税进行改进。[17] 在数字经济背景下,该方案的意义在于能够将数字化交易囊括在内,以统一的税率对电子商务征收预提税,解决了数字经济环境下征税困难的问题。同时,该方案可以由国家单方面制定实施,不需要修订既存的双边税收协定,具有简便性。

尽管预提税方案有针对性地解决了数字化交易的征税问题,但存在逻辑无法自洽、操作难度大等缺陷。首先,预提税方案违背中性原则。具体体现在以下几个方面:第一,根据该方案,仅仅针对跨境数字化交易所涉及的货物与服务课征预提税,而对国内相同交易却不征税,从而在跨境和国内交易形成区别对待。第二,预提税是按企业收款的总额而非纯利润课征。以总额作为税基,提高了数字产品的成本,甚至在预提税率比较高的情形下,可能出现税负高于纯利润,导致税前盈利业务转化为税后亏损,造成经济扭曲。

其次,预提税的扣缴主体仍有待商榷。按照预提税的制度设计,扣缴预提税的责任通常转移到款项结算的代理人,如客户或第三方中介机构。该机制运作的前提是负责扣缴的主体能够清楚地获知与交易相关的信息。在B2B和B2C交易中,尽管消费者或者非居民企业能够掌握充分的信息,但将其规定为扣缴主体,客观上会造成高昂的交易成本。数字经济下的交易对象多为普通的消费者,具有个体性和零散性的特征。消费者没有任何纳税申报的经验,也没有任何代扣代缴的

---

〔15〕 张智勇:《数字经济与国际税法的变革:路径与方案的思考》,载《国际经济法学刊》2014年第3期。

〔16〕 前引6,OECD报告,p. 113。

〔17〕 See Pinto, Dale, “The Need to Reconceptualize the Permanent Establishment Threshold”, *Bulletin for International Taxation* 60.7, 2006, p. 266.

激励。在这种情形下,极易出现不申报的现象。这无异于将预提税制度架空。倘若将负责结算的中介机构,如银行列为扣缴主体,则不得不重视由信息不对称所带来的管理成本和挑战。作为中介机构,银行往往看到的是交易的金额,无法获知交易的具体内容。由于无法识别交易的具体信息,银行无法确定交易是否属于跨境数字化交易、是否属于扣缴对象。针对这种情况,可能存在的解决方案是增加强制性非居民企业登记制度,要求所有远程货物和服务销售商指定专用银行账户用于收取当地客户价款。但这种解决方法是在法律没有规定并且没有授权的情况下为远程货物和服务销售商施加义务,同时也为第三方的中介机构增加了合规义务,在实践中并不具有可行性。[18]

2. 衡平税

所谓衡平,是指在不同商业模式或者不同税收管辖权保持税收中性。为了避免显著经济存在规则产生的利润归属难题,衡平税可以被视为解决数字经济挑战的替代方法。尽管衡平税可以以多种方式实现,但为了向所有利益相关者提供确定性和公平性,避免给中小企业造成不必要的负担,衡平税一般仅对有显著经济存在的非居民企业征税。[19]

为了应对数字经济的挑战,印度从 2016 年 6 月 1 日起,对数字广告征收 6% 的衡平税。开征衡平税的原因与近年来数字经济的发展趋势密切相关。近年来,数字经济的发展开拓了数字广告的市场,数字广告成为 Google、Facebook、Twitter、Linkedin 等数字企业的重要业务。但是这些数字企业的设立地点往往不在印度境内。由于在印度没有设立常设机构,印度没有权力对其征税。这意味着,数字企业从印度所获得的这些收入免于所得税,客观上给印度造成税基侵蚀。为了规制这种现象,印度当局颁布通告,针对印度居民从非居民企业获得的特定服务征收 6% 的衡平税。衡平税的征税对象仅包括在线广告和其他用于在线广告的设施和服务。同时规定了衡平税的例外条款:拥有常设机构的非居民企业以及收入总额低于 100,000 卢比的非居民企业可以免征衡平税。[20]

衡平税虽然能够针对在线广告等数字交易课征税收,但是存在双重征税的风险。目前引进衡平税的国家为数不多。如果各国单方面实行衡平税,未与相

〔18〕 参见前引 6,OECD 报告,p. 114。

〔19〕 参见前引 6,OECD 报告,p. 115。

〔20〕 See THE FINANCE ACT,2016,Sec. 165.

关国家协商签订税收协定,则很容易引发国际双重征税的问题。被征收衡平税的企业在其居民国需要缴纳所得税,并且无法依据税收协定进行抵免。这意味着企业同一笔收入需要在居住国和来源国同时缴税,无疑加重了企业的负担,阻碍了自由贸易的发展。以印度为例,衡平税并非隶属于印度税收体系内的所得税(income tax)或服务税(services tax)。有学者提到,衡平税不属于印度所得税法的一部分,这意味着需要课征衡平税的收入不需要缴纳所得税。因此,目前并不清楚负有缴纳衡平税义务的非居民企业是否可以享受条约利益(如税收抵免或豁免)。[21] 笔者认为,税收协定主要是针对所得税、公司税和资本利得税提供税收抵免。由于衡平税并不属于以上税种,因此原则上,衡平税并不在税收协定的范围内。在这种情形下,非居民企业是无法享受条约利益的。同时,目前开征衡平税的国家甚少,要求对方国家提供衡平税的税收抵免并不现实。

此外,衡平税与现行国际贸易规则不相兼容。虽然衡平税是以净额为基础征税,但这样的规定可能违反《服务贸易总协定》(General Agreement on Trade in Service,GATS)和《关税及贸易总协定》(General Agreement on Tariffs and Trade,GATT),与现行的贸易规则相悖。

GATT 和 GATS 分别是国际货物贸易和国际服务贸易的框架性法律文件。两者在内容上最为核心的是国民待遇和最惠国待遇条款。在国民待遇方面,GATS 在第14条(d)项规定了一般例外条款,只要措施"在同等情况下,不构成任意或不合理的歧视,或者对服务贸易的变相限制……并且规定差别对待以确保公平和有效地对其他成员的服务和服务提供者课征直接税为限"。[22] 也就

〔21〕 See Sagar Wagh, "The Taxation of Digital Transactions in India: The New Equalization Levy", Bulletin for International Taxation, 2016.

〔22〕 GATS 脚注6对平等和有效的课征直接税进行解释:(a)非居民服务提供者的纳税义务是由来源于该成员境内的应征税项目决定;(b)为保证在该成员领土内课税或征税,而对非居民实施的措施;(c)为防止避税或逃税而对非居民或居民实施的措施;(d)为了确保对来源地税收的征收,对在另一国境内提供的,或来自另一国的服务的消费者采取的措施;(e)把具有世界范围应征税项目的服务提供者与其他服务提供者加以区别的措施,承认他们在课税性质上存在差异;(f)为了保障该成员的税基而采取的确定、分配或分摊居民或分支机构的,或有关联的人员之间或同一人所拥有的分支机构之间的收入、利润、收益、亏损、扣除或抵免的措施。See General Agreement on Trade in Services, Note 6.

是说,在不构成歧视的前提下,GATS 允许成员国突破国民待遇的限制,对服务提供者课征直接税。与 GATS 不同的是,GATT 并没有规定国民待遇的例外条款。GATT 第 3 条第 2 款规定:"对于进入其他成员国的产品,直接或间接课征的国内税费和规费,不得超过国内同类产品。"[23] 该条款非常清楚地表明,在同等情况下,不允许对进口产品课征更多的税费。目前,关于跨境提供数字产品属于服务还是货物在国际社会上并无定论。[24] 当跨境提供数字产品被视为货物而课征衡平税时,跨境数字产品要比国内同类产品缴纳更多的税费,这与成员国所负担的国民待遇义务是相违背的。实际上,上文所提到的预提税方案也同样面临这个问题。

有观点认为,GATT 条文中所提到的课征对象是货物而不包括单位或个体。在税收体系内,对货物所征收的税种主要有增值税(value added tax)、商品与服务税(goods and services tax)和消费税(consumption tax)。而所得税是对单位或者个人所得所征收的税种,不属于第 3 条所涵盖的范围。[25] 但这是否意味着,衡平税和预提税是对所得征税,故而不受第 3 条第 2 款的约束?从文义解释的角度,第 3 条第 2 款确实不包括所得税。但在实务中,WTO 争端解决机构通常采取扩大解释的方法,扩大其适用范围,避免成员国通过所得税措施规避第 3 条。典型例子如阿根廷对进口皮革预征所得税案件。在该案中,专家组的裁决逻辑在于,阿根廷所课征的预征所得税是以产品的价格为基础,因此属于对产品适用的措施,进而裁定阿根廷所采取的预征所得税措施适用第 3 条第 2 款。[26] 因此,由于衡平税和预提税的所得跟产品的价格相挂钩,实务中一旦发生争议,WTO 争端解决机构很有可能通过扩大解释的方法,将衡平税和预提税纳入第 3 条第 2 款的管辖范围。在这种情形下,衡平税和预提税方案仍然面临着违反国民待遇义务的诘难。

3. 转移利润税

为了打击跨国公司避税,英国从 2015 年 4 月 1 日起,开征转移利润税

---

〔23〕 General Agreement on Tariffs and Trade, art. 3, cl. 2.

〔24〕 See *Work Ppogramme on Electronic Commerce*, Progress Report to the WTO General Council WT/L/274, Sept. 30, 1998, p. 5.

〔25〕 参见龙英锋:《GATT 中的国内税问题探析》,载《法学》2006 年第 2 期。

〔26〕 参见韩立余:《WTO 案例及评析》,中国人民大学出版社 2001 年版,第 118 页。

(diverted profits tax),对人为从英国转移利润至国外的情形征收25%的税负,高于19%的公司税。该税被认为是英国当局针对谷歌等大型跨国公司通过人为转移利润方式避税所采取的单边应对措施,亦称其为"谷歌税"。如何判断该行为是人为转移在英国产生的利润,主要依赖以下两个规则:规避常设机构规则(avoided permanent establishment rule)和替代规则(alternative provision rule)。[27] 所谓规避常设机构规则,指的是非居民企业是否通过人为安排规避常设机构,重点针对海外开票公司(billing company)架构。海外开票公司通过当地人员在英国本土设立子公司或分支机构,表面对外经营,实际上是由海外开票公司和消费者直接对接,从而实现开票公司绕开常设机构的目的。例如,一个消费者在网上购买了商品或服务。该网站的服务器不在境内,拥有该服务器的境外公司通过其他人在境内开展营销。最终,由于该服务器不在境内不构成常设机构,从而逃避了税收监管。而替代规则关注的是居民与非居民企业的集团内部交易(通常涉及知识产权许可或转让、设备租赁和管理服务),防止通过缺乏经济实质的交易或实体创造税收优势。例如,一家英国公司A将其知识产权转让给一家设立在低税收地区的非英国公司B。B公司再将知识产权许可给A公司。通过该交易架构,A公司在计算公司税负时可获得特许权使用费的进项税额扣除,而B公司则以低税率缴纳转让费。

笔者认为,转移利润税的最大问题在于,法理上无法解释与税收协定的关系,进而引发与现行规则冲突的危机。关于转移利润税和税收协定的关系问题,立法文本和相关指引中并没有明确的规定。但英国税务机关曾公开对外表示,转移利润税不受税收协定的约束,因此无法根据税收协定获得豁免。[28] 并且认为,英国所开征的转移利润税并不违反避免双重征税协定的义务。其理由主要基于以下两点:第一,转移利润税仅适用于利用税收协定逃税的交易安排。在国际法的框架内,英国并没有义务对该类交易安排提供救济;第二,转移利润税并不在英国双重征税协定的救济范围内,因为这些条约仅针对所得税、公司

〔27〕 See Finance Act 2015, part 3, Diverted profits tax.

〔28〕 See Ben Jones & Cathryn Vanderspar, "Twenty Questions on the Diverted Profits Tax", https://www.taxjournal.com/articles/20-questions-diverted-profits-tax-24092015, July 5, 2018.

税和资本利得税提供救济。[29] 该观点源于英国税务局对于转移利润税的定位。英国税务局认为转移利润税是一种新税种,不属于上述税种,因此转移利润税并不属于税收协定的约定范围。

英国税务局关于转移利润税不违反税收协定的论证并不充分。转移利润税是新税种并不当然地推出其不在税收协定的救济范围内的结论。英国特许公认会计师公会(The Association of Chartered Certified Accountants)的税务主管 Chas Roy-Chowdhury 也提到:"虽然英国方面声称转移利润税不是公司税,但这并不意味着其他管辖区会接受这样的观点"。[30] 以英国和美国的税收协定为例,该协定第 2 条第 4 款规定:"本公约同样适用于签署日期后所开征的相同或者实质相似(identical or substantially similar)的税收以及代替现行税收的税种"。[31] 这里需要界定的是转移利润税究竟属不属于跟公司税相同或实质相似的税种。从功能上看,转移利润税针对人为转移利润课征 25% 的税收。为发挥反避税的效果、督促纳税人自觉纳税,转移利润税的税率远高于 19% 的公司税,具有一定的惩罚性质。从这个维度看,转移利润税是公司税的补充。两者构成非居民企业征税、维护英国税基的两大堡垒。正因为这个原因,有学者提到:"转移利润税和公司税两者唯一的可识别性差异在于征管的管辖范围不同(jurisdictional standard)。"[32] 由此可见,转移利润税并非当然被排除出税收协定的救济范围。

三、我国场所型常设机构制度完善的立法思路

在澳大利亚布里斯班举行的二十国集团(G20)峰会上,习近平主席指出,我国要"严厉打击国际逃避税,全面深入参与应对税基侵蚀和利润转移(BEPS)

---

〔29〕 See HMRC, "Diverted Profits Tax", *The Royal Society*, Jan 8, 2015.

〔30〕 Calum Fuller, "Google tax may be extra-territorial, warns ACCA", https://www.accountancyage.com/aa/news/2386020/-google-tax-may-be-extra-territorial-warns-acca, july 5, 2018.

〔31〕 UK/USA Double Taxation Convention, art. 2, cl. 4.

〔32〕 MacLennan, Stuart, "The Questionable Legality of the Diverted Profits Tax Under Double Taxation Conventions and European Union Law", *Intertax* 44. 12, 2016, p. 909.

行动计划,构建反避税国际协作体系"。[33] 完善场所型常设机构规则,积极回应BEPS项目是我国承担大国税收责任、参与国际税收规则制定的重要机会。鉴于我国是成文法国家,且场所型常设机构规则主要规定在税收协定中,我国可通过修改税收协定的方式,具体包括引进显著经济存在的判断标准和在豁免条款中新增准备性或辅助性测试,对场所型常设机构制度进行完善。

(一)引进显著经济存在的判断标准

随着数字经济的发展与推进,传统认定场所型常设机构的关键要素"实体性存在"成为逃避监管的重要缺口。越来越多的跨国利益实体借助信息和通讯技术实现数字交易。考虑到目前技术发展日新月异,针对数字经济制定专门的法律法规在立法成本上显得不切实际。因此,扩大场所型常设机构的内涵和外延显得极其重要。鉴于数字交易的运行高度依赖用户、数据、在线合同等数字因素,我国宜乘着数字经济的浪潮,引进显著数字经济存在的判断标准,填补场所型常设机构认定出现的漏洞。

1. 定性与定量之争

目前,关于显著经济存在的界定是国际税收领域正在积极探讨的话题。与传统场所型常设机构注重定性有所不同,显著经济存在本身是一个模糊的概念,其借助量化的指标(如数字、收入和用户)予以确定。因此,我国在引进显著经济存在的判断标准时,面临的第一个问题便是定性和定量之争。

对于常设机构,有学者认为应该进行定性测试,[34] 也有学者认为应该进行定量测试。[35] 笔者认为,定性和定量标准各有优缺点。但在确定性和合规成本方面,定量标准相对占优。无论对于纳税人还是税务部门而言,非居民企业是否构成场所型常设机构都具有重要意义。这涉及纳税负担和财政收入的问题。为了减少税务纠纷,提供确定性的判断标准无疑是消解纷争的制度性保障。与定性标准相比,定量标准可表征于客观的数据,为利益相关者提供最大限度的确定性。除了在确定性方面有所不同,两者在合规成本方面也有所差异。在定

[33] 贺艳、厉征:《合作共赢:大国税务应势而为》,和讯税务,2016年1月7日。

[34] See Hinnekens, Luc, "Looking for an appropriate jurisdictional framework for source-state taxation of international electronic commerce in the twenty-first century", *Intertax* 26.6, 1998, p. 197.

[35] See Avi-Yonah, Reuven S. and Halabi, Oz, "A Model Treaty for the Age of BEPS", *Law & Economics Working Papers* 1, 2014, p. 103.

性标准的框架下，税务部门和企业需要花费时间讨论非居民实体是否构成常设机构。而定量标准则不然。通过客观数据的衡量，税务部门和企业可以快速地确定是否构成常设机构。因此，从这个维度看，定量标准的遵从成本要比定量标准的遵从成本低。

虽然说定量在确定性和合规成本方面略占优势，但并不意味着笔者赞同完全抛弃传统对场所型常设机构认定的路径，用显著经济存在的定量标准加以取代。目前数字企业和非数字企业并存。显著经济存在规制的对象主要是数字企业。非数字企业可能在定量指标上并不突出。在这种情形下，如果仅采用显著经济存在的标准，这些经营传统业务的企业有可能因达不到指标的阈值而不构成常设机构。为了避免这种情况，目前比较合适的方法是在定性的基础上辅之定量，在现行税收协定第5条的基础上增设第8款：

如果其在某一企业的数字化活动满足以下任一条件或所有条件的，将被认定为在我国拥有数字化常设机构，我国有权根据国内法对该公司在其境内通过数字化常设机构取得的利润征收企业所得税：

(a)该公司及其关联公司在该成员国提供数字化服务，并在纳税年度实现营收超过[X]元；

(b)在纳税年度，该成员国接受该公司的数字化服务的活跃用户超过[Y]；

(c)在纳税年度，该公司与该成员国的用户达成的线上合同数量超过[Z]。[36]

从前文阐述可知，对于这些指标，印度、意大利、以色列均主要着眼于定量指标，而关于定量的阈值仍在探讨之中。定量本身关涉税收的确定性问题。如果没有清晰和确定的标准，势必会给纳税人带来困扰，进而引发一系列的税务纠纷。因此，我国在引进显著经济存在时，需要从定量指标和定量阈值两个角度确定显著经济存在。在定量指标方面，我国应将收入、用户、在线合同签订量纳入统计指标的范畴。而阈值方面，则需结合信息学科和统计学进行确定，有赖进一步研究。

2. 依托区块链技术实现税收征管

引进显著经济存在时，面临的第二个问题是，如何实现对这些定量指标的

〔36〕 See *Tax Challenges Arising from Digitalisation-Interim Report* 2018: *Inclusive Framework on BEPS*, OECD Publishing, Mar. 16, 2018.

监管。笔者认为,数字经济在商业领域不断创新模式。相应地,税收征管对数字经济也要有相应的创新模式。将信息和通讯技术融入国际税收管理中,可以有效提高税收征管效率。以区块链技术为例,区块链是近年来兴起的分布式记账新技术,能够帮助交易双方直接进行点对点交易。由于该技术具有去中心化、公开透明性和可追溯性等特点,且拥有强大的记录和防篡改功能,目前正在逐步探索将其应用于税收监管领域。笔者认为不妨利用该契机,将区块链技术应用到常设机构监管区域。为此,下文结合区块链的技术特点和财税理念,分析区块链技术利于显著经济存在的实施。

表1　区块链技术与财税理念对比〔37〕

特点	区块链技术	财税理念
去中心化	各个节点地位相同	财务部门、管理层、治理层、税务部门信息对称
公开透明性	单一节点无法篡改数据	财税数据不可篡改、真实有效
可追溯性	数据按时间顺序冗余保存	会计记账的不可逆
智能合约机制	自动执行条款	收入确认、纳税义务发生及时确认

如表1所示,区块链技术的首要特点是去中心化,有助于共享跨境交易数据。去中心化是相对中心化而言的。目前的税收管理存在上下层级以及平级之间沟通协调的障碍与迟滞,导致信息不通畅。在区块链去中心化实施后,跨境交易所形成的数据将被各个节点记录并且实现共享。对于各级税务机关而言,其能够获得更多的数据、信息,打破信息孤岛现象,从而提高税收征收管理的效率性和针对性。

其次,区块链技术具有公开透明性的特点,有利于跨境交易数据保持真实性。自然人税收管理的难点在于税务机关对于自然人信息掌握的不充分。“在区块链网络中,任何单一节点提出的数据修改申请,都需经过其他节点的确认,从而实现了账簿的公开透明。”〔38〕通过区块链,一旦将资产记录到分类账中,基

〔37〕 参见张之乐:《以区块链技术促进纳税遵从的设想》,载《税务研究》2017年第12期。

〔38〕 同上,张之乐文,第108页。

于链条的环环相扣,完整的审计跟踪将自动跟踪所有权、地点甚至税单的变化。

此外,区块链技术具有可追溯性。区块链的分布式账本使每项跨境交易都会被清楚地记录,从而使其具有很强的可追溯性。追本溯源的存在使得每一项交易的真实性能够最大限度地得到保证。伪造的交易容易被识别出来。因此,一旦出现纳税失信交易记录,税务机关可以快速锁定交易方和关联方,打击逃税避税。

最后,基于区块链技术的智能合约可以应用到税收征管领域。智能合约是一种计算机程序,可促进、执行使用区块链技术的个人和组织之间的协议。当预先编程的条件被触发时,智能合同执行相应的合同条款。在降低合约履行成本的同时,税务机关也掌握了较为充分的信息,可以通过系统自动计算每一笔收入或纳税人某一期间所得的纳税义务。

由此可见,通过运用区块链技术,税务机关可以运用互联网技术完成税收预缴、网上缴税等服务。区块链技术也可以帮助税收部门收集和记录企业交易数据,并且形成无法更改的证据链,保证税收信息的完整性,从而堵塞逃避税漏洞。

(二)新增准备性或辅助性测试

如前所述,OECD 提出修订豁免条款,对(a)至(d)项活动作补充规定,规定其所开展的活动属于准备性或辅助性活动。笔者赞同 OECD 所提出的方案。修订豁免条款,规定所有豁免活动需要经过准备性或辅助性测试是解决我国现行豁免条款过于宽泛的举措。我国曾在中智税收协定采取了此思路,但之后其他税收协定都没有采用该种做法,其中缘由尚无从考察。

通过分析立法初衷,笔者发现:之所以在税收协定第 5 条第 4 款规定豁免条款,是因为"准备性或辅助性活动虽然对企业的生产性有一定贡献,但因其企业利润的实现较远,以致在利润分配时难以向其分配利润"。[39] 从这里可以看出,豁免条款设立的依据是坚持生产性标准。构成常设机构本身意味着其从事的生产性活动对营业起到核心的帮助。在规则制定的初期,仓储、展览、采购等活动确实处于价值链的末端,并非整个生产经营活动的核心部分。但是随着数字经济的发展,当对接、签订合同等业务可以在线完成时,实地的仓储、展览、采购等豁免活动就成为交易成功的关键要素,居于生产经营的主要地位。此时如

〔39〕 前引 12,Commentary on Article 5。

果继续坚持原来的条款,一方面,与立法初衷有违;另一方面,我国对这些核心业务所取得的利润无法课税,造成税基侵蚀。因此,考虑到既有框架和立法目的,我国宜在第5条第4款增加准备性或辅助性测试,将"条件是上述活动属于准备性质或辅助性质"作为第5条第4款的限制性规定。通过该种立法,强调实质重于形式,只有性质上属于准备性或辅助性活动才得以豁免,防止非居民企业假借准备性或辅助性活动之名绕开常设机构。

如何判定非居民企业所从事的活动是否具有准备性或辅助性性质呢?BEPS第七项行动计划对关键词"准备性"和"辅助性"进行了解释:发生在企业活动的基本部分或重要部分之前的相对较短时间内的活动一般都具备准备性质;辅助性活动则是为了支持上述基本活动,而不构成该基本活动的任何部分,并以案例的形式明确指出用于储存或交付通过互联网销售的产品的仓库作为线上商店的"重要资产",在人员和资金投入上都具有相当的规模,是企业销售活动的"关键部分",因此这些仓库的活动不具有准备性或辅助性特征。〔40〕结合国家税务总局文件〔41〕来看,笔者认为,在进行准备性或辅助性测试时,可以从以下几个方面进行考察:第一,场所是否依附于总机构从事经营活动,对外并不直接营利;第二,场所的业务性质与总机构的业务性质是否一致;第三,场所服务的对象是否仅为总机构服务还是也为其他人服务;第四,场所的业务是否仅限于事务性服务,进而判定场所是否成为总机构业务的重要组成部分。如果以上四个条件均满足的话,那么非居民企业所从事的活动具有准备性或辅助性性质,适用第5条第4款,反之则不适用。

结　论

综上所述,数字经济给我国现行常设机构规则造成巨大的冲击,反映出过于依赖实体性存在、豁免条款过于宽泛的问题,容易诱发税基侵蚀。因此,我国

---

〔40〕 参见前引11,OECD报告,pp. 30-31。

〔41〕 《国家税务总局关于税收协定常设机构认定等有关问题的通知》(国税发〔2006〕35号)对"经营性"的判断方法作出了明确规定:一是看固定基地或场所的业务性质是否与总机构一致;二是看固定基地或场所是否仅为总机构服务,还是也为其他人服务;三是看固定基地或场所的业务是否成为总机构业务的重要组成部分。

有必要对常设机构规则进行相应调整。在调整的各种方案中,本文认为,显著经济存在方案是在保留经济关联原则的基础上结合数字经济的特点,对传统认定规则进行革新;而预提税、衡平税、转移利润税等方案,实际上已经抛弃了常设机构的规范框架,采用新增税种的路径对数字交易进行规制。由于目前采用这种制度的国家不多,且没有成熟的避免双重征税制度,新增税种的路径往往面临中立性原则的质疑,存在与现行国际规则不相兼容的危机。

在国际比较研究的基础上,本文提出了完善我国场所型常设机构规则的思路:其一,在修订双边税收协定时引进"显著经济存在"的判断标准,为了增强显著经济存在标准的可操作性,我国可借助区块链技术进行税收征管;其二,修订豁免条款,规定所有豁免活动都必须具有准备性或辅助性性质。

(责任编辑:郑恺歆)

虚构未来事实的诈骗行为证成

——基于刑法论证的研究视角

韦春发*

摘要：

单向度的刑法解释研究路径基于其理念上的分歧与方法论上的障碍已然陷入了巨大的危机之中，该理论模型无法为“虚构未来事实”之诈骗行为的纷繁争议找寻合理出路。适时实现固有范式的转型是我国刑法学研究应有的方法论觉醒。在以罪刑法定主义为根本遵循的刑法解释的基础上展开刑法论证或将指引“虚构未来事实”之诈骗的理论纷争走出相关误区。以兼顾保障与保护功能的合理性为诉求的刑法论证要求在不放弃对财产法益保护的同时，应在一定限度内承认虚构未来事实之诈骗行为。而未来事实的不确定性特质以及刑法论证具备的最大限度达成共识的固有属性，则要求承认“真伪可辨的未来事实”与“盖然性未来事实”是诈骗行为虚构的对象。

关键词：

刑法论证；虚构未来事实；诈骗行为

我国《刑法》第266条诈骗罪客观构成要件的核心要素当属“诈骗行为”，然而向来的研讨重心多置于被骗人基于认识错误处分财物等诈骗罪的其他客观要件，对作为诈骗行为构成要素的“虚构事实，隐瞒真相”在既有学术研究及司法实务上均缺乏应有的理论关照。因此，本文拟从这一角度为切入点，就“虚构未来事实”能否成为诈骗罪的客观行为方式展开初步研究，以求教于学界师友。

---

* 韦春发，中南财经政法大学刑事司法学院2016级硕士研究生。

一、问题的提出

"虚构事实,隐瞒真相"是我国刑法学界对诈骗行为方式所做界定的主流观点。[1] 学理上通常从形式的字面意义出发将此不成文的要素解释为:"这里的虚构事实是指捏造不存在的事实,隐瞒真相是指掩盖客观存在的事实,从而使被骗人陷入错误认识。"[2]但是这种纯粹的文理解读对于在理论上深化对诈骗行为的认知以及指导刑事司法实践而言,显然意义有限。尤其是我国当前面临着诈骗犯罪高发的基本态势,各种新类型的诈骗行为层出不穷,固守形式意义上的既有解释结论未免有隔靴搔痒之感。故而有必要对该构成要素进一步展开研讨,以期实现对诈骗罪欺诈行为的合理解读。

以"虚构事实"为例,如何理解这里作为虚构对象的所谓"事实"便成为一个无法回避的重要问题。如果以时间维度为观察的视角,事实可以区分为过去的事实,现在的事实以及未来的事实三者,是否虚构上述任何一种事实均可成立诈骗行为不可避免地引起人们的困惑。首先可以明确的是,就前两者亦即过去和现在的事实而言,由于可被证实或证伪,所以可成为虚构的对象自不待言。但作为"未来的事实"因为无法明确其真实性,故而可否予以虚构便存在疑问。有学者梳理德国司法判例后认为:"这里的'事实'必须是过去或现在的事实。行为人向他人谎称将来会发生的事实的,原则上不成立诈骗。因为未来的事实欠缺确定性以及与当前状态的关联性。"[3] 由于基本符合我国刑法理论对"事实"概念的理解加之近年来德国刑法学理被不断引介,这种观点对我国大陆刑法学界理解诈骗行为的"虚构事实"产生了一定范围的影响。以前述我国传统解释为例,所谓"捏造不存在的事实"与"掩盖客观存在的事实"都是指向过去以及现在的"事实"而言的,未来的事实无法判定真伪则无所谓捏造与否,更遑论掩盖"未来事实"。应当指出的是,在我国台湾地区亦有部分刑法学者持类似的见解,如有研究者指出:"仅有能与事实相对应时方可断定是否为虚假;而针

---

〔1〕 参见王作富主编:《刑法分则实务研究》,中国方正出版社2001年版,第1119页。

〔2〕 陈兴良:《规范刑法学》,中国政法大学出版社2003年版,第384页。

〔3〕 王钢:《德国刑法诈骗罪的客观构成要件——以德国司法判例为中心》,载《政治与法律》2014年第10期。

对未来的事实,在实施行为之际不存在可以对照的事实基础,故而无法成立诈骗。"[4]"更何况,所谓事实,必有真伪的内涵,未来之事于当前无法检验真假,所以对于未来之事无法传递不实的信息。"[5]美国刑法理论上也认为:"为构成诈骗罪,虚假陈述必须关系到对现在的或者过去的事实(present or past fact),但不是将来的事实。因为'现在'(审案时)无法证明'将来'究竟怎样,既可能是'虚假'的,也可能是'真实'的。"[6]

然而同以上各国观点截然不同的是,日本刑法学说以及判例却对"虚构未来事实"成立诈骗行为积极地予以肯定。具有代表性的观点,如大塚仁教授认为:"欺骗行为不限于就有关过去的事实和现在的事实进行欺骗,只要行为人违反现在的意思状态进行告知,足以使对方陷入错误,即使就未来的事实进行欺骗也可以。"[7]此外,日本判例也指出:"成立诈骗罪所要求的欺骗,只要通过虚伪的意思表示,使他人陷入错误就够了,其意思表示不以与现在或者过去的事实有关为必要,即使关于未来的事项,如果违反自己现在的意识状态而告知他人,足以使他人陷入错误,也不能认为欠缺诈骗罪的欺骗手段。"[8]

综合以上论述,针对是否可以承认"虚构未来事实"的诈骗行为这一问题,德国和美国持否定论的观点,而日本则持肯定论的见解。我国目前虽然基本上与德美两国相同,否定论的看法相对处于主流的地位,但也有部分学者提出了不同意见,如周光权教授明确指出:"虚构的事实,可以是过去或者现在的事实,也可以是将来的事实;欺诈行为的手段方式没有限制,可以是对事实作出虚假描述,也可以是对事物作出虚假的价值判断或者其他意思表示。"[9]在笔者看来,此问题绝非纯粹的事实真伪的判定,而是在相当程度上还包含着价值的衡

[4] 蔡律师:《刑法分则》,高点文化事业有限公司2001年版,第347页。

[5] 林东茂:《一个知识论上的刑法学思考》,中国人民大学出版社2009年版,第145页。

[6] 储槐植、江溯:《美国刑法》,北京大学出版社2012年版,第203页以下。

[7] [日]大塚仁:《刑法概说(各论)》,冯军译,中国人民大学出版社2003年版,第242页。

[8] [日]日本《大审院刑事判决录》第23辑,第1621页。转引自张明楷:《诈骗罪与金融诈骗罪研究》,清华大学出版社2006年版,第63页。

[9] 周光权:《刑法各论》,中国人民大学出版社2016年版,第125页。

量与选择。肯定说与否定说在根本上所体现的是对刑法功能理解的不同侧重,亦即对刑法的人权保障功能与法益保护功能偏重差异。长久以来,刑法的保障功能与保护功能之间一直存在对立紧张的关系;如果侧重于前者,强调保障功能,则如前述德美两国倾向于否定"虚构未来事实"之诈骗行为;而若偏重于后者,重视保护功能,则如日本主流见解倾向于肯定"虚构未来事实"之诈骗。此外,除却"未来事实"能否被虚构的学理之争以外,对该问题的解答终究无法逸脱于本国的刑事立法与司法实践,同时与本国的刑法理念以及刑法文化等诸多复杂因素均存有一定的关联,亦即是否认可"虚构未来事实"的诈骗实际上体现着刑法解释的基本理念的不同以及在根本上彰显着各国研究者的刑法观的差异。因此,下文拟就我国当前的学术语境下是否应当以及应在何种范围内承认"虚构未来事实"的诈骗行为展开初步研讨。

二、问题背后的刑法解释理念分歧与出路

虽然"法的理念作为真正的正义的最终的和永恒的形态,人在这个世界上既未彻底认识也未充分实现,"[10]但这并不妨碍我们基于刑法论证的研究方法对既有文本做出相对合理的分析解读借以实现刑罚法规的规范保护目的,因为"法律人的技艺就在于论证"。[11] 而厘清"虚构未来事实"诈骗之争背后的解释理念分歧是展开具体的刑法论证的前提,以兼顾保护功能与保障功能的合理性诉求为价值取向的刑法论证或将为解决本文论题提供一条新的路径。

之所以出现本文所提出的"虚构未来事实"之诈骗行为的肯定说与否定说之争,根据笔者的观察,首先集中映射的是我国当前在刑法解释理念上呈现出的以陈兴良教授为代表的形式解释论[12]与以张明楷教授为代表的实质解释论[13]之争。对构成要件要素的解释究竟应立足于何种立场当前尚处于激烈的论争之中,这种学理之争实际上涉及的是刑法解释的边界究竟应当如何加以妥

〔10〕［德］H. 科殷:《法哲学》,林荣远译,华夏出版社 2003 年版,第 10 页。

〔11〕［德］英格博格·普珀:《法学思维小学堂》,蔡圣伟译,北京大学出版社 2011 年版,原著前言第 1 页。

〔12〕参见陈兴良:《形式解释论的再宣示》,载《中国法学》2010 年第 4 期。

〔13〕参见张明楷:《实质解释论的再提倡》,载《中国法学》2010 年第 4 期。

当界定的问题。不少学者纷纷站边表态以致基本形成了两大阵营。在此之前必须指出,本文无意介入这场学术论争之中,只是简要地指出其背后或许存在的一定程度上的学术关联,因为学者们在对诈骗犯罪的构成要件的研究过程中分别以各自的解释理念为指引。实质解释论者认为,如果脱离了构成要件的法益保护目的而对其要素展开纯粹文理意义上的形式解释,如前文所述将“虚构事实”解释为“捏造不存在的事实”是无法得出其准确含义的,毋宁说只是一种用语的简单转换而已;而且这种“字面论”的严格解释态度也无法适应日新月异的社会生活事实,体现在当前的风险社会中则更是如此,因此对“虚构未来事实”的诈骗行为方式在解释论的视域中必须始终在不违背罪刑法定原则的前提下以财产法益的保护目的为指引和依归。而形式解释论者则认为前述实质论者的观点本身即存在违背罪刑法定的嫌疑,其本质上是应受刑罚惩罚性的社会危害性理论在作祟;刑法文本对诈骗行为规定的用语既是解释的出发点,也应当成为解释的最终归宿。不同研究者以各自所秉持的解释理念为指导自然会在具体问题上形成相异的结论,但是,使这场旷日持久的论争变得更为复杂的是,针对具体的构成要素的解释,部分形式解释论者可能会与实质解释论者得出相同的结论;反之亦然,也存在实质论者赞同形式论者的观点,而反对本阵营其他论者见解的现象。诚如邓子斌教授指出:“某位学者所持的观点可能更接近于他的对手,而不是号称与他同一战壕的战友。”〔14〕面对如此硝烟弥漫的论辩,有研究者敏锐地指出:“形式解释论与实质解释论仅仅是一种口号之争,争论依赖于大量的误解而存在,不仅浪费了大量的智力资源,还可能对刑事司法实践产生不利影响。”〔15〕这种论断应当说颇有其合理之处,实际上“只要解释法律就可能会产生多解的结果,会呈现出多种可能的意义。”〔16〕

具体到本文论题,乍看起来,似乎基于形式解释论则应否定“虚构未来事实”之诈骗行为,而若采实质解释似应肯定“虚构未来事实”之诈骗。但本文并不认同此种判断,单就前述我国传统学说为例,将虚构事实形式化地解释为“捏造并不存在的事实”从语义上来说仍能得出“虚构未来事实”的结论,因为“未

〔14〕 邓子斌:《中国实质刑法观批判》,法律出版社2009年版,第7页。

〔15〕 陈坤:《形式解释论与实质解释论刑法解释学上的口号之争》,载陈兴良主编:《刑事法评论》(第31卷),北京大学出版社2012年版,第301页。

〔16〕 陈金钊、焦宝乾:《法律解释学》,中国政法大学出版社2006年版,第15页。

来事实”亦属尚“不存在的事实”,仍有被捏造的空间。反之,实质解释论者也完全可能认为“未来事实”已经超出了“事实”用语所可能具有的含义射程,因而否定其成为虚构对象。由此可见,无论以何种解释理念为依归,都可能对本文论题形成不同观点;这足以说明虚构未来事实可否成立诈骗行为与形式及实质解释理念之间所存在的错综复杂的学术关联。

造成前述复杂现象的原因,在本文看来,表面上是因为现有研究本身对诸如“形式”与“实质”之类的抽象概念尚存在不同理解。除去上述表面上所体现的解释理念上的分野外,如果对本文论题所涉争议进一步深究的话,即可发现更为深层次的原因在于单纯强调主体对文本的解释的固有研究范式已经陷入了巨大的危机之中。追求“真实性”的刑法解释建立在两个基础上:第一,假定并相信解释主体具有发现法律真实的理性能力;第二,假定解释客体即刑法文本的完善与科学。遗憾的是,这两个前提都是不存在的。首先,作为解释主体的人本身只具有相对的理性,即人的理性是有一定的限度的,诚如哈耶克所说:“实际上,对于有意识理性之作用的真正符合理性的洞见,就在于明确指出,理性所具有的最为重要的作用之一便是承认理性控制着自身固有的限度。”[17]其次,刑法文本自身所固有的各种瑕疵终究是我们无法回避的,而且相对稳定的刑法规范与不断变动的社会生活事实之间必然存在脱节现象,所以才导致“法学的永久的重大任务就是要解决生活变动的要求和既定法律的字面含义之间的矛盾”。[18] 因此,纯粹强调刑法解释的传统研究范式已然陷入了目标不明确,根基不可靠与结论不可信等危机之中,有关本文论题的“虚构未来事实”可否成为诈骗行为的纷繁争议所体现的主体差异性即是适例。换言之,第266条的刑法规范本身只能提供一般性的目的,而更具体的目的则应借助于“自由—秩序”的权衡,且难以获得确定性保证,这也是笔者前文所谓有关本文论题实则包含着价值衡量与选择的基本考量。

面临前述刑法解释的困境,本文主张与其沉浸在抽象的理念纷争之中,不如在恪守罪刑法定原则的基础上,对具体构成要件要素的含义展开论证更为妥

---

〔17〕 [英]哈耶克:《哈耶克论文集》,邓正来编译,首都经济贸易大学出版社2001年版,第218页。

〔18〕 [奥]欧根·埃利希:《法社会学原理》,舒国滢译,中国大百科全书出版社2009年版,第442页。

当。实际上"无论采取什么样的立场最终都不可能绕过罪刑法定原则的实质考量;明确这一点之后,就应该将精力放在如何论证刑法解释没有违背罪刑法定原则和没有超过国民的一般预测可能性的问题上。"〔19〕易言之,摒弃以探求文本"真实性"为唯一诉求的解释进路;转换到另一种新的研究范式,即以遵循罪刑法定原则为前提的解释基础上的刑法论证,此种论证应当以"合理性"为价值诉求,同时具有在特定时空条件下最大限度达成共识的固有属性。根据笔者的观察,刑法理论界长期以来实际上已经在以"刑法解释"之名行"刑法论证"之实,因为学者们通常关注的所谓"刑法解释",其重心早已非结论"是什么",而是在探讨何种结论才是"可接受的"或者说是"正当合理的";然而这种以"刑法解释"为名的"刑法论证"实践似乎只是在凭直觉进行,并没有自觉地以刑法论证理论为指导,因而论证失范的局面难以避免。实际上,刑法解释属于"发现"的范畴,而刑法论证则属于"证立"的领域。因此,在刑法适用方法论上必须有所觉醒,应当强调"从'发现'到'证立'的转换以及由'独白式理解'到'沟通式理解'的转变。法律论证理论无疑为此提供了一条可能的进路;这就要求从传统对刑法文本规范的解释转移到对刑法裁判规范的理性证成上。"〔20〕诚如有学者指出:"刑法解释并不能完成刑法适用的任务,刑法适用方法除了涵摄、解释以外,还应当包括论证。"〔21〕实际上,与传统的封闭式的刑法解释模式相比,刑法论证则具有合理性诉求、对话方式以及开放性结构等优势,这为我们解决本文论题的"虚构未来事实"的诈骗提供了基本的方法论指引。

三、虚构未来事实的诈骗行为之刑法论证展开

如前所述,既然刑法的保护与保障功能二者间存在天然的紧张关系,那么试图解决这种对立则是不明智的选择,因为对刑法学理的诸多问题的探讨无外乎在此二者间寻求平衡与折中,从而实现前述双重功能的兼顾。具体到本文论

---

〔19〕 罗世龙:《形式解释论与实质解释论之争的出路》,载《政治与法律》2018年第2期。

〔20〕 武良军:《文本规范的解释到裁判规范的证成——刑法方法论的一种觉醒》,载《法治研究》2018年第3期。

〔21〕 童德华:《外国刑法导论》,中国法制出版社2010年版,第12页。

题亦概莫能外。一概否认对未来事实的虚构实际上是对刑法保护财产法益功能的放弃;诚然,全部肯定此种诈骗行为也存在着刑法过分干预国民行动自由的风险。因此,基于刑法论证的基本研究方法,根据相应的论据在一定范围内肯定“虚构未来事实”的诈骗行为,从而使得本文论题所涉争议达至最大限度的相对共识,借以实现刑法保护与保障功能的同时发挥的合理性诉求是本文的基本目标,以下予以具体展开。

首先,单纯从文本上看,我国《刑法》第 266 条所规定的是“诈骗公私财物,数额较大……”这里并没有明确限定诈骗行为的手段或方法,而“虚构事实,隐瞒真相”本就是从学理上所界定的不成文的构成要件要素,不过这种要素获得了较为普遍的认同而已。因此如果只认可对过去和现在事实的虚构而否认对未来事实的虚构,实际上是在无合理根据的前提下对第 266 条做了限缩解释,这种断然的否定论无益于本条款对财产法益的保护,因而其合理性值得怀疑。其次,既然“虚构事实”本就是不成文的要素,那么将其转换表述为“虚构事件”在本文看来亦未尝不可,进而行为人以非法占有为目的,对“未来事件”进行虚构也是完全有可能的,这也正说明即使只对“虚构事实”做文理解释也不存在肯定“虚构未来事实”的障碍。最后基于体系化的论证方法,纵观我国《刑法》分则的规定,实际上有相当部分条款都蕴含着“虚构未来事实”的意义;比如,第 224 条之一规定的组织、领导传销活动罪,传销组织通常以“未来的重利”诱骗被害人身陷其中,进而实现条文中所明确规定的“骗取财物”,这也正说明传销行为本就是对“未来事实的虚构”,未将其作为诈骗犯罪处理,只是立法者出于刑事政策的考量而只处罚组织者和领导者;再如,第 300 条第 3 款规定:组织、利用会道门、邪教组织、利用迷信诈骗财物等犯罪行为的,依照数罪并罚的规定处罚,而实际上利用邪教或迷信骗取财物通常是就“未来事实”进行虚构的。因此,肯定“虚构未来事实”的诈骗行为也符合我国刑事立法的基本精神。

通常否定“虚构未来事实”是因为未来的事实无法确定其真实性,即无法被证实或者证伪。因此如果认可虚构未来事实的诈骗,一旦后续该事实被客观地实现了,那么将意味着案件定性有误,因而存在一定的审判风险与侵犯人权之虞。然而未来事实果真始终无法判断真伪吗?本文认为未必如此。诚然,“自 1926 年德国科学家海森堡提出测不准原理以来,使得科学界觉察到不确定性是世界上一个基本的不可回避的性质,这对人类世界观产生了非常深远的影响。"[22]未来事实固然有其不确定性的基本特质,但因而便放弃对"虚构未来事实"的认定,这在充满价值判断的刑法学研究中实际上是犯了方法论混淆的错误。恰如齐文远教授指出:"价值判断是整个刑法问题的核心,司法者的利益衡量、目的考量与价值评价贯穿刑法问题的始终。"[23]而且根据笔者的理解,未来事实在一定程度上也是可以判断其真伪的。首先,根据当前公认的科学法则和已经积累的生活经验法则,社会一般公众对于某项未来事实的真伪性可以做出倾向性判断的,行为人对此予以虚构时,当然可径直认定其属"虚构未来事实"的诈骗。再者,如果对某项未来事实虽然在行为之际无法明确其性质,但事后能有充分证据证明行为人系虚构的话,亦可认定其系"虚构未来事实"。换言之,若将"虚构未来事实"的诈骗行为性质本身与对其的证明问题二者予以区分,在一定意义上也可得出"虚构未来事实"的诈骗行为的肯定结论。

如前所述,否定"虚构未来事实"的诈骗行为实则是不当的限缩解读,因而就限制了诈骗犯罪的处罚范围。然而同样是"虚构事实"的骗取财物行为,对一部分行为人认定为诈骗犯罪,而对另一部分则予以放纵,这显然是因为文本解释的差异而导致对部分行为人的不公平对待。再者,同样是针对被害人财物所实施的骗取行为,仅因手段的些微差异便放弃认定,这在相当程度上既是对被害人财产法益之保护的放弃,也有引诱行为人以此方式实施诈骗的嫌疑。例如,"如若未来事实同过去或者现在事实存在一定的牵连关系,故而虚构过去或者现在事实,使被害人针对未来事实的判断陷入错误认知,亦是有可能的。在此场合中,未来事实也可成为诈骗行为的内容。"[24]或者如有学者谨慎地指出:"若是对未来事实发表陈述,虽是一种臆测,但若提供虚伪的资料,作为推测未来事实的佐证的话,仍可认为是使用诈术。"[25]因此,不当缩小诈骗犯罪成立范围的"虚构未来事实"之否定论观点实难为本文所认可。

---

〔22〕 [英]史蒂芬·霍金:《时间简史——从大爆炸到黑洞》,许明贤、吴忠超译,湖南科学技术出版社1996年版,第60页。

〔23〕 齐文远、苏彩霞:《犯罪构成符合性判断的价值属性辩证》,载《法律科学》(西北政法大学学报)2008年第1期。

〔24〕 刁荣华:《刑事判决评释》,汉林出版社1983年版,第212页。

〔25〕 林钰雄:《论诈欺罪之施用诈术》,载《台湾大学法学论丛》2003年第3期。

明确诈骗犯罪的实质，亦能对本文论题的具体论证发挥启发意义。典籍中对于“诈骗”的释义为：“以假冒身份、伪造证明、虚构事实或隐瞒真相等欺诈手段来骗取公私财物以及其他招摇撞骗的行为。”[26]实际上，作为取得型财产罪的诈骗罪，其关键之处在于“骗”，亦即使被骗者陷入错误认知。正如有学者所指出的那样：“诈骗犯罪的核心就在于主观上具有非法占有目的，客观上实施了能够致使他人产生错误认识从而骗取他人财物的行为，欺骗的方法不仅可以是虚构事实或者是隐瞒真相，还应包括‘致他人产生错误认识’的方法。”[27]因此即便行为人针对未来的事实进行陈述和表达，只要其出于非法占有的目的，足以使被骗者陷入处分财物的错误之中，在此种场合承认其属于“虚构未来事实”的诈骗行为亦与诈骗犯罪的精神实质相吻合。甚至有学者在此方面更进一步指出：“因为对将来事实的欺骗也会使人发生错误认识并交付财产，因此，只要符合诈骗罪的犯罪构成，就没有必要区分是过去、现在的事实还是将来的事实。”[28]

日本刑法学界部分对“虚构未来事实”之诈骗持否定论的学者，通常会主张：“如若针对未来事实之‘可能性’实施欺诈，此时应当属于就现在的事实进行的欺骗。”[29]但是，试图明确界分虚构未来事实的可能性与真伪性之间的关系的做法是无法取得成功的，因为此二者间本就存在模糊不清的边缘地带；而且在许多场合，这种观点在最终的结论上与日本主流的肯定“虚构未来事实”之诈骗行为的观点取得了一致。虽然德国主流意见否认“虚构未来事实”的诈骗行为，但是根据笔者的思考，德国学界实际上是将部分针对未来事实进行的虚构转化认定为对过去或现在事实的虚构加以处理的。比如行为人谎称某日将会出现日食奇观，进而高价向被害人兜售天文望远镜的行为；德国学界将此认定为诈骗行为的理由在于：“因为这种科学意义上的未来事件，实际上是以当前的事实(目前相应天体的位置)为基础。基于这一原因，行为人以存在自然规律相

[26] 《辞海》(上册)，上海辞书出版社1989年版，第1023页。

[27] 卢建平：《诈骗行为并不限于“虚构事实隐瞒真相”——以短信诈骗为例》，载《法治研究》2011年第11期。

[28] 黎宏、刘军强：《被害人怀疑对诈骗罪认定影响研究》，载《中国刑事法杂志》2015年第6期。

[29] [日]林幹人：《刑法各论》，东京大学出版会1999年版，第229页。

欺骗,或声称基于科学知识的推断在某时某地会出现某种自然现象时,依然属于就现在的事实进行欺骗。"[30]但是在本文看来,基于被害人的角度,由于根本无法希冀一般公众当时掌握天文科学知识,因此行为之际对此种未来事实的真伪性根本无从判断,故而就此未来事实陷入错误亦是不可避免的,所以将其转化认定为被害人可以判定的现在事实未免牵强。更为重要的是,当无法转化认定之时就将意味着被害人的财产法益不再受到刑法保护。因此,与其转化认定,似不如径直承认"虚构未来事实"的诈骗行为,从而更为周全地实现对财产法益的保护。

在恪守罪刑法定原则的前提下,基于具体解释展开的上述刑法论证表明本文在基本立场上是支持"虚构未来事实"诈骗行为的。简言之,行为人虚构过去及现在的事实无疑成立诈骗,但若针对"未来的事实"进行虚构,足以使被骗人陷入处分财物的错误认知时,当然亦可认定其为"虚构未来事实"的诈骗行为;应当将"虚构未来事实"的诈骗行为本身与对其的证明问题二者予以严格区分,不能因为未来事实存在证明真伪上的困难,便否定对其虚构行为具有的诈骗性质。

四、有限范围内"虚构未来事实"的诈骗行为厘定

基于前述理由虽然应当积极地肯定虚构未来事实的诈骗行为,但是根据刑法论证研究所要求的兼顾保护与保障功能之合理性诉求,为有效避免刑法过度干预的风险,因而在不放弃对财产法益保护的同时只能在有限范围内对此予以承认,如此方能达至前述刑法论证所要实现的最大限度共识。下文拟就这一"有限范围"展开简要讨论。

(一)基于"不确定性"对未来事实的再分类略论

我们对"客观事实"这一概念本身实际上长期存在一定程度的误解。我国台湾地区有学者指出:"事实是指现在或者过去的具体历程或者状态,并且具有可以验证其为真或伪之性质者;虚构事实是指对被害人宣称虚伪的事实,操弄或扭曲事实真相,经由断章取义等手法将事实的某些部分予以添加或省略,以

[30] 王钢:《德国判例刑法(分则)》,北京大学出版社2016年版,第196页以下。

达成掩盖事实整体真相的目的。"[31]而实际上,所谓现在或过去的具体历程与状态,单纯看来好像是明确和单义的,但这并非代表着我们可以将存在于某一时点的全体事实描述出来。换言之,即使针对过去或者现在的事实,"有鉴于事实环节的不可穷尽性以及人类认知能力的局限性,在现实世界中不可能会有一种完整的事实描述,亦即当我们在描述一个'客观事实'时,绝对不可能观察到所有的细节,只可能描述整体事实的极小片段。"[32]由此我们即可发现,其实"不确定性"并非"未来事实"所独有的特质,所谓的"客观事实"本身都多少存在一定程度上的不确定性,只是"未来事实"的"不确定性"表现得至为明显罢了。所以,在研究诈骗罪特殊行为方式的"虚构未来事实"的场合,有必要对"未来事实"的范围做出基本限定,以免因其鲜明的"不确定性"特征而有碍国民自由的刑法保障。如前所述,诈骗罪所谓"虚构事实"本就是不成文的构成要素,其实将其表述为"虚构事件"或者"虚构信息"亦未尝不可。比如,在证券期货等资本市场中,"每一个证券交易的完成都必然涉及大量证券信息的披露、搜集、整理和分析,证券投资本质上就是关于信息的处理和博弈过程。"[33]而这些投资与交易中通常存在大量的真假信息,其中亦不乏涉及未来的真伪"信息"或者说"事实"。因此,如果对作为诈骗行为虚构对象的"未来事实"缺乏应有的合理界定,则势必导致国民行动自由在相当程度上的萎缩,而这已然背离了诈骗罪的立法初衷。

在前述基于时间的维度将事实划分为过去、现在以及未来三者的基础之上,本文提倡将"未来事实"根据其可被判断程度的高低为标准进一步划分为:真伪可辨的未来事实、盖然性未来事实以及或然性未来事实三者。此分类首先实现了在概率论的意义上对未来事实的把握,其次也助益于对虚构未来事实之诈骗行为的具体范围的权衡,更为重要的是其与未来事实最为显见的不确定性特征相契合。既然应当将对虚构未来事实的证明问题与虚构未来事实本身相区分,那么针对以上三种可被不同程度判断的未来事实,自然应当提出不同的证明标准要求。

---

〔31〕 林钰雄:《论诈欺罪之施用诈术》,载《台湾大学法学论丛》2003年第3期。

〔32〕 蔡圣伟:《重新检视因果历程偏离之难题》,载《东吴法律学报》2008年第1期。

〔33〕 于秀峰:《证券犯罪经济学分析》,法律出版社2008年版,第19页。

(二)虚构未来事实之诈骗的有限范围廓清

首先,在对未来事实作进一步分类基础上,我们发现虽然无法在对案件定性之际完全明确某项具体未来事实的真伪性,但对此也绝非无据可查。在科学技术高速发展的当下,根据相应的科学知识、自然规律以及社会公众一般予以认可的日常生活经验法则,如果对于某项未来事实的真伪性可以做出相对明确的倾向性判断意见,此种事实我们称其为"真伪可辨的未来事实";行为人若对该未来事实予以虚构,足以使被骗人陷入处分财物的错误认识时,可以认定其属于"虚构未来事实"的诈骗行为。这方面比较典型的案例有如前文所述的传销行为,现实中的传销手段固然是千变万化的,但其共同的特点在于向被骗者虚构短期的未来时段能获得重大收益;然而根据普通民众的生活经验以及经济学常识,此种显然违背经济运行规律的所谓"投资收益"实则就是行为人对"真伪可辨的未来事实之虚构";如果否定对此种未来事实的虚构,实际上是模糊了传销行为所暗含的诈骗性质。再如,现实中常见的利用迷信手段骗取财物的行为,通常也是就"未来事实"进行虚构的。例如,算命者向被害人谎称其在近期将有灾祸临头而骗取财物的,根据理智的社会公众的一般智识,对该所谓的未来灾祸明显可以做出其系虚构的倾向性判断意见,因而认定其属于"虚构未来事实"的诈骗行为无论在学理抑或经验上都并不存在障碍。概言之,如果某项未来事实的真伪性可以根据现有智识得出相对明确的倾向性判断结论时,在行为人对该"真伪可辨的未来事实"予以虚构使得被骗者陷入错误的场合,应当认定其行为系"虚构未来事实"的诈骗行为。应当强调的是,对虚构"真伪可辨的未来事实"的诈骗行为,在证明标准上必须由控诉一方提供确实充分的判断资料与判断依据。

其次,如果某事项立足于当下的认真考量,对其真伪性能做出高度盖然性的把握时,即某事实在未来实现或者不实现可能性显著偏高而能被我们掌握的场合,对此我们称其为"盖然性未来事实"。此种未来事实的真伪性虽然无法像前述真伪可辨的那样能够做出相对明确的倾向性判断意见,但由于在概率的意义上仍然能就其做出一定程度上的把握,所以当行为人基于非法占有的目的,虚构此种"盖然性未来事实"使被骗者陷入错误时,可以将其定性为"虚构未来事实"的诈骗行为。应当附带指出的是,司法实践中对虚构"盖然性未来事实"之诈骗行为的证明标准应达到排除合理怀疑的程度,这既是《刑事诉讼法》第53条的明确规定,也是对某项未来事实的"高度盖然性"所提出的应然证明要求。其所追求的"目的在于确保疑罪从无的人权保障理念的彻底实现,减少案件错判风险。"[34]

最后,所谓"或然性未来事实"则是指某事项在当前完全无从判断其未来实现与否的可能性,亦即不存在充分可供判定的资料与判断依据。行为人对此种未来事实的叙述,本文主张不成为虚构未来事实的诈骗行为。基本的理由在于,既然对该或然性未来事实的真伪性完全无从判断,那么该项事实在未来同时具有实现或者不实现的可能,此时动辄将行为人对此种未来事实的主观评估性叙述以诈骗行为论处,既存在前文中所提出的司法误认的定性风险,亦不免因刑法的过分干预而导致不当地限制了国民的行动自由。易言之,对于"或然性未来事实"这种疑点利益应当归属于被告人所享有;之所以如此,是因为对此种案件事实的疑问,坚守有利于被告的原则"根植于其深厚的神学、道德、法学与人权理论之中,并得到了法官的良心、社会的宽容、国家的责任与个人的自由等多种理念的支撑"。[35] 否认此时的"虚构或然性未来事实"之诈骗亦可谓在尊重《刑法》第266条对财产法益的保护之基础上,同时为行为人的人权保障留下了相当的空间。实际上,许多否定"虚构未来事实"之诈骗行为的论者所反对的大多应是这里所提出的"或然性未来事实",而未必是前述两种"真伪可辨"以及"盖然性"未来事实。诚然也会有论者质疑本文对未来事实所进行的前述"盖然性"与"或然性"的区分缺乏可供明确判断的标准,进而无法得出相应结论;但是笔者窃以为以此为由否定本文以上对未来事实的划分实则是陷入了相对主义的泥潭之中了,因为对任何一种事实的评判终究都要由人们根据自身理性与经验做出判定。

结合以上讨论,本文主张,有鉴于未来事实所具备的鲜明"不确定性"特征,应当将其进一步划分为真伪可辨的未来事实、盖然性未来事实以及或然性未来事实三者;而虚构未来事实的诈骗行为仅能在前两种未来事实的有限范围内予以承认,对于真伪可辨的未来事实在对其证明上要求控诉一方提供确实充分的判断资料与判断依据,而对于盖然性未来事实在证明标准上则要求至少达到刑事控诉的最低限度即排除合理怀疑的程度,而且应当允许被告人对其予以反证

---

〔34〕 何荣功:《刑法适用也应遵循"排除合理怀疑"》,载《检察日报》2017年7月6日,第3版。

〔35〕 邢馨宇:《存疑时有利于被告的根据》,载《法学》2013年第11期。

进而推翻指控。至于或然性未来事实,既然对其无从把握与判断,则应坚持将此类案件事实的疑点利益归属于被告,不再将行为人对此种未来事实的叙述与评判认定为"虚构未来事实"之诈骗行为,借以实现有效避免司法定性风险的同时切实保障国民的基本权利与行动自由。

五、余论:刑法论证理论的研究前景展望

基于刑法论证的研究视角与方法,上文对"虚构未来事实"的诈骗行为做了初步的分析与解读。虽就该具体论题已然得出相应结论,但仍有必要从一般意义上对"刑法论证"这一尚未引起学界足够重视的刑法适用方法略作说明与展望,以为后续研究之基础。

以"虚构未来事实"之诈骗行为的理论争议为例,我们可以清晰地窥见以真实性作为唯一诉求的刑法解释路径有鉴于理念上的分歧必将陷入目标不明确、根基不可靠与结论不可信等巨大的危机之中,单向度的刑法解释已然无法承担起指导具体问题研讨的使命。因此,必须实现刑法方法论的适时转型,本文提倡在以恪守罪刑法定原则为根本遵循的刑法解释基础上展开具体的刑法论证。此种论证以"主体间"的对话之基本方式实现兼顾刑法的人权保障功能与法益保护功能的合理性诉求,而且这一合理性诉求实际上内含法律论证所具有的最大限度达成共识的固有属性。虽然有学者对"主体间性"这一概念尚抱持质疑态度,如刘艳红教授指出:"德日刑法教义学中的一些概念,如'主体间性'等可能与中国刑法理论及实践之间存在水土不服。"[36] 但是本文以为,我国刑法学界目前盛行的主客体间的刑法解释是"独白式"的,其在结构上是封闭的;而本文倡导的主体间的刑法论证则是"商谈式"的,具有开放性的结构特征;在解释的基础上建构多边的对话、商谈与论证机制对于走出诸多刑法学理的困境颇有益处。上文对"虚构未来事实"诈骗行为的初步论证与探讨正是适例。再者,诚如德国学者阿图尔·考夫曼等指出:"法的发现不仅仅是一种被动的推论行为,而是一种构建行为。法的发现者一同进入行为过程,这意味着法不是实体的事物;毋宁是,一切法具有关系特征,法是某种联系的事物,它存在于人的相互关

---

〔36〕 刘艳红:《中国刑法教义学化过程中的五大误区》,载《环球法律评论》2018年第3期。

系中。至于这种法思维，只能存在一种敞开的体系，在敞开的体系中只能存在‘主体间性’乃是不言而喻的。”〔37〕

展望未来对刑法论证理论的后续研究，本文窃以为应当着重注意以下几点。首先，“实在法规范是刑法的基础，应该理解刑法规范，但更重要的是应该规范地理解刑法”。〔38〕因此，任何形式的刑法论证都必须以规范化的刑法理念为指引，脱离刑法规范本身的所谓论证终将成为无本之木，且有背离罪刑法定原则的倾向。其次，在法哲学层面上继续深化法律论证的相关基础理论探讨以为具体的刑法问题论证奠定理论根基。例如，虽然在法律论证中经常遭遇“无限倒退，循环论证以及武断地中止论证”〔39〕的“明希豪森—三重困境”，但是我们也应当充分注意到当代德国思想家哈贝马斯通过提出交往行动理论与交往理性概念，认为生活世界中的真理就是一种共识，以“真理共识论”取代“真理符合论”。易言之，实践中验证法律规则与司法决定的正确性往往依靠一定范围的“共识”。总之，“‘正确性’意味着合理的、由好的理由所支持的可接受性。确定一个判断有效性的，当然是它的有效性条件被满足，不可能通过直接诉诸经验证据和理想直接提供的事实，而只能以商谈的方式，确切地说通过以论辩的方式而实施的论证过程”。〔40〕以上这些观念不失为展开具体刑法论证的重要理论指引。最后，刑法论证作为刑法适用的理性的实践活动，需要一系列的论证规则来保证。这些规则的作用在于保证在刑法论证的过程中，主体间能够理性地讨论相关论题，使论证活动得以理性地进行，使具体的刑法适用可以避免武断的意见并建立在充分论证的基础上，即对刑法论证的具体规则与方法的探讨应成为后续的研究方向之一。

概言之，在法哲学维度的法律论证理论的基石上，立足于刑法规范本身，以具体的论证规则与方法为保障的建立在解释基础上的刑法论证应当成为刑法

---

〔37〕［德］阿图尔·考夫曼、温弗里德·哈斯默尔：《当代法哲学和法律理论导论》，郑永流译，法律出版社2002年版，第146页。

〔38〕冯军：《刑法问题的规范理解》，北京大学出版社2009年版，第62页。

〔39〕参见［德］罗伯特·阿列克西：《法律论证理论——作为法律证立理论的理性论辩理论》，舒国滢译，中国法制出版社2002年版，第221页、代译序，第1页以下。

〔40〕［德］哈贝马斯：《在事实与规范之间——关于法律与民主法治国的商谈理论》，童世骏译，生活·读书·新知三联书店2003年版，第278页。

适用方法论的重要研究课题。在价值多元化时代,摒弃固有的单向度的刑法解释研究范式以适时实现刑法适用方法论的理论转型,充分挖掘刑法论证这一富矿应当成为我国刑法学界的理论自觉。最后,必须承认的是,笔者以"虚构未来事实"的诈骗行为为切入点对刑法论证理论的探讨仍旧颇为粗浅,观点与逻辑的挣扎或仍隐于其中,若有幸成为批判的对象亦可谓实现了本文的价值;而对于刑法论证这一论域中的更多困惑,尚有待后续研究不断予以推进。

(责任编辑:秦喆予)

驰名商标权利边界初探

陈 铄*

摘要：

驰名商标的特殊保护制度——跨类保护制度，在适用过程中容易出现驰名商标权利边界被不当扩大的问题，为了准确把握驰名商标的权利边界，可以从立法和司法两个角度着手。立法方面，提高驰名商标认定的公众范围标准，采用“一般公众标准”。司法方面，在认定驰名商标时，应当坚持“全国范围标准”，将驰名商标淡化的证明标准确定为“实际损害标准”。最后，司法人员才可以对满足相应条件的驰名商标进行跨类保护。

关键词：

驰名商标；权利边界；全国范围标准；实际损害标准；一般公众标准

引　言

驰名商标作为一种享有盛誉的商标，不仅用于区分商品或者服务来源，其还代表着优质的商品质量与良好的企业形象。因此，《中华人民共和国商标法》（以下简称《商标法》）以及最高人民法院颁布的相关司法解释等都对驰名商标特殊保护问题作了专门规定，赋予其更大的权利边界。

但是在司法实践中，却出现不当扩大驰名商标权利边界的问题，这与商标法立法本意背道而驰，极大地损害了社会公共利益。要解决这一问题，笔者认为重中之重在于对驰名商标的权利边界予以准确、清晰的界定。

* 陈铄，中山大学法学院 2018 级硕士研究生。

一、驰名商标权利边界不当扩大

(一)驰名商标权利边界不当扩大的表现

随着经济的发展,市场经营者不再满足于在经营范围内使用商标,并开始利用商标形成的影响力开展跨行业经营。此时,如果其他经营者在不相同、不相类似的商品或者服务上使用相同或者近似商标,会使得具有极大影响力的商标的商誉被降低。因此,跨类保护制度应运而生。

我国目前涉及驰名商标保护制度的法律法规众多。2002年最高人民法院发布的《关于审理商标民事纠纷案件适用法律若干问题的解释》第1条列举规定了究竟何种行为属于对驰名商标的侵权行为;[1]最高人民法院2009年在《关于审理涉及驰名商标保护的民事纠纷案件应用法律若干问题的解释》中第9条通过对"容易导致混淆"以及"误导公众,致使该驰名商标注册人的利益可能受到损害"作出详细的解释,更加细化了跨类保护的相关规定。[2] 正式阐述驰名商标的跨类保护制度,标志着跨类保护制度的建立的是2013年全国人大修订的《商标法》;[3]2017年最高人民法院在《关于审理商标授权确权行政案件若干问题

---

〔1〕《关于审理商标民事纠纷案件适用法律若干问题的解释》第1条:

下列行为属于商标法第五十二条第(五)项规定的给他人注册商标专用权造成其他损害的行为:……(二)复制、摹仿、翻译他人注册的驰名商标或其主要部分在不相同或者不相类似商品上作为商标使用,误导公众,致使该驰名商标注册人的利益可能受到损害的……

〔2〕《关于审理涉及驰名商标保护的民事纠纷案件应用法律若干问题的解释》第9条:

足以使相关公众对使用驰名商标和被诉商标的商品来源产生误认,或者足以使相关公众认为使用驰名商标和被诉商标的经营者之间具有许可使用、关联企业关系等特定联系的,属于商标法第十三条第一款规定的"容易导致混淆"。足以使相关公众认为被诉商标与驰名商标具有相当程度的联系,而减弱驰名商标的显著性、贬损驰名商标的市场声誉,或者不正当利用驰名商标的市场声誉的,属于商标法第十三条第二款规定的"误导公众,致使该驰名商标注册人的利益可能受到损害"。

〔3〕《中华人民共和国商标法》第13条:

为相关公众所熟知的商标,持有人认为其权利受到侵害时,可以依照本法规定请求驰名商标保护。

就相同或者类似商品申请注册的商标是复制、摹仿或者翻译他人未在中国注册的驰名商标,容易导致混淆的,不予注册并禁止使用。

就不相同或者不相类似商品申请注册的商标是复制、摹仿或者翻译他人已经在中国注册的驰名商标,误导公众,致使该驰名商标注册人的利益可能受到损害的,不予注册并禁止使用。

的规定》中也强调,对于驰名商标的保护必须要与其驰名度相适应。[4] 除此之外,《中华人民共和国反不正当竞争法》等其他法律法规也对驰名商标的跨类保护作了详细的规定,这些内容构成了驰名商标的跨类保护体系。

制定跨类保护制度,除有利于弥补传统商标法适用的混淆理论的不足之外,也可更好地维护消费者的合法利益。

但是,面对驰名商标的跨类保护制度,不少驰名商标持有人开始将其当作自己的"尚方宝剑",试图绝对禁止其他市场竞争主体在相同、类似或者不相同、不类似的商品上注册或者使用与自身商标相同或者近似的商标,妄图建立起自己的"商标霸权"。

本文从北大法宝、中国裁判文书网、威科先行以及无讼网等权威数据库收集最高人民法院及全国各地法院审理的关于驰名商标跨类保护的案件,表1列出相关典型案例的裁决文书,具体情况见表1、表2。

表1 认定不构成商标淡化的案件

案号	涉及商标	驰名认定	裁判结论	具体理由
北京知识产权法院(2016)京73行初2882号行政判决书	飞科	是	不构成淡化	争议商标指定使用的电动自行车等商品与原告商标据以知名的剃须刀等商品在功能、用途、销售渠道、销售场所以及消费对象等方面差距明显。原告亦没有证据证明其剃须刀商品与电动自行车商品之间具有关联性。相关公众在看到电动自行车上的争议商标时很难联想到飞科公司所提供的剃须刀产品,二者之间缺乏关联性。不会导致相关公众的混淆、误认,致使飞科公司的利益受损

[4] 《关于审理商标授权确权行政案件若干问题的规定》第13条:

当事人依据商标法第十三条第三款主张诉争商标构成对其已注册的驰名商标的复制、摹仿或者翻译而不应予以注册或者应予无效的,人民法院应当综合考虑如下因素,以认定诉争商标的使用是否足以使相关公众认为其与驰名商标具有相当程度的联系,从而误导公众,致使驰名商标注册人的利益可能受到损害:

(一)引证商标的显著性和知名程度;

(二)商标标志是否足够近似;

(三)指定使用的商品情况;

(四)相关公众的重合程度及注意程度;

(五)与引证商标近似的标志被其他市场主体合法使用的情况或者其他相关因素。

续表

案号	涉及商标	驰名认定	裁判结论	具体理由
北京知识产权法院(2016)京73行初7030号行政判决书	槟卡	是	不构成淡化	本案中广州紫曦公司主张引证商标构成驰名的商品主要为"服装"商品,与诉争商标核定使用的第29类"香肠"等商品类别差异较大。因此,诉争商标使用在指定商品上,不致误导公众,致使广州紫曦公司的利益可能受到损害

纵观上述案件可知,跨类保护制度的立足点依然在于标识与特定商品或服务之间的联系,而非致力于形成"强者通吃"的局面。如表1所列案例,虽然原告所持有的商标都被认定为驰名商标,但是对其并非绝对进行跨类保护,应当综合考虑涉案商标的驰名程度、被诉商标与原告驰名商标核定使用的商品或者服务类别的关联性等因素。

表2　认定构成商标淡化的案件

案号	涉及商标	驰名认定	裁判结论	具体理由
湖北省武汉市中级人民法院(2005)武知初字第31号民事判决书	好太太	是	构成淡化	被告的上述行为足以使相关消费者混淆两件商品生产者的来源,给原告的利益造成损害
云南省昆明市中级人民法院(2005)民六初字第77号民事判决书	吉利	是	构成淡化	被告未经原告许可,擅自在其生产销售的衬衫上使用原告的"吉利"商标,并且在对其商品的宣传中采用使公众误认其商品与原告有关联性的宣传语句,其行为已构成对原告驰名商标的侵犯
广东省揭阳市中级人民法院(2006)揭中法民三初字第4号民事判决书	榕泰	是	构成淡化	被告未经原告许可,擅自将"榕泰"作为商品标识使用在其销售的雨伞上,误导公众,致使原告的利益可能受到损害,被告的行为已构成侵权

续表

案号	涉及商标	驰名认定	裁判结论	具体理由
山东省淄博市中级人民法院(2006)淄民三初字第3号民事判决书	扳倒井	是	构成淡化	被告将与原告商标近似的标识使用在其商品、包装材料等之上,就是想利用原告的良好声誉,这种行为将会降低原告的商标在公众心目中唯一且独特的商标形象,损害原告的利益,淡化原告的商标
北京市第一中级人民法院(2009)一中行初字1589号行政判决书	伊利	是	构成淡化	“伊利”商标系驰名商标,被告将“伊利”商标用在水龙头等商品之上,尽管这类商品在生产、销售等方面与伊利公司并没有太大的联系,一般情况下很难引起公众的混淆,但被告的这种行为客观上减弱了“伊利”作为驰名商标的显著性
上海市浦东新区人民法院(2012)浦民三(知)初字第330号民事判决书	Cartier	是	构成淡化	被告的上述行为极大可能会吸引相关公众对其商品的注意并产生错误认识,在客观上会造成减弱原告商标的显著性、降低原告商标标识作用的严重后果
最高人民法院(2013)行提字第3号行政判决书	全友 QUAN YOU	是	构成淡化	被异议商标的申请注册足以误导相关公众,致使全友家私公司的利益受到损害,违反了《商标法》第13条第2款的规定,故不应予以注册
北京市高级人民法院(2014)高行(知)终字第2201号行政判决书	中信	是	构成淡化	当相关公众看到使用在玻璃钢容器、非金属容器等商品上的被异议商标时,容易联想到驰名的引证商标(核准使用于第36类金融服务),并误认为二者的提供者之间存在投资、合作等关联关系,弱化驰名的引证商标与中信集团之间的对应关系,在客观上利用了驰名引证商标的市场声誉,从而损害中信集团的利益
北京市高级人民法院(2017)京民终76号民事判决书	老干妈	是	构成淡化	将“老干妈”字样标注在涉案商品包装上的行为,客观上造成的后果是消费者会误认为涉案商品与“老干妈”字样所指向的贵阳老干妈公司之间存在特定的联系

续表

案号	涉及商标	驰名认定	裁判结论	具体理由
最高人民法院(2017)最高法行申1038号行政裁定书	吉普JEEP	是	构成淡化	被异议商标使用在关联度较高的广告等服务类别上,易导致相关公众误以为上述服务与引证商标一、二所指向的“汽车”商品存在某种特定联系,从而减弱和淡化该在先驰名商标的显著性
北京知识产权法院(2018)京73行初1733号行政判决书	来福士	是	构成淡化	第三人住所地处于上海,与原告的“来福士广场”项目同处一地,其注册诉争商标“来福士”明显具有攀附他人商标的不正当意图。且引证商标二在“不动产管理;不动产出租”服务项目上经过长期使用和宣传在诉争商标申请日前已构成驰名商标,诉争商标在核定使用办公家具等商品上的注册构成对他人驰名商标的复制、摹仿,容易误导公众,从而使该原告的利益可能受到损害

但是笔者发现,在涉及驰名商标跨类保护问题的案件之中,一些涉案的驰名商标的权利边界被不合理地扩大了。

具体而言,如“榕泰”商标权纠纷一案中,[5]原告“榕泰”注册商标的核定使用商品为第1类多聚甲醛等化学品,因此其消费群体显然不是普通大众消费者;而被告所销售的商品为“榕泰”牌雨伞,恰恰是面向普通大众进行销售的商品。即便“榕泰”在其所处的特定行业享有较高的声誉,但是对于被告商品的相关公众——日常消费者来说,他们很难知晓该商标,被误导的可能性非常小。但在该案中,主审法院却给予了广东“榕泰”跨类保护,这非常值得商榷。

再如表2中曾引起广泛关注的吉利汽车状告“吉利”衬衣侵权案件中,[6]原告吉利公司在第12类商品上注册了“吉利”商标,此外,还在其他30多种类

〔5〕 参见广东省揭阳市中级人民法院“榕泰”商标权纠纷一审民事判决书,(2006)揭中法民三初字第4号。

〔6〕 参见云南省昆明市中级人民法院“吉利”商标侵权纠纷案民事判决书,(2005)民六初字第77号。

别的商品上分别进行了注册，但并未涵盖被告生产销售的衬衫这个类别的商品。“吉利”牌汽车具有较大的特殊性，与衬衫这类商品相比属于“奢侈品”，“吉利”衬衫的消费者不一定知道“吉利”牌汽车，若将相对较小的相关公众扩大到更大范围的相关公众，则认定的保护范围将无疑被扩大。因此，对于法院在此案中给予的保护跨类，我们不难得出该裁决在一定程度上是对“吉利”商标不合理地进行跨类保护的结论。

存在类似问题的还有“吉普”商标纠纷案。[7] 驰名商标“吉普”核定使用的商品类别是汽车类商品，但是被异议商标指定使用的是第 35 类商品，即“广告；进出口代理；推销（替他人）；拍卖；替他人采购（替其他企业购买商品或服务）”等服务。法院将“吉普”商标的权利边界从汽车类商品跨越到第 35 类商品，但是在说理部分存在严重的不足，并没有将被异议商标的这种使用将会带来的“误导公众，致使该驰名商标注册人的利益可能受到损害的”这一侵权要件论述清楚。毕竟这两类商品服务类别是存在较大的不同的，究竟“吉普”商标的影响力是否可以有如此大范围的跨越，法院的论述仍然不具有较大的说服力。

（二）驰名商标权利边界不当扩大的危害

我国商标法旨在维护多方权益，进而促进社会主义市场经济的发展。[8] 其赋予商标权人的权利只是在合理范围内对注册商标享有的使用并且禁止他人使用的权利，而非致力于形成“一统天下”的局面，否则将带来极大的危害。

1. 对于市场秩序的危害

（1）限制其他经营者的自由

以上文的“榕泰”一案为例，法院在审判时，忽略了原告商标所核定使用的商品类别与被告商品类别存在的极大的差距，笼统地给予该商标跨类保护的权利，将原告驰名商标的权利边界从第一类化学品延伸到雨伞之上，进而认定被告侵权。这将导致其他经营者失去正当使用“榕泰”这个商标的自由。

（2）片面追求驰名商标的认定

在驰名商标权过度扩张的刺激下，将会产生这么一种恶性循环——商标权

[7] 参见最高人民法院“吉普”商标纠纷案行政裁定书，（2017）最高法行申 1038 号。

[8] 《中华人民共和国商标法》第 1 条：为了加强商标管理，保护商标专用权，促使生产、经营者保证商品和服务质量，维护商标信誉，以保障消费者和生产、经营者的利益，促进社会主义市场经济的发展，特制定本法。

人为了在这种市场垄断中获得一席之位,将开始迷信驰名商标的作用,想方设法来做好自己的商标宣传,不惜投入巨资来营造品牌形象,甚至舍本求末,将很多本应该用于研发或者提高产品质量的投资纳入这种广告宣传中,忽视了竞争硬实力的提高。

据新闻报道,某知名品牌主要依靠广告投资来打开市场,品牌的广告投资居然占据该公司募股所集资金的90%以上,而真正投入研发的费用不超过3%。更值得玩味的是,这家公司也因为巨额的广告投资而获得业绩的迅速上升。[9]

2. 对于消费者权益的危害

驰名商标权利边界不当扩大的问题愈演愈烈,其实,市场中的消费者才是最后的受害者。

如上文所述,不少市场竞争者会开始投入大量资金用于打造自己的驰名商标,甚至因此忽视了对于产品质量、性能等的研发投资。也就是说,驰名商标所标识的商品的质量将会慢慢与驰名商标的"盛名"脱节,最后,面对市场上琳琅满目的"驰名商标商品",消费者就不得不在心里打上一个问号,自己究竟是否可以相信这些所谓的驰名商标商品。这在无形中会增加消费者的购买成本和搜寻成本。

可见,为了维护驰名商标,我们可以对之进行特殊保护,进行一定的权利边界扩张,但是驰名商标的权利边界不可过度扩大也不可模糊化,否则便是在放纵"权利灌木丛"的生长。

二、驰名商标权利边界不当扩大的原因

对于驰名商标权利边界不当扩大的原因,我们主要从理论、立法以及司法3个方面进行探讨。

(一)理论基础的缺陷

《商标法》第13条第3款中规定的"误导公众"一词,一般看来,是体现了混淆理论。但是通过体系解释,我们可以观察到,最高人民法院于2009年颁布的《关于审理涉及驰名商标保护的民事纠纷案件应用法律若干问题的解释》中,对

〔9〕 参见姚鹤徽:《商标法基本问题研究》,知识产权出版社2015年版,第260页。

"误导公众"进行了详细的解释,一旦足以让相关公众认为被告使用的商标与原告被认定驰名的商标具有某种程度的联系,进而降低驰名商标的显著性、市场声誉,或者不正当利用其市场声誉的,就构成了"误导",这正好与淡化理论中的弱化及丑化这两种表现形式相对应,是典型的商标淡化情形。这已经不再是简单停留在混淆理论之上了,可以说明,我国已经引入了淡化理论,我国的跨类保护制度就是建立在淡化理论的基础之上的。

同时,通过对适用跨类保护制度的裁判文书的梳理,我们不难发现,法院在处理驰名商标跨类保护案件时,大多都不约而同采用了"淡化"一词。可见,在我国司法实践中,法院开始越来越多地间接甚至直接适用淡化理论。

淡化理论有其合理之处,我国引进淡化理论对驰名商标进行跨类保护是符合时代潮流的。但是我国目前的驰名商标权利边界不当扩大的问题与淡化理论本身的缺陷有着不可分割的关系。

1. 淡化理论还未足够成熟

淡化理论在现今还未真正发展成熟,对于淡化的主要表现形式如弱化、丑化等至今仍然没有较为统一且明确的定义,McCarthy 教授就曾经公开感慨,在其与知识产权法接触的四十多年中,会像"商标淡化"的概念一样,产生如此多的学说困惑和司法误读的商标法内容,是从未有过的。[10]

司法人员在适用淡化理论进行跨类保护的大多数情况下,对于究竟是否造成淡化、这种淡化是如何体现的,都说不出一二。那么这种跨类保护的适用就成了经不起推敲的结论。驰名商标的权利边界被不正当地扩大也是难以避免的了。

2. 淡化理论可能带来的商标垄断

适用淡化理论根本无需证明消费者是否产生混淆,商标权人可以在不证明混淆甚至根本不存在混淆的情况下以行为人的行为误导公众、损害自身商标权益为由以跨类保护制度为请求权基础寻求司法救济。

可以说淡化理论在一定程度上抛弃了混淆理论,其直接赋予某些商标更大的权利边界,使得市场上不同商标的保护程度有了更大的差异,这有时候就会与其他厂家正当参与市场竞争的权益相冲突。比如,一个新的市场主体为了降

---

〔10〕 See Thomas McCarthy,"Dilution of A Trademark: European and United States Law Compared",*The Trademark Reporter* 6,2004,p. 1163.

低进入市场的难度,可能会选择一个与某个驰名商标相同或者相似的商标,将之使用于与该驰名商标不相同、不相类似的商品之上,通过区别宣传让消费者意识到自己与原先的市场主体不存在联系,从而消费者亦不会发生混淆,该驰名商标的显著性与识别性也并没有因此受到影响,商誉也不会受到破坏,同时也有助于该市场主体进入不相关市场。

但是淡化理论之下,如果没有严格把握好判断尺度,这样的行为就很大可能被认定构成淡化,需要承担商标侵权责任。驰名商标权人在无形中垄断了其所持有的驰名商标。[11]

可见目前的淡化理论在适用中还是亟待完善的,而目前这些缺陷的存在将使驰名商标的权利边界划定问题变得更加扑朔迷离。

(二)配套立法的缺陷:驰名商标认定标准中公众范围标准

从驰名商标保护制度的历史发展沿革可以看出,驰名商标的保护体系正在不断地完善,但是,作为进入保护体系的敲门砖——驰名商标认定制度,却存在一定的缺陷。

1. 我国驰名商标认定标准中的公众范围标准:“相关公众标准”

驰名商标认定标准中的公众范围标准是涉及驰名商标认定的重要影响因素。究竟商标要在多大的公众范围内驰名才可以称为驰名商标。我国对此问题较明确地采用了“相关公众标准”,即商标只需要在其使用的商品的消费者和业界人士中驰名即可。

2. “相关公众标准”的缺陷

(1)“相关公众标准”违背淡化理论的初衷

跨类保护制度是建立在淡化理论的基础之上的,而非传统的混淆理论。如“伊利被注册成水龙头商标”一案,[12]被告在冲水马桶、水龙头等卫生设备上申

---

〔11〕 杜颖认为:对知识产权的过度保护有可能导致少数人掌控威胁力,造成社会分配不公平。对商标权的过度保护严重威胁着社会福祉,并将商标法原来以欺诈为基础建立起来的竞争平衡关系置于险境,因为以财产权为基础确立的商标法律制度呈现反竞争特性,它制造市场控制力——商标垄断,带来效率损失。参见杜颖:《商标法律制度的失衡及其理性回归》,载《中国法学》2015年第3期。

〔12〕 参见北京市第一中级人民法院伊利商标侵权纠纷一审行政判决书,(2009)一中行初字第1589号。

请注册“YiLi + 伊利”商标,本案原告所持有的“伊利”商标被认定为驰名商标,被告在水龙头等商品上申请注册了“伊利”商标,尽管这些商品类别与伊利公司“伊利”商标核定使用的商品类别并没有太大的关联,但是伊利商标具有的极高知名度,不仅局限于奶制品等行业,已经扩大到更大的行业范围,其中便包括被告所处的行业。因此法院认定被告的行为构成侵权,给予原告驰名商标跨类保护。

商标的影响已经跨越到其他类别的商品上,这是我们构建以淡化理论为基础的跨类保护制度的直接原因。但目前我国适用跨类保护的前提是商标为驰名商标,而我国认定驰名商标时又采用“相关公众标准”。

如果商标仅仅在相关公众中驰名,就可以适用跨类保护,那么被认定驰名的商标的显著性、知名度以及公众范围等要素将具有较大的局限性,很可能实际上其影响力并无法跨越到其他类别的商品之上,或者并无法跨越到具体案件中所涉及的特定其他类别的商品之上,这时候如果我们还坚持对这样的驰名商标进行跨类保护,那么将违背淡化理论的初衷,进而违背跨类保护制度的设立宗旨。

(2)“相关公众标准”加剧淡化理论的垄断之忧

如前文所述,淡化理论由于自身的局限性,有导致商标垄断的风险。如果我们对于驰名商标的认定坚持采用“相关公众标准”,那么被认定的驰名商标的数量将会难以控制。据相关数据显示,我国目前经行政认定的驰名商标累积至目前已接近1000件,司法认定的数量更是惊人。

在这个较低标准的刺激下,商标权人会更加想方设法跨过驰名商标的门槛,接受获得跨类保护的审查。同时跨类保护适用的“决策者”——司法人员,在这么大的“驰名商标”跨类保护审查压力之下,其“把关能力”自然也会下降。那么越来越多的被认定驰名的商标获得跨类保护将成为难以避免的事实,“商标霸权”将不断建立、巩固。

(三)司法适用中的偏差

目前,在适用驰名商标跨类保护制度司法实践中,由于驰名商标淡化的构成要件不明确,以致出现了适用上的偏差,不当地扩大了驰名商标的权利边界:

1. 我国驰名商标认定标准中的地域范围标准

(1)“全国范围标准”和“部分地区标准”

我国《驰名商标认定和保护规定》中将在中国为相关公众广为知晓的商标

界定为驰名商标。[13] 其中对于“在中国”应该作何理解至今并不明确。是指在全中国范围内广为知晓,还是在部分地区广为知晓即可,这样的问题并没有统一的答案。因此在司法实践中,对于驰名商标认定的地域范围标准往往会有不同,也就是存在两个标准——“全国范围标准”和“部分地区标准”。

(2)“部分地区标准”加剧驰名商标权利边界不当扩大的问题

由于统一标准尚未建立,不少法院仍沿用“部分地区标准”,如“松本”商标侵权纠纷一案,被告将原告注册在开关、插座商品上的“松本”商标注册于与开关、插座不相类似的第19类商品上,原告向法院提起诉讼,主张商标侵权救济。一审法院在认定该商标是否驰名时,提出“松本”商标2000年被评为广东省著名商标,并被广东省工商局推荐为驰名商标,因此认定“松本”商标为驰名商标。[14]

但是二审法院提出,商标局并未认定“松本”商标为“驰名商标”,这说明原告的“松本”商标虽然是广东省著名商标,但该商标尚未达到在全国全行业的范围内驰名的程度,因此对“松本”商标不予认定为驰名商标。二审法院主要从“全国范围标准”对一审法院的驰名商标认定结果进行纠正。[15]

两审对于驰名商标的认定存在截然相反的结果,同样,对于该商标是否适用跨类保护自然也完全相反。最终二审法院撤销了一审法院的判决,并且驳回了原告的诉讼请求,不予其跨类保护。

尽管现在交通发达、信息交流迅速,但是商标的传播速度、传播范围是有限的,这个时候,如果我们采用部分地区标准,给予一个地方著名商标辐射全国大部分地区、跨越其本身所属行业的权利,实属不当。

且在这种小地域范围的驰名标准之下,被认定驰名的商标的数量将会难以控制,不少地方著名商标也会被纳入驰名商标之中,那么这种不当扩张权利边界的问题将会越发严重,进而严重损害公平的市场竞争秩序。

---

〔13〕《驰名商标认定和保护规定》第2条第1款:本规定中的驰名商标是指在中国为相关公众广为知晓并享有较高声誉的商标。

〔14〕参见广州市中级人民法院“松本”商标侵权纠纷一审民事判决书,(2002)穗中法民四初字第118号。

〔15〕参见广东省高级人民法院“松本”商标侵权纠纷二审民事判决书,(2004)粤高法民三终字第102号。

2. 司法实践中驰名商标淡化的证明标准

(1)"可能淡化标准"

我国已经依据淡化理论建立起跨类保护制度,[16]但是究竟淡化的证明标准是什么,相关法律法规并没有给出明确的规定。面对立法上的这一模糊不清的规定,司法人员在适用跨类保护制度的时候,对驰名商标淡化的认定标准都是进行自由裁量的,而且从表1、表2等相关案件的研读可知,司法人员大多采用"可能淡化标准"。

美国在2006年10月6日的《2006年商标淡化修正法案》(TDRA)中正式确立了"可能淡化标准"。且美国《兰哈姆法》(Lanham Act)第43条(C)(1)也强调了该标准。[17]

"可能淡化标准"其实并没有明确的判断标准,同美国司法实践一样,我国司法人员在适用这一标准时也都是通过对诸如"驰名商标的显著性""涉案商标的相似性""消费者的熟悉程度"等相关因素的分析来判断是否有淡化的可能。

如"来福士"一案,[18]法院通过对比被告使用的商标与原告"来福士"这两个商标近似的程度,被告行为对原告所有的驰名商标显著性可能导致的负面影响等因素推导出被告对原告的驰名商标权益可能有一定的损害,可能会导致原

---

〔16〕《中华人民共和国商标法》第13条第3款:就不相同或者不相类似商品申请注册的商标是复制、摹仿或者翻译他人已经在中国注册的驰名商标,误导公众,致使该驰名商标注册人的利益可能受到损害的,不予注册并禁止使用。

〔17〕15 U. S. C. 1125 (Section 43 of the Lanham Act): False designations of origin, false descriptions, and dilution forbidden

(c) Dilution by blurring;

(1) dilution by tarnishment Subject to the principles of equity, the owner of a famous mark that is distinctive, inherently or through acquired distinctiveness, shall be entitled to an injunction against another person who, at any time after the owner's mark has become famous, commences use of a mark or trade name in commerce that is likely to cause dilution by blurring or dilution by tarnishment of the famous mark, regardless of the presence or absence of actual or likely confusion, of competition, or of actual economic injury.

〔18〕参见北京知识产权法院凯德置地有限公司与国家工商行政管理总局商标评审委员会一审行政判决书,(2018)京73行初1733号。

告商标的淡化。

再如郑州宇通客车股份有限公司诉陈继发商标侵权纠纷案,[19]法院同样也是从原被告商标的相似度等指出被告的行为致使原告的商标权益可能受到损害,判定构成侵权。

诸如此类的判决说理比比皆是,从这部分内容可以看出,法院在认定驰名商标淡化的时候,都仅仅根据对相关因素的分析得出有淡化的可能,进而认定驰名商标受到淡化,并因此给予反淡化保护(也即跨类保护)。

(2)"可能淡化标准"的缺陷

对上述这些因素进行综合考量,固然有利于分析究竟被告的行为有无造成淡化的可能性,但是不可否认的是,这样的"可能淡化标准"的认定在实践中会出现许多问题。

首先,我国目前驰名商标出现"满天飞"的现象,司法人员在堆积如山的涉及跨类保护的案件面前,或多或少会做出不尽如人意的裁决结果。

其次,这些因素广泛而且复杂,难以分清其中的主次,在判断时具有极大的不确定性。从法院对这部分的说理可以看出,究竟这种淡化的可能性是怎么产生的、是否真实存在、可能性究竟有多大,法院在对这些因素的分析中,大多时候并无法提供足够的令人信服的论据,因为这些因素究竟与驰名商标淡化的成立各自有多大的关联我们无从知晓。

最后,这些因素在个别考量的时候也具有一定的问题,对这些因素的考量标准进行设定存在较大的困难。在此以商标显著性大小为例进行说明。

驰名商标的显著性有大小之分,显著性越大则商标被淡化的可能性就越大。根据显著性大小判断商标被淡化的可能性有其合理之处。美国在司法实践中,按照商标固有显著性的强弱,将商标划分为四大类,由强到弱分别是:臆造性标志、任意性标志、暗示性标志和描述性标志。其中臆造性标志、任意性标志和暗示性标志都具有内在显著性的标志;描述性标志的显著性相对来说,要弱得多。[20]

目前司法实践中,司法人员主张借鉴美国这一做法,对驰名商标进行分类,按照驰名商标本身显著性大小的不同来综合判断是否构成淡化以及淡化的程

[19] 参见河南省开封市中级人民法院州宇通客车股份有限公司诉陈继发商标侵权纠纷一审民事判决书,(2006)汴民初字第47号。

[20] 参见李明德:《知识产权法》,法律出版社2014年版,第218页。

度。但是,商标具有的显著性根据来源可以分为内在显著性和获得显著性两种的,内在显著性是指特定的标志因其独一无二的设计而本身具有的显著性;获得显著性是指有的标志虽然不具有内在显著性,但是通过在市场上的使用,逐步获得了显著性或者第二含义,具备了识别能力。

内在显著性的判断采用美国上述做法在理论上具有可操作性,但是对于具有获得显著性的描述性标志,如果采用这种判断标准则会有失公允。这种标志通过被使用而获得"第二含义"进而成为具有显著性的商标,在具体个案中,通过商业使用和广告宣传,这类商标的显著性很大可能会超越具有内在显著性的商标。显然根本不可简单按照上述排列来衡量其显著性大小。这时候判断起来具有极大的难度,根本难以量化,无从设定标准。

可见,"可能淡化标准"并不是一个严格的法律标尺,其在适用过程中会面临较大的不确定性,而这种不确定性恰恰就为驰名商标权利边界不当扩大提供了萌发生长的土壤。

司法是立法之外最后一道平衡不同利益关系的工具,需要我们谨慎利用这一工具。在驰名商标跨类保护中更是如此。因为在这种效力更强的司法保护中,存在驰名商标权人、社会公众(消费者)、其他商标权人三方主体。一旦司法人员在司法适用中过分将利益的天平不当地倒向驰名商标权人,那么这个司法保护体系就会走向畸形,驰名商标权人将会把自己的权利边界肆意扩大,在其他主体权利边界内横行。

三、驰名商标权利边界不当扩大的克服

面对跨类保护制度在司法适用过程中出现的驰名商标权利边界被不当扩大的问题,当务之急是准确把握驰名商标的权利边界,我们可以从立法和司法两个角度着手。

(一)立法建议:驰名商标认定的公众范围标准采用"一般公众标准"

正所谓"小智治事,中智用人,大智立法",要解决目前的驰名商标权利边界不当扩大的问题,我们必须坚持立法先行,通过改革我国的相关制度,力求从根本上解决问题。因此关键在于完善驰名商标认定制度。

纵观国际社会关于驰名商标认定标准中公众范围标准的规定,除了我国采用的"相关公众标准"之外,还存在另外一种标准,即"一般公众标准"。

1."一般公众标准"

从《关于驰名商标保护规定的联合建议》(以下简称《联合建议》)第2条的规定可知,[21]《联合建议》在认定驰名商标时采用的也是"相关公众标准"。但是该建议在第4条(c)中又提出,[22]在对商标进行反淡化保护时,应采用另一种驰名商标认定标准——"一般公众标准"。换言之,世界知识产权组织(WIPO)在《联合建议》中规定了一种双重标准。

美国《兰哈姆法》也是采用这一标准,[23]其要求必须在一般公众中享有盛

〔21〕《关于驰名商标保护规定的联合建议》第2条(1)(b):尤其是,主管机关应对向其提交的有关能据以就该商标驰名或不驰名作出推理的因素的信息加以考虑,包括但不限于涉及以下内容的信息:(1)相关公众对该商标的了解或认识程度;(2)该商标的任何使用的持续时间、程度和地理范围;(3)该商标的任何宣传工作的持续时间、程度和地理范围,包括在交易会或展览会上对使用该商标的商品和/或服务所作的广告或公告及介绍;(4)该商标的任何注册和/或任何注册申请的期限和地理范围,以反映使用或认识该商标的程度;(5)成功实施该商标权的记录,尤其是该商标由主管机关认定为驰名商标的范围;(6)与该商标相关的价值。

〔22〕《关于驰名商标保护规定的联合建议》第4条(1)(b):无论商标所使用、提出注册申请或注册的商品和/或服务如何,只要该商标或该商标的主要部分构成对驰名商标的复制、模仿、翻译或音译,且至少符合下列条件之一的,即应认为该商标与该驰名商标发生冲突:(i)该商标的使用会暗示该商标所使用、提出注册申请或注册的商品和/或服务与驰名商标注册人之间存在某种联系,并且可能会使驰名商标注册人的利益受到损害;(ii)该商标的使用可能会以不正当的方式削弱或淡化驰名商标的区别性特征;(iii)该商标的使用会不正当地对驰名商标的区别性特征加以利用。(c)尽管有第2条第(3)款(a)项第(iii)目的规定,为适用本条第(1)款(b)项(ii)目和(iii)目的目的,成员国可要求该驰名商标必须为全体公众所熟知。

〔23〕 See 15 U.S.C. 1125 (Section 43 of the Lanham Act): False designations of origin, false descriptions, and dilution forbidden

(c) Dilution by blurring;

(1) dilution by tarnishment Subject to the principles of equity, the owner of a famous mark that is distinctive, inherently or through acquired distinctiveness, shall be entitled to an injunction against another person who, at any time after the owner's mark has become famous, commences use of a mark or trade name in commerce that is likely to cause dilution by blurring or dilution by tarnishment of the famous mark, regardless of the presence or absence of actual or likely confusion, of competition, or of actual economic injury.

誉才可以被认定为驰名商标。

如2001年的Toro商标异议一案就是美国适用“一般公众标准”的典型案例。Toro商标的所有人从1914年开始使用该商标,使用历史已经有80多年,而且商标所有人非常注重该商标的宣传工作,每年投入巨额资金用于打造该商标的崇高声誉。经过商标所有人的辛苦运营,该商标所标识的商品(草坪和园林景观维护以及精确灌溉设备)几乎已经覆盖整个美国。毋庸置疑,该商标在草坪以及园林景观维护行业已经建立起强大的声誉,并且为该领域的公众所熟知。但是该案的司法人员提出,Toro商标被其所标识的商品所涉及的公众熟知并不意味着其被一般公众所熟知,因此也就不具备被认定为驰名商标的资格。〔24〕

除了美国,日本在此处也采用了“一般公众标准”。在日本商标法中规定了著名商标、周知商标(也即我国的驰名商标),其必须是“为消费者广泛熟识”的商标。〔25〕可见,日本对于“驰名商标”的认定采用的也是“一般公众标准”,必须在日本一般公众中具有较大的知名度才可以被认定为“驰名商标”。

2. 给我国的立法启示

(1)采用“一般公众标准”

驰名商标认定制度就是驰名商标保护的前提,其中认定标准中的公众范围标准就如同一道不可跳过的门槛。这个标准的高低与驰名商标的保护息息相关。因此笔者认为驰名商标认定标准中的公众范围标准的设置是目前立法的重中之重。

WIPO在《联合建议》中规定了一种双重标准,〔26〕根据驰名商标不同的保护动因,针对不同的驰名商标保护情景采用不同的标准,〔27〕而不是绝对地采用

---

〔24〕 See Toro Co. v. Toro Head, Inc., 61 U. S. P. Q. 2d 1164 (T. T. A. B. 2001).

〔25〕《日本商标法》第4条[不能进行商标注册的商标]:

……

(一)下列商标虽符合前条的规定,但不能取得商标注册:

(10)与表示他人业务有关商品、且为消费者广泛熟识的商标或与之类似的商标,并且用于相同或类似商品上的商标……

〔26〕 See Martin Senftleben, “The Trademark Tower of Babel-Dilution Concepts in International”, *US and EC Trademark Law* 40, 2009, pp. 45－77.

〔27〕 参见王太平:《论驰名商标认定的公众范围标准》,载《法学》2014年第10期。

“相关公众标准”或者“一般公众标准”。笔者认为这种做法的出发点是好的,但是对于结论,笔者并不完全赞同。因为按照这种思路,对于同一个商标,在不同情境下,由于涉及不同保护动因,其认定结果很可能会因为标准的不同而不同。这个矛盾认定结果的存在将会给商标保护带来一定的困扰。

综上所述,笔者认为,我国可以借鉴国际社会的做法,同时结合我国的具体国情,对我国的驰名商标认定的公众范围标准予以修改完善,适用“一般公众标准”。

(2)我国采用“一般公众标准”的合理性

将“一般公众标准”运用到我国的驰名商标认定制度之中,驰名商标的准入门槛将会极大地提高,必须在一般普通公众中建立起强大的声誉才可以被认定为驰名商标,具有跨越其他类型的商品的影响力,进而才可以进入驰名商标的跨类保护体系,获得更大的权利边界,这也就是所谓的“高标准,宽口径”。

一个商标一旦在一般公众中享有盛誉,那么这个商标的显著性、知名度以及所涉及的公众范围等自然都可以涵盖被告的商标,那么被告的使用行为导致驰名商标的淡化的可能性将会大大地提高,这种情况下,给予驰名商标跨类保护便是不可或缺的,同时也可以避免司法人员由于判断不当而“跨类太远”“不当跨类”的问题。

如前述说到的“好太太”一案,该案中,原告的商标“好太太”所具有的商标影响力并没有跨越到被告商品之上,但是法院却给予其跨类保护,这一做法无疑就是由于判断偏差而引发的“跨类太远”。虽然我们可以说是司法人员判断偏差而导致的,但是我们无法保证世界上存在绝对不会判断偏差的司法人员,更何况是在如此大的审查压力之下。但是如果按照“一般公众标准”,该案中“好太太”这个商标或许不会被认定为驰名,那么也就不存在由于司法人员判断偏差而“跨类太远”,进而不当扩大商标权利边界的问题了。

当然,有人会说,我们不可以一竿子打死,通过将驰名商标的认定标准设置成“一般公众”这样的高标准,以此来希求从根本上减少由于司法人员判断偏差而“跨类不当”或者“跨类太远”等问题,这样对一些在特定公众范围(但并未涵盖一般公众)享有盛誉的商标来说,可能会存在保护不足的嫌疑。对这个疑问,笔者认为可以从以下3个方面来加以论述:

首先,这个商标毕竟仅仅在特定几个行业中具有较大的声誉,一般公众对之并不熟悉,这时如果被告在原告商标驰名度没有涵盖的行业中的商品上使用与原告商标相同或者近似的商标,其实从一定意义上来说,是对原告商标的一种强化,而非淡化,那么就无须给予反淡化保护。例如为众多中国法学生再熟悉不过的司考培训机构——“厚大法考”所采用的商标——“厚大”,该机构的商标“厚大”在教育、图书印刷等行业取得了一定的知名度,如果这时候第三人将“厚大”商标注册于面包生产销售行业并且开始使用,那么这时候是否应该给予厚大机构该商标的跨类保护呢?其实不然,因为“厚大”商标固然具有其一定的知名度,但是也仅仅在特定行业中,并未涵盖一般公众,第三人在面包生产销售行业使用该商标,其实从本质来说,并不会导致该商标的淡化,相反,会强化该商标在一般公众尤其该商标本身并未涉及的其他行业中的公众的知名度。这时候,我们并不需要认定其为驰名商标,给予其跨类保护。

其次,如果被告恰巧就是在原告商标驰名度涵盖的行业中的商品上使用原告的商标,那么这个时候,其实原告可以事先采取措施予以预防,例如注册防御商标。我国目前尚未建立防御商标制度,但是日本在这一制度层面已经做了较多的尝试,[28]我们大可借鉴日本的这一制度。例如上文所提及的“厚大”商标,其商标权人“厚大机构”便是采用了注册防御商标的方式来防止自己的商标遭受淡化。根据在中国商标局的查询可知,[29]厚大机构已经在图书印刷、教育、电子出版物、学习用品等行业申请注册了“厚大”商标。此时根本无需通过将其认定为驰名商标,给予其跨类保护的方式来维护商标权人的合法权益。

最后,在“一般公众标准”下,驰名商标的认定数量必然会得到控制甚至减少,这样一来,尽管跨类保护制度会因为司法适用的种种偏差而被不当适用,进而带来驰名商标权利边界不当扩大的风险,但是毕竟驰名商标的数量已经得到控制,这时候我们可以说已经从立法上将这种风险产生的可能性降到最低了。

---

〔28〕《日本商标法》第64条:商标权人在表示自己业务上的指定商品的注册商标,已广为消费者所熟知的情况下,为了防止他人在其注册商标的指定商品以及类似商品以外的商品上使用该注册商标,而该商品又有可能与自己业务上的商品发生混淆的危险时,可以在这些可能有混淆危险的商品上进行与其注册商标相同标志的防护商标的注册。

〔29〕国家知识产权局商标局、中国商标网:http://sbj. saic. gov. cn/,最后访问日期:2018年4月15日。

当然驰名商标保护体系中除了跨类保护,还有另一个更加重要的保护制度,即注册豁免。[30] 有人也许会提出一旦采用"一般公众标准",那么将会导致许多本应该获得保护的但是还未注册的商标无法获得相应的保护。但是笔者认为,注册豁免设立的初衷是为了防止已经使用并且积累起一定商誉的商标被竞争者不正当地加以利用。我国目前仍然是处于注册取得商标权的体制之中,首先还是应当维护这种注册制度,那么对于这种"例外的商标权取得"的情形设定一个更高的标准,笔者认为是无可厚非的。

(二)司法对策

1. 驰名商标淡化的证明标准采用"实际损害标准"

(1)"实际损害标准"

对于驰名商标淡化的证明标准,除了"可能淡化标准",国际上还有另一种标准——"实际损害标准"。这一标准要求商标权人必须证明自己受到了实际的损害。这是一种更高的证明标准。

2003年,美国最高法院曾借助"Moseley案"[31](维多利亚的秘密),正式确立"实际损害标准"。但是3年后,美国以TDRA推翻了在"Moseley案"中确立的"实际损害标准",[32]正式确立了"可能淡化标准",并且沿用至今。

但是,目前还有不少国家在立法中采用"实际损害标准"。如在法国《知识产权法典》第三章中规定了商标淡化的表现和法律后果,其中对于淡化行为的

---

[30] 《中华人民共和国商标法》第13条第2款:就相同或者类似商品申请注册的商标是复制、摹仿或者翻译他人未在中国注册的驰名商标,容易导致混淆的,不予注册并禁止使用。

[31] See Moseley v. V. Secret Catalogue, Inc., 518 U.S. 418, 428 (2003).

案情介绍:被告维克多·莫斯里在伊丽莎白镇开设了一家名为"维克多的秘密"(Victory's secret)的零售店,主营男女内衣、色情音像制品和性玩偶等商品。以出售女性内衣闻名的"Victoria's secret"公司认为被告情趣用品商店使用"Victory's secret"侵害其商标专用权并淡化其商标。在接受"Victoria's secret"的律师函后,被告即将其商店的名称改为"Victory's Little secret"。不过,"Victoria's secret"公司认为被告仅增加一字,且字体较其他两个字小很多,但仍有淡化其商标的可能,所以向法院提起诉讼。

[32] See Federal Trademark Dilution Act (2006).

认定,其采用的就是“实际损害标准”,〔33〕必须给商标权人造成实际损害,相应的救济条款才可以予以适用。

再者,同我国一样,司法实践中对于驰名商标淡化的证明标准适用不明的国家还有加拿大。虽然加拿大商标法的相关规定〔34〕表面看来似乎规定了“可能淡化标准”,但是通过对加拿大相关司法案例的研究可以发现,加拿大法院在适用这条规定的时候,秉持着十分谨慎的态度。有的法院直接按照法条字面意思,采用“可能淡化标准”,有的法院则更多受到美国“Moseley 案”的影响,倾向采用“实际损害标准”。〔35〕

(2)我国司法实践中应当采用“实际损害标准”

鉴于“可能淡化标准”的适用在我国引发的驰名商标权利边界不当扩大的问题,我国司法人员在驰名商标淡化的证明标准方面,可以借鉴其他国家的立法、司法实践,采用“实际损害标准”这一更加具有确定性的标准,只有实际导致商标淡化,带来实际经济损失,才可以诉请跨类保护,将驰名商标的权利边界控制在一个合适的范围之内。

至于究竟应该如何将这一标准适用到我国司法实践中,笔者认为,可以从国内外适用该标准裁决驰名商标淡化侵权纠纷的案件入手。其中,最为典型的

---

〔33〕《法国知识产权法典》第 3 章 713 – 5:在不类似的商品或者服务上使用著名商标给商标所有人造成损失或者构成对该商标的不当使用的,侵害人应当承担民事责任。前款规定亦适用于保护工业产权巴黎公约第六条之二所称的驰名商标。

〔34〕《加拿大商标及反不正当竞争法》第 22 条　商誉的贬低:

(1)任何人不得以可能贬低他人商标信誉的方式使用他人注册商标。

(2)对违反上述(1)中规定的商标使用人,法院可在告知其注册商标所有人对其使用行为已提起诉讼的同时,拒绝判决行为人赔偿注册商标所有人经济损失,也可允许被告继续销售其现存或在其控制下的附有该商标的商品。

〔35〕最为典型的案例就是加拿大最高法院于 2006 年发布的“Barbie”案 Mattel U. S. A. ,Inc. v. 3894207 Canada Inc,23 C. P. R. 395 (T. M. O. B. 2002)。

在该案中,被告欲在其经营的小餐厅的招牌和广告上申请注册“Barbie”商标,持有芭比娃娃商标“Barbie”的美泰公司得知后,立即对该商标申请提出异议,但是商标审查局并没有支持美泰公司的异议,并且准许了被告的注册申请,因此美泰公司提起诉讼。该案法院认为原告持有的“Barbie”商标仅仅只是在玩具行业驰名,并没有扩及其他行业,且原告无法提出证明被告的使用行为会给自己的商标带来实际损害的证据,因此美泰公司还是败诉告终。

莫过于对驰名商标淡化证明标准进行了诸多探索的美国的相关裁决。

正如上文所提及的美国"Moseley 案",美国最高法院在该案的裁决中适用"实际损害标准",其提出原告若想胜诉,则必须提出足够的证据证明被告的行为给其造成了实际损害,构成驰名商标淡化行为。同时,最高法院在该案裁决中提出,证明实际淡化并不要求原告一定要去证明由于淡化而导致的销售量或者利润的减少。[36] 其主张,可以用消费者调查问卷、产品销售量下降、专家证言等间接证据来证明淡化的实际存在,虽然这些方式要么耗费成本极大,要么需要耗费极多时间,且也存在造假的可能性,但是不论难度有多大,都不可以成为违背正当性的借口,如果根本不存在淡化,那根本无需给予反淡化保护。同时其指出如果被告使用的商标与原告商标是完全相同的,那么这时候依靠这种间接证据,原告更容易证明淡化的实际存在。

美国法院适用"实际损害标准"对驰名商标进行反淡化保护的典型案例还有"Ringling Brothers 案"。[37] 由于原告无法提出足够的证据证明自己所遭受的实际经济损失,因此一审法院认定,被告的行为并非驰名商标淡化行为,原告的淡化诉讼请求被全部驳回了。该案二审法院在一审裁决的基础上,进一步提出,在认定驰名商标淡化行为成立的时候,必须证明"被告的商标使用行为对驰名商标所有人造成了实质性的经济损失"。因此还是维持了一审的裁决结果。但是二审法院对于究竟应该如何证明原告遭受的实质性的经济损失提出了三方面的参考意见:

(1)除了提出自己的商业利润遭受实际损失,原告还应该提出足够的证据,

---

〔36〕 参见邓宏光:《美国联邦商标反淡化法的制定与修正》,载《电子知识产权》2007 年第 2 期。

〔37〕 案情简介:原告 Ringling Brothers 是一家由 Bamuln&Bialey 联合创办的娱乐演出公司。该公司自 1872 年起就使用"The Greatest Show on Earth"作为他们的商业宣传口号并将其作为商标于 1961 年获得联邦商标注册。本案的被告 Uhat 是一家犹他州的旅游发展集团公司。在没有得到原告允许的情况下,被告在 1962 年开始使用"The Greatest Show on Earth"并将其用于旅游服务行业。并且在 1975 年取得犹他州的商标注册。被告 Utha 用此商标 1985 年和 1995 年分别两次获准在犹他州续展,并于 1997 年在原告 Ringling Brothers 提出反对的情况下仍然获得联邦商标注册。原告 Ringling Brothers 因此向犹他州地区法院提起诉讼,请求获得反淡化保护。

将可能导致商业利润减少的其他可能性因素予以排除；

(2)原告可以通过消费者调查问卷的方式对消费者进行调查，证明由于被告的商标使用行为，原告的商标遭受到了淡化；

(3)同时原告还可以提出其他辅助性证据，如原告商标的知名度，原告、被告商标的相似程度，等等。

据有关数据记载，在"Moseley 案"之后，在 TDRA 之前，非常多的法院适用了"实际损害标准"，包括之前那些一直坚持"可能淡化标准"的法院。这些案例都为我国采用"实际损害标准"作为驰名商标淡化的证明标准提供了宝贵的经验教训，同时这些案例也为我们提供了不少具有较大可行性的证明路径。

2. 驰名商标认定的地域范围标准采用"全国范围标准"

正如前文所述，如果我们采用"部分地区标准"，那么将赋予一个覆盖范围有限的商标以辐射全国各地各类市场的权利，这将会不当扩大这类商标的权利边界，进而损害公平的市场竞争秩序。

为了解决这个问题，司法人员在认定驰名商标时，应当采用"全国范围标准"。

美国在此处的规定就十分清楚，其在《兰哈姆法》中对驰名商标的定义进行了明确的界定，[38]规定中的"美利坚合众国"便将驰名商标认定的地域范围标

---

[38] 15 U. S. C. 1125 (Section 43 of the Lanham Act): False designations of origin, false descriptions, and dilution forbidden.

(2) Definitions

For purposes of paragraph (1), a mark is famous if it is widely recognized by the general consuming public of the United States as a designation of source of the goods or services of the mark's owner. In determining whether a mark possesses the requisite degree of recognition, the court may consider all relevant factors, including the following:

(i) The duration, extent, and geographic reach of advertising and publicity of the mark, whether advertised or publicized by the owner or third parties.

(ii) The amount, volume, and geographic extent of sales of goods or services offered under the mark.

(iii) The extent of actual recognition of the mark.

(iv) Whether the mark was registered under the Act of March 3, 1881, or the Act of February 20, 1905, or on the principal register.

准予以严格的限定,必须是在美利坚合众国的整个地域范围来说具有比较高的知名度的商标才可以被认定为驰名商标。

因此,我国驰名商标定义中的“在中国”应当理解为全中国范围,但是这样的理解并不等同于要求某商标必须在全部行政区域内驰名,但是正如魏森教授提出的,至少必须在绝大多数的省级行政区域内驰名。〔39〕

采用“全国范围标准”作为认定驰名商标的地域范围标准,目前在司法实践中已经得到不少法院的肯定。如“蒙娜丽莎”案件中,〔40〕法院提出,原告所持有的“蒙娜丽莎”商标在全国大部分地区拥有广泛和稳定的用户群,在2006年先后经行政认定和司法认定为驰名商标后,仍然持续通过中央电视台、全国各地的主流报纸、陶瓷行业报、户外广告、网络等进行有步骤、大规模的宣传,因此应当认定为驰名商标。可见,法院在此处就是坚持了“全国范围标准”,特定商标必须在全国绝大多数地区享有较大的知名度才可以被认定为驰名商标。

通过提高对驰名商标享有知名度的地域范围的要求,一来可以限制驰名商标的认定数量,防止将许多仅仅在小部分地区驰名的商标认定为驰名商标;二来可以保证被认定驰名的商标享有的知名度所涵盖的地域范围是较大的,这样当国内其他市场竞争者将该商标用于其他类别的商品上时,我们对该商标进行跨类保护是不会轻易导致过度扩大其权利边界的。

结　　语

商标法的趣旨是发挥商标的来源识别功能,而商标权利保护仅仅是一种手段。一旦这种保护过度,则会形成一片一片的“权利灌木丛”,不断挤压公共领域。

因此,我们应当从立法、司法两个角度着手,积极寻求对策解决目前我国司法实践中出现的驰名商标权利边界不当扩大的问题。立法方面,提高驰名商标认定的公众范围标准,采用“一般公众标准”,只有当商标在一般公众中享有较

〔39〕 参见魏森:《商标侵权认定标准研究》,中国社会科学出版社2008年版,第155页。

〔40〕 参见广东省高级人民法院广东蒙娜丽莎新型材料集团有限公司、广州蒙娜丽莎建材有限公司与佛山市贝佳斯洁具有限公司侵害商标权纠纷二审民事判决书,(2015)粤高法民三终字第143号。

大的知名度才可以被认定驰名。司法方面，在认定驰名商标时，应当坚持“全国范围标准”，也即是驰名商标享有盛誉的地域范围应当是在全国绝大多数的省级行政区域之内；将驰名商标淡化的证明标准确定为“实际损害标准”，只有证明实际经济损失的存在才可以证明淡化的存在。双管齐下，对驰名商标的权利边界予以清晰、准确的界定，进而真正实现我国商标法的趣旨。

（责任编辑：曹亚君）

司法实践与制度剖析

“执行难”的概念变迁

——以我国三十年执行政策为视角

张　琛*

摘要：

如何化解“执行难”这一“沉疴顽疾”，是全国法院三十余年来的重点工作。而不同时期对于“执行难”概念的不同理解，反映在该时期的执行政策之中。近两年来，随着“基本解决执行难”工作的推进，法院对于什么是“执行难”进行了新的解读，强调将“执行难”与“执行不能”进行区分。一方面，法院对于“执行难”问题的理解与评估标准都更为理性；而在另一方面，从当事人的视角出发，其对解决“执行难”的理解是只要是生效判决所确定的权益便能得到实现，所谓“执行不能”归根结底还是属于“执行难”之范畴。本文通过结合执行政策实际运行中产生的现象，根据不同时期对“执行难”的不同理解将之划分为三个阶段，梳理20世纪80年代中期以来我国执行相关政策的变迁，尝试探寻“执行难”作为一个司法概念的变迁过程。

关键词：

“执行难”；执行政策；执行权；政策导向

一、引言：作为概念的“执行难”

20世纪80年代中期，经济审判工作中判决难以执行问题日益突出，“执行

---

* 张琛，中山大学法学院2018级研究生，中山大学司法体制改革研究中心研究人员。

难”问题已引起实务界与法学界等有关方面的重视。[1] 1987年全国法院工作会议对此问题进行了专门讨论,1988年《最高人民法院工作报告》则首次于官方层面明确指出“执行难”问题的存在,这里所说的“执行难”即为经济审判工作中判决难以执行,[2]经生效判决确定的权利在相当长的一段时期内难以得到实现。

至今三十余年间,以最高人民法院为代表的相关部门机构在解决执行难问题道路上的探索从未停歇,国家出台诸多政策并采取相应举措,且多次在全国范围内开展了执行积案清理活动。十八届四中全会明确提出“切实解决执行难”以保障当事人及时实现权益。2016年3月,最高人民法院院长周强在十二届全国人大四次会议上报告最高人民法院工作时承诺:“用两到三年时间基本解决执行难问题”,[3]两年时间已过,各地法院亦叫响“决胜执行难”的口号,以广东省佛山市中级人民法院为例,该院将基本解决执行难的日期倒计时精确到某分某秒。

最高人民法院的决心也许能让各界看到化解“执行难”的曙光,但可能使得大众产生一种错觉,即在各级法院的努力下,“执行难”问题便能迎刃而解。真实的情况远非如此简单,解决“执行难”问题依然任重而道远。《最高人民法院公报》2013年至2016年公布的数据显示,2013年至2016年,民商事执行案件的受案数量呈井喷式增长之态,其中2013年为231万件,2014年为264万件,

---

[1] 该时期已有学者就某一地区法院的执行案件现状进行实证调查,并归纳总结“执行难”的原因与解决方式。各地法院亦针对“执行难”问题召开会议,针对执行问题进行专题研究。值得一提的是,这一时期在异地执行的问题上,已开始进行有益探索,如1987年北京市崇文区人民法院协助江苏省盐城市城区法院完成数万元执行标的额的案件执行。参见柯焕锐、叶国均:《经济纠纷案审结后执行难问题探讨》,载《政法学刊》1986年第2期;《人民司法》评论员:《狠抓“执行难”》,载《人民司法》1987年第5期;丁海湖:《解决民事“执行难”之管见》,载《当代法学》1988年第4期。

[2] 1988年4月1日,时任最高人民法院院长郑天翔在第七届全国人民代表大会第一次会议上的报告中指出:“当前,经济审判工作中最突出的问题是判决难以执行。”对这个问题,1987年的全国法院工作会议进行了专门讨论,指出了法院工作中重审判、轻执行的缺点,强调了要加强执行力量,对有些案件要及时采取诉讼保全措施、为执行创造条件,在必要时强制执行,大力扭转执行难的局面。

[3] 海伟:《周强主持召开最高人民法院专题会议强调:坚决打赢基本解决执行难这场硬仗》,载《人民法院报》2016年3月29日,第1版。

2015年为350万件,2016年为411万件。[4] 虽然执行案件的结案数与之成正比关系,但如何有效在消化积案、解决新案方面有所突破,仍然是法院面临的极大考验:若不着重于提升执行效率,执行工作可能陷入"积了又清、清了又积"的循环。值得关注的是,根据《最高人民法院公报》统计数据,作为执行期限内结案率即为法定期限内结案数与案件执结数之比的法定期限内执行结案率在2015年已高达99.03%,在2013年甚至达到99.52%的峰值。客观而言,如果年执结率已能达99%,那么"执行难"的问题基本上可以消除。然而,最高人民法院在2016年又另行召开破解"执行难"的专题会议,审议并通过了《关于落实"用两到三年时间基本解决执行难"问题》的工作纲要,说明执行问题不容小觑。

从当事人的角度看,解决"执行难"问题的标准在于实现胜诉判决确定的权利,这一理解反映在申请执行的金额能够实现多少,即对执行案件实际执行到位率的关注。但从全国法院司法统计公报与各地法院公布的数据来看,实际执行到位率并不乐观,大部分法院执行案件的实际执行到位率[5]仍处在40%左右,甚至更低数值。一方面,是高达99%的年执结率与"四个90%,一个80%"[6]的目标;另一方面,是常年处于40%左右的实际执行到位率,[7]"两到三年内基本解决执行难"的愿景应当如何实现?

---

[4] 参见2013年至2016年《中华人民共和国最高人民法院公报》刊载的《全国法院司法统计公报》。

[5] 根据《最高人民法院关于建立执行考核指标体系的通知》(法〔2017〕302号),实际执行到位率=实际执行到位金额(执行完毕案件结案金额+终本案件执行到位金额+其他方式结案金额+未执结案件已执行到位金额)÷首次执行案件申请执行标的总额。

[6] 最高人民法院将"四个基本"具体化为"四个90%,一个80%"的核心指标要求,作为阶段性目标,即90%以上有财产可供执行案件在法定期限内执结,90%以上无财产可供执行案件终结本次执行程序符合规范要求,90%以上执行信访案件得到化解或办结,全国90%以上法院达标,近三年执行案件整体执结率超过80%。参见周强:《最高人民法院关于人民法院解决"执行难"工作情况的报告》,载中国法院网:https://www.chinacourt.org/article/detail/2018/10/id/3542564.shtml,最后访问日期:2019年6月5日。

[7] 从公开发布的数据来看,各级法院公布其实际执行到位率的情况相对罕见。安徽省和县人民法院曾公布其"实际执行到位率高达49.02%"。实际上,全国各级法院案件的实际执行到位率将远低于这个数值。参见《和县法院"六个强化"提升实际执行到位率》,载http://ahhxfy.chinacourt.gov.cn/article/detail/2018/06/id/3374361.shtml,最后访问日期:2019年6月5日。

在此背景下,就有必要厘清“执行难”的内涵。现有文献中关于“执行难”基础概念的研究成果颇丰,但往往是以静态的视角解读某一时期的“执行难”。本文结合20世纪80年代中期至今不同时期的最高人民法院工作报告及报纸、期刊等其他文献对于“执行难”概念研究成果,以我国三十余年来执行相关政策的变迁为线索,采用动态的研究思路,探寻“执行难”概念发生嬗变的原因以及因此而产生的现象,并提出“执行难”属于社会问题而非司法问题,以端正社会对执行的认知,理性看待“执行难”问题。

二、“执行难”概念的含义演变

(一)1987~1992年:“执行难”概念的提出阶段

改革开放以来,民事审判案件数量逐年增多。20世纪80年代中期,执行案件积压现象开始出现。此外,1987年与1988年的实际执行到位的案件比例经历了一次“断崖式”的滑坡:据不完全统计,经济纠纷案件判决后未能执行的比例,[8]1985年、1986年均为20%左右,1987年上升到30%左右,有的省则为40%以上。[9] 在执行案件数量增加、难度加大的背景之下,最高人民法院在1988年年度工作报告中明确提出了“执行难”的概念与“执行难”的问题。

关于“执行难”概念的理解,法院这一时期还处于相对模糊的状态,仅指出了经济审判中判决难以执行的情况客观存在,但并未对什么是“执行难”做出清晰界定,导致具体执行政策也不成熟。虽有《民事诉讼法》关于执行程序的规定,[10] 最高人

[8] 关于“未能执行”的具体含义,最高人民法院并未做出明确阐释,且相关司法数据缺失。笔者认为,20%等数据反映的是未能执行的案件数量,即该数据更趋近于反映当时的“实际执结率”(包含无财产可供执行的案件在内)。

[9] 1988年《最高人民法院工作报告》。

[10] 1991年《民事诉讼法》在执行部分有了较大程度的完善,在“一般规定”这一章中增加了关于执行机构的设置、执行和解、暂缓执行以及具有我国特色的执行回转等内容的规定。在“执行的申请和移送”这一章中,规定了法院对仲裁裁决进行审查监督的权力。在“执行措施”这一章中,增加规定了拍卖被执行人财产、加强查明被执行人财产的若干措施,以应对执行实践中已经存在的“执行难”问题。然而民事执行内容过于庞大和复杂,仅通过《民事诉讼法》中原则性的规定无法达到体系化、规范化的效果。参见张卫平:《中国民事诉讼法立法四十年》,载《法学》2018年第7期。

民法院也就执行问题发布了一些贯彻意见与批复,但总体看来过于原则,可操作性不强,不能为执行工作提供充分的法律依据。通过当时对“执行难”成因的分析可见,认为“执行难”问题的根源在于“地方保护主义和部门主义”。[11] 这体现了当时法院在国家机构及社会结构中的尴尬地位:权大于法、权高于法。为了改变这一现象,之后我国相当长时期内的执行体制改革均围绕着加强法院执行权来进行。此外,当事人履行能力不足在当时还不是破解“执行难”的最大障碍。因为这一时期申请执行人和被执行人多数是国有企、事业单位,集体组织,机关团体等,案件类型与执行对象相对单一。当时关于化解“执行难”的具体对策尚停留在学理研究层面,以国家执行政策为导向的具体对策研究明显不足。[12]

值得一提的是,1987 年之前案件实际执行到位比例一直维持在 80% 左右,在 1987 年时骤降至 60% ~70% ,[13] 这一现象背后包含了从计划经济向市场经济转型过程中社会经济结构初步发生转变等诸多复杂的体制因素。易言之,法院提出“执行难”问题,起因并非法院内部执行力量不足,而是随着社会经济发展而产生的客观现象。这为我们研究在之后 30 年“执行难”问题为何长期存在提供了思路:从问题根源上看,“执行难”问题恐难仅仅依靠法院之力得到根本解决。此外,虽然这一阶段针对“执行难”的理解还停留在“摸着石头过河”的表象阶段,然而历年《最高人民法院工作报告》中均指出,化解“执行难”的目标在于保障当事人的合法权益,维护法律的威严,其中,债权人的合法权益便体现为生效判决赋予的权益实现了多少。可见,致力于突破执行困境,帮助申请人实现生效判决确认的权利才是法院强调解决“执行难”问题之初衷。

---

〔11〕 1988 年的《最高人民法院工作报告》中强调“执行难”的主要原因在于“地方保护主义和本位思想严重”;1989 年《最高人民法院工作报告》则强调,“对这些(指‘执行难’)问题,人民法院今后一定要严肃执法,排除地方保护主义和本位主义的干扰,坚决依法办事”;1990 年《最高人民法院工作报告》指出“造成执行难的因素很多,其中主要是地方保护主义和本位主义的干扰”。

〔12〕 但仍有一些法院为破解“执行难”采取了创造性的举措。如 1990 年,深圳市中级人民法院对一些国有企业存在的债务问题创造性地实施了“放水养鱼”的执行方式,使一批国有企业逐步解脱债务困境,重现生机,同时也保护了债权人的利益。参见陈乾:《敢为天下先——深圳法院 30 年改革成绩素描》,载《中国审判》2010 年第 11 期。

〔13〕 参见 1988 年《最高人民法院工作报告》。

(二)1993~2016年:"执行难"概念的稳定期

随着市场经济的迅速发展,人们的权利观念得到空前的强化,通过审判解决纠纷日益普遍,纠纷解决后的执行自然成为一个后续的法律现象。[14] 然而随着案件数量与类型的激增,"执行难"状况愈演愈烈,未结执行案件数量与标的金额极高。[15] 在此背景下,法院为化解"执行难"问题进行了诸多尝试:路径方面,从通过执行权内外部分离完成法院内部权力归正,到2008年后致力于实际执行中的困难突破;手段方面,采取了集中清理执行积案、执行信息化建设与社会诚信体系建设等方法化解"执行难"。

20世纪90年代中期,最高人民法院明确指出了执行工作的重点在于"提高队伍素质,加大执行力度,规范执行秩序,严肃执行纪律,加强执行监督",[16] 拉开了从执行权力内外部分离入手,进而出台具体执行政策指引解决"执行难""执行乱"问题的序幕。1999年《中共中央关于转发〈中共最高人民法院党组关于解决人民法院"执行难"问题的报告〉的通知》(1999年11号文件)也提出了"加强执行工作的统一管理和协调"的工作要求,2007年《民事诉讼法》的修订[17] 标志着"审执分离"的格局基本建立。从1993年到2007年这段时期内,执行工作方向相较于前一阶段来说更为明确,即以法院内部改革为方向,从厘清审判和执行的关系模式入手进而对执行体制进行合理分化与重构。这一时期法院对于执行概念的理解相较于之前也更为明确:执行是指对人民法院发生

〔14〕 汤维建:《关于破解"执行难"的理性反思——以执行体制的独立化构建为中心》,载《学习与探索》2007年第5期。

〔15〕《司法部关于积极支持和配合人民法院解决"执行难"问题的通知(1999年9月8日)》。参见郑刚、雷运龙:《"执行难"的法律反思》,载《法制日报》2000年8月13日,第2版;李旭兵:《执行难,难在哪儿?》,载《河南日报》2000年8月4日,第2版。

〔16〕 1996年4月,最高人民法院召开了全国法院第一次执行工作会议,对全国法院"八五"执行工作进行了总结分析,针对面临的问题和任务,提出了"坚持审执分立的原则,坚持严肃执法,努力提高执法水平,充分发挥执行工作的职能作用,维护国家法制的权威和统一,为改革、发展和稳定服务"的指导思想,确定了"提高队伍素质,加大执行力度,规范执行秩序,严肃执行纪律,加强执行监督"的工作重点。

〔17〕 根据2007年《民事诉讼法》的规定,执行工作由执行员进行;根据需要可以设立执行机构。

法律效力的判决,在当事人不能自觉履行其法定义务的情况下,由法院专门工作人员在国家强制力的保障下加以执行。[18] 关于执行中公正问题的衡量标准是责令债务人履行债务,满足债权人的权利要求。[19] 同时,在执行权力内部修正之外,法院还着力加强直接关系人民群众切身利益和社会安定的案件的执行[20],并对执行困难的案件采取针对性举措。由此可见,在这一阶段法院解决“执行难”的工作目标与民众的心理预期并无二致。

2008 年,执行权力的内部修正基本完成,解决“执行难”由“向内认知”开始转向“向外行走”,重点针对实际执行中的困难进行突破。2008 年至 2016 年,为了破解实际执行中面临的困境,以最高人民法院为代表的相关部门机构针砭时弊,在不同节点采取了不同的举措。这一阶段涉及解决“执行难”的具体政策较多,其中集中清理执行积案活动、社会信用体系建设、法院系统内部绩效考核制度的建立等突出反映了这一时期执行工作的动态。2008 年,法院系统内部开始建立绩效考核制度,并在相当长的时间内影响了法院破解“执行难”工作的导向,法院解决“执行难”的工作重心向如何调整执行数据指标倾斜,这使得包括每隔几年就要进行一次的集中清理积案活动在内的一系列执行工作都围绕绩效考核指标进行。

需要说明的是,虽然 2007 年至 2015 年的执行工作方向与之前有差异,但对“执行难”概念的理解并无太大变化。如图 1 所示,从《最高人民法院公报》全国法院司法统计公报所公布的执行案件实际执行率[21] 来看,2007 年至 2015 年,实际执行率虽呈波动趋势,但在较长一段时期内呈逐年增长之态,并于 2012

---

〔18〕 苏宁:《少喊执行难、多想怎么办——全国法院执行情况述评》,载《人民日报》1996 年 6 月 5 日,第 3 版。

〔19〕 参见汤维建:《关于破解“执行难”的理性反思——以执行体制的独立化构建为中心》,载《学习与探索》2007 年第 5 期。

〔20〕 参见 2002 年《最高人民法院工作报告》。

〔21〕 执行标的到位率虽能有效展示解决“执行难”的进展,但由于数据缺失,难以作为纵向分析指标,故本文选取实际执行率作为研究样本。实际执行率为执行完毕、和解并履行完毕的案件之和与案件执结总数之比,实际执行率越高,反映出法院的执行效果越好。需要说明的是,最高人民法院公布的实际执行率数据虽然不仅包含民事案件,但由于民事执行案件在执行案件总数中占据绝大多数的比例,其差别并不影响整体结果。

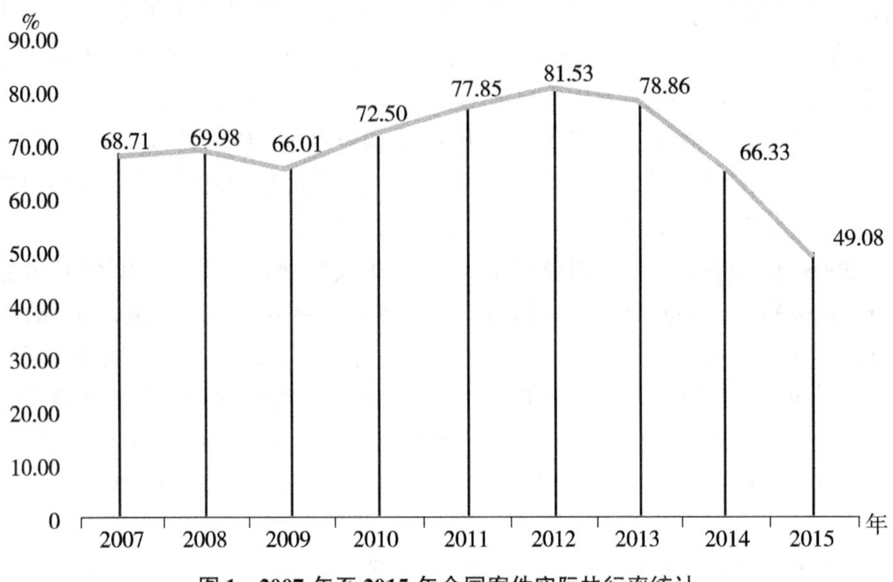

图1 2007年至2015年全国案件实际执行率统计

资料来源:2008年至2016年《中华人民共和国最高人民法院公报》刊载的《全国法院司法统计公报》。

年曾达81.53%的峰值。不可否认,实现生效判决确定的当事人权利仍是法院执行工作的主要努力方向。综上,从这一时期的执行政策、官方文件及报刊对于解决"执行难"工作的宣传来看,整体而言,执行工作并未偏离提升实际执行率与执行标的到位率的大方向。[22] 换言之,这二十余年间,法院对于"执行难"概念的理解处于相对稳定的时期。

(三)2016年至今:"执行难"与"执行不能"的概念分离

自2016年3月最高人民法院院长周强提出"用两到三年时间基本解决执行难"的目标以来,最高人民法院等相关部门单位的执行政策以及各级法院多样式的执行手段层出不穷,这段时期内执行工作有了明显的进展,执行效率显著提升。在这一阶段,执行工作的政策导向化更加显著。此外,随着执行政策的变迁,这一阶段法院对于"执行难"概念的解释也发生了变化,对于"执行难"

[22] 虽出现过以"法定期限内结案率"高达99%强调解决"执行难"工作质效的情况,但整体而言对于执行工作重心的理解并未偏离。

数据的统计口径也发生了变化。其中最显著的变化是"执行不能"从"执行难"中分离,延伸到实际执行工作中将两者相互区分。

通过对《人民法院报》[23] 2010 年至今提及"执行不能"的频次进行统计[24]——2016 年之前,也有少数研究文献认为有必要对"执行难"与"执行不能"概念作出区分,[25]但并未强调需要将二者作为两个独立的概念来看待。如 2015 年 9 月的一篇报道提出,执行工作面临着"案件增多、执行不力、执行不能"等困难,[26]这体现了对于"执行不能"的理解还包含于"执行难"的范畴之内。自 2016 年以来,强调分清"执行难"与"执行不能"已成为最高人民法院到各级法院的工作趋势:2016 年,河南省被确定为解决"执行难"工作重点推进地区,同年 10 月河南省政协委员冯军义提出厘清"执行不能"与"执行难"的界限的必要性;[27] 2018 年关于分清"执行难"与"执行不能"的宣传力度空前,"三个 90%,一个 80%"[28]的核心指标针对有无财产可供执行的案件进行了分别规定;9 月 13 日最高人民法院联合新浪司法、新浪微博共同推出的"决胜执行难"

---

〔23〕 由于研究样本难以穷尽,笔者选取相对而言更具有权威性与代表性的《人民法院报》作为研究样本。

〔24〕 笔者在《人民法院报》官方网站首页检索系统中全文检索"执行不能"关键词,共得到 283 条结果,其中共有 63 条涉及文中所述"执行不能"。资料来源:《人民法院报》官网:http://rmfyb.chinacourt.org/paper/html/2018-09/26/node_2.htm,最后访问日期:2018 年 9 月 26 日。

〔25〕 如张新阶:《外科医生与执行法官》,载《人民法院报》2014 年 6 月 6 日,第 6 版;闫继勇:《临沂:打造"沂蒙司法品牌"》,载《人民法院报》2014 年 5 月 13 日,第 8 版;余冬冬:《影响执行难的外部因素及应对建议》,载《人民法院报》2015 年 9 月 2 日,第 8 版等。

〔26〕 余冬冬:《影响执行难的外部因素及应对建议》,载《人民法院报》2015 年 9 月 2 日,第 8 版。

〔27〕 刘勋:《正确区分执行不能与执行难》,载《法制日报》2016 年 10 月 27 日,第 7 版。

〔28〕 "三个 90%"的要求是指:有财产可供执行案件在法定期限内实际执结率达到 90%;无财产可供执行案件终结本次执行程序合格率达到 90%;执行信访案件办结率不低于 90%。另一个核心指标是"一个 80%",即三年内整体执结率不低于 80%,也就是说,以终结本次执行程序方式结案率加上法定期限内实际执结率的总和不低于 80%。

专栏则将“执行不能”作为列示的主要内容之一。[29]

“执行难”,是被执行人有财产可供执行但由于各种原因难以执行,而“执行不能”则是指被执行人无财产可供执行、经执行法院穷尽手段仍不能执行。[30]当“执行不能”作为一个与“执行难”平行的法律概念被提出,相应带来了“执行难”作为法律概念的变动,这种变动体现在其内涵与外延两个方面:就“执行难”的内涵而言,法院要解决的“执行难”是指有财产可供执行案件的执行困难,无财产可供执行或仅有部分财产可供执行而无法实际执行到位的案件将不再属于“执行难”案件之列,而长期以来此类案件在所有执行案件中占比居高。最高人民法院《2017年全国法院司法统计公报》公布的数据显示,2017年度,全国法院共受理民事执行案件3,943,595件,结案3,785,201件,其中以终结本次执行程序方式结案的共1,844,118件,占民事执行案件结案总数的48.72%;[31]从其外延来看,在解决“执行难”的过程中,当区分“执行难”与“执行不能”已成为明确的政策导向之时,各级法院通常会更致力于审查案件是否符合终止本次执行程序的条件,执行的人力、物力的投入亦会有所选择。由此产生的现象是对于有财产可供执行但不予履行、逃避履行的案件所能给予的人力、物力有所缩减,而此类案件才是实际执行到位率难以提升之症结所在。此外,在我国,表象下的“执行不能”往往是债务人有履行能力却仍能通过各种途径逃避履行,无论是法院或是政府均难以规制。虽最高人民法院提出了无财产可供执行案件终结本次执行程序的合格率应达到90%之要求,但在当前关于是否符合终结本次执行程序的审查条件、相应的财产调查机制以及对法院终结本次执行工作的监督机制等尚不甚完备的背景下,区分“执行不能”的可操作性尚有待时间的检验。

---

〔29〕 最高人民法院:《“决胜执行难”专栏正式上线》,载http://www.court.gov.cn/zixun-xiangqing-118471.html,最后访问日期:2018年9月14日。

〔30〕 刘建国:《分清“执行难”与“执行不能”》,载《人民法院报》2018年7月13日,第2版。

〔31〕 参见2017年《中华人民共和国最高人民法院公报》刊载的《全国法院司法统计公报》。

三、"执行难"概念分离之制度实效的评估

(一)评估重心从实体走向程序

"执行难"三十年来一直是各级法院攻而不破的顽疾,在解决"执行难"的过程中,无财产可供执行的案件绝非近两年才出现,为何直至2016年法院才开始着重强调"执行难"与"执行不能"的区分,并对"执行难"概念作出了新的诠释?究其原因,不外乎是为"两到三年内基本解决执行难"开辟路径。通过对三十年来执行政策变迁的梳理以及对近年来法院执行工作重点的解读可见,近两年化解"执行难"的阻力与之前相比并无本质变化。如公布失信被执行人名单、限制出行与高消费等实体措施,实则属于在全社会构建诚信体系的范畴,而要在全社会建立起一套完备的信用制度,是难以毕其功于一役的。在此背景下,如何实现"两到三年内基本解决执行难"之目标?正如前述,随着时间的推移与对于"执行难"问题理解的深化,执行工作越来越呈现出政策导向型的趋势,"四个90%,一个80%"的核心指标与第三方评估机制的引入使执行评估体系优化成为本阶段执行政策的核心,而优化执行评估体系归根结底是从程序方面着手进行的调整。近两年来,尤其是2018年第三方执行评估机制启动以来,各级法院的执行工作均以"由四大核心指标[32]以及200多项基础性指标共同构成的五大板块"为圆心展开,以广东省规定的基层法院第三方评估指标为例(见图2、图3)。

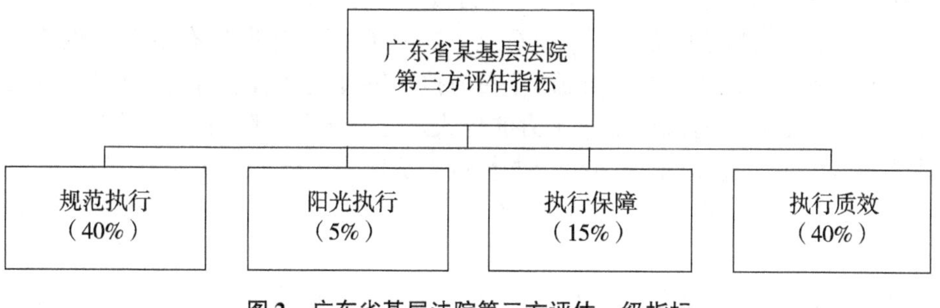

图2 广东省基层法院第三方评估一级指标

---

[32] "四大核心指标"指"四个90%,一个80%"的要求:即"终本案件合格率"、"有财产可供执行案件法定期限内实际执结率"、"信访办结率"和"结案率"。其中"结案率"虽未纳入第三方评估指标体系,但也是基本解决执行难的重要评价标准。

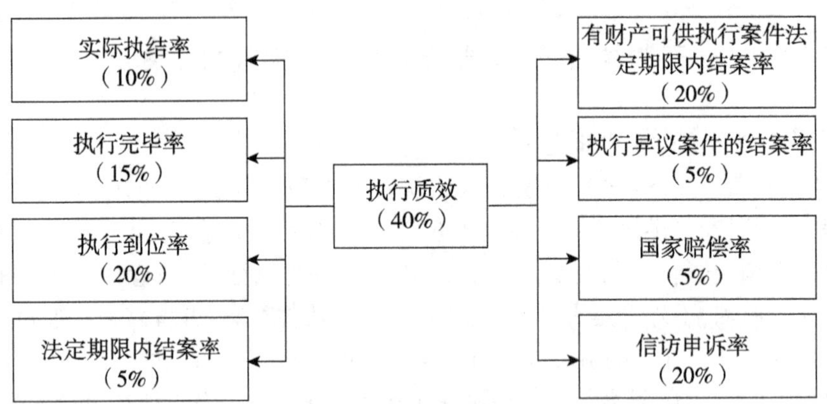

图3 广东省基层法院第三方评估二级指标

首先,关于法院执行工作绩效进行评估的一级指标(见图2),"规范执行"、"阳光执行"与"执行保障"均是对法院执行工作的程序性规制,已占绩效考核60%的比重。将剩余40%"执行质效"下属的二级指标展开来看(见图3),其中民众最为关注的执行到位率只占执行质效评估的20%,这在第三方评估中整体仅占8%的比重。在引入第三方评估机制之前,法院内外部对执行工作的评估呈现无体系之样态,但一般而言,主要依据法定期限内结案率、实际执结率、执行到位率等实体指标进行考核。相较于之前,当前执行工作评估机制的显著特征是以程序评价为主,而非针对实际执行效果方面的评价。

其次,对于法院来说,区分"执行难"与"执行不能",即将有财产可供实行案件与无财产可供执行案件分流,意在为执行案件创造合法合理的退出程序,不失为一种缓解当前执行工作压力的方式。这意味着法院对于执行工作的态度不再是大包大揽,对于穷尽执行力量也无法解决的无财产可供执行案件,不再赋予民众过高的期待。在此背景之下,当前法院对于执行工作的评估标准亦更切合实际。根据最高人民法院《关于建立执行考核指标体系的通知》等文件的规定,以执行到位率的计算为例,申请标的额不仅包括执行完毕结案的案件,还涵盖以终结本次执行方式结案的案件。一方面,这表示了法院对于执行问题的认识更加趋于理性,对确实无财产可供执行的案件不再回避;另一方面,也促使法院规范终结本次执行案件的审查,加大有财产可供执行案件的执行力度,以提升执行到位率回应民众期待。

此外,需要明确的是,即便以法院对“执行难”概念的解读为出发点,重点关注有财产可供执行的案件,实现“有财产可供执行案件法定期限内实际执结率达到90%”这一核心指标也并非易事。以广东省为例,在执行指挥平台“三个90%”和“一个80%”模块中,全省法院2016年1月至2018年8月17日有财产案件法定期限内实际执结率为87.47%,距离达标还有2.53个百分点。而且,对被执行人财产调查权以及最终确定被执行人是否有财产可供执行的权利由法院掌握,在当前“执行难”与“执行不能”的区分标准不明确的情况下,容易产生寻租空间。诚然,将无财产可供执行的案件归类为“执行不能”能够避免有限的司法资源的浪费,然而问题在于,“执行难”与“执行不能”的区分标准应当如何把握?这对致力于达到解决“执行难”核心指标同时又缺乏终结本次执行工作监督机制的法院来说是较大的考验,若把握不好,则极易造成实际执行工作中的乱象。如今年7月底安徽省某基层法院“一元拍卖黑色水性笔”事件引发热议,相关执行裁定书[33]显示,执行标的额为17.7万元。从案件的实际情况来看,应当归入“执行不能”一类,法院耗费司法成本进行一元拍卖的做法,实则是通过拍卖使之在形式上成为“有部分财产可供执行”且已执行,可以计入实际执结率的案件。虽说该做法是决胜“执行难”关键时期的无奈之举,但从其造成的社会影响来看,无论是对于解决“执行难”还是保障司法权威的公信力,均无任何实际意义,恐有舍本逐末之嫌。

(二)民众“执行难”认知与法院执行定位的差异

前述关于各阶段“执行难”概念的梳理、执行政策的制定、执行工作评估指标的确立,都是建立在法院视角之下的。虽说执行工作应当以保障当事人的利益为出发点,但从客观情况来看,民众对于“执行难”的认知历来未成为引导执行政策制定之主流。换言之,民众认知的“执行难”不一定与法院的执行工作定位在任何情况下都具有一致性和同步性。在“执行难”概念的提出阶段与稳定时期,这种差异并不显著,但从2016年至今强调“执行难”与“执行不能”的概念区分,并以程序性指标作为执行工作评估的重点开始,法院对“执行难”的界定便与民众的理解出现了偏差。

执行工作的基本出发点在于实现胜诉当事人经由生效判决确定的利益,因此,民众对于执行工作的直观评价系基于涉执标的金额到位程度而进行的,当

[33] (2017)皖0302执1177号之一执行裁定书。

执行标的不能全部或者大部分到位时,该案便是民众理解之下的"执行难"案件。诚然,执行标的不能到位存在两种情况:第一种是有财产可供执行,但因法院执行力度不足或其他客观原因,案件标的尚未执行到位;第二种则是该案"先天不足",被执行人并无财产可供执行。而后者即为近年来强调从"执行难"概念中区别开来的"执行不能"案件。如果以民众视角下的"执行难"案件作为本次基本解决"执行难"的基数,由于无财产可供执行的案件现实存在,想要达到政策既定的目标显然是不现实的。民众视角下的"执行难"是涵盖了法院所界定的"执行不能"案件的,法院"基本解决执行难"的工作重点在于解决法院界定的"执行难"案件,该范围并不涵盖"执行不能"。虽然这种区分更为理性,然而,若从当事人的视角来看,法院为执行工作付诸的努力却未能达到其对于解决"执行难"的期许。案件标的是否执行到位关系当事人切身利益,因此,当事人对"执行难"的理解并不会随着时间推移与执行工作重心转变而发生变化,结合近来法院等有关部门自上而下对于区分"执行难"与"执行不能"的重视程度来看,民众与法院对于"执行难"概念理解的偏差仍将长期存在。

这种观念的偏差很大程度上是法院长期以来把解决"执行难"当作一个司法问题来处理而形成的必然结果。对于司法问题,司法机关往往能够通过加强内部工作队伍,集中司法系统内部工作力量的方式加以解决。然而对于一项社会问题,就有必要结合系统外部力量,以及其他相关部门和社会公众对于该项问题的理解来进行综合治理。由于"执行难"问题涉及面广,司法机关也早已意识到解决"执行难"不能仅凭借法院一己之力,但从其相关执行政策出发点来看,仍然是将"执行难"作为一个司法问题来处理,而非社会问题。近两年来,执行工作有了很大进展,内外部联动机制逐渐完善,然而司法机关作为执行政策的制定者,在制定相关政策、推进执行工作的同时,民众对于"执行难"工作的期许同样不容忽视。在强调区分"执行难"与"执行不能"的背景之下,一方面,对于有财产可供执行的案件要尽可能执行到位;另一方面,对于所谓"执行不能"的案件,首先要综合各方力量确认其是否真实的无财产可供执行,只有确实无财产可供执行的案件,才能进入终结本次执行程序,还需要一套完备的恢复执行程序与之配套,一旦发现被执行人有财产可供执行,应当尽快恢复执行,保障当事人权益。

四、结 论

随着2016年至今法院执行工作评估标准由重视实体性评估转向着重实现法院执行工作的透明化、合法化、规范化的程序性评估,并引入“执行不能”概念以来,法院对于“执行难”概念的理解也发生了根本性的变化,并更加趋于理性。当前法院所解读的“执行难”案件,指的是有财产可供执行但实际难以执行到位的案件,而无财产可供执行的案件,则属于“执行不能”的范畴。

事实上,即使针对有财产可供执行的案件,要提升实际执行到位率,也是一个缓慢而漫长的过程。“执行难”绝非一个简单的司法问题,而是长期存在的涉及方方面面的复杂社会问题,难以仅仅通过法院自身加强执行力量的方式解决。如何从提升国家治理能力的角度出发,摆脱解决“执行难”过程中法院“单打独斗”的现象,探索把执行局从法院系统中剥离出来,建立具备社会联动机制的独立于司法系统之外的执行局,从体制与机制上根本解决“执行难”,才是今后相当长一段时期内需要研讨的话题。

(责任编辑:彭箫剑)

股东签名被伪造形成的股东会决议效力问题探究*

李正洋**

摘要：

伪造股东签名形成的股东会决议剥夺了相关股东参与公司决策的权利，同时也违背了公司决议形成的正当程序原则。最高人民法院《关于适用〈中华人民共和国公司法〉若干问题的规定（四）》引入了公司决议不成立制度，但是对于股东签名被伪造形成的股东会决议效力问题并未作出明确规定。准确认定伪造股东签名形成的股东会决议不成立，需要在正确划分股东签名被伪造形成的股东会决议在司法实践中呈现出的两种不同情形的基础上，充分考虑公司决议形成的过程是否符合法律、行政法规和公司章程的规定，保障股东意思表示的自由与公司决议的真实性和正当性，同时结合民法中有关法律行为和意思表示的一般理论加以分析，更好地实现私法自治与社会公正，推动市场经济主体健康发展。

关键词：

股东会决议；效力瑕疵；决议不成立；签名伪造；瑕疵治愈

一、引　言

2017年9月1日，最高人民法院《关于适用〈中华人民共和国公司法〉若干问题的规定（四）》（以下简称《公司法司法解释（四）》）正式施行。这部司法解

* 本文受国家社会科学基金青年项目“改革开放40年来中国重要经济立法的方法论研究”（项目编号：19CFX064）资助；同时为中国政法大学（2019年）研究生教育教学改革项目（项目编号：YJLX1904）的成果。

** 李正洋，中国政法大学民商经济法学院2018级硕士研究生。

释在现行《中华人民共和国公司法》(以下简称《公司法》)第22条所确立的决议无效、决议可撤销的基础上,新增了确认决议不成立之诉,形成了我国公司决议效力的"三分法"格局,即决议不成立、决议可撤销和决议无效。"三分法"格局的确立,在很大程度上弥补了《公司法》对于公司决议效力形态规定的漏洞,区分了决议的成立与生效这两个环节,使法官在处理司法实践中一些公司决议本未成立的案件时,有了统一的法律适用依据。

但是,对于股东签名被伪造所形成的股东会决议效力问题,最终通过的司法解释并没有作出明确规定,而是回避了在2016年年底最高人民法院颁布的《公司法司法解释(四)》(原则通过稿)所采用的处理方式——在决议无效、可撤销的基础上,增加了"决议不存在"和"未形成有效决议"两种情形,并将股东签名被伪造的情形明确认定为决议不存在。最终通过的版本中并未再明确提及股东签名被伪造的效力问题,而是做了模糊化处理——将原则通过稿中的第4条、第5条合并为"决议不成立",并在第5条的最后一项使用"导致决议不成立的其他情形"这一兜底条款进行立法处理。这样一来,股东签名被伪造形成的股东会决议效力成了这部司法解释中的一个空白点。

然而,在有关公司诉讼的司法实务案件中,股东会决议股东签名被伪造这一现象却层出不穷,对于这一现象所产生的股东会决议的效力应当如何认定?应当认定为决议不成立,还是适用《公司法》第22条认定其为无效的决议或者可撤销的决议?在不同情形下的伪造股东签名形成的股东会决议应当如何适用法律和司法解释的规定?

一般而言,股东签名被伪造形成的股东会决议包括两种情形,一种是股东会根本未曾召开或者形式上虽然召开了股东会,但是并未形成会议决议,行为人伪造部分股东的签名而炮制出所谓的股东会决议;另一种是股东会实际召开,但是部分股东对股东会拟决议事项持反对意见,行为人通过伪造股东签名在股东会决议上署名同意(包括决议上的部分签名系无权代理人未经股东授权为之的情形)。

在《公司法司法解释(四)》颁布施行之前,对于前述两种情形产生的案件不胜枚举,但是如何认定不同情形下的股东会决议效力,法官往往是在尊重案件客观事实的基础上,对法律的适用进行变通:有的将其认定为无效——违反《公司法》关于人事制度的强制性规定无效,[1]违反《公司法》关于修改公司章

---

〔1〕 参见姜敏诉北京城建弘诚物业管理有限责任公司公司决议撤销案,北京市西城区人民法院(2013)西民初字10876号民事判决书。

程表决比例的强制性规定应属无效;[2]有的将其认定为可撤销——侵害了股东所享有的《公司法》第4条赋予的参与重大决策权,且会议程序严重违反法律和公司章程的规定,应当予以撤销。[3] 甚至有的法院为了案件真实,立足于案情本身,突破了《公司法》第22条的规定,在判决主文中直接认定股东会决议不存在。

前述认定为无效或者可撤销的判决虽然以《公司法》本身作为裁判依据,达到了有关无效或者可撤销决议法律适用的效果。然而就其本质而言,上述判决仍是立足于股东会决议已经存在的基础上进行的分析,难以经得住推敲。[4] 被认定为决议不成立的判决,虽然判决说理逻辑清晰,但是仍是对现有法律的突破,且我国并非判例法国家,这种做法不能得到普遍适用的效果,有违法律的预测功能。"法律作为一种公认的、有确定内容的规定,使人们依据法律就可以判断自己行为是否合法,是否能够得到国家机关的支持和保障。"[5]

通过前述对于司法实践的现状分析不难看出,对于股东签名被伪造形成的股东会决议,大多数法院的判决由于缺少法律、司法解释的裁判基础,产生了以下两个方面的问题:其一,把决议不存在混同为决议可撤销,大大增加了原告的举证责任,并且对原告的起诉时间提出了更高的要求,同时法院也会基于意思自治、商业效率和交易安全的考量,对于违反法律的程序性规定和公司章程的做法,不区分程序瑕疵的严重程度一概予以驳回,损害了公司股东的合法权益;其二,将严重的程序瑕疵认为是违反法律、行政法规的强制性规定,实质上将会议程序与会议内容这一实体要素进行混同,容易导致司法权力过度介入商事活动,不利于维护商事交易的安全性和稳定性。

上述两个方面的问题实则属于对伪造签名决议效力的不正确认识而产生的两个极端。解决上述问题,仅从《公司法》及《公司法司法解释(四)》的相关条款中并不能直接得到答案,需要结合该问题的不同情形进行分析,进而解决

---

[2] 参见于英海与沈阳天之源市场管理有限公司公司决议效力确认纠纷案,沈阳市中级人民法院(2014)沈中民三终字第1240号民事判决书。

[3] 参见刘书云诉井冈山盛泰通讯技术有限责任公司公司决议撤销案,江西省吉安市吉安县人民法院(2014)吉民初字第63号民事判决书。

[4] 参见步兵、孟星宇:《股东会决议不存在探析——以〈公司法〉第22条为中心》,载《东南大学学报》(哲学社会科学版)2014年第2期。

[5] 姚建宗:《法理学》,科学出版社2010年版,第192页。

当前司法实践中处理相关问题时的尴尬境况。在《公司法司法解释(四)》实施之后,公司决议不成立制度已经得到了最高审判机关司法解释的认可,在类似案件中,法官的判决有了法律的依据,这无疑是公司法领域的一大进步。对于存在伪造股东签名的股东会决议的效力问题,尽管司法解释中没有明确规定,但是从民商法的基本原理和法律解释的角度出发,也应当归入该解释第5条所规定的决议不成立的范围中,根据案件的不同情形,适用相应的条款。

本文将立足于公司决议瑕疵的形态以及公司决议与股东意思表示的一般理论,从公司决议不成立的制度价值出发,结合公司决议的性质、股东意思表示和公司决议效力瑕疵的基本理论,分别对前述股东签名被伪造的两种情形进行讨论,并结合司法判例,为司法实践提供参考。准确认定该决议的效力对于相关利害关系人向法院提起公司决议瑕疵之诉,保障股东依法参与公司经营管理事项的决策权力,维护私法自治和商事秩序具有重要的意义。〔6〕

二、股东签名被伪造与决议不成立

股东签名被伪造属于股东会决议在效力上存在瑕疵,由于不同瑕疵所涉及的程度不同,《公司法》和《公司法司法解释(四)》确立了公司决议效力瑕疵"三分法"的格局。但是对于股东签名被伪造这一情形应当属于何种瑕疵形态,法律和司法解释条文中并未明确列举,因此需要从理论上对决议不成立制度本身以及其与其他两种瑕疵形态之间的区别进行分析。

(一)股东会决议效力瑕疵的基本形态

股东签名被伪造所形成的股东会决议在效力上是存在瑕疵的,因此,明确股东会决议效力瑕疵的基本形态,是认定伪造股东签名形成的股东会决议不成立的基础和前提。

作为社团自治下的产物,股东会决议的成立与生效取决于程序和内容两个方面,其中程序包括了召集程序和议事方法。只有程序和内容均合法的股东会决议,才能够充分保障股东在公司的重大事项决策权,维护公司的利益。当前

〔6〕 为了写作方便,本文之后的公司决议的效力分析将主要围绕有限责任公司的股东会决议进行,董事会决议、股份有限公司的股东大会决议分析思路同本文相似,故不再单独论述。

述两个内涵中的任何一个部分出现违反章程或法令的部分,股东会决议则存在瑕疵,法律应当对其效力予以否定性的评价,此即股东会决议瑕疵制度。

作为一项单一团体的意思,股东大会决议是“资本多数决”规则的产物,其本质是资本多数出资者的意思决定。[7] 在大陆法系国家,《德国商法典》对股东会决议瑕疵制度和有关情形进行了系统的规定,将其分为无效和可撤销两类,其他大陆法系国家如日本、韩国在制定商法典时也效仿了德国的做法,采取两分的模式,但是由于司法实践中商事活动的多样化以及法学理论的不断发展,日韩等国在20世纪后期相继修改了商法典,在两分的基础上引入了决议不成立制度,形成瑕疵决议三分的格局。德国虽然没有修改其商法典,但是学术理论界和司法判例中已经承认了决议不成立这种决议形态,形成实质上的三分法格局。

1. 无效与可撤销的二分法格局

根据民法的基本原理,民事法律行为产生拘束力的基础在于意思自治。意思自治作为法律行为的核心,不仅要求内容上符合法律规定、不违背公序良俗和不侵害社会公共利益,还要求意思表示内容的真实性。决议作为民事法律行为的一种,其拘束力同样也源于意思自治,只不过此时不再是参与表决者的意思自治,而是社团的意思自治。因此意思机关一旦通过法定程序作出选择,无论社团还是其成员均应受该自由选择的拘束,即使此时真理掌握在少数人手中,或者多数决形成的意志对社团明显不利,亦是如此。[8]

我国现行《公司法》第22条前两款确立了决议效力的无效与可撤销的二分法结构,尽管在法律适用的过程中思路简洁明了,但是该条法律规范的适用前提是决议已经成立。当公司未曾召开股东会形成一份所谓的股东会决议,或者股东未出席股东会却被伪造签名形成股东会决议,在事实判断上如果将前述情形归属于决议无效或者决议可撤销,则割裂了决议“形成—生效”这一逻辑顺序,忽视了决议在形成阶段存在的重要瑕疵。同时,在采取二分法立法例的国家中,其普遍逻辑认为决议的瑕疵程度是二分法的适用基础,即对于瑕疵严重者,已经达到违反法律、行政法规的强制性规定的程度时为决议无效;对于瑕疵相对轻微,仅在程序上违反法律、行政法规或内容上违反公司章程的程度时为决议可撤销。这种简单以实体和程序瑕疵的异同来区分决议效力的方式过于

〔7〕 参见钱玉林:《股东大会决议瑕疵的救济》,载《现代法学》2005年第3期。

〔8〕 参见徐银波:《决议行为效力规则之构造》,载《法学研究》2015年第4期。

形式主义,缺乏坚实的法理基础。

在本文的引言部分,笔者简要介绍了股东签名被伪造形成的股东会决议的两种情形,这两种情形涉及股东会形成过程的不同阶段:第一种处于股东会决议的成立阶段,因为没有股东对待决议事项作出同意、反对或者弃权的意思表示,因此此种情形下伪造的股东会决议欠缺成立要件,类似于民法中法律行为的成立阶段;第二种涵盖了股东会决议的成立和生效阶段,即股东做出了意思表示,但是行为人通过伪造部分或者全部股东的签名篡改其本身的意思表示,导致最终的股东会决议满足《公司法》或者公司章程规定的投票比例,〔9〕类似于民法中法律行为的生效阶段。

《公司法》第22条对公司决议效力"二分法"的设计是立足于公司决议已经成立的基础之上的,但是前述两种情形都有在公司决议的形成阶段就存在瑕疵的情况,即涉及公司的决议是否实际成立的问题,对此《公司法》《公司法司法解释(四)》都没有提出明确的处理方式,尽管在之前的司法解释原则通过稿中有部分涉及,但也仅是昙花一现,对这一问题最高人民法院并没有给出明确的解释。

2.决议不成立制度的引入:"三分法"的内涵与其合理性〔10〕

虽然表面上看"三分法"只是在"二分法"格局的基础上增加了"决议不成

〔9〕 根据《公司法》第43条的规定,有限责任公司股东会的议事方式和表决程序,除《公司法》另有规定外,由公司章程规定。

〔10〕 关于公司决议瑕疵形态,学界还有一种观点认为是采用四分法,即在三分的基础上增加"未形成有效决议"(或者决议未生效)这一情形,2016年年底《公司法司法解释(四)》(原则通过稿)也采用了这种形式,但是后来的正式稿仍然选择了三分法,一些主张四分法的学者认为,其理论基础在于在决议的效力层面增加决议如何执行这一环节,因此对应决议瑕疵方面还应得到不同的价值判断结论。但是决议的执行问题本身涉及的是公司法的另一个问题,即三机关的相互关系问题,且不同类型的公司其公司章程也会做出更加具体的规定。尽管二者表面上处于不同阶段,即是否已经召开过相关会议,但是生活事实上的差别不一定一一对应地反映在法律条文中,法律条文恰恰是对生活事实的抽象概括归纳。参见王轶:《论民事法律事实的类型区分》,载《中国法学》2013年第1期;王雷:《公司决议行为瑕疵制度的解释与完善》,载《清华法学》2016年第5期;张旭荣:《法律行为视角下公司会议决议效力形态分析》,载《比较法研究》2013年第6期。

立”作为一种新的决议瑕疵类型,但是这种体系的架构和逻辑上的分离是有充分理由的:依照“三分法”的观点,股东会决议本质上是一种民事法律行为,而法律行为的成立和生效是两个不同阶段的不同概念。相应地,股东会决议的成立和生效也应与民法中有关法律行为的理论相吻合。[11]

2017年10月1日起正式施行的《中华人民共和国民法总则》(以下简称《民法总则》)也采纳了法人决议的法律行为说,认为决议行为是民事法律关系主体之间基于共同的意思表示而意图实现一定私法上法律效果的行为,其满足民事法律行为的所有条件,是一种民事法律行为。[12] 当欠缺成立要件时,该民事法律行为不成立;同理,当股东会决议欠缺成立要件时,该股东会决议亦不成立。故在公司法中,决议不成立(或者决议不存在)应当解释为“决议在程序上的瑕疵十分明显,以至于无法认定该决议在法律上存在的情形”。[13]

区别于民法中一般的单方、双方和多方法律行为,股东会决议作为一项法人的意思表示,其形成过程需要经过两个阶段,首先需要形成股东们的个人意思表示,在此基础上形成一个意思表示的集合体,即“在重大问题上,在对外从事行为之前,还必须先在内部形成社团的意思”,[14] 经过会前的召集程序、会上的充分讨论后,按照法定的表决程序形成最终的股东会决议,然而“决议的根本目的不在于调整参与制定决议的个人之间的关系,而是构建他们所共同拥有的权利领域或者他们所代表的法人的权利领域”。[15]

---

〔11〕 前引7,钱玉林文。

〔12〕 《民法总则》第134条规定:(第1款)民事法律行为可以基于双方或者多方的意思表示一致成立,也可以基于单方的意思表示成立。(第2款)法人、非法人组织依照法律或者章程规定的议事方式和表决程序作出决议的,该决议行为成立。参见李适时:《中华人民共和国民法总则释义》,法律出版社2017年版,第42页。

〔13〕 李建伟:《公司决议效力瑕疵类型及其救济体系再构建——以股东大会决议可撤销为中心》,载《商事法论集》2008年第2期;吴建斌编译:《日本公司法》,法律出版社2017年版,第436页。

〔14〕 [德]迪特尔·梅迪库斯:《德国民法总论》,邵建东译,法律出版社2000年版,第841页。

〔15〕 [德]卡尔·拉伦茨:《德国民法通论》(下册),王晓晔译,法律出版社2003年版,第433页。

"三分法"以股东会决议这一特殊的法律行为作为分析起点,类推适用了民事法律行为的一般法理,虽然具体细节上存在不同,但是在股东会决议的成立和生效问题上,二者包含了相同的法理。如此,在判断一份股东会决议是否存在瑕疵时,应当遵循的判断步骤是:先从事实层面判断决议是否成立,例如修改公司章程必须经过代表2/3以上的表决权的股东表决通过,如果低于该比例,该项股东会决议不能成立;之后再从效力层面判断该项决议是否有效,例如该项决议的内容是走私,则该项决议因违反《中华人民共和国刑法》而自始无效;或者公司章程明确规定修改公司章程必须经过代表100%表决权的股东通过,而实际票决结果仅为4/5,虽高于《公司法》的最低限度,但因为未满足公司章程的规定,相关利害关系人可以提起决议撤销之诉。

(二)将伪造股东签名认定为决议不成立的依据

1.伪造股东签名形成的股东会决议不属于决议无效

如前所述,法律行为的成立与生效是两个不同的概念,尽管在法律效果上不成立与无效具有一定的相似属性,但这种效果上的趋同性并不能就此将二者画等号,不能因此认定二者在构成要件、行为指引意义和其他方面不存在任何差别,法律行为成立制度具有其独立的内容要求和价值意义,公司决议行为成立制度亦是如此。[16]

公司的决议行为包括了内容和程序两个维度,决议程序的合法合规有利于保障实体内容的公正,同时决议程序本身也有其独立价值——维护企业的运行秩序和商事效率,因此公司决议的成立意味着该项决议必须是法定主体依据法定职权或者章程的授权,在符合法律或章程规定的召集程序和表决方式下作出。当公司决议在前述过程中有任何一个环节严重违反既定规则时,在此基础上形成的决议也不能称为公司决议,即公司决议并未成立。此时无需对其效力进行探究,因为从程序上该项决议就不符合公司会议的正当程序。同时,也正是因为该项决议未能成立,公司之后还可以依据法定和既定章程重新召集会议作出内容相同的决议来治愈程序上的瑕疵;然而若一项决议被认定为无效决议,该项决议自始不会发生效力,公司也不能再次作出包含相同内容的决议。伪造股东签名所形成的决议虽然在公司决议的成立阶段就因为股东意思表示

〔16〕 参见王雷:《公司决议行为瑕疵制度的解释与完善》,载《清华法学》2016年第5期。

存在瑕疵而导致公司决议缺乏成立要件,但是这种情况完全可以通过重新按照正当程序进行决议的方式予以治愈,并且如果治愈后的决议结果与之前瑕疵决议的结果相同,也能够保护公司外交易相对人的交易预期,不会因直接认定为无效而导致善意相对人交易安全处于一种不稳定的状态。况且有时并非所有伪造股东签名的行为都一定会损害股东的利益,例如增加公司注册资本的决议等。如若对那些明知股东权益受到侵害但却长期不主张伪造决议无效的股东予以放任,任随其毫不受限地其诉请决议无效,必将导致对这些股东的投机心理的纵容,导致权利的滥用,并在第三人要求股东承担责任时逃之夭夭。[17]

2. 伪造股东签名形成的股东会决议不属于决议可撤销

股东签名被伪造这一行为发生于公司意思表示的形成阶段,尽管根据实际的情形不同,可以将其认定为是程序违法抑或是行为人侵犯了有关股东的实体权利,但是归根结底最终形成的公司决议仍然欠缺成立要件;公司决议可撤销的原因大多也包含程序上的瑕疵,因此认定伪造签名形成的股东会决议不成立,首先应明确其与决议可撤销之间的关系,这往往也成为司法实践中的核心问题,笔者认为,二者主要体现在如下两个方面:

一是制度价值不同。法律行为是否成立涉及事实层面的判断,而法律行为是否有效却是价值层面的衡量。如前所述,股东签名被伪造属于公司决议成立阶段,缺乏被伪造签名股东的意思表示意味着该项公司决议违背了公司决议的基本原理——基础成立要件缺乏,自无所谓效力评价问题。[18]

二是瑕疵的程度和内容不同。程度上,不成立的决议的程序瑕疵严重程度要强于可撤销决议,前者的程序瑕疵严重程度更高以至于决议根本不能成立;内容上,决议不成立的事由仅包括程序存在瑕疵,而决议可撤销事由还包括决议的实质内容违反公司章程。[19] 对此,日本的立法例甚至直接认为,决议不成立的瑕疵就是指“高于决议撤销事由,同时对该瑕疵的诉讼主张设置三个月的

〔17〕 参见袁辉根:《伪造公司决议的效力认定》,载《人民司法·案例》2010年第6期。

〔18〕 参见杜万华主编:《最高人民法院公司法司法解释(四)理解与适用》,人民法院出版社2017年版,第138页。

〔19〕 参见李建伟:《公司决议效力瑕疵类型及其救济体系再构建》,载王保树主编:《商事法论集》(总第15卷),法律出版社2009年版。

不变期间实为不当的程度上的瑕疵”。[20] 股东签名被伪造不仅仅对公司决议的是否成立造成了影响,同时也对股东参与公司决策的权利造成了侵犯。如果仅仅将其认定为可撤销决议,事后通过一些股东追认等补救措施予以完善,混淆了股东个人意思表示和公司意思表示。

三是股东权利保护期限不同。根据现行《公司法》的规定,股东可在法定期间内向法院诉请撤销。[21] 这 60 日属于法定不变期间,不能够中止、中断和延长。由于决议不成立本身属于法律行为形成阶段的一个环节,在伪造决议的情形下,股东甚至不知道决议作出的真实日期,更何谈保护股东权利。更需要提出质疑的是,既然决议是伪造的,那么该份决议的根本不存在一个“作出”的行为,又怎能够认定决议作出的日期?这一点更加凸显了决议可撤销说的内在矛盾和局限性。[22]

三、未召开股东会而伪造股东签名所形成的股东会决议的效力

股东会未曾召开,意味着股东没有经过法定程序表达其真实意思,因此判断该种情形下伪造股东签名形成的股东会决议应当先从该种行为的形态进行——分析股东会决议构成的要件,进而结合公司和股东个人意思表示的形成过程来分析其效力形态。

(一)行为形态

公司股东会的决议须满足如下四个要件:决议机关确有举行会议,有法定人数出席会议,会议曾做出表决,表决结果达多数决要求。[23] 如果公司股东会未曾召开股东会,则无法形成社团意思,更无法形成决议。具体而言,这主要包括两种情形:一种是根本未曾召开股东会,股东在毫不知情的情况下被伪造签名形成了股东会决议;另一种是股东聚集在一起开会,但并不知道或者并不认

---

〔20〕 张凝:《日本股东大会制度的立法、理论与实践》,法律出版社 2009 年版,第 303 页。

〔21〕《公司法》第 22 条第 2 款规定:……股东可自决议作出之日起六十日内,请求人民法院撤销决议。

〔22〕 前引 17,袁辉根文。

〔23〕 前引 8,徐银波文。

为现在是股东会,或没有认识到是在进行表决,在此基础上形成的所谓决议——二者的核心在于缺乏决议法律行为的"成立"这一过程。

(二)认定为决议不成立的依据

如前文所述,作为一种法律行为,应当严格依照法律或者章程所规定的议事方式和表决程序进行,这是股东会决议成立的前提。对于第一种情形,公司的意思表示形成机关根本未曾做出任何意思表示即形成所谓的"决议",此种行为类似于两个自然人之间订立买卖合同,一方当事人未曾发出要约,另一方即要求对方按照"合同"履行给付义务。这种伪造股东签名的行为,实质是在股东会会议的召集程序上和表决过程中存在的重大瑕疵,属于《公司法司法解释(四)》第5条第1项和第2项所列决议不成立的情形。因此,在没有召开股东会的情况下,伪造股东签名进而伪造股东会决议,无法满足前述决议成立的四项基本要件,同时这一行为也侵害了其他股东的合法权益和利益,严重违反了法定程序,故此类决议因不满足决议成立的要件而不成立。[24]

意思表示作为法律行为的核心,包含了行为意思、表示意思和效果意思三个方面。适用于公司决议,则要求做出公司决议的主体只有满足上述三个层面的内容才能够形成最终的意思表示。股东会作为有限责任公司的权力机关,是有限公司的决议主体,因此有限公司股东会的决议只能体现股东会的意思,而不能是个别或者少数股东的个人意思。故即使召开了公司会议,但是即使行为人通过伪造他人签名形成了"书面决议",最终也会因不满足决议成立的形式要件而被认定不成立。此种情况下,虚构决议行为并非公司股东或者董事共同作出的法人意思表示的体现,仅反映了虚构者的个人意志,实际上是以个人意思代替公司意思,不能产生法律约束力。[25] 故对于第二种情形,因为没有真正的决议存在,类似于根本未曾召开过实质意义上的股东会,因此也应当认定为决议不成立。

相较于决议无效,认定为决议不成立还能够更好地保护善意第三人的合法权益,保障交易的稳定和安全。决议无效说的问题是,即使被伪造签名的股东事后已经知道或应当知道伪造决议的内容,并在公司经营中以明示或者默示的方式实施或者遵守了该决议的内容,他也可以在决议作出后的任何时间诉请确

〔24〕 前引18,《最高人民法院公司法司法解释(四)理解与适用》,第134页。

〔25〕 前引18,《最高人民法院公司法司法解释(四)理解与适用》,第135页。

认决议无效并废弃决议内容指向的既成事实，进而对第三人构成抗辩，损害第三人的合法权益。[26] 然而决议不成立的本质并不涉及价值判断，故不能和决议无效等同，仅是决议未成立，不存在决议的效力有无问题，前述情形完全可以按照法定程序重新形成一份体现之前被伪造签名股东真实意思表示的股东会决议。

相较于决议可撤销，认定决议不成立更能符合被伪造的公司决议的本质，同时也能够更好地保护股东和公司的合法权益和利益。决议不成立说要求公司全体股东对这份未通过法定程序形成的决议予以追认才能够认定其成立并对其效力进行评价，故只要公司股东没有对其进行追认，则在法定诉讼时效期间内股东均可向法院提起确认之诉。这样能够使企图通过伪造股东签名损害其他股东利益的行为不受法律保护，同时还给予了相关股东对其受到侵害的权利以救济途径。决议可撤销规定的法定 60 日不变期间，在期间届满之后决议便有效，这对于维护其他股东的股东权益是明显不利的。尤其是在一种更为极端的情形下——被伪造签名的股东根本不知道或者根本没有机会知道伪造的决议已经存在这一事实——就更难以保证公平，而决议不成立说恰恰填补了这一漏洞。[27]

（三）司法实践中的法律适用与评析

在《公司法司法解释（四）》正式颁布之前，由于缺乏决议不成立的法律适用依据，司法实践中对于未召开股东会而伪造股东签名形成的股东会决议的主要态度取决于决议本身的内容：如果决议内容本身严重侵害股东的权利的行使，则判定其为无效；此外还有部分法院则在判决中直接判令决议不存在。

在“古某与湖南中油鄱阳汽车加气站有限公司公司决议纠纷、股权转让纠纷案”中，长沙市中级人民法院认为，有限责任公司通过股东会决议的方式进行公司章程的变更、决定股权的转让等行为实质是股东通过股东会行使股东权利、决定变更自身与公司的民事关系的法律行为，故股东实际参加股东会并作出真实有效的意思表示是股东会及其形成的决议有效的必要条件。[28] 被告公

〔26〕 王林清：《公司纠纷裁判思路与规范释解》（第 2 版），法律出版社 2017 年版，第 873 页。

〔27〕 同上，王林清书，第 873 ~ 874 页。

〔28〕 参见长沙市中级人民法院（2013）长中民四终字第 01997 号民事判决书。

司章程明确规定公司变更注册资本,必须召开股东会并由全体股东通过并作出决议,而诉争的股东会决议中原告的签名系伪造,因此不能认定该次会议形成的为有效的股东会决议,即相关工商登记所依赖的股东会决议并不存在。

在“王某与黄某、南黄海旅游服务公司等公司决议效力确认纠纷案”中,江苏省高级人民法院认为,陆某向任益明转让股权之事项亦未书面通知黄某,陆某表示其与王某没有股权转让的关系,南黄海公司从未开过股东会。王某和南黄海公司没有通知所有股东,便自行召开股东会并伪造股东黄某的签名,故基于此形成的股东会决议的行为违反《公司法》的规定,侵害了黄某的股东权益,法院不予认可其效力。[29] 该案的核心在于股东向公司股东以外的人转让股权,但未曾召开股东会,且伪造其他股东同意转让的股东会决议签名,侵害了公司现有股东的优先购买权,其伪造股东会决议的行为违反《公司法》第72条关于有限责任公司股东优先购买权的规定,侵害了原告的股东权益,不产生法律效力。

在“毕某等与南京中兴公司公司决议效力确认纠纷案”中,一审、二审法院均认为,中兴公司办理公司营业期限变更登记的依据,实质是公司控股股东的个人意思表示的产物,所谓的“股东会决议”严重侵害了三位原告作为股东的合法权益,且在本案诉讼中,毕某等三位原告明确表示对此股东会决议拒绝予以追认,所以该决议不能发生法律效力。[30] 有限公司的股东会应当依照法定和章程规定的召集和议事方式进行,在股东会拟对相关事项作出决议时,应当由股东会按照法定和公司章程所规定的程序进行,且结果须达到法定和章程规定的表决权比例,此时股东会决议才能够形成。通过股东会决议对公司营业期限等章程内容的变更,实质是股东通过参加股东会行使表决权的民事法律行为,是变更股东个人与公司民商事法律关系的过程,其核心是股东的参与行为及其意思表示的客观存在,包括以口头明示或行为参加股东会、进行表决的表示。尽管各股东的表示与最终形成的决议可能并不一致,但是股东会的组织形式,以及会议最终形成的文件理应包含这一形成过程和实质。

上述判决在说理部分把握了股东会决议瑕疵这一节点,有的虽然维护了股东的权益,但混淆了决议的成立与生效两个环节;有的虽然抓住了决议未成立

〔29〕 参见江苏省高级人民法院(2014)苏审二商申字第00393号民事裁定书。

〔30〕 参见南京市中级人民法院(2013)宁商终字第1001号民事判决书。

这一事实，但因缺乏法律依据而缺少普遍的适用性和参考价值。但是，上述问题在《公司法司法解释（四）》出台之后得到了解决，该解释第5条第1项和第2项明确列举了前述情形所形成的决议不成立。[31] 未召开股东会或者股东大会、董事会而虚构决议的，以及会议未对决议事项进行表决而形成的公司决议不成立。决议不成立制度的设立，弥补了我国《公司法》有关公司决议瑕疵制度的立法漏洞，较全面地体现了实践中公司决议瑕疵的多样性，赋予了当事人在符合法定条件时提起确认决议不成立之诉的权利，也有助于法官确定裁判依据和裁判路径。[32]

四、已召开股东会决议而伪造股东签名形成的股东会决议的效力

股东会已经召集意味着在形式上股东有做出意思表示的行为，但是在内容上与最终公示或者发生效力的股东会决议不符，该情形跨越了公司决议的形成和生效两个阶段，并且与民法理论中的无权代理行为有相似的地方，实践中认定此种情形下股东会决议的效力也往往存在“剔除法”和“一概认定为决议不成立”这两种较为极端的做法，但是为了保持司法对公司自治介入的客观和公正，应当将处理的焦点回归到被伪造签名股东本身的真实意思与其所谓伪造的决议生效之后的行为上。

（一）行为性质

在公司运行的过程中，还会出现股东会决议上股东签名被伪造的另一种情形，即股东会已经按照法定和章程规定的程序召开，且股东会会议记录上表明股东或者其代理人出席，然而最后形成并在工商备案的股东会决议上，该股东的意思表示被篡改或者部分签名系无权代理人签署，至于其意思表示被篡改的原因可以是事后篡改，也可以是事前个别股东及其代理人受到了行为人的欺诈或者胁迫导致其在股东会决议时，做出了不真实的意思表示，这种情形类似于

---

〔31〕《公司法司法解释（四）》第5条（节选）：股东会或者股东大会、董事会决议存在下列情形之一，当事人主张决议不成立的，人民法院应当予以支持：（一）公司未召开会议的，但依据公司法第三十七条第二款或者公司章程规定可以不召开股东会或者股东大会而直接作出决定，并由全体股东在决定文件上签名、盖章的除外；（二）会议未对决议事项进行表决的。

〔32〕前引18，《最高人民法院公司法司法解释（四）理解与适用》，第134页。

民事法律关系中的无权代理。[33] 结合上文对法律行为与公司决议之间的分析，笔者认为，此种情形可以类推适用民法中的无权代理对其进行定性。但是民法中的代理行为属于双方法律行为，而公司决议作为一种独立的法律行为类型，尽管可以类推适用无权代理，但是对于公司瑕疵的治愈方法却不能直接照抄民法。

同时，需要明确的是，这种情形与前一部分论及的一种情形不同，其既存在于公司决议的形成阶段即股东作出意思表示的阶段，又存在于公司决议的生效阶段。尽管在公司决议的成立阶段，该项决议客观上已经符合公司决议成立的一般构成要件，但是在公司决议的生效阶段，因为行为人伪造相关股东签名的行为，导致有关股东意思表示不真实，其实质是排除了股东个人的真实意思表示在公司决议中所发挥的作用。反映在公司决议的形成过程中，即是缺乏公司法和公司章程所要求的公司决议成立的主观要件——股东就特定事项做出意思表示，因而在满足一定条件时，也应当认定该种情形下形成的公司决议不成立。

（二）理论上的两种处理方法及评述

在理论上，对于前述情形的处理方式主要有两种，分别是“剔除法”和“一概认定为决议不成立”。这两种方法分别站在效率和公平的角度，对股东签名被伪造的情形做出了价值层面的判断，为解决这一问题提供了思路。但是，这两种方法站在两个极端的层面，且都是从结果出发逆向对过程进行评价，忽略了在股东意思表示形成过程中和公司决议过程中的行为细节，同时也没有实现公平和效率二者在法律效果上的价值均衡。

1. 剔除法

剔除法的分析思路主要从公司的资本多数决这一前提入手，首先承认被伪造签名的股东属于意思表示不真实，但是出于决议的效率考量，如果在剔除该股东的表决权比例后公司决议仍然能够符合法律或者公司章程规定的表决比例，该项决议仍然是有效的。剔除法认为，对于一些股权结构较为分散的公司，一些小股东为了自己的利益，可能会阻挠公司的正常经营计划和投资方案，因此以种种理由找出公司股东会决议在程序上存在的瑕疵，并诉诸法院认定决议

---

[33] 根据《民法总则》第171条规定，“行为人行为人没有代理权、超越代理权或者代理权终止后，仍然实施代理行为”属于无权代理。

不存在。但是,假设前述股东的确在决议本身没有任何瑕疵的情况下参加了股东会决议,并且投了反对票,但仍然不会影响股东会决议最后的结果时,此种情形下这些股东的个人意思表示对公司决议的最终成型并不会产生举足轻重的影响。

剔除法站在宏观经济运行的角度,立足于商法外观主义的特点,保障公司的运行效率和相对人的交易安全。但是这种做法忽略了股东作为社团成员的决策权,公司作为社团法人,其存在的基础在社团成员之间的合作,特别是有限责任公司这种人资两合性的企业,其决议的形成有赖于社团内社员的参与,直接剔除某个股东的表决结果的做法完全忽略了股东的社员权利。

2. 一概认定为决议不成立

公司民主是一种参与式民主,强调股东之间的协商、讨论以达成共识,力求最大限度地保护绝大多数股东的利益。[34] 股东参会不仅能够行使表决权,同时还可能通过会议上的陈述影响其他股东的表决行为,从而影响最终的投票结果。此种观点假设了另一种情形,就是对于股东人数较少的有限责任公司,股东之间的人和性是公司运营的重要基础之一,因此股东的签名被伪造或者篡改,实质上是对公司中人合性因素的严重破坏,有损公司的重要根基,也不利于今后公司的发展。同时,如果在会前或者会中部分股东受到了来自控股股东或者利害关系人的欺诈或胁迫,一方面他在股东会上做出了虚假的意思表示,另一方面他也有可能丧失了在会上了解真实情况、判断决议的潜在风险并说服其他股东改变其意志或者向其他股东揭穿决议隐藏目的的机会[35]。此时对于一些跟风投票的股东而言,虽然他们的意思表示并非虚假,但却为支配股东所利用。

因此,一概认定为决议不成立的做法强调股东会决议不能仅看被伪造签名的股东的股权比例,资合性只是公司决议形成的一个方面。这种观点站在股东的社员权角度出发,维护了股东的权利和公司产生的重要基础——人,具有一定的可取之处。但是如果任何决议都一律认定为决议不成立,特别是对于一些对股东实体权利并不会造成重大影响的决议,直接认定为决议不成立有些过于

〔34〕 参见张闽:《资本多数决的滥用与纠正》,山东大学出版社 2014 年版,第 13 页。

〔35〕 参见赵心泽:《股东会决议效力的判断标准与判断原则》,载《政法论坛》2016 年第 1 期。

极端,一定程度上也不利于公司决议效率的提高。

(三)根据个别股东对决议结果的影响来认定决议的效力

通过分析上述两种处理方式,不难发现,二者在事后对于被伪造签名的股东本身的意思和行为关注度并不够。即我们在类推适用这种情形为无权代理时,应当关注这种决议瑕疵实质上更多的是立足于委托人和代理人之间的内部关系,因此运用民法中的代理法律制度,这种瑕疵也是能够得到治愈的。

民法中,被代理人的追认可以补足行为人无权代理的效力瑕疵,在无权代理行为未得到被代理人的追认的情况下,其对被代理人不发生效力。[36] 类推适用于公司决议中,应当根据个别股东对决议结果的影响来认定决议的效力:第一,如果该被伪造的具有瑕疵的意思表示(无论无效还是可撤销)的表决比例被剔除后,剩余的表决比例仍能够满足公司章程的规定,说明该股东的投票行为并未对其他股东产生实质影响,该决议有效;第二,如果该股东意思表示本身即是无效的(参考股东个人意思表示无效的民法规则,例如行为人与第三人恶意串通而形成的意思表示等情形)且其对其他股东的投票造成了实质性影响,此时决议不成立;第三,"如果该股东的意思表示具有可撤销的原因并且其表决权重对资本多数决原则产生了实质性影响,那么此时的决议为可撤销的决议,并非无效决议,这是根据意思表示的基本理论,在撤销前该个人表决行为是有效的,除非其表决行为被撤销才会影响最终的决议效力",[37] 例如股东受到欺诈或者胁迫而作出的意思表示在其意思表示通过司法途径被撤销前仍然是有效的。

因此,如果委托人(被伪造签名的股东)在知道相关股东以自己的名义进行投票这一事实后一定时间内没有提出异议或者明示接受投票结果,即代理行为没有被撤销则无权代理投票行为有效,符合法定或者章程规定的比例的,股东大会决议则成立生效。[38]

最高人民法院在起草《公司法司法解释(四)》的过程中,对于这一问题,产生了较大的分歧。但是,在最终确定的司法解释中,对于该类型行为司法解释

---

〔36〕 参见张新宝:《〈中华人民共和国民法总则〉释义》,中国人民大学出版社2017年版,第370页。

〔37〕 前引26,王林清书,第923页。

〔38〕 参见前引18,《最高人民法院公司法司法解释(四)理解与适用》,第145页。

并没有做出明确的规定。笔者认为,这样做的立足点在于司法解释的制定者希望这一类案件应当采取个案分析的方法,不能一概而论,即在某种意义上否认了前述两种较为极端的做法,而是关注在伪造签名的股东会决议作出后股东是否对其进行追认,或者以明示的方式接受了决议内容。这种明示的接受主要体现在按照决议的内容行事等方面。当然这其中也包括一种情形,即如果股东未曾参加过股东会会议即"被伪造签名"形成股东会决议时,如果伪造签名的人能够举证证明原告有充分的可能知道或者应当知道决议内容的存在并对决议内容表示接受,则基于此形成的公司决议仍然是成立的。否则,则属于股东会决议程序出现了严重瑕疵,应当适用《公司法司法解释(四)》第5条的兜底条款,认定决议不成立。

(四)司法实践中的法律适用与评析

在《公司法司法解释(四)》颁布之前,对于此类案件,一些法院也采取了与笔者的分析思路相近似的方法来认定决议的效力。例如,在"张某诉北京中西多远教育咨询中心公司决议效力确认案"中,北京市第二中级人民法院认为,虽然涉案决议中"张某"的签名并非本人所签,但在涉案决议作出时,在无相反证据证明的情况下,可以认定张某系多元中心公章的控制人或支配人,决议内容系其真实意思表示,原告张某上诉称其于2011年10月查询工商档案时才知道涉案内容决议,该上诉主张与常理明显不符,法院不予采信。[39] 该二审判决分别从张某的身份、决议的内容、印章的控制及盖章情况、决议的履行情况等方面,论证了原告知道并同意相关的决议事项。法院通过对举证责任的分配和证明标准的把握,一方面使法律事实尽可能趋近客观事实,另一方面也逐步引导当事人减少乃至杜绝代签名行为的发生。

有关股东对决议上签名进行追认的问题,在"张某诉江苏万华公司等股东权纠纷案"中,法院认为,虽然被告万华拥有工贸公司绝对多数的表决权,但并不等同万华可以利用控股股东的地位,将个人决策行为与公司决议行为相混同,更不意味着万某的个人意志可以代替股东会决议的效力,故不能认定工贸公司召开了股东会并形成了真实有效的股东会决议……诉争的所谓股东会决议,系万某所虚构,实际上并不存在,当然不发生法律效力……对于由此形成的

〔39〕 北京市第二中级人民法院(2013)二中民终字第4357号民事判决书。

股权转让协议,事后张某亦拒绝追认,故该股权转让协议依法不成立。[40]

上述判决根据案件的实际情况,把握了原告股东的行为是否构成追认或者其是否做出追认的明示意思表示这一关键点,在合理划分举证责任的基础上,运用民事诉讼法中证明责任的理论,合理解决了诉争的股东会决议的效力问题。但是在《公司法司法解释(四)》正式实施之后,对于实践中存在的股东签名被伪造且明确拒绝追认的案件,在明确案件事实确属公司决议缺乏成立要件的前提下,应当适用决议不成立的兜底条款,判定决议不成立。

五、结　语

《公司法司法解释(四)》通过对《公司法》第22条进行限缩解释,创设了公司决议不成立制度,形成了公司决议瑕疵“三分法”的制度架构,这对于保障公司作为营利性社团法人在进行团体决策时遵循正当程序原则具有重要意义。符合法律规定的决议行为可以保障公司这一团体的决策避免沦为少数存在表决权优势地位的人滥用股东权力的工具,促进公司所有的表决权人更加自由地表达意志,进而提高合意形成的效率。[41]

股东签名被伪造形成的股东会决议,在实践中呈现出的两种不同的情形,其中一种已经为《公司法司法解释(四)》第5条的前两项内容所吸收,认定为决议不成立;对于“无权代理”条件下的伪造股东签名形成的股东会决议,虽然司法解释并没有明确地将其认定为决议不成立的一种情形,但是通过本文对决议不成立制度价值的分析,立足于公司决议行为的性质、意思表示与法律行为基本理论以及公司运行的效率,笔者认为,在今后的司法实践中法官应当灵活地根据案件实际情况运用决议不成立制度的兜底条款判定决议不成立。同时在适用法律、司法解释的过程中,应当注意决议瑕疵的治愈。

对于存在轻微瑕疵或者当事人在事后通过其行为已经认可决议内容的决议,法院不应当一概认定为决议不成立,而是应当对被伪造签名股东的事后个人意志及其行为是否已经认可了伪造的股东会决议予以充分考虑。程序正义

[40] 参见《最高人民法院公报》2007年第9期(总第131期),江苏省南京市玄武区人民法院(2006)玄民二初字第1050号民事判决书。

[41] 前引16,王雷文。

与公司的经营成本、商事交易的效率和法律关系的稳定之间存在内在的张力——程序正义、经营成本与司法处理的严格化呈正相关性,相比之下商事效率、法律稳定与司法处理的严格化呈负相关性。[42] 司法权对公司决议行为的合理介入,有助于纠正市场经济本身存在的不足,同时也可以最大限度地保障公司股东的合法权益与公司决策效率之间的平衡。在审理公司决议瑕疵纠纷案件中,既要充分关注少数参与方,又要平衡地协调公司和多数参与方,二者的正当利益对于实现股东与公司利益的和谐发展具有重要的意义。[43] 因此,法官在适用法律的过程中,应当把握好各种价值、原则之间的冲突和焦点,寻求它们之间的平衡,最大限度地维护经济效率和交易安全。

法律行为的高度抽象性能够使其贯穿于私法的各个方面,并适用于丰富的社会生活,进而最大限度地实现私法自治。[44] 《公司法》作为维护我国社会主义市场经济稳定运行、保障市场经济活力的重要商事法律,对于公司这一市场经济主体的生存和发展具有重要的意义。民商法之间的紧密联系,公司决议行为的法律行为性质的认定使得公司决议瑕疵的体系构建也更加完整,准确诠释决议效力形态,妥善治愈公司决议瑕疵,必然能够实现民商法体系下的私法和谐。

(责任编辑:余依晴)

---

〔42〕 前引35,赵心泽文。

〔43〕 前引26,王林清书,第858页。

〔44〕 参见张旭荣:《法律行为视角下公司会议决议效力形态分析》,载《比较法研究》2013年第6期。

化学专利案件中补交实验数据的审查标准

金　宁*

摘要：

化学专利案件中的补交实验数据的审查标准一直以来争议不断，对其尺度宽松的把握会影响申请人与社会公众之间的利益平衡。根据专利法的先申请制度与公开换保护原则，允许补交实验数据的本质在于技术贡献在申请日前已作出，并且已被充分公开，因此，公开充分和创造性问题应适用同一审查标准。具体来说，对充分公开问题，技术方案需要实验数据加以证实的，补充实验数据不能被接受；对创造性问题，本领域技术人员从原申请文件中不能得出预料不到的技术效果的，则对比实验数据不应被采纳。我国一直以来的严格审查标准符合专利法本质，不必借鉴美欧的宽松标准。

关键词：

化学发明；补交实验数据；充分公开；创造性；审查标准

一、问题的提出

化学专利案件补交实验数据的问题是近年来专利领域争议很大的一个问题。化学属于实验科学，其技术效果可预见性远低于机械、电气领域，仅根据技术方案的描述往往无法推测发明能够产生预期的技术效果，因此，多数情况下，化学发明需要以能够实现预期技术效果的实验证据来反推其技术方案的成立。

在专利复审或无效程序中，机械、电气领域中的申请人可以通过结合发明的结构特征和作用方式，以说理和论证的方式证明自己的发明具有预期效果或预料不到的技术效果，来克服发明未充分公开或创造性不足的问题；而化学领

* 金宁，华东政法大学知识产权学院 2017 级硕士研究生。

域则不同,大多数情况下,化学发明需要通过补交实验数据来进行证明。[1] 而由于补交的实验数据可能是对化学发明的进一步改进研究,甚至是该化学发明的核心,此时采纳该实验数据则可能与先申请制产生矛盾,补交实验数据的审查标准问题也因此在化学领域尤为突出和复杂。我国专利复审委员会和法院对化学发明补交实验数据则一贯采取一种严格的态度,要求实验数据欲证明的技术效果在原申请文件中必须有所记载,不轻易允许申请人在申请日后补交实验数据。

在这一问题上,欧洲和美国的判断尺度则较为宽松:欧洲专利局(European Patent Office,EPO)审查指南规定:在某些情况下,尽管不允许加入申请中,审查员仍然可以将后提交的实施例或新效果作为支持要求保护的发明专利性的证据。假如所述新效果在原申请中隐含或至少与原申请公开的效果有关,则该新效果可以作为支持创造性的证据。[2] 在 EPO 的一个案例中,申请人补交的实验数据显示要求保护的组合物具有预料不到的低毒性,但低毒性在原文件中并没有记载,该证据被采纳,原因是"药物活性和毒性对于本领域技术人员是常常可以预期联系在一起的两个方面"。[3] 美国专利商标局的审查指南规定:可使用申请日后提交的证据支持如何使用该发明。如果本领域技术人员通过阅读说明书认为仅是提出一种假设以及确定该假设是否准确,这并不足够。即使证据形成于申请或授权后,也有可能反驳显而易见性。如果预料不到的技术效果可从公开的方法隐含得出,或与公开产品的预期用途有紧密联系,后提交的实验证据应被考虑。[4] 在美国的一个案例中,申请人补交了发明和现有技术在毒性和治疗指数方面的对比实验数据,法院认为化合物的毒性是与公开的作为药物的用途无法分离的特性,尽管对比实验数据在专利申请日前未提交,但在考虑要求保护的化合物专利性时仍必须考虑。[5] 可以看出,美欧对补交实验数据的要求不拘泥于原说明书的记载,而是更注重对发明是否存在客观技术效果的要求。

在我国化学专利无效案件中,经常有申请人主张不应强求申请人在申请文

---

[1] 《专利审查指南》(2010)第二部分第二章 2.2.4。

[2] 《欧洲专利审查指南》(2013)Part G V I I.11。

[3] 田芳、卢士燕:《对申请日后补交的证明预料不到的技术效果的实验数据能否考虑》,载《中国发明与专利》2012 年第 12 期。

[4] 《美国专利程序审查手册》2100.2124 节。

[5] See Ex parte Sasajima,212 USPQ 103,104 - 105(Bd. App. 1981).

件中就对引用的现有技术准备好所有反证,应允许申请人补交实验数据进行争辩,发明相对于现有技术到底有没有效果,这个客观事实是无法改变的,不能因为在提交专利申请时没有提交相应的证据就认为发明没有该效果。学界亦有学者认为申请人在申请专利时不可能预见到所有技术,我国要求实验数据欲证明的技术效果必须在原申请文件中有明确记载的做法过于严苛,损害了申请人的利益,应当适当放宽标准,借鉴欧美的审查标准。

笔者认为,在申请日后补交实验数据涉及专利法的先申请制度和公开换保护原则,因此有必要立足于申请日后补充证据的本质,结合专利法的基本原理,对申请人和社会公众的利益进行评价衡量,在此基础上确定我国究竟应采取怎样的审查标准和尺度。

二、相关规定和实践中的审查标准

(一)《专利审查指南》与相关文件对此规定不一致

1.《专利审查指南》相关内容修改变化

表1 《专利审查指南》及《关于修改〈专利审查指南〉的决定》相关内容

版本	是否可以补入说明书	审查专利性时的参考问题
1993年版《专利审查指南》	不允许将补交的实施例写入说明书,尤其是其中与保护范围有关的内容,更不允许写进权利要求	可以供审查员审查专利性时参考
2001年版《专利审查指南》	同上	可以供审查员审查新颖性、创造性或实用性时参考
2006年版《专利审查指南》	判断说明书是否充分公开,以原始说明书和权利要求书记载的内容为准,申请日之后补交的实施例和实验数据不予考虑	删除
2010年版《专利审查指南》	同上	同上
2017年《关于修改〈专利审查指南〉的决定》	判断说明书是否充分公开,以原说明书和权利要求书记载的内容为准。对于申请日之后补交的实验数据,审查员应当予以审查。补交实验数据所证明的技术效果应当是所属技术领域的技术人员能够从专利申请公开的内容中得到的	未修改

从表1可以看到,《专利审查指南》对补交实验数据的态度经历了从宽容到严厉,再回归宽容的变化:1993年版的《专利审查指南》虽然规定不允许将补交的实验数据纳入说明书和权利要求中,但该数据可以供审查员在审查专利性时予以参考;2001年版的《专利审查指南》有所趋严,将专利性参考限缩到了新颖性、创造性或实用性;2006年版的《专利审查指南》则全面趋严,直接规定补交的实验数据不予考虑;但在2017年《关于修改〈专利审查指南〉的决定》(以下简称《决定》)中,审查标准又回到了宽容态度上,规定对于补交的用于证明说明书充分公开的实验数据,审查员应当予以审查。

针对《决定》中的修改,北京高院知识产权庭2017年发布的《当前知识产权审判中需要注意的若干法律问题》明确了如下几点意见:第一,补充提交的实验数据所证明的技术效果在原专利申请文件中要有明确的记载,并且其证明的事实不能超过原始申请文件公开的范围,不能用于证明新的技术事实;第二,无论权利人提交补充实验数据是用于克服说明书未充分公开,还是用于证明本专利具备创造性,该补充证据的采信标准是一致的;第三,补充实验数据的内容虽然规定在《专利审查指南》关于化学领域审查章节,也适用于其他技术领域;第四,该实验数据应当是采用专利申请日前的实验条件、设备和实验手段所获得的。

由此可以看出,北京高院明确指出充分公开和创造性的审查标准应当是一致的,具体来说,能被接受的实验数据必须是在原说明书中有明确记载的。

2. 最高人民法院征求意见稿

针对补充实验数据的问题,最高人民法院于2018年6月1日发布的《关于审理专利授权确权行政案件若干问题的规定(一)(公开征求意见稿)》(以下简称征求意见稿)第13条对此作出了规定:"化学发明专利申请人、专利权人在申请日以后提交实验数据,用于进一步证明说明书记载的技术效果已经被充分公开,且该技术效果是本领域技术人员在申请日根据说明书、附图以及公知常识能够确认的,人民法院一般应予审查。化学发明专利申请人、专利权人在申请日以后提交实验数据,用于证明专利申请或专利具有与对比文件不同的技术效果,且该技术效果是本领域技术人员在申请日从专利申请文件公开的内容可以直接、毫无疑义地确认的,人民法院一般应予审查。"

在这份征求意见稿中,最高人民法院的做法与《专利审查指南》不同,其区分了补交实验数据的不同证明目的,二者采取不同的审查标准:对于充分公开采取较为宽松的审查标准,要求结合说明书和现有技术能够被确认即可;而针对创造性则采取更为严格的审查标准,要求从专利申请文件中能够被直接、毫无疑义地确认。

(二)审查实践的审查规则不清晰

表2 我国相关审查案件的简要情况〔6〕

案例简称	裁判文书编号	裁判机关主要意见	对补交实验数据的态度			
			专利复审委	一审法院	二审法院	再审法院
贝林格尔公司“溴化替托品单水合物”	第12206号决定;(2010)高行终字第751号;(2011)知行字第86号	本领域技术人员根据涉案专利公开的信息以及现有技术,得不到任何有关专利权人声称的技术效果的指导,这一效果不能作为认定涉案专利具备创造性的依据	不接受	不接受	不接受	不接受
武田药品工业株式会社“治疗糖尿病的药物组合物”	第12712号无效决定;(2010)高行终字第566号;(2012)知行字第41号	当专利申请人或专利权人欲通过提交对比实验数据证明其要求保护的技术方案相对于现有技术具备创造性时,接受该数据的前提必须是针对在原申请文件中明确记载的技术效果	不接受	不接受	不接受	不接受
赛尔金“一种化合物”	(2013)第21646号,2015年高行(知)终字第00309号	补交的实验数据显示的技术效果在原说明书中已经有含蓄的揭示,从而使所属领域的普通技术人员能直接推论出用途和效果,“或者”能直接从现有技术中推论出用途和效果	不接受	不接受	不接受	—

〔6〕 笔者在无讼案例网站上以“补充实验数据”为关键词,检索到37份判决书,检索日期为2018年7月16日。在此基础上,按照以下三个标准选取了7份案例作为分析样本(标准一:争议焦点中包含对“补交实验数据”的判断;标准二:诉讼程序较为完整,至少经历了专利复审、一审、二审程序;标准三:判决书说理较为充分)。

续表

案例简称	裁判文书编号	裁判机关主要意见	对补交实验数据的态度			
			专利复审委	一审法院	二审法院	再审法院
卫材公司“制备1,2－二氢吡啶－2－酮化合物方法”	(2016)最高法行申1878号	专利申请人卫材公司申请日后提交的实验数据所要证明的技术效果在原申请文件中并无明确记载,不能作为评价创造性的依据	不接受	不接受	不接受	不接受
细胞基因公司“作为抗肿瘤剂的5－取代的喹唑酮衍生物”	(2014)第73780号;(2017)京行终1642号	补充实验数据可以接受的前提是不破坏先申请原则,如果接受补充实验数据会破坏先申请原则,就不能接受。 如果接受补充实验数据,会引入原说明书未记载的发明人未实现的新的技术内容,则会破坏先申请原则;如果不会引入新的技术内容,则不会破坏先申请原则	不接受	不接受	不接受	—
吉联亚公司“核苷酸类似物”	(2017)京行终1806号	虽然反证Ⅲ－13是本专利申请日之后形成的实验数据,但能够客观反映本专利的技术贡献,接受该实验数据并不会为专利权人带来不当利益	不接受	不接受	接受	—
贝林格尔公司“治疗肺病药物”	(2015)京知行初字第3431号;(2017)京行终2470号	所谓“明确记载的技术效果”,应当理解为记载的技术效果是明确具体的、可验证的,通常情况下应当有实证数据的支持,不能是泛泛的、断言性的,本领域技术人员根据该记载就足以明确其具有何种程度的有益的技术效果	不接受	不接受	不接受	—

从表2我国相关审查实践来看,实践中绝大多数补交实验数据都未被采

纳,我国对申请日后补交实验数据普遍采取一种严格的态度,强调补交实验数据欲证明的技术效果不能超出原说明书记载。

在创造性问题上,大多数法院采用的措辞是"说明书明确记载的技术效果",在贝林格尔公司"治疗肺病药物"案中,北京高院具体解释了何为"明确记载",但该解释更像是一种方向性的宣示,实践指导上的意义并不强;而在赛尔金"一种化合物"案中,北京高院认为:补交的实验数据显示的技术效果在原说明书中已有含蓄提示,从而使本领域技术人员能直接推论出用途和效果或者能直接从现有技术中推论出用途和效果。"明确记载"较"含蓄提示"来说是一种更为严格的审查标准,"明确记载"囿于说明书的书面记载,会受专利申请人描述的技术效果限制;而"含蓄提示"则可以结合现有技术内容对说明书中的技术效果做出合理的推测。可以看出,在补交实验数据的审查问题上,虽然《专利审查指南》对此作出了规定,但专利复审委和法院的具体审查规则却并不清晰。

三、补交实验数据的正当性与合理限制

(一)允许补交实验数据的正当性

专利的说明书公开充分不仅要求本领域技术人员能够实现技术手段,解决技术问题,还必须要取得该技术方案所预期取得的技术效果。[7] 由于化学发明的技术效果可预见性低,在缺少实验数据支持时,审查员会质疑发明的技术方案能否产生预期效果,这时申请人就会通过补交实验数据以证明自己的发明可以实现预期效果;在化学发明领域,常用"发明取得了预料不到的技术效果"作为判断创造性的辅助性因素。在实践中,审查员经常会以发明与现有技术的结构非常接近,发明的技术效果显而易见来指出申请不具有创造性,申请人往往会通过补交对比实验数据来证明发明具有预料不到的技术效果。

在审查中,审查员应当站在本领域普通技术人员的视角来审视发明的专利性,但由于专利法上的"本领域的普通技术人员"是一个假设的概念,现实中的审查员不可能对每个技术领域的全部技术知识都有所了解,审查员可能由于专业知识的不熟悉或者对技术方案的内容理解出现了偏差,而导致其对专利申请的专利性产生误判:如结合现有技术知识,不需要结合实验数据也能推导出技

---

〔7〕 参见石必胜:《专利说明书充分公开的司法判断》,载《人民司法》2015年第5期。

术方案能够产生预期的技术效果,但审查员不了解这一方面的知识;或者由于审查员缺乏某方面的技术知识,其对现有技术的结构或实验条件理解出现偏差,导致其错误地得出技术效果显而易见的结论等。申请人补交实验数据有现实需要,此时如果不允许申请人补交实验数据等于是让申请人为审查员的不足承担后果,对申请人过于苛刻,损害了申请人的合法权益。〔8〕

(二)对价理论对补交实验数据的限制

根据对价理论,专利不是对创造性的嘉奖或对公民的奖励,而是发明人和社会公众之间订立的一种契约,发明人以公开其最新的发明创造作为对价,来获得一定期限内对该技术的垄断权。〔9〕 作为获得专利权的对价,专利权人向社会公众提供的专利信息必须足够完整、准确,〔10〕完整、准确具体有以下两点要求:第一,申请人公开的信息必须是对社会公众有实质性利益的,公开的内容应当是直接具有实用性的信息,事实上,申请人公开的内容必须真正地丰富公众的科技知识;第二,申请人必须在说明书中诚意地提供所有必要信息,使本领域技术人员根据说明书可以直接实施发明的技术内容。只有达到此种程度的公开对价,使社会公众获得了直接、现实的益处,申请人才能获取到排他垄断权。〔11〕

为鼓励发明人尽早将其发明公之于众,专利法先申请原则旨在保护最先对发明创造提出申请的人,因此申请人能够获得专利权的发明只能是最初申请的部分,如果发明人能够通过修改原申请文件的方式改变原技术方案,就会使申请日后的研究工作提早享有了权利。先申请原则和公开换保护的制度有严密的利益平衡考量,〔12〕此种利益平衡的考量决定了专利申请人所得到的专利权保

---

〔8〕 参见李越:《与充分公开有关的实验证据问题的探讨》,载国家知识产权局条法司编:《专利法研究》(2010),知识产权出版社 2011 年版,第 303 页。

〔9〕 参见刘春田:《知识产权法》,高等教育出版社、北京大学出版社 2003 年版,第 150 页。

〔10〕 参见杨德桥:《专利权社会契约理论及其对专利充分公开制度的证成》,载《北京化工大学学报》(社会科学版)2018 年第 2 期。

〔11〕 参见何艳霞:《Teva Canada 诉 Pfizer Canada 案——说明书充分公开的判定》,载甘绍宁主编:《国外专利诉讼要案解读》,知识产权出版社 2013 年版,第 128 页以下。

〔12〕 参见国家知识产权局专利复审委员会:《专利行政诉讼概论与案例精解》,知识产权出版社 2011 年版,第 195 页。

护应与其所做出的贡献相一致,专利先申请原则和公开换保护制度决定了申请人只能对其最初公开的技术贡献获得垄断权。如果申请人在后补交的实验数据是对原专利申请的改进,属于新的技术内容,此时若采纳此部分实验数据,会导致申请人在后的技术内容获得了较早的保护日期,申请人得到的保护范围超出其当初对现有技术的贡献。

因此,如果说明书中的技术效果必须有实验数据加以证实才能得到,而最初的说明书中没有记载任何实验数据,此时表明效果实验及其实验结果才是相关研究的核心,[13]这部分才是对公众有用的实质性信息,而申请人补交实验数据等于是在原申请文件中加入了新技术内容,真正的技术贡献是在申请日后才公开,这时若接受该数据实际上是对申请日后的技术贡献赋予了申请日的权利;相同地,对于创造性问题,申请人针对审查员检索到的现有技术,补交了对比实验数据以证明原申请较现有设计确实具有更有益的技术效果,若该技术效果在原说明书中没有体现,则该实验就是申请人在后的研究工作,对比实验也即申请人在后的技术贡献。

虽然补交的实验数据证明该效果确实是存在于原技术方案中的,但是真正发现技术问题并公布技术效果的技术贡献是申请人在申请日后才完成的,不能对此部分予以采纳。如同专利法允许第二医药用途获得专利,化合物本身的物化性质是固有的,发明人通过发现基于该物化性质的某种药理学或病理学作用机理,实现其第二医药用途。第二医药用途是客观存在的效果,但发现并公开该化合物新的作用机理才是新的技术贡献,不能因为某人发明了一项化合物,指出了其一项技术效果,就让其垄断对该化合物之上的所有技术效果。因此,补交的实验数据只能是对原说明书中记载的技术信息的确认、支持,而不能是新的技术内容。

客观合理地认定申请人在申请日后补交的实验数据,对于恰当平衡专利权人和社会公众之间的利益十分重要。[14] 从这一角度来说,2017年4月1日《专利审查指南》的修改值得肯定:有条件地允许补交实验数据既公平地肯定了申

---

〔13〕 卢阳:《医药化学领域说明书充分公开问题探析》,载《中国知识产权报》2014年12月31日,第11版。

〔14〕 参见尹昕:《发明专利创造性判断中对试验数据及技术偏见的司法认定》,载《人民司法》2013年第4期。

请人技术贡献,有利于鼓励发明创造,同时也避免了申请人通过抢占申请人来打击同业竞争者。[15] 这一看似严格的审查标准实则正确地维护了先申请原则和公开换保护制度,亦实现了平衡专利权人和社会公众利益的目标。

美欧认为即使在原申请文件中对相关技术效果没有记载,只要该效果与发明用途有密切联系就可以接受该补交的实验数据,美欧宽松的审查标准与其国情是有着密切关联的,目前发达国家通过百年的苦心经营在化学医药领域占据绝对优势,对补充实验数据采取较低的标准从而放松对实验证据的要求,最大的受益者是那些医药巨头以及发达国家自身。但事实上,我国现有的要求实验数据欲证明的技术效果在原申请文件中必须有所记载的审查标准才符合专利法制度本质。

四、补交实验数据的标准和规则完善

(一)充分公开与创造性的审查标准应当一致

前文已述,公开充分问题中补充实验数据的情形一般是审查员指出根据原说明书中的描述不能推导出该发明具备预期技术效果,申请人会通过补交实验数据以证明发明能够实现预期效果,此时补充的内容一般是针对发明本身的实验数据;而创造性问题一般是审查员检索到现有技术,该现有技术与发明结构非常近似,审查员据此认为原说明书中描述的技术效果没有创造性,此时申请人会通过补交对比实验数据证明发明较现有技术有预料不到的技术效果,补充的内容是针对发明和现有技术不同的效果的实验数据。有学者据此认为,公开充分问题和创造性问题补充实验数据的情形、内容均不相同,不应当对二者适用相同的审查标准。[16] 笔者认为,此种观点只注意到了二者表层的区别,没有看到化学专利案件中补交实验数据的本质。

对于申请日后补交的实验数据而言,接受该实验数据是因为申请人在申请日前就发现了该技术问题,并提出了技术手段,能够解决技术问题,即该技术贡

[15] 参见张清奎:《化学及药品专利审查中的热点问题回顾和展望——关于实验数据的要求及补救措施》,载《中国发明与专利》2018 年第 8 期。

[16] 参见刘梦玲:《生物医药领域补充实验数据的考量和标准构建——以创造性为视角》,载《科技与法律》2017 年第 5 期。

献在申请日前已完成;而拒绝接受实验数据是因为申请人实际上并未真正发现存在的技术问题并实现技术效果,却企图通过在后补交数据(之后的进一步研究)提早获得对这一部分的专利权。因此,对补交实验数据的判断关键看该技术贡献究竟是在申请日前就已经完成,还是在申请日后完成。对于审查员和社会公众来说,判断技术贡献是不是在申请日完成的,其只能通过判断该技术贡献是否在原说明书中有所体现。

因此,虽然为克服公开充分问题或创造性问题补充实验数据的内容、情形不同,但在这方面,二者的本质是相同的,应当使用相同的审查标准。

由此,最高人民法院征求意见稿对补交的实验数据证明充分公开和创造性问题,采取不同标准的做法有失妥当。笔者建议最高人民法院在适用《中华人民共和国专利法》第26条第3款和第22条第3款时,对当事人补交的实验数据应采取相同的审查标准。具体而言,建议征求意见稿将第13条修改为:化学发明专利申请人、专利权人在申请日以后提交实验数据,用于进一步证明发明符合专利法第22条第3款和第26条第3款的规定的,若该实验数据系采用涉案专利申请日前的实验方法获得,其所证明的技术效果是本领域技术人员从原专利申请说明书中可以明确得到或者推导得出的,人民法院应当予以审查。[17]

(二)实验数据证明充分公开的规则完善

尽管化学领域的发明可预见性低是事实,仅根据化学结构推测某些化合物的药理活性,结果充满了未知与可能,因此通常情况下新化合物的技术效果需要相关的实验数据加以证实,然而化学发明的效果并非完全无法预期,基于化合物的化学结构预测其相关特性也并不是全然无规律可循。事实上,化合物个性因素的改变对效果的影响不可忽视,但共性的特点也始终存在,现有技术对化合物共性认识水平在不断提高,相应地效果预测可能性也在提高。但具体的化合物现有技术的水平以及个性因素变化带来的影响是否可预知,需要本领域技术人员在详读技术方案的基础上结合现有技术综合判断。[18]

---

〔17〕 参见刘庆辉:《医药专利案件中补交实验数据的审查标准》,载"中国知识产权杂志"微信公众号:https://mp.weixin.qq.com/s/xer-CN2fIhwXAOCburHzWw,最后访问日期:2018年7月12日。

〔18〕 参见许钧钧、潘珂:《实验数据的缺乏会导致说明书公开不充分吗?》,载《中国知识产权报》2015年8月19日,第10版。

针对化学发明的充分公开,《专利审查指南》指出如果说明书中给出了具体的技术方案,但没有提供任何实验数据,若本领域普通技术人员无法根据现有技术预测发明能够实现预期效果,即该技术方案必须依赖实验结果加以证实才能成立的,将被视为发明无法实现。由此,并非所有的化学发明都必须在说明书中给出实验数据。当审查员对说明书充分公开问题提出质疑时,申请人往往通过提交实验数据证明自己的发明确实存在说明书中明确记载的技术效果,以证实发明的可实现性。申请人强调存在技术效果通常属于以下两种情形:

1. 说明书中对发明的技术效果有明确记载,缺乏效果实验,但该效果是本领域技术人员可以推测出的。

2. 说明书中对技术效果有明确记载,但所属领域技术人员即根据技术方案本身无法确定其可以产生该技术效果。

对于情形1,本领域技术人员在说明书已有公开内容的基础上,结合现有技术知识,完全可以预料到该发明的化学物能够产生说明书中记载的技术效果,即使说明书中没有记载相关实验数据,该预期技术效果均是本领域技术人员可以预期的。此时申请人补交的实验数据只是对说明书中描述的技术内容的确认和支持,接受这些实验数据并不会给申请人带来不当利益。

对于情形2,所属领域技术人员根据说明书的内容,无法确定发明涉及的技术方案能否解决技术问题,若说明书中未给出相应实验数据证实,那么即使说明书中明确记载了该发明的技术效果,这里的“明确记载”并不符合说明书充分公开所要求的“记载”。这种结论性或断言性的描述,仅仅是可供研究人员进一步探索的研究方向,在后补交的实验数据才是明确的、有实质性的技术贡献,因此若接受补交的实验数据则会使申请人不当受益,损害了社会公众的利益。

由此可见,审查员判断发明的技术方案是否必须依赖实验结果这一结论,对申请人日后能否补交实验数据有着决定作用。因此,审查员在将发明归为必须依赖实验证据的证实才能成立的情形时应当更加慎重:在判断实验数据的缺乏是否会导致说明书公开不充分时,需要在准确理解现有技术的整体状况的前提下,密切联系发明相对于现有技术所做的改进等因素综合、整体进行考量,而不是仅局限于申请文件所陈述的内容。审查员认为专利申请因没有实验数据而存在公开不充分的问题时,其负有初步举证责任,通过说理或举例证明该发明必须依赖实验数据才能成立,而不能笼统地以“化学领域可预测性低”为理由想当然地认定说明书未记载实验数据就是公开不充分;对于申请人来说,当审查员认定发明因缺乏实验数据而公开不充分时,这一结论不是无法逾越的,申请人此时应当提供现有技术知识来证明该技术方案无需实验数据亦可成立。[19]

(三)实验数据证明创造性的规则完善

无论是原始申请文件,还是补充实验数据,都是对申请日前申请人已完成发明并将其进行充分公开这一客观事实的证明。因此,补交的实验数据也必须满足这两点要求才可以被接受采纳:即证明的技术贡献是申请日之前已完成的和在原申请文件中被公开。[20] 补充的实验数据只能是一种补强性证据,结合说明书中已有的内容或现有技术证明技术效果可以实现。《专利审查指南(2010)》规定,基于最接近的现有技术重新确定的该发明实际解决的技术问题,可能不同于说明书所描述的技术问题。作为一个原则,发明的任何技术效果都可以作为重新确定技术问题的基础,只要本领域技术人员从该申请说明书中所记载的内容能够得知该技术效果即可。[21] 是否能够"得到"应站位本领域技术人员,而非取决于原申请对该技术效果是否有文字记载或记载形式本身。[22] 因此补充实验数据欲证明的内容必须是在原说明书中已经有所"记载"的内容,它可以是文字明确记载的技术效果,也可以是有含蓄地提示,从而使所属领域的普通技术人员能直接推论出来的用途和效果。[23]

当审查员检索到与要求保护的化合物结合非常接近的现有技术,并以此质疑发明的创造性时,申请人往往会通过提交与现有技术的对比实验数据来证明发明具有预料不到的技术效果。申请人强调技术效果可分为以下三种情形:

---

〔19〕 参见前引8,李越文。

〔20〕 参见王扬平、张宇:《申请日后补交对比实验数据证明创造性的判例思考》,载中华全国专利代理人协会编:《〈专利法〉第22条和第23条的适用》,知识产权出版社2016年版,第161页。

〔21〕 参见原学宁:《关于化学领域对比实验数据的一点探讨》,载中华全国专利代理人协会编:《〈专利法〉第22条和第23条的适用》,知识产权出版社2016年版,第154页。

〔22〕 参见朱宁、王荣霞:《补交实验数据在创造性评判中的探析》,载《专利代理》2017年第3期。

〔23〕 参见吴文英:《涉及制药用途的说明书充分公开的考量》,载《中国知识产权报》2015年10月21日,第9版。

1. 对比实验数据欲证明的技术效果在说明书中从未提及，本领域技术人员根据现有技术也无从得知。

2. 对比实验数据欲证明的技术效果在说明书中有明确记载，该技术效果属于需要实验数据加以证实，原说明书中给出了实验数据；或者虽没有效果实验，该效果是本领域技术人员可以预料的，但缺乏与现有技术的对比实验证据。

3. 对比实验数据欲证明的技术效果没有文字记载，但该效果是本领域技术人员根据说明书描述和现有技术可以得出的。

对于情形 1，补交的对比实验数据想要证明的技术效果在原说明书中从未提及，且本领域的技术人员由原申请文件中不能推知，那么这一技术效果就是新技术效果，这部分技术内容不是申请人在申请日时已获得的，加入新的效果会产生一项新的发明，超出了原申请记载的范围，因此补交的实验数据不应予以承认和考虑。

对于情形 2，申请人欲证明的更有益的技术效果实际上在原说明书中就已有记载并被充分公开，只是由于审查员对现有技术的结构或实验条件理解出现偏差，导致其错误地得出技术效果显而易见的结论，申请人提供对比实验数据并非是对原申请发明的改进，而是为了强调自己的技术方案确实具有更优的技术效果。

如在吉联亚核苷酸案中，专利化合物与现有技术的结构极为类似，原说明书实施例记载了关于化学稳定性、生物利用度以及对 HIV－1 的抗逆转录病毒活性方面的实验数据。专利复审委和一审法院认定由于专利公开的是 IC50、CC50、SI（CC50/IC50）值，现有技术中公开的是 ED50、IC50、SI（IC50/ED50）值，二者之间试验条件不同，获取的数据形式也不同，不能进行直接的比较，因此专利技术方案是显而易见的，不具备创造性。二审法院推翻了上述裁判：根据本专利说明书和现有技术的记载可知，两者实验都在 MT－2 细胞中测定抗病毒活性效果。虽然本专利说明书实施例 16 和现有技术使用的指标不同，但上述数据形式都是表征化合物抗病毒活性和细胞毒性水平的指标，对比实验数据显示了本专利在抗病毒活性和细胞毒性水平上的改善情况。最终二审法院认定虽然对比实验数据是申请日之后形成的实验数据，但能够客观反映本专利的技术贡献，接受了该补交的实验数据。

对于情形 3，由于发明的技术方案往往包含多个技术特征，申请人不太可能在申请文件中以详细的实验数据描述每个技术特征对应的技术效果。如果补充的实验数据并非对发明的改进和完善,而是其在申请日时确已完成的技术内容,且这部分内容在原申请文件已经充分公开,本领域的技术人员可以相信或推知其能产生更有益的技术效果,则可以允许以实验数据加以证明,并以此作为判断创造性的依据。

五、结　　语

化学发明专利申请人、专利权人在申请日后补交实验数据,用于证明发明符合说明书公开充分和创造性的,其所证明的技术效果必须是从原申请文件中可以明确得到或推导得出的。我国的审查标准总体上较欧美来说是趋严的,欧美国家采用较为宽松的标准有出于国情的考量,而我国的审判标准更符合专利制度的本质。

我国的审查标准本质上是考量技术贡献是否是在申请日前作出,这一点对于充分公开问题和创造性问题都是一样的,两者应当采用一样的标准,因此建议最高人民法院的征求意见稿对此应予以修改;在具体对标准把握的规则上,对于充分公开问题,能不能接受补交的实验数据关键看技术方案是否需要实验数据加以证实,如果需要实验数据加以支持,则补交的实验数据是新技术贡献,不应予以采纳;对于创造性问题,关键看实验数据欲证明的技术效果有无在说明书中被“记载”,“记载”不应拘于文字记载或记载的形式,而应当取决于本领域技术人员根据说明书和现有技术能否得出该技术效果。这样的理解才能真正实现申请人和社会公众之间的利益平衡。

(责任编辑:曹亚君)

论“离婚协议房屋产权归属约定”之排除强制执行

黄丹琳　李展豪*

摘要：

在被强制执行房屋的登记所有权人已通过离婚协议约定将房屋所有权转让给原配偶的案外人异议之诉中，原配偶基于离婚协议而对房屋享有的权利是否为“足以排除强制执行之实体权益”，现行法尚未明晰。法官在个案中应综合考量原配偶之债权及申请执行人之债权的权利性质、成立时间、权利形成根源等因素，进行利益衡量并作出价值判断，以实现个案公正。第一，在性质上，基于离婚协议之房屋产权归属约定而产生的权利为债权而非物权。而该债权能否对抗申请执行人，需考察申请执行人对房屋享有的权利为金钱债权还是非金钱债权以及能否适用公示公信原则。第二，在成立时间上，如果离婚协议成立先于申请执行人与被执行人之债权，推定被执行人无利用离婚协议逃避债务的恶意；如果离婚协议成立于房屋被强制执行之后，应认定原配偶对房屋所享有的债权不能对抗申请执行人；而当离婚协议成立于申请执行人之债权成立之后，且在房屋被申请强制执行前，推定被强制执行人不具有逃避债务之恶意。第三，在权利形成的根源上，自然人所享有的“生存利益”应优先于债权人之债权，故需考量被执行房屋于原配偶方及跟随其生活之子女而言是否是其唯一生活住所，而决定是否需要对前者的“生存利益”优先保护。

关键词：

离婚协议；房屋产权归属约定；案外人异议之诉；排除强制执行

* 黄丹琳，中央财经大学法学院2017级硕士研究生；李展豪，中央财经大学法学院2017级硕士研究生。

强制执行以效率为首要价值追求,其审查被执行人之责任财产时原则上遵循“表面权利规则”。[1] 然而,执行机关既系依标的物之“权利外观”为强制执行,自然难以避免因执行标的物“名实不符”而致使作为实际权益人的案外第三人之财产处于被强制执行的危险中。有鉴于此,我国民事诉讼法设置了案外人异议之诉制度以救济权利受损的案外人,即当案外第三人主张其对执行标的物有足以排除强制执行之实体权益时,可请求法院作出不得强制执行或撤销执行程序之判决。[2] 但何为“足以排除强制执行之实体权益”并非明朗,司法实践中对离婚后房屋“名实不符”时作为房屋实际权益人的原配偶享有的不动产权益是否为“足以排除强制执行之实体权益”的争议尤为突出。不同法院相关判决存在较大差异,即使是公报案例,对该问题的态度似乎也摇摆不定。个中争议,究其本质主要围绕两方面:一是基于离婚协议之分割房屋条款而产生的实体权益之性质;二是该实体权益是否为“足以排除强制执行之实体权益”之认定。

一、典型案例判决要旨

在实践中,本文所研究的“基于离婚协议约定房屋产权归属所产生之权利能否排除强制执行”之案件的案情大致可抽象概括为:夫妻(A和B)在婚姻存续期间购买房屋并登记于一方(A)名下,后夫妻感情不和协议离婚,通过离婚协议约定房屋产权归属于非登记产权人一方(B)但未办理产权变更登记。随后A因个人债务无法偿还,该房屋基于“权利外观规则”被认定为登记产权人(A)之责任财产而被第三人申请强制执行,非登记人一方(B)提出执行异议并提起执行异议之诉,请求停止执行。然该类案件之判决要旨产生了较大分歧,主要体现在两方面:一是基于夫妻离婚协议中有关房屋产权的约定而形成的权利是债权还是物权;二是该权利是否为“足以排除强制执行之实体权益”,能否

〔1〕 参见雷运龙:《强制执行之基本定位》,载《民事程序法研究》2016年第2期。

〔2〕 参见张卫平:《民事诉讼法》,法律出版社2009年版,第450页。

对抗申请执行人。本文借助三则典型案例"付某华案"[3]"钟某玉案"[4]"王某英案"[5]之判决要旨展开具体分析。

(一)判决要旨之分歧

关于权利的性质问题,付某华案与钟某玉案的法官均认为,基于夫妻离婚协议中有关房屋产权归属的约定产生的权利为债权,即请求办理房屋过户登记的权利;而王某英案的法官则认为,夫妻离婚协议对房屋归属的约定在夫妻双方之间直接发生物权变动之效力,产生的权利的性质为物权。该物权因未经房屋产权变更登记不能对抗主张物权的善意第三人,但优先于债权人。

关于权利是否能对抗申请执行人,王某英案的法官认为因离婚协议有关房屋产权的约定能产生物权变动效力而自然而然地推导出能对抗享有金钱债权的申请执行人;付某华案和钟某玉案在认定基于离婚协议中房屋产权条款而产生的权利为债权而非物权上相一致,分歧主要体现在分析基于离婚协议之分割房屋条款而产生的实体权益是否为"足以排除强制执行之实体权益"时,究竟是止步于债权具有相对性,不能对抗因物权公示公信制度而产生信赖的申请执行

[3] 《付某华与吕某白案外人执行异议之诉》,载《最高人民法院公报》2017年第3期。在该案中,付某华与刘某锋于2007年离婚,其离婚协议约定婚姻存续期间购买的两处房屋之所有权归付某华(其中一房屋登记在刘某锋名下,另一房屋登记在两人名下),离婚后未办理房屋过户登记。后两房屋因刘某锋于2012年与吕某白发生的股权转让纠纷而被查封。付某华申请执行异议被驳回,遂提起案外人异议之诉,请求确认系争房屋的所有权属于付某华,解除对系争房屋的司法查封并停止对该房地产的执行。

[4] 《钟某玉与王某、林某达案外人执行异议纠纷案》,载《最高人民法院公报》2016年第6期。在该案中,钟某玉与林某达于1996年7月达成离婚协议,约定讼争房屋归钟某玉及其四名子女所有。离婚后,钟某玉多次要求林某达变更房屋登记未果。2011年,该房屋因林某达与王某之间的股权转让纠纷而被申请强制执行,钟某玉对此申请执行异议,被法院以执行标的房屋登记于林某达名下,房屋产权人未变更登记为钟某玉,物权尚未变动为由驳回,故其随后提起案外人异议之诉,请求确认讼争房产归钟某玉所有,解除对该房屋的查封并停止执行。

[5] 北京市大兴区人民法院(2016)京0115民初11974号民事判决书。在该案中,2010年12月,王某英与赵某阳协议离婚,约定讼争房屋全部归原告所有,未办理房屋变更登记。2013年12月,该房屋因赵某阳与王某之间的借款合同纠纷而被申请执行。王某英申请执行异议被驳回,提起执行异议之诉,请求解除对房屋的查封,停止执行。

人,还是进一步分析两个债权,对其进行利益衡量以确定保护顺位。付某华案认为应严守公示公信制度,保护申请执行人的信赖利益。离婚协议确定的债权未经物权变动登记,仅约束夫妻双方,对第三人不发生效力。享有债权的案外配偶不享有排除信赖物权登记的申请执行人申请查封和执行被执行人名下责任财产的权利;而钟某玉案则认为,相较而言,无过错的案外配偶之权利更值得保护。判断作为案外第三人享有的债权能否对抗申请执行人应综合考虑其是否有过错,权利形成时间、内容、性质、形成根源等,以确定保护顺位,而不能仅仅考虑物权公示公信制度。案外配偶对讼争房屋享有请求权,而申请执行人仅为金钱债权时,可参照最高人民法院《关于审理买卖合同纠纷案件适用法律问题的解释》第10条的精神,认定请求变更房屋产权登记的请求权优先于申请执行人的金钱债权。

(二)判决要旨分歧之实质

上述案例判决要旨之分歧,究其本质,首先在于如何理解我国《物权法》第9条与离婚协议中关于房屋产权的约定之关系,进而厘清基于离婚协议中关于房屋产权归属之约定而产生的权利之性质为债权抑或物权。其次,如该权利属于物权,则该类执行异议之诉的处理即拨云见日;如该权利属债权,则须进一步探析物权公示公信制度于执行异议之诉中的适用可能性,关键在于物权公示公信制度中的第三人是否排除执行程序这一非交易领域中的第三人。最后,如果物权公示公信制度仅保护交易领域的善意第三人,则需明晰申请执行人之债权与实际权益人之债权的保护顺位,厘清最高人民法院《关于适用〈中华人民共和国民事诉讼法〉的解释》(以下简称《民事诉讼法司法解释》)第312条第1项"足以排除强制执行的民事权益"之含义,以判定实际权益人享有的实体权益是否满足其条件。

二、离婚协议中关于房屋产权之约定的权利性质

判断基于离婚协议中房屋产权归属之约定而产生的权利之性质为债权抑或物权,核心在于厘清我国《物权法》第9条与离婚协议中关于房屋产权的约定之关系。我国《物权法》第9条规定了不动产物权变动原则上遵循登记生效主义,仅在法律另作规定时例外处理。故判断离婚协议中关于房屋产权之约定能否直接引起物权变动之关键在于其是否属于《物权法》第9条中的"法律另有规

定的除外”。

王某英案引用《婚姻法》第 19 条“夫妻约定财产制”之规定，推导出案外第三人王某英基于离婚协议中房屋产权的约定直接取得了房屋的所有权，该观点值得商榷。从体系上解释，《婚姻法》第 19 条并非规定在婚姻法有关离婚的第四章中，而是规定在家庭关系一章，其与夫妻法定财产制相对，调整的对象为婚内财产分割协议，即夫妻双方可以约定夫妻财产共有、个人所有、部分共有或部分个人所有。故离婚协议中有关房屋产权的约定不属于第 19 条调整。而根据最高人民法院《关于适用〈中华人民共和国婚姻法〉若干问题的解释（二）》（以下简称《婚姻法解释（二）》）第 8 条的规定，离婚协议中的约定仅在夫妻双方之间产生拘束力。问题之关键在于该约定产生的是物权效力抑或债之关系。[6] 换言之，婚姻法中的规定是否能成为物权法不动产登记生效主义的例外，而使夫妻双方的约定直接产生物权变动之效力。

对于涉及婚姻法领域的物权变动，目前主要有两种学说：一是认为婚姻法作为身份法，其调整的夫妻之间的财产关系有别于一般的财产交易，此时物权法宜保持谦抑性，进而认为婚姻法中的规定为特别规定，夫妻之间有关财产的约定可直接在夫妻内部发生物权变动；[7] 二是认为应当适用物权法的规定，我国不动产物权变动采登记要件主义，未经登记，不发生物权变动，无变通适用之余地，此为物权法定之要求。[8] 本文支持第二种观点，理由主要有如下两点：

第一，从学理分析的角度来看，我国物权变动模式采债权形式主义，即物权

---

〔6〕 最高人民法院《关于适用〈中华人民共和国婚姻法〉若干问题的解释（二）的补充规定》第 8 条：离婚协议中关于财产分割的条款或者当事人因离婚就财产分割达成的协议，对男女双方具有法律约束力。

当事人因履行上述财产分割协议发生纠纷提起诉讼的，人民法院应当受理。

〔7〕 参见裴桦：《夫妻财产制与财产法规则的冲突与协调》，载《法学研究》2017 年第 2 期；姚辉：《夫妻财产契约中的物权变动论》，载《人民司法（案例）》2015 年第 4 期；程啸：《婚姻财产分割协议、夫妻财产制契约的效力与不动产物权变动——唐某诉李某某、唐某乙法定继承纠纷案》，载《暨南学报》（哲学社会科学版）2015 年第 3 期。

〔8〕 参见贺剑：《论婚姻法回归民法的基本思路——以法定夫妻婚姻财产制为重点》，载《中外法学》2014 年第 6 期；王毓莹：《离婚协议关于房屋产权的约定能否对抗申请执行人》，载《人民法院报》2017 年 11 月 22 日，第 7 版。

变动法律效果的发生,除存在债权意思外,还必须按照法定方式进行登记或交付,但对当事人之间是否作出物权变动的意思表示不作要求。该模式又被称为意思主义与登记或交付相结合的物权变动模式。[9] 在该模式下,不动产物权变动之发生,需满足"债权意思 + 登记",物权变动的意思表示不单独作要求,而"登记"则为不可或缺的必备要素之一。从本质上而言,离婚协议中有关房屋产权的约定仅为债权意思表示,未经登记则物权变动之要素未齐备,无法引起物权变动之效果。故离婚协议有关房屋产权之规定能否引起物权变动的问题可以转换为其是否属于《物权法》第9条的例外。

第二,从规范性分析的角度来看,《物权法》第9条的"法律另有规定",主要指的是《物权法》第28条至第30条的规定,即非基于法律行为的物权变动。[10] 无论是法院生效判决、征收、继承抑或是合法建造、拆除房屋,其作为不动产登记生效要件之例外情形,均具有以下两个特点:(1)必须依据法律的规定,而不取决于当事人的意思;[11] (2)具有某种程度上的公示性。[12] 例如,房屋的继承者已经占有了被继承的房屋,合法建造房屋的建房人已经占有房屋等。应当承认,这些情况会形成权利外观,并在一定程度上彰显了物之归属。此为特定的法律事实未经登记而得发生物权变动的部分考量因素。按照同类解释,离婚协议中有关房屋产权的约定若要归为不动产物权变动登记生效主义之例外,应至少同时满足上述两个特征。而事实上,在离婚协议中,夫妻对房屋产权归属之约定是基于双方当事人的意思,难寻法律明文规定其不适用物权登记生效制度。即使是《婚姻法解释(二)》第8条,也仅仅规定了离婚协议发生效力的范围,而不是直接规定离婚协议可发生物权变动的效果。尽管承认婚姻法如第一种学说所言,规范的法律关系具有身份属性,但夫妻身份之特殊并未改变其有关财产的约定为财产契约的本质;加之该契约不具有公示性,无法形成权利外观以表现物权的归属,故

---

[9] 参见王利明:《物权法研究》修订版(上卷),中国人民大学出版社2007年版,第255页。

[10] 《中华人民共和国物权法》第9条:不动产物权的设立、变更、转让和消灭,经依法登记,发生效力;未经登记,不发生效力,但法律另有规定的除外。依法属于国家所有的自然资源,所有权可以不登记。

[11] 参见陈华彬:《物权法原理》,国家行政学院出版社1998年版,第155页。

[12] 参见王利明:《物权法研究》修订版(上卷),中国人民大学出版社2007年版,第286页。

离婚协议中有关房屋产权的约定仅在夫妻双方之间发生合同效力，其为要求房屋登记名义人进行房屋变更登记的债权请求权，而非物权。[13]

分析至此，我们可以得出离婚协议中有关房屋产权归属之约定为债权，不发生物权变动之效果。以这一结论为案件分析的前提，进一步探讨涉及离婚协议不动产归属的执行异议之诉中，案外第三人享有的权利能否对抗申请执行人。

三、案外第三人基于离婚协议享有的债权能否对抗申请执行人

根据我国《民事诉讼法司法解释》第312条的规定，[14]执行标的得以免于强制执行的理由为案外第三人享有的权利“足以排除强制执行”。而何为“足以”，我国《民事诉讼法》没有规定，但在最高人民法院《关于适用〈中华人民共和国民事诉讼法〉执行程序若干问题的解释》第15条作了原则性的规定，即“所有权及其他足以阻止强制执行的权利”。[15] 我国通说认为，这些权利以所有权为典型，同时包括用益物权、特定债权、特定权益比如占有使用等。[16] 从世界各国和地区有关案外人异议之诉诉讼事由的相关规定[17]来看，其大多也仅作原则性的规定，将诉讼事由表述为：“对标的物享有阻却强制执行之进行的权利。”而

〔13〕 参见郑晓剑：《案外人异议之诉遭遇物权公示的问题及出路》，载《南都学坛》2014年第6期。

〔14〕 最高人民法院《关于适用〈中华人民共和国民事诉讼法〉的解释》第312条：

对案外人提起的执行异议之诉，人民法院经审理，按照下列情形分别处理：

（一）案外人就执行标的享有足以排除强制执行的民事权益的，判决不得执行该执行标的；

（二）案外人就执行标的不享有足以排除强制执行的民事权益的，判决驳回诉讼请求。

案外人同时提出确认其权利的诉讼请求的，人民法院可以在判决中一并作出裁判。

〔15〕 最高人民法院《关于适用〈中华人民共和国民事诉讼法〉执行程序若干问题的解释》第15条：

案外人对执行标的主张所有权或者有其他足以阻止执行标的转让、交付的实体权利的，可以依照民事诉讼法第二百零四条的规定，向执行法院提出异议。

〔16〕 参见江必新：《执行规范理解与适用》，中国法制出版社2015年版，第126页。

〔17〕 例如：《日本民事执行法》第38条、《德国民事诉讼法》第771条、《韩国民事执行法》第48条、我国台湾地区“强制执行法”第15条。

该原则性规定依赖于法官在司法实践中“根据第三人对于执行标的物所得主张之实体法权利之性质效力及执行之目的或方法之情况而决定”。[18]

着眼于付某华案和钟某玉案,在夫妻通过离婚协议对婚姻存续期间共有的房屋产权约定归一方而未办理房屋产权变更登记时,作为非登记名义人的原配偶一方对被执行人享有的权利仅为债权,既不是典型的排除强制执行的“所有权”,也不是法律规定的特殊债权。而债权具有平等性,加上该房屋登记于被执行人名下,产生了公信力,故案外第三人此时享有的债权不足以对抗申请执行人。此为付某华案之判决思路。论证有理有据,但该判决理由也存有一定漏洞:第一,物权公示公信原则之目的在于维护交易秩序和交易安全,而其是否一概适用于执行异议之诉是值得探讨的;第二,在这种情况下,案外第三人已经实际占有房屋,如果在其正在办理房屋产权变更登记或者其对未能办理登记无过错的情况下,其离获得房屋之所有权仅差登记一步。若第三人享有的仅为金钱之债,两个债权是否应区分保护顺位以及区分保护顺位之依据为何也值得进一步分析。

(一)案外人异议之诉中物权登记能否发挥公信效力

判断在案外人异议之诉中的物权登记是否产生公信力,需要厘清该原则之内涵及功能目的。物权公示原则是指物权之变动须以法定的第三人可知之方式予以公示,[19]其设立之功能目的在于考虑到物权为支配权,其优先效力和排他效力使之具有无论辗转于何人之手均可追及之效力,可能会影响第三人的利益。[20] 故物权之设立、移转力求公开、透明,[21]彰显物权的归属,维护交易秩序及交易安全,以定分止争。物权公示原则系物权公信原则的基石。物权公信原则是指第三人有理由相信物权公示显示的内容即为权利人真实的权利状态,并与之为交易行为,其信赖利益得为法律所保护。[22] 如果保护真实物权人,第三人需要花费相当多的成本对物权的真实权利状态予以审查,徒增交易成本,故出于提高效率、保护交易安全的目的,有必要规定公信原则。[23] 由是观之,公信

[18] 赖来焜:《强制执行法总论》,元照出版有限公司2007年版,第654页。

[19] 参见王利明:《物权法》,中国人民大学出版社2015年版,第29页。

[20] 参见史尚宽:《物权法论》,中国政法大学出版社2000年版,第10页。

[21] 参见崔建远:《物权:规范与学说》(上册),清华大学出版社2011年版,第172页。

[22] 参见谢在全:《民法物权论》(上册),中国政法大学出版社1999年版,第85页。

[23] 参见崔建远:《物权法》,中国人民大学出版社2009年版,第57页。

公示原则旨在维护交易秩序和交易安全。

那么,在上述案外人异议之诉中公示公信原则是否有适用的空间?易言之,能否直接依据物权公示公信原则判定案外原配偶基于离婚协议中有关房屋产权的约定不能对抗申请执行人?此时不能一概而论,而应根据申请执行人对执行标的享有的债权之特性进行分类探讨。如果其享有的债权会对房屋产生直接的支配作用,则为非金钱债权,否则为金钱债权。当申请执行人享有的仅为金钱债权时,由于申请执行人是在债权无法履行而提出强制执行申请之时,才根据物权公示状况确定被执行人的责任财产,故申请执行人与被执行人之间并非物权交易,更谈不上基于对物权公示的信赖而为交易行为。公示公信原则在申请执行人享有的债权为金钱债权的执行异议之诉中不存在适用的前提。申请执行人不能主张其对执行标的有信赖利益而当然排除案外第三人的权利。换言之,此时案外配偶基于离婚协议中有关房屋产权的约定不会因为物权登记公信力而无法对抗申请执人。而当申请执行人享有非金钱债权时,其与被执行人之间系物权交易关系,此时满足物权公示公信原则适用的前提,申请执行人的信赖利益应得到保护。

虽然物权公示公信原则在执行异议之诉中并非一概适用,但物权公示公信原则与强制执行的关系仍有必要厘清,以确定案外人异议之诉中审查标准与"权利外观""物权公示公信原则"的关系。物权公示公信原则在强制执行中发挥作用的环节应当在于以法定公示的物权确定被执行人的责任财产。如果案外人针对被执行人的责任财产提出执行异议,考虑到"强制执行以效率为首要价值追求",执行异议仍应坚持"权利外观"规则,作形式审查。若案外第三人对执行异议不服,提起执行异议之诉,其审查标准应与执行异议中对权利外观有较高要求不同,更应注重进行实体审查,运用利益衡量规则,寻求案外第三人与申请执行人之间利益保护的"黄金分割点"。否则,若执行异议与执行异议之诉坚持同一"权利外观"审查标准,执行异议之诉就丧失了存在的必要性。故物权公示公信原则适用于强制执行过程中确定被执行人的责任财产以及执行异议中的形式审查,但不应适用于执行异议之诉。

回归付某华案,该案的审理法官直接以案外第三人与被执行人之间的债权具有相对性,不能对抗信赖物权登记的申请执行人为由驳回付某华诉讼请求的做法,值得商榷。第一,物权公示公信制度只适用于交易领域。在该案中,申请执行人享有的是金钱债权,被执行人与申请执行人之间不涉及物权交易,公示公信原则无适用的前提。第二,本案为案外人异议之诉,应作实体审查。而付某华案严格遵循权利外观规则,审查标准不与执行异议中的形式审查作区分,相当于是执行异议的重复,使案外第三人异议之诉"流于形式",无法发挥其制度作用。第三,现实生活中,夫妻离异后基于种种原因,在离婚协议上约定房屋产权而不作变更登记的情形并不少见,且目前我国不动产登记仍不完备。如果一律坚持依据物权公示公信原则作统一的处理,可能与现实不适应。由此,我们至少可以得出一个结论:公示公信原则不能用以论证申请执行人之金钱债权优先于案外第三人之债权。

(二)案外第三人基于离婚协议享有的债权之特殊性

案外第三人基于离婚协议之房屋归属约定而享有的债权系请求被执行人进行房屋产权变更登记的权利,在案外第三人已经实际占有房屋的情形下,其距离成为真正意义上的所有权人仅仅差变更登记一步。虽然这并不能改变案外第三人享有的权利为债权的性质,但该债权与申请执行人之金钱债权相比,确实存在一定的特殊性。如在钟某玉案中,法官通过对比案外第三人之债权请求权与申请执行人之债权请求权,认为在时间上,案外第三人之离婚协议的成立先于申请执行人申请强制执行,内容上前者系对执行标的的请求权,而后者仅为金钱债权等,故因此而具有排除强制执行的效力。问题之关键在于该债权之特殊性能否成为案外第三人之债权足以对抗申请执行人的理由且其是否具有正当性?

1. 规范性分析角度

现有法律对基于离婚协议之房屋归属约定而产生的债权是否能对抗申请执行人的债权并没有明文规定。但从现有规定来看,案外第三人享有的债权类似于我国最高人民法院《关于人民法院民事执行中查封、扣押、冻结财产的规定》(以下简称《查封规定》)第17条[24]中的未进行房屋产权变更登记的房屋买受人。根据该规定,当房屋买受人同时满足三个要件时(①已经支付部分或全部价款;②已经实际占有该房屋;③对未办理过户登记无过错),法院则不能查封该房屋。如此,随之而来的问题在于涉及离婚协议约定房屋产权的案件中能否类推适用该条款?事实上,通过离婚协议约定房屋归属与房屋买卖合同有很

[24] 最高人民法院《关于人民法院民事执行中查封、扣押、冻结财产的规定》(以下简称《查封规定》)第17条:被执行人将其所有的需要办理过户登记的财产出卖给第三人,第三人已经支付部分或者全部价款并实际占有该财产,但尚未办理产权过户登记手续的,人民法院可以查封、扣押、冻结;第三人已经支付全部价款并实际占有,但未办理过户登记手续的,如果第三人对此没有过错,人民法院不得查封、扣押、冻结。

多相似之处,前者甚至内含更值得保护的价值。

首先,二者权利变动情况相似。房屋买卖合同和离婚协议分割房屋条款的目的均在于变动房屋的所有权。在婚姻存续期间,房屋虽然仅登记在夫妻一方名下,但为夫妻双方的共同财产。在离婚时二人约定房屋归未登记一方,旨在将房屋所有权由共同共有变更为单独所有,非登记一方配偶享有请求登记名义人进行房屋产权变更登记的权利。房屋买卖合同签订后,买受人是从对房屋不享有权利到对房屋享有要求出卖人进行房屋产权变动的请求权。

其次,虽然在离婚协议约定房屋产权归属的语境之下,要件①中“已经支付部分或全部价款”可能并不直接体现为财产对价的给付,但离婚协议中的财产分割往往隐含着相应的对价。在离婚的场合下,夫妻通过协议进行财产分割时,其考量并非严格按照市场交易。很多情况下,夫妻分割财产体现为夫妻财产之间的互易,甚至会出现不以财产作为对价的情况,如体现为一方对另一方情感的填补。故在离婚协议约定房屋产权归属的情况下,可以对“已经支付部分或全部款项”要件①作扩大解释为“已经支付部分或全部对价”并认定其已经满足。

再次,对于要件②“已经实际占有该房屋”,在离婚协议约定房屋产权归属的情形下,该占有为持续占有。由于实践中离婚后房屋往往约定归于抚养孩子的一方配偶,故相较于买受人而言,非登记名义人配偶一方的持续占有更体现“房屋乃安身立命之场所”及“生活保障”之意义。

最后,对于要件③“对未办理过户登记无过错”,离婚协议约定房屋产权归属的情形与房屋买卖的情形的审查标准类似,主要为债权人是否在合理期限内请求变更登记。在钟某玉案中,作为案外第三人的非登记名义人钟某玉多次请求前夫进行房屋产权变更登记未果,其对未办理房屋过户登记不存在过错。

综上所述,在法律对基于离婚协议之房屋归属约定而产生的债权是否能对抗申请执行人的债权无明确规定的情况下,可以参照我国《查封规定》第 17 条的规定,举轻以明重。房屋买受人满足三个要件时尚且能够获得救济,离婚配偶一方基于离婚协议而享有的对房屋的请求权更应得到保护。

2. 学理分析角度

执行异议之诉的目的在于通过赋予案外第三人举证证明其享有足以排除强制执行的实体权益的权利,以平衡申请执行人与案外第三人的利益。[25] 这就

---

〔25〕 参见唐力:《案外人执行异议之诉的完善》,载《法学》2014 年第 7 期。

决定了执行异议之诉的审理过程中要坚持利益平衡原则。不同于执行程序中“效率优先、兼顾公平”的理念,执行异议之诉作为审判程序,更注重公平。[26]因此,执行异议之诉的审理并不仅仅适用“权利外观原则”。在权利人“名实不符”的情况下,若能通过实体审查查明被执行标的的实际权利人,则实际权利人之权益也应受保护。此时“利益平衡原则”则意味着需要结合实体法的规定比较案外第三人与申请执行人享有之权利,并对二者权利之性质进行甄别,确定在实际权利人与申请执行人之利益发生冲突时的权利实现顺位。易言之,在权利人“名实不符”的情况下,难以依据单一的因素确定统一的裁判标准,个案的公平正义有赖于法官结合实体法综合考量案外第三人和申请执行人享有的权利之性质、权利取得的来源及时间等,进行利益衡量并作出价值判断。

具体到上述典型案例,如前文所述,在权利性质上,法官应首先甄别案外第三人基于离婚协议而享有的对房屋的请求权为债权而非物权。其次,应判断申请执行人享有的权利为金钱债权抑或非金钱债权。若申请执行人享有的债权为要求被执行人交付房屋的非金钱债权,则满足适用公示公信原则的前提,案外第三人享有的债权不足以对抗申请执行人。若申请执行人享有的是金钱之债,其与案外第三人享有的债权相比无法定的优先顺位。故在二者权益相互冲突的情况下,法官需要对两个债权的优先保护顺位作出价值判断。如在时间上,钟某玉案中的法官认为,钟某玉夫妻离婚协议成立于申请执行人与被执行人之债权成立之前,足以排除案外第三人与被执行人有恶意串通逃避债务的可能。对此,笔者深以为然。此外,如果离婚协议成立于房屋被查封之后,因查封具有公信力,自然也能推导出案外第三人的恶意而不支持其排除强制执行的诉讼请求。那么,如果离婚协议成立于申请执行人债权债务关系成立之后,而在查封之前,是否也认为案外第三人有过错?笔者认为,如果该情形下夫妻之间系恶意串通逃避债务,申请执行人可通过第三人撤销之诉等寻求救济,此时的“时间”因素不宜作过于严格的认定。故该种情形也不宜认定案外第三人有过错。此外,从权利形成的根源来看,夫妻离婚时将房屋约定归于一方所有,往往同时兼顾了财产补偿、情感补偿及保障对方和孩子生活的考量。故保护案外第三人(非登记名义人配偶)的权利对案外配偶及孩子具有生活保障之意味,符合

[26] 参见刘贵祥、范向阳:《〈关于人民法院办理执行异议和复议案件若干问题的规定〉的理解与适用》,载《人民司法》2015年第11期。

执行异议之诉的“生存利益优先原则”。综上,案外第三人基于离婚协议享有的债权如果满足上述特殊性,应考虑优先保护该债权。

四、结　　语

在房屋权利人“名实不符”的情形下,基于离婚房屋分割协议而产生的债权能否对抗申请执行人,现行法仅有原则性规定,司法实践中法院无法仅凭单一的因素形成统一的裁判规则。该类案件有赖于法官在个案中综合考量案外第三人及申请执行人之债权的权利性质、成立时间和权利来源等因素,从而进行利益衡量并作出价值判断。

具体而言,在权利性质甄别上,基于离婚房屋分割协议而产生的权利为债权而非物权。依据债权的主要权利内容是否涉及金钱给付为标准,申请执行人享有的债权可分为金钱债权和非金钱债权。物权公示公信原则旨在保障交易安全和交易秩序,故当申请执行人享有的债权为非金钱债权时,该原则存在适用的空间,此时基于离婚房屋分割协议而产生的债权不能对抗申请执行人。而当申请执行人享有的债权为金钱债权时,因不涉及物权交易,此时物权公示公信原则无适用之空间,由此至少可以得出申请执行人的债权不具有优先于案外第三人(离婚原配偶一方)所享有的债权的结论。于此情形下,本文主张以《查封规定》第 17 条为基础,对基于离婚房屋分割协议而产生的债权和申请执行人享有的债权进行比较,综合考虑债权成立的先后及形成的根源。在成立时间上,如果离婚协议成立于申请执行人与被执行人之债权形成之前,推定案外第三人无利用离婚协议逃避债务的恶意;如果离婚协议成立于房屋被查封之后,应认定案外第三人所享有的债权不能对抗申请执行人;而当离婚协议成立于申请执行人之债权成立之后,且在房屋被申请强制执行前,同样推定案外第三人不具有逃避债务之恶意。在权利形成的根源上,则要考量该房屋于案外第三人而言是否具有生活保障之意味,而决定是否需要对“生存利益”优先保护。

总而言之,基于离婚房屋分割约定而产生的债权能否对抗申请执行人,需要对上述各因素综合进行价值衡量,从而实现个案的公平正义。

(责任编辑:缪子仪)

病假旅行严重违反规章制度的判定

戴　婷*

摘要：

病假旅行是劳动者自主安排病休期间用于旅行的行为。判定其是否严重违反规章制度，首先应当明确：一方面，劳动者自由行使病休权的行为不应受到限制。另一方面，单位有权依据内容明确合理的规章行使病假管理权。以劳动者病假旅行构成严重违反规章制度为由解除合同的，必须同时满足以下条件：一是按照法定程序制定的规章已对病假期间的行为做出明确限制；二是规章关于病假管理的内容具有合理性；三是劳动者病假旅行行为满足严重违规性的要求。在判定行为的严重违规性时，不应随意适用诚信原则，而应当综合考虑病休需求的真实性、违规行为的数量性、违规行为的顽固性、隐藏理由的合理性等因素。

关键词：

病假旅行；劳动合同；严重违反规章制度

引　　言

规章制度是用人单位在经营管理中普遍采取的一种制度安排，"严重违反用人单位规章制度"作为解雇劳动者的一项重要事由被频繁适用。然而，如何认定劳动者行为构成严重违反规章制度一直是理论界与实务界的难题，学界对此进行了深入探讨。比如，全国人大法工委提出参考劳动法规和合理的规章制度规定。[1] 又如，有学者建议引入交易习惯与行规作为判断规章合理

---

* 戴婷，中央财经大学法学院 2017 级硕士研究生。

〔1〕 参见信春鹰：《中华人民共和国劳动合同法释义》，法律出版社 2007 年版，第 138 页。

性的标准。[2] 再如,有学者指出应综合衡量劳动者的主观故意、行为性质、行为后果、补救措施等四个方面。[3] 还有学者论证比例原则在判断劳动者严重违反规章制度中的可适用性。[4]

上述学者的研究,集中于从宏观角度进行探讨,却较少涉及对劳动者病假旅行这一特殊行为性质的分析。现有对病假旅行的研究,分散于病假制度的相关研究中,且主要是从企业实务管理的角度进行分析,[5]零散而不系统。事实上,以"阿里巴巴员工病假旅行解雇案"为代表的劳动者病假旅行案件不断涌现,[6]已经引发了社会的广泛关注与思考。同时,随着社会经济发展,病假纠纷形式日益多样化,此类案件数量呈现上升趋势,一直是司法实践中的热点问题。因此,有必要对劳动者病假旅行这一特定行为是否构成严重违反规章制度进行系统性的分析。

作为判断病假旅行是否构成严重违反规章制度的典型案例,"阿里巴巴员工病假旅行案"颇有值得探讨之处,该案中劳动者丁某因颈椎病向公司请假,却

---

〔2〕 参见郑尚元、王艺非:《用人单位劳动规章制度形成理性及法制重构》,载《现代法学》2013年第6期。

〔3〕 参见胡大武:《严重违反单位规章制度之严重性边界的实证分析——以〈劳动合同法〉第39条第(二)款为视角》,载《中国劳动》2016年第12期。

〔4〕 参见穆随心:《试论比例原则在惩戒解雇制度中的适用》,载《兰州学刊》2014年第1期。

〔5〕 参见尹明生:《职工休病假的条件与程序研究》,载《中国劳动关系学院学报》2015年第4期;唐付强:《企业如何做好员工病假的管理》,载《上海法治报》2018年9月17日,第7版;林纲:《企业病假管理制度要点分析》,载《人力资源管理》2018年第6期;张纯煦:《病假管理有讲究》,载《中国劳动保障报》2018年3月2日,第5版。

〔6〕 笔者以"病假""旅游"为检索词,在无讼网上检索到大量涉及劳动者病假旅行严重违规性判断的案例,参见南京市中级人民法院(2014)宁民终字第497号民事判决书,上海市徐汇区人民法院(2014)徐民五(民)初字第492号民事判决书,上海市浦东新区人民法院(2016)沪0115民初1295号民事判决书,北京市第三中级人民法院(2017)京03民终1702号民事判决书,上海市第一中级人民法院(2010)沪一中民三(民)终字第3066号民事判决书,上海市普陀区人民法院(2017)沪0107民初5105号民事判决书,北京市第一中级人民法院(2015)一中民终字第650号民事判决书,北京市高级人民法院(2017)京民再65号民事判决书等。

在当日前往巴西旅行,被阿里巴巴公司以"提供虚假申请信息并恶意欺骗公司,行为严重违反公司规章制度"为由解除劳动合同。[7] 其实,劳动者病假旅行案件的基本案情大抵如此,以小见大,此类病假旅行案件具有共同的争议焦点,即劳动者在病假期间旅行的行为是否适用《劳动合同法》第39条第2项。[8] 本文认为,要想回答这一问题,一方面应当明确病假旅行的性质,因其直接关系到能否适用规章;另一方面,还应当结合用人单位规章制度的内容与劳动者行为的客观表现,判断行为是否构成严重违规,才能得出比较恰当的答案。本文将试图对以上问题做出回应。

一、病假旅行的法律性质

病假休息权指劳动者在伤病(非因职业病或者因工负伤)期间停止工作、休息和就医的权利,[9]其关系到劳动者的生命健康权,属于劳动者的基本人权之一。首先应当明确,规章制度是否有权对劳动者在病假期间旅行的行为做出规定?对于病假旅行的法律性质,学者们观点不一,这是导致病假旅行现象不断蔓延的原因之一,故而应当厘清病假旅行的法律性质。

(一)病假无权旅行说

持"病假无权旅行说"的学者认为,劳动者在病假期间无权旅行,故单位完全有权制定规章限制病假期间的旅行行为。至于劳动者为何无权旅行,存在不

---

[7] 一审判决书参见北京市海淀区人民法院(2013)海民初字第26371号民事判决书,二审判决书参见北京市第一中级人民法院(2015)一中民终字第650号民事判决书,再审判决书参见北京市高级人民法院(2017)京民再65号民事判决书。

[8] 《劳动合同法》第39条规定:"劳动者有下列情形之一的,用人单位可以解除劳动合同:(一)在试用期间被证明不符合录用条件的;(二)严重违反用人单位的规章制度的;(三)严重失职,营私舞弊,给用人单位造成重大损害的;(四)劳动者同时与其他用人单位建立劳动关系,对完成本单位的工作任务造成严重影响,或者经用人单位提出,拒不改正的;(五)因本法第二十六条第一款第一项规定的情形致使劳动合同无效的;(六)被依法追究刑事责任的。"

[9] 参见刘焱白:《如何处理劳动者病休权与单位病假管理权的冲突》,载《中国劳动》2011年第11期。

同的解释:第一种观点认为,劳动者在病假期间的行为附有一定的义务,这项义务的内容就是"劳动者安心养病,恢复身体以便更好地为单位服务",故劳动者不得从事其他有害身体的行为,包括旅行。暂且不论旅行是否有碍于养病义务的履行,认定劳动者承担养病义务的缘由有二:一是"病假工资对价说",该观点认为劳动者的养病义务来源于用人单位支付的病假工资。〔10〕 由于患病期间的劳动者不能提供任何劳动,按照"无劳动无报酬"的观念,用人单位本不应提供给劳动者工资,但根据现行法律规定,用人单位仍需支付劳动者在病假期间的工资,且不得低于最低工资标准的 80%,〔11〕从权利义务对等的角度出发,劳动者享受领取工资的权利就应当履行对应的义务,故劳动者在病假期间附有养病义务。

二是"劳动合同义务说",该观点认为,劳动者休养身体的义务基于劳动合同本身。作为典型的持续性债务关系,劳资双方互负的权利义务并不因劳动者休病假而停止。比如,原劳动部《关于加强企业伤病长休职工管理工作的通知》(劳险字〔1992〕14 号)规定:"禁止伤病休假职工从事有收入的活动",就是对劳动者忠实义务的要求。域外也有对工作时间外劳动者的行为进行约束的规定,比如,德国《联邦休假法》明确规定:劳动者不得从事与休假目的相悖的营利活动,原因在于该行为违反了劳动合同中的从义务。〔12〕 日本法上则规定劳动者负有诚信规则上不损毁雇主的业务利益和信誉的义务,这意味着劳动者在工作场所之外的行为并非完全不受限制,若其行为损害了企业利益,仍可作为惩戒的对象。〔13〕 从这个意义上来说,劳动者在病假期间休养身体是其诚信履行劳动合同的应有之义。换言之,用人单位规章的合理性限制内容是对劳动者应遵守的

〔10〕 参见前引 5,尹明生文。

〔11〕 根据原劳动部发布的《关于贯彻执行〈中华人民共和国劳动法〉若干问题的意见》第 59 条规定:"职工患病或非因工负伤治疗期间,在规定的医疗期间内由企业按有关规定支付其病假工资或疾病救济费,病假工资或疾病救济费可以低于当地最低工资标准支付,但不能低于最低工资标准的 80%。"

〔12〕 参见[德]雷蒙德瓦尔特曼:《德国劳动法》,沈建峰译,法律出版社 2014 年版,第 218 页。

〔13〕 参见谢增毅:《用人单位惩戒权的法理基础与法律规制》,载《比较法研究》2016 年第 1 期。

合同义务的具体化,劳动者在病假期间应当而且必须从事用人单位期待的“养病行为”。

第二种观点认为,病假期间的行为可成为规章规定的客体。众所周知,规章可对与单位管理秩序紧密联系的事项做出规定,[14]休假制度关系到企业能否正常运转,而病假制度作为休假制度的组成部分,其对于管理秩序的重要性自不待言。良好的管理秩序是用人单位有效运作的前提,试想一下,若用人单位无权对劳动者“以病假之名,行旅行之实”的行为加以制止,那么其他劳动者将争相效仿此种行为,打着休病假的旗帜不劳而获,损害用人单位的合法权益,最终可能导致单位管理秩序出现混乱,不利于企业发展目标的实现,因此,规章必须有权对劳动者在病假期间的行为做出限制。

第三种观点认为,病假旅行违背诚信原则,应被禁止。由于病假旅行的劳动者并未就病假期间的行为据实告知用人单位,名为休病假,实则私自旅行,因此违反诚信原则。劳动者擅自在病假期间旅行导致其身体难以得到恢复,违背了用人单位批准病假的初衷。司法实践中,法院据此认定劳动者病假旅行违背诚信原则的判决并不少见。

(二)病假旅行自由说

劳动者有权在病假期间旅行,规章无权对病假期间的行为做出限制。持“病假旅行自由说”的学者主要基于以下考虑:第一,病休权作为一种权利,本身意味着对劳动者工作义务的豁免,既然单位已经批准病假,那么“在何地休病假、如何休病假”属于劳动者自主决定的内容,单位无权干涉。劳动者出卖的仅为劳动力使用权,而非将自己卖身为奴。[15] “自主支配”是休息权的应有之义,也是劳动者实现休息权的保证,唯有尊重劳动者在休息时间内的自主支配权,劳动者才能真正地实现尊严。[16] 既然劳动者在病假期间旅行是权利,该行为自然与违反诚信原则无关。

---

〔14〕 参见沈建峰:《论用人单位劳动规章的制定模式与效力控制——基于对德国、日本和我国台湾地区的比较分析》,载《比较法研究》2016年第1期。

〔15〕 参见中共中央马克思、恩格斯、列宁、斯大林著作编译局编译:《马克思恩格斯文集》(第5卷),人民出版社2009年版,第195页以下。

〔16〕 参见尹明生:《劳动者休息权制度的基础法理探析》,载《石油大学学报》2015年第4期。

第二,劳动者附有养病义务的说法不成立。与“病假无权旅行说”不同,持该观点的学者认为,尽管单位支付病假工资,但支付工资并非单位管理病假行为的合理理由。按照民法思维,因债务人个人原因导致无法给付,债权人免于对应的给付,其以对等、理性的个人之间的交易为前提,有其正当性。不过,该思维却不能适用于劳动法领域,〔17〕这是因为,劳动合同异于一般的民事合同,具有继续性与生存依赖性的特点,适用该项原则对劳动者极为不利。由于劳动合同并非一时给付而完成,客观上无法期待劳动者不生病,劳动者对于工资报酬却具有高度的依赖性,工资是其安身立命的根本。故相比于具有雄厚的经济实力和熟练的风险转移能力的单位,劳动者显然处于弱势地位。因此,劳动者具有社会保护的必要性,带薪休假在一定程度上是对劳动者的社会性保护,而非劳动者负有义务的对价。

第三,限制劳动者在病假期间的行为将进一步压缩劳动者的休息自主权。其一,现阶段我国对劳动者休息权利保障不足。由于我国休假制度不健全,劳动者在空闲时间学习、游玩、娱乐、陪伴家庭等精神需求难以满足,故其利用病假期间从事其他行为也属情理之中。如德国劳动法上专门规定了员工照顾时间和父母假期,目的在于改善家庭与职业照顾的关系,且该休假期间雇主不得解除劳动关系。〔18〕 而我国则无此类制度,一直以来,我国劳动者“请假难”“假期短”,利用正常休假自我发展的时间远远不足,休息权难得保障,这才导致劳动者在病假期间进行旅行等休闲活动。其二,赋予规章对病假期间限制的权利,存在限缩劳动者休息自主权的风险。众所周知,用人单位相对于劳动者处于优势地位,若允许规章对劳动者在病假期间的行为做出限制,很难期待用人单位不会滥用管理权损害劳动者休息权,致使原已保障不足的休息权进一步被限制。

(三)本文的观点

首先,劳动者应当享有一定的自主决定权。为了更好地理解这一点,我们可以将劳动者“病假旅行”与“出差旅行”进行对比分析:毫无疑问,劳动者在病假期间的约束显然应当少于出差期间的要求。然而,即使在正常履行劳动合同

---

〔17〕 参见胡玉浪、石丽芳:《台风假法律问题之探讨——基于台湾地区相关立法的考察与借鉴》,载《海峡法学》2016 年第 3 期。

〔18〕 参见前引 12,雷蒙德瓦尔特曼书,第 219 页。

的出差期间,劳动者也并非全天候处于工作状态。一般认为,只要劳动者行为未对合同义务履行造成障碍,用人单位无权对劳动者的私人活动进行干预,故劳动者在工作时间外的聚餐娱乐活动应属正当。既然劳动者在出差期间都具有一定的行动自由,病假期间的行动自由权自不待言。

不过,用人单位应当享有病假管理权。现有法律规定了单位进行病假审批的权利,防止劳动者虚构事实骗取病假工资,但对于劳动者在病假期间的具体行为,只有原劳动部等部门发布的《关于加强企业伤病长休职工管理工作的通知》作出了规定,要求"伤病休假职工不得从事有收入的活动"。至于规章是否有权对病假期间的其他行为做出限制,则未置可否。笔者认为,以劳动者为视角并主张对其在病假期间的行为附义务,固然提供了一种解释的思路,但似有扩大用人单位干涉劳动者私人生活权力之嫌疑。毕竟在很多情形下,证明病假旅行与单位业绩或秩序具有直接关联非常困难。本文认为,从用人单位管理利益的角度似乎更容易理解这一问题,事实上,用人单位之所以想要约束真实病休劳动者在病假期间的行为,是因为担忧劳动者休假返岗后工作效率降低,从而影响合同的继续履行。比如,劳动者旅行之后,病情不但未好转反而恶化,会对整个单位的生产业绩造成不良影响。诚然,对于劳动者病假旅行返岗后损害单位利益的行为(比如劳动者休假返岗后因病情加重导致出现严重工作失误的情形),用人单位自然可以解除劳动合同而保护自身的利益,但基于追求利润最大化及优化员工管理水平的考虑,用人单位可以对病假期间做出一定的限制,提前预防劳动者病假旅行的负面影响。

其实,承认单位规章对病假期间行为作出规定的权利,并不一定会严重损害劳动者的自由行动权,甚至是对劳动者权利的保护。具体而言,劳资双方地位不平等的问题一直存在,并非因规章制度的限制性规定而产生。有观点担忧,规章规定休假方式会导致资方滥用管理权,进而致使劳资冲突进一步加剧。但本文认为,由单位规章对病假期间的行为明确做出限制,反而将单位约束休假权的内容置于光亮之处,从而有利于司法者对其做出公正的评价。诚然,对于休假行为的限制也可以依据一定的观念,但对于病假期间旅行的性质这一极具争议性的话题,相比于主观随意性强、内容变动的社会观念,客观、规范、明确的规章内容可为劳动者行为提供较为具体的指引,而规章制定程序的要求在一定程度上也可以提高劳动者的参与度。此外,规章合理性审查制度也有利于平衡劳资双方的利益,限制资方管理权的滥用。由此可见,由规章对病假期间的行为作出限制对保护劳动者休假权更为有利。

此外,鉴于“修养身体”内涵的丰富性,判断规章是否有权禁止旅行,还需具体分析。尽管劳动者应当遵守规章的相关内容,但并不等同于被限制行动自由。在旅行有利于休养身体的场合,“一刀切”式地禁止病假旅行并不妥当,因此,对于这种特殊情况,应由司法实践区别对待,但这并不意味着用人单位无权对病假期间的行为做出合理限制。

综上所述,“病假旅行自由说”旨在倾斜保护劳动者休息权的观点固然值得理解,但其忽视单位的管理利益,未免过于偏激,脱离实际。劳动者病休权具有两面性:一方面,病休权的权利属性赋予劳动者病假期间一定的自主决定权。另一方面,单位的用工管理权要求其对病休行为进行适当的监督,重点是在劳动者休息自主决定权与用人单位用工管理权之间实现平衡。用人单位对于劳动者在病假期间的行为,并非完全没有管理权限,单位规章则可以为劳动者行为提供具体的指引,从而有利于劳动者休假权的保护。较为恰当的做法是:承认用人单位在规章中对劳动者在病假期间的行为作出规定的权利,同时通过内容的合理性审查制度限制单位管理权的滥用。

二、规章存在程序上瑕疵对病假旅行性质认定的影响

司法实践中,规章制度的效力一直是当事人争议的焦点问题,也是法院审判关注的重点。根据《劳动合同法》第4条,对于直接涉及劳动者切身利益的规章制度,用人单位在制定、修改或决定时应“与工会或者职工代表平等协商确定”,同时应当“公示或者告知劳动者”。用人单位以严重违反规章制度解除劳动合同的,自然必须有明确的规章内容作为依据。然而,对于规章制度是否必须满足“民主程序”和“公示程序”方可发生效力,实践和学界并未形成统一意见,形成了“劳资双决”与“资方单决”两种不同的看法。二者的重要区别在于:对于制定程序存在瑕疵的规章制度,“劳资双决说”一律认定其无效,“资方单决说”则并非全然否定其效力。

(一)程序瑕疵无效的劳资双决说

从文义出发,“劳资双决说”认为“平等协商确定”就是指劳资双方在平等的地位上,就争议内容达成一致意见。“劳资双决说”强调劳动者享有最高程度的程序参与权——“共同决定权”,以劳资双方的意思合致作为规章效力的来

源,旨在保护弱势劳动者的利益,原因在于若由资方单决,劳动者必然受到资方强势地位的压迫,完全陷入被动,致使规章最终沦为资方肆意合法侵害劳动者权益的工具。因此,规章内容必须经过民主程序保障合意达成,以及公示程序使劳动者知情后,才能发生效力。若单位规章制定程序存在瑕疵,规章不发生效力,劳动者就不构成严重违规,但“劳资双决说”的缺陷在于过于理想化,无法反映劳资双方在实践中的真实情况。

(二)内容合理性审查的资方单决说

持“资方单决说”的学者的主要理由是:从立法角度来说,《劳动合同法》第4条之所以未采取《劳动合同法(一审稿)》中的“共同制定”字眼,而采用“平等协商确定”的表述,这意味着:“立法者意图将职工的参与程度降至不影响‘资方单决’的‘讨论,提出方案和意见’。”[19]故对于职工代表大会的意见,用人单位可以采纳也可以不采纳,最终由用人单位自决。从实践角度来说,要求规章对所有事项都作出事无巨细的规定并不现实,“告知并征求劳动者意见”的生效要件也不利于单位实现社会化生产经营,且与规章追求效率的价值相悖。[20] 何况实践中由于工会、职工代表缺乏独立性与主动性,在制度环境缺失的背景下,民主程序仅仅是“走过场”,最终是否采纳实际上完全取决于用人单位。因此,对于形式性的走过场程序,不如放弃。从司法实践来说,各地法院出台的相关意见或者裁判指引均突破了民主程序的要求,而把内容合理性作为判断是否有效的标准。[21] “资方单决说”常以“概括的同意”推定劳资双方已达成合意。在特定情形下,即使规章存在程序瑕疵,只要内容合理合法,不影响规章效力,单位

[19] 朱军:《〈劳动合同法〉第4条“平等协商确定的再解读”——基于劳动规章制度的中德比较》,载《华东政法大学学报》2017年第6期。

[20] 参见朱军:《论我国劳动规章制度的性质——性质二分说提出与证成》,载《清华法学》2017年第3期。

[21] 比如,广东省高级人民法院、广东省劳动争议仲裁委员会联合制定的《关于适用〈劳动争议调解仲裁法〉、〈劳动合同法〉若干问题的指导意见》第20条第1款规定:“用人单位在《劳动合同法》实施前制定的规章制度,虽未经过《劳动合同法》第四条第二款规定的民主程序,但内容未违反法律、行政法规及政策规定,并已向劳动者公示或告知的,可以作为用人单位用工管理的依据。”

仍可以严重违规解除合同。[22]

（三）本文的观点

“劳资双决说”的缺陷在于过于理想化，基于现行立法与实践，本文赞同“资方单决说”，但本文认为，其对规章制定程序要求的突破应当谨慎。绝对的“劳资双决”固然无法实现，但片面否定乃至抹杀劳动者的程序参与权更不可取。换言之，“资方单决”绝不意味着程序无用，郑尚元指出：“《劳动合同法》第4条意欲增强职工参与度的立法目的不可不察。”[23]在资方单独决定规章内容的现实场合，用人单位完全有能力履行法律规定的程序制定要求。

关于规章的法律性质，学界发展出“格式合同说”“法规授权说”“性质二分说”等不同的看法，但笔者认为无论采取何种学说，最终目的是实现劳资双方利益的平衡，故应当重点分析规章制定程序对劳资双方利益的影响。站在劳动者的角度，民主程序是其行使程序参与权的重要途径。虽然民主程序不能绝对保障规章内容的合理性，但却是证明其合理性的重要证据，重视多数劳工的意见在学术及判例中已发展成主流观点。[24] 公示程序则是劳动者了解规章内容并具以指引自身行为的前提条件。在劳动者对于规章内容无决定权的场合，程序参与的权利应当被保障。当然，即使是制定程序完善的规章，还需经过合理性审查才能确定其效力。

对于用人单位而言，履行规章制定程序并不会导致其陷入不利地位。第一，既然是形式性的“走过场”程序，按照程序规定制定规章自然并非难事，因为单位只需要履行一个集思广益的过程即可，无需获得劳动者的同意，并未增加单位的制定规章的负担，故其拒绝履行程序要求的理由难以成立。第二，严格的程序要求可以给单位施加压力，激励单位尽心尽力地制定“明确、透明、稳定”的规章制度，防止单位滥用管理权限，从而有利于企业规章制度的规范化管理。[25] 由此可见，用人单位履行规章制定程序并不会导致劳资双方权利义务的失衡。

---

〔22〕 参见沈同仙：《试论程序瑕疵用人单位规章制度的效力判定》，载《政治与法律》2012年第12期。

〔23〕 前引2，郑尚元、王艺非文，第81页以下。

〔24〕 前引2，郑尚元、王艺非文，第81页。

〔25〕 2015年《中共中央国务院关于构建和谐劳动关系的意见》中提出加强企业民主管理建设，鼓励劳动者通过民主程序参与规章制度完善的价值取向内含其中。

另外,需要注意的是,实践中虽有突破规章制定程序乃至内容要求的判决,但仅限于例外情形。通览法院相关文件与司法案例可以发现,此类案例中劳动者大多存在"恶劣违规"的行为,仅在个案中具有价值,故在居于绝对地位的一般情形下,应当尊重"程序瑕疵推定无效"的一般效力认定规则。

之所以允许恶意违规的例外情形,是因为,若坚守规章制定程序存在瑕疵无效的规则,用人单位将陷入无法辞退劳动者的困境,任由恶意违规者肆意妄为,对于用人单位而言显失公平,故此时可突破程序要求,认定规章制度有效,将用人单位从合同履行中解脱出来。此时即使规章存在程序瑕疵乃至未明确规定,由于劳动者的行为违反劳动合同的基本义务,用人单位解除合同的行为仍然合法。比如,在最高法院指导性案例"熊某与曼宁家屋面系统(成都)有限公司劳动争议案"中,劳动者多次实施性骚扰行为,经单位告诫不知悔改,性质极为恶劣,规章制度的要求虽未明确规定,法院认定劳动者的行为违反劳动纪律,认定解除行为合法。〔26〕 该指导性案例中,由于劳动者存在极端恶劣的行为,严重扰乱了单位的工作秩序,为了保障用人单位的权益,当且仅当规章的内容无法约束恶劣违规行为,而规章又存在程序瑕疵时,才需要法院对规章的内容进行扩大解释。对于病假旅行行为而言,笔者认为不存在"严重恶劣"的性质,原因在于:存在真实病休需求的劳动者在病假期间的行为并不会给单位造成严重的损害,即使造成严重损害(如因病情加重导致工作失误),用人单位完全可以其他理由解除合同,而不必依据病假旅行构成严重违规解除合同。

故此,用人单位行使病假管理权应当以规章的明确规定为前提,在规章制度存在程序瑕疵时,应当倾向于认定规章制度无效。

三、病假旅行严重违反规章制度的判断标准

前文从规章制定的程序角度,探讨了规章本身效力对病假旅行性质判定的影响。若规章已经生效,鉴于"严重违反规章制度"在内涵上的模糊性,用人单位在解除合同时还应当考虑哪些因素?下文将结合司法实践中的经验,对判定严重违规的要素进行梳理。结合规章内容和劳动者行为的实际情况,具体分析单位在不同情形下是否具有解除权。

---

〔26〕 参见四川省成都市中级人民法院(2009)成民终字第2216号民事判决书。

众所周知,劳动者的行为包括主观与客观两个方面。判定劳动者的行为是否构成"严重违反规章制度",必须综合劳动者行为的主客观方面。具体而言,客观方面需结合行为客观违规性判断,主观方面则需要结合行为的挑衅性、数量性和隐藏理由来判断。在界定"严重违反规章制度"的标准时,既要防止制度异化导致劳动者恶意违规,也要考虑对单位管理权进行约束,更好地保护劳动者权益。

(一)规章内容的合理性

作为解雇依据的事由应当具有正当性,仅限于与履行工作义务相关的事由,[27]不能无限放大乃至超越劳动管理的范围,否则将损害劳动者的自由权利。规章有权对病假期间的行为做出限制,但其内容必须合理。既然规章制定的目的是实现病假管理权,那么作为手段的惩戒内容应当与达成该目标具有合理的关联性,[28]规章中与实现目标无关的内容,对劳动者不发生效力。

其一,规章不应不合理地增加劳动者的休假成本。这不仅是为了保护劳动者就诊自由的权利,更是为了防止单位干涉私人生活、变相阻碍劳动者行使休假权。其二,完全限制劳动者在病假期间的自由行为并非合理。正如"阿里巴巴员工病假解雇案"中一审法院判决中提到的:"休假"与"旅行"在内容和目的上存在交叉关系,若劳动者能够实现病假休养的目的,对于"休养附带旅行"或者类似的行为应持宽容态度。其三,若规章的内容并未增加劳动者负担,亦未偏离病假休养之目的,劳动者应当遵守。其四,交易习惯与行规具有重要的参考价值。[29] 病假旅行能否解除合同可以参照普遍实践的行规与交易习惯。

尽管以上标准提供了判断规章合理性的一些思路,但仍然比较模糊,在司法实践中难以把握,可操作性不强。为细化这一标准,判断病假旅行是否构成严重违规可从病休事实、主观状态、行为数量、隐藏理由、诚信原则的适用等五个维度展开,下文将展开详细论述。

(二)病休需求的真实性

以严重违规解除劳动合同的,必须以劳动者存在客观违规行为为前提,用人单位负有提供充分的证据证明劳动者实施违规行为的证明责任。劳动者享

---

〔27〕 参见王倩:《我国过错解雇制度的不足及其改进——兼论〈劳动合同法〉第 39 条的修改》,载《华东政法大学学报》2017 年第 4 期。

〔28〕 参见前引 4,穆随心文。

〔29〕 参见前引 2,郑尚元、王艺非文。

受病假休息权以存在客观休息需求为前提,根据原劳动部《关于加强企业伤病长休职工管理工作的通知》(劳险字〔1992〕14号),[30]劳动者申请病假应当提交医疗证明材料,用人单位进行审核并做出是否批准的决定。

通过对相关裁判文书的梳理,我们发现,法院在长期司法实践中,对于如何认定病休事实已经形成了一套相对完整的判断标准,可供我们思考并借鉴。

其一,劳动者负有在合理期间内及时提供医疗证明材料的义务,未及时提供材料的行为应认定为旷工。具体而言,劳动者提交材料的"合理期间"一般为"休假前",提交的医疗材料内容应当使单位信服其确需休病假。需要注意的是,囿于医疗知识的专业性和技术性,用人单位在认定病假材料的真实性时,仅具有形式审查权。

其二,用人单位基于"合理怀疑"可以推翻医疗证明材料的效力。[31]此种"合理怀疑"主要包括:证明材料存在程序上的瑕疵或者内容上的不合理。其中,"程序上的瑕疵"仅包括足以引起真实性判断的重大瑕疵,规章中不合理的程序要求不发生效力。比如,孙某案中,证明材料遭到涂改且缺少主要责任人的签章,因其足以影响对内容真实性的判断而构成合理怀疑。[32]但对于劳动者未提供指定就诊医院材料的行为,在真实性无异议的情形下应当承认其效力。"内容上相对不合理"应当以一般人在特定情形下可能产生疑问为标准,而不包括用人单位的主观揣测。比如,病假休假时间过长、[33]含有重要内容的证明材料缺失、[34]证明材料经单位核实系伪造[35]等。

〔30〕《关于加强企业伤病长休职工管理工作的通知》(劳险字〔1992〕14号)中规定:"职工因伤病需要休假的,应凭企业医疗机构或指定医院开具的疾病诊断证明,并由企业审核批准。"

〔31〕参见前引5,尹明生文。

〔32〕参见山东省威海市中级人民法院(2017)鲁10民终92号民事判决书。

〔33〕参见江苏省高级人民法院(2016)苏民申4198号民事裁定书,"严曙霞与阿特斯阳光电力科技公司劳动争议案"中劳动者虽提交证明材料,但病假长达九周且缺少检查报告。

〔34〕参见江苏省高级人民法院(2017)苏民申2505号民事裁定书,"蔡倩与南京浦福机车组装有限公司劳动合同纠纷申诉案"中劳动者仅提供病假条,无法提交疾病诊断证明。

〔35〕参见浙江省绍兴市中级人民法院(2016)浙06民终1878号民事判决书,"庄某与上海必胜客有限公司劳动争议案"中,用人单位向医疗材料出具单位核实后,发现诊断证明书上的病休建议系伪造。

其三,若劳动者突发炎症或者其他特殊情形亟须休假治疗的,事后应补交相关的证明材料。出于保护劳动者正当病休权的目的,对于事后补交证明材料的行为应予认可。

故此,在劳动者未按程序提交证明材料或者材料真实性存疑,单位无法确认劳动者存在确需休假的理由时,当然可直接以严重违规解除劳动合同。反之,用人单位不得以任何理由拒绝批准休假。这是实现劳动者休假权同时保障用人单位权益的必然要求。

(三)违规行为的数量性

过错解雇以不当行为存在主观过错为归责基础,[36]无论学界抑或实务界,均认可不同等级的过错行为对应不同的法律效果。违规行为的次数与行为的过错性密切相关,违规行为的次数越多,主观过错越大,初次违规行为难以认定为严重过错。劳动者初次病假旅行亦如此。我国台湾地区法院细化解雇适用的标准为:劳动关系受到严重干扰且难以继续维持,用人单位适用其他惩戒方法均无法解决。[37] 一般来说,劳动者的初次违规行为无论在主观过错还是实际损害方面,都难谓造成"严重干扰"。对于劳动者的初犯行为,单位可以采取警告、减薪、降职等对劳动者损害较少的惩戒手段,[38]既可保全劳动者就业,又能达到惩戒目的。

但若劳动者多次违规,单位可以严惩。如美国雇佣法认为,劳动者"大错不犯,小错不断"的工作状态构成解雇的正当性理由。[39] 因此,较为合理的规章制度是对违规行为做出阶梯式惩戒的规定,仅在违规行为达到"数量上"的满足时,才可解除劳动合同。

(四)违规行为的顽固性

在判断劳动者的过错程度方面,违规行为的顽固性与数量性相辅相成。不过,"行为的顽固性"强调的是主观状态存在拒不改正的恶意挑衅心理,而"行为的数量性"更多的是从客观行为推断出劳动者主观方面的恶意。之所以强调劳

---

〔36〕 参见黎建飞:《解雇保护:我国大陆与台湾地区之比较研究》,载《清华法学》2015年第5期。

〔37〕 参见前引4,穆随心文。

〔38〕 参见前引4,穆随心文。

〔39〕 穆随心:《论惩戒解雇制度的正当性原则——基于美国雇佣法的思考》,载《河北学刊》2016年第1期。

动者的主观状态,是因为劳动合同具有人身性和继续性的特点,故对劳资双方的相互信赖与配合提出了更高的要求,明知故犯的违规行为不仅动摇作为合同履行基础的信任关系,而且使合同目的蒙上阴影,对合同履行有害无利,[40]故劳动者的恶意挑衅行为将打破信赖基础,为合同履约所不容。

在合同履行过程中,如若劳动者对单位的警告或者批评指正充耳不闻,继续故意实施可能损害单位利益的不当行为,则为《劳动合同法》第39条第4项规定的"经用人单位提出,拒不改正的"情形,具有严重的挑衅意味,可以认定劳动者具有严重过错,单位可以解除劳动合同。

需要注意的是,过错解雇还应当遵循公平原则,对所有劳动者应一视同仁、没有歧视,综合考虑本单位的管理秩序。具体而言,如果此种故意不当行为"时有发生",而用人单位一直处于置之不理的消极状态,"突然袭击式"的解雇行为并不公平。比如,用人单位是食品包装企业,长期以来,单位对员工偷吃水果行为一直持放任态度。由于公司疏于管理的行为给了劳动者不合理的预期,那么,即使规章规定此种行为属于严重违规行为,也难以认定劳动者构成严重违规。[41] 也就是说,若用人单位一直放任劳动者病假旅行的行为,则不能以此为理由解除劳动合同。

(五)隐藏理由的合理性

判断劳动者的主观过错,还应当考虑减轻过错的情形。若劳动者病假旅行是基于合理的隐藏理由,可减轻对劳动者过错程度的判断。马克思曾指出:"自由时间用于娱乐与休息从而为劳动者开辟更广阔的天地"。[42] 劳动者除工作谋生存之外,还应当拥有追求幸福生活的权利。但要想真正实现这一点,必须以充足的权利保障为前提,使得劳动者休息的权利"独立且不依附于他人"。[43] 实际情况却恰好与之相反:在用人单位占尽优势地位的买方市场中,迫于就业及生存压力,签订合同时劳动者权利受到诸多限制。而单位采取的"减员增效"

[40] 参见前引27,王倩文。

[41] 参见黄昆:《如何判定严重违纪行为》,载《中国劳动》2011年第10期。

[42] 中共中央马克思、恩格斯、列宁、斯大林著作编译局编译:《马克思恩格斯全集》(第26卷),人民出版社1974年版,第281页。

[43] 参见蓝寿荣:《休息权何以成为权利——劳动者休息权的属性与价值探析》,载《法学评论》2014年第4期。

等一系列激励措施更加重了劳动者的竞争压力。[44] 凡此种种,使劳动者在行使权利时多有顾虑,往往被迫采取"非常手段"获取休假权。

鉴于此,若劳动者病假旅行是基于合理的隐藏理由,则单位无权解除劳动合同。具体而言,隐藏的理由不仅包括用人单位拖延批准、拒绝批准劳动者正当休假的情形,还包括设置竞争机制变相压迫劳动者放弃休假等其他足以影响劳动者正当休假权行使的情形。

(六)诚实信用原则的可适用性

劳动者病假旅行是否适用诚信原则,司法实践存在争议。比如,阿里巴巴员工病假解雇案中,一、二审判决均未适用诚信原则,而再审法院却认为劳动者行为违反诚信原则,致使对同一案件的裁判结果不同。因此,有必要厘清诚信原则在此类案件中的可适用性。

不同于民法推崇绝对的契约自由,双方必须严守合同,在劳动法领域,为实现平等保护劳动者,使其免受就业歧视等原因,劳动者隐瞒事实并不必然构成欺诈,据实回答以存在"释明义务"为前提。对于单位的非法提问,劳动者享有拒绝乃至给予不实回答的权利。比如,在雇主提问劳动者是否已婚时,由于此种提问不被允许而劳动者无释明义务,故违背事实的回答完全合法。[45]

具体到病假旅行案件中,分为两种情况。第一,在规章未对病假期间的行为做出限制时,对具有真实病休需求的劳动者不应适用诚信原则。从劳动者角度来看,其谎称病假期间的行为并不构成非法欺诈,这是因为病假管理权应由规章明确规定,在规章未规定休假方式时,单位询问劳动者病假期间的行为已属"非法提问",故劳动者拒绝回答或者编造谎言完全合法,不违反诚信原则。对于用人单位而言,其往往根据经验推断劳动者申请病假的目的并非休假。但这也只是用人单位的主观推断,若能提供充分的证据证明劳动者提供的病假材料系伪造,单位自然有权解除劳动合同,否则单位无权询问劳动者在病假期间的行为,更不用说在此基础上对行为做出价值判断。

第二,在用人单位对病假期间的行为做出限制,而劳动者的行为违反规章的限制性规定时,劳动者隐瞒病假期间的行为可能违反诚信原则。然而笔者认为,在适用法律时,法院应当尽可能地寻找法条及制度依据,而不应向基本原则

〔44〕 参见张志伟:《劳动者休息权之检视》,载《江西社会科学》2010 年第 11 期。

〔45〕 参见前引 12,雷蒙德瓦尔特曼书,第 142 ~ 143 页。

逃逸。若规章已经做出了明确规定,法院完全可以依据规章做出解除劳动合同是否违法的判断,而不需要适用“诚实信用”原则。

(七)小结

解雇作为最为严厉也是最终的惩戒手段,[46]不仅关系到劳动者自身的生存与发展,而且与社会稳定密切联系。因此,单位在适用该项惩戒措施时更应谨严、审慎。劳动者的行为包括主观与客观两个方面,判定劳动者的行为是否构成“严重违反规章制度”,必须综合劳动者行为的主客观方面考虑。

首先,劳动者的违规行为必须客观存在,用人单位的主观推断不能作为判断劳动者违规行为存在的依据。内容明确且程序合法的规章是依法解除劳动合同的前提。单位以严重违规解除合同的,一般要求造成的损失具有严重性。违规行为的后果包括造成单位财产损失、名誉损失或者损害单位的生产经营秩序。对于一般性的损失,比如数额较小的财产损失、限于单位内部的名誉损失或者影响不大的生产秩序混乱等都不构成解雇的合理理由。同时,损失“重大性”的判断应当结合行业特点、岗位特点与行为发生的特定情形。[47]

其次,考虑劳动者的过错程度,劳动者的主观状态可以从以下几个方面判断:一是违规行为的次数越多,主观过错越大,而初次违规行为则难以认定为严重过错。二是故意挑衅的不当行为以损害单位利益为目的,构成严重过错。三是考虑其他可能减轻过错判断的情形。若违规行为存在隐藏的理由可以减轻对行为过错程度的判断,当且仅当劳动者行为存在严重过错且无其他理由时,方可解除劳动合同。四是劳动者解雇应当遵守公平原则。

最后,用人单位因劳动者严重违反规章制度解除劳动合同的,应当给予劳动者充分的机会。若单位采取降薪、调职等其他替代惩戒措施亦可达到惩戒目的,则不应以严重违规解除劳动合同。只有当特定事由已重大且持续地危害到合同履行且对劳动者已经无法形成合理的期待时,即行为满足违规后果的严重性、主观状态的恶意性要件,用人单位才可以解除劳动合同。

总之,在判定劳动者病假旅行的法律性质时,出于倾斜保护劳动者的理念,

---

[46] 参见谢增毅:《用人单位惩戒权的法理基础与法律规制》,载《比较法研究》2016年第1期。

[47] 参见张朴田:《惩戒解雇:案例分析与规则建构——以〈劳动合同法第〉三十九条第二款为核心》,载《法律适用》2017年第18期。

应当反复检验上述各要件,当且仅当劳动者满足全部违规要件时,方可认定解雇行为合法。

结　语

通过前文分析,可以总结出,法院在判定劳动者病假旅行的性质时,应当先审查规章对于病假旅行是否做出了明确的规定:若规章并无规定,劳动者行为合法;反之,则需要进一步检验劳动者是否存在需要休假的客观事实、违规行为的次数、违规行为的顽固性、有无隐藏的理由等因素。法院判定病假旅行性质的裁判思路如图1所示:

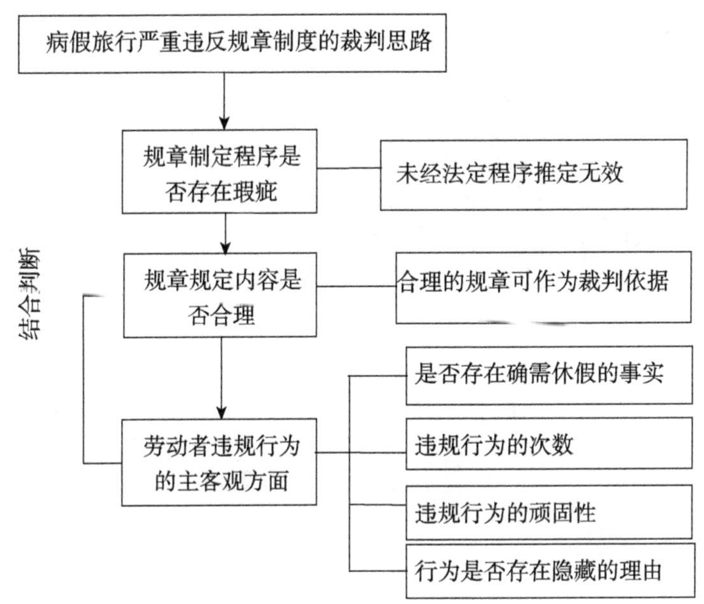

图1　病假旅行严重违反规章制度的裁判思路

当然,随着社会实践的不断发展,影响行为严重违规性判定的因素将不断丰富。因此,法院在司法实践中,需要不断归纳和总结相关因素的具体适用,增强可操作性,实现用人单位与劳动者权益保护的平衡。

(责任编辑:郑恺歆)

国际法治的多维图景

美国“航行自由计划”的国际法分析与思考

徐琬晴*

摘要：

美国并非《联合国海洋法公约》(以下简称《公约》)的缔约国，但它自1979年推出“航行自由计划”以来，一直以维护《公约》下的航行自由之名，挑战他国与美国立场不符的海洋权利主张。近年来，美国频繁派遣军舰于南海海域开展所谓的“航行自由行动”，此等行动缺乏充分的国际法依据。面对美国日趋频繁且不断演进的“航行自由行动”，中国应采取更为有效的应对之策。此外，各方关于航行自由的意见分歧也反映出《公约》规定存在模糊之处和缺陷。鉴于此，国际社会应完善《公约》以从源头上遏制美国“航行自由计划”日趋常态化的实施，防止航行自由权利的滥用。

关键词：

美国“航行自由计划”；《联合国海洋法公约》；南海；领海；专属经济区

自20世纪末以来，美国以维护《联合国海洋法公约》(以下简称《公约》)中的航行自由权利为名，频繁派遣军舰于我国相关海域开展所谓的“航行自由行动”，挑战我国的海洋权利主张，严重危害我国的国家安全。近三年，在所谓的“南海仲裁案”背景之下，美国更是把“航行自由行动”的重点转向南

---

* 徐琬晴，中山大学法学院2018级硕士研究生。本文是国家社科基金重大项目《南海断续线的法理与历史依据研究》(14ZDB165)的阶段性成果。

海海域,先后十余次于南海开展"航行自由行动",[1]无视我国的国家安全与海洋权益。"航行自由行动"是美国1979年出台的"航行自由计划"(Freedom of Navigation Program)政策的重要组成部分。自该计划实施以来,美国持续以军事宣示行动的方式对沿海国的所谓"扩张性海洋权利主张"(Excessive Maritime Claims)进行挑战,损害沿海国的海洋权益。因此,对"航行自由计划"背后涉及的国际法问题进行研究、梳理中美两国关于航行自由的相关分歧、分析美国所谓的"扩张性海洋权利主张"理论存在的缺陷、为中国探寻应对美国在南海的"航行自由行动"的策略显得刻不容缓。本文拟从国际法的角度出发,以美国南海"航行自由行动"为切入点,对"航行自由计划"的法律依据、理论基础、国家实践等方面进行分析。

一、美国"航行自由计划"的提出及其依据

(一)美国"航行自由计划"的提出

"二战"之后,美国发布《杜鲁门公告》首次提出对大陆架底土和海床自然资源主张管辖权。该举措促使沿海国家的海洋意识逐渐觉醒,越来越多的沿海国家试图将管辖权扩张至领海之外,对丰富的海洋资源主张权利。

作为海洋大国,美国自建国以来,就宣称维护海洋自由是美国一项重要的国家利益。[2] 沿海国家试图主张更为宽广的领海以及其他更多的海洋权益的

---

[1] 2015年10月27日,"拉森"号驱逐舰进入渚碧礁12海里之内;2016年1月29日,"阿蒂斯·威尔伯"号驱逐舰进入中建岛12海里之内;2016年5月10日,"劳伦斯"号驱逐舰进入永暑礁12海里之内;2016年10月21日,"迪凯特"号驱逐舰进入中建岛12海里之内;2017年5月24日,"杜威"号驱逐舰进入美济礁12海里之内;2017年7月2日,"斯坦塞姆"号驱逐舰进入中建岛12海里之内;2017年8月10日,"麦肯恩"号驱逐舰进入美济礁12海里之内;2017年10月10日,"查菲"号驱逐舰进入西沙群岛内水;2018年1月17日,"霍珀"号驱逐舰进入黄岩岛12海里之内;2018年3月23日,"马斯廷"号驱逐舰进入美济礁12海里之内;2018年5月27日,"希金斯"号驱逐舰和"安提塔姆"号巡洋舰进入西沙群岛12海里之内;2018年9月30日,"迪凯特"号驱逐舰进入南沙群岛有关岛礁邻近海域。以上整理自外交部例行记者会与发言人表态和问答。

[2] See U. S. Department of Defense, "DOD Freedom of Navigation (FON) Program Fact Sheet", http://policy. defense. gov/Portals/11/DoD%20FON%20Program%20Summary%2016. pdf? ver =2017 -03 -03 -141350 -380, October 11, 2018.

行为，导致受沿海国主权控制的海域扩大，公海海域相应地减少，这使得传统的海洋自由得以适用的空间减少。因此，在第三次联合国海洋法会议谈判期间，为了在大会无法达成令美国满意的协议之时，美国能够走出《公约》的框架确保其海洋权益得以维护，美国就已经开始筹备出台“航行自由计划”的工作。

1979 年，卡特政府正式出台“航行自由计划”。[3] 所谓的“航行自由计划”，即是通过军事宣示行动（“航行自由行动”）与外交磋商和抗议，对美国所认为的沿海国旨在限制甚至是消灭航行自由的与国际法不符的主张进行挑战，以保障所有国家的航行和飞越自由等海洋权利的一项政策计划。[4] 随后的历届美国政府亦均有出台相应的政策文件对计划背后的美国海洋权益主张予以强化。被称为美国海洋政策基础的 1983 年《美国海洋政策声明》（Statement on United States Oceans Policy）指出，在“航行自由计划”之下，美国将“以与《公约》相一致且符合各国利益的方式在全球范围内行使和维护海洋权利和海洋自由”。对于一些沿海国声称的与《公约》不相符的“扩张性海洋权利主张”，美国表示“不会默许这些国家旨在限制国际社会航行飞越权利和自由的单方行为”。[5] 而现今美国在南海海域开展的“航行自由行动”正是美国“航行自由计划”的一部分。

美国之所以会出台“航行自由计划”，一方面，从政策的角度来看，是为了维持美国海军在全球海域的机动性，维护美国的海洋霸权。《公约》不仅明确

---

[3] See U. S. Department of State, Bureau of Ocean and International Environmental and Scientific Affairs, “Limits in the Seas No. 112 United States Responses to Excessive National Maritime Claims”, p. 6, https://www. state. gov/documents/organization/58381. pdf, October 11, 2018.

[4] See U. S. Department of Defense, “DOD FON Program Fact Sheet”, *supra* note 2; U. S. Department of State, Office of the Legal Adviser, *Digest of United States Practice in International Law* 1989 – 1990, p. 440, https://www. state. gov/documents/organization/139393. pdf, October 11, 2018; U. S. Department of State, “Limits in the Seas No. 112”, *supra* note 3, p. 6.

[5] See Ronald Reagan, “Statement on United States Oceans Policy (10 March 1983)”, https://www. reaganlibrary. gov/sites/default/files/archives/speeches/1983/31083c. htm, October 11, 2018.

了12海里的领海宽度,而且还确立了200海里专属经济区等新制度,致使沿海国管辖控制的海域面积扩大而美国能够行使公海航行自由的范围缩小,这种变化所带来的复杂性导致航行自由未来的发展走向难以预测。另一方面,从海洋法秩序的层面来看,美国实施"航行自由计划"是为防止因自身不积极行使海洋权利,而默许了其他国家与其海洋权利主张不相符的"扩张性海洋权利主张",随着时间的推移,这些"扩张性海洋权利主张"最终发展成为具有约束力的习惯国际法规则。简言之,美国试图通过国家实践对《公约》中模糊条款的解释以及海洋法的发展产生影响,使得海洋法领域的国际法规则的发展与美国的海洋权益相一致。除此之外,由于美国未加入《公约》,美国亦需要通过"航行自由计划"向国际社会明确其海洋权利主张。因此,"航行自由计划"应运而生。

(二)美国"航行自由计划"的依据

1.法律依据:1982年《公约》和习惯国际法规则

美国指出,"航行自由计划"的法律依据是国际法的两个主要渊源:条约法和习惯国际法。[6] 具体而言,主要是指1982年《公约》和海洋法领域的习惯国际法规则。

美国虽然并非《公约》的缔约国,但它在主张海洋权利、认定他国的扩张性海洋权利之时,始终是参照《公约》进行的。[7] 美国认为,《公约》中与航行自由和海洋传统利用相关的条款,都是对现有的习惯国际法规则和正在形成的习惯国际法规则的编纂。[8] 即便其中些许条款仍未正式形成习惯国际法规则,但其

---

[6] See William J. Aceves, "The Freedom of Navigation Program: A Study of the Relationship between Law and Politics", *Hastings International and Comparative Law Review* 19 (1996), p. 264; J. Ashley Roach and Robert W. Smith, *Excessive Maritime Claims*, 3rd Edition, Leiden, Martinus Nijhoff Publishers, 2012, pp. 6-7. 注:J. Ashley Roach是前美国国务院法律顾问,Robert W. Smith是前美国国务院海洋事务办公室地理顾问。

[7] 参见何志鹏、王艺罂:《对历史性权利与海洋航行自由的国际法反思》,载《边界与海洋研究》2018年第5期。

[8] See David Lawrence Treat, "The United States' Claims of Customary Legal Rights under the Law of the Sea Convention", *Washington and Lee Law Review* 41 (1984), p. 253; 前引6, William J. Aceves文, p. 301。

内容至少也反映了国际社会对相关海洋法问题的一致观点,随着国家实践的发展,这些条款在未来也必将演变成习惯国际法规则。原因在于,一方面,《公约》的内容基本上是对国家实践的反映,在第三次联合国海洋法会议谈判期间,已有不少国家通过立法等国内程序将《公约》的相关内容转化成国内法予以实施;另一方面,1982 年《公约》中的不少条款都是对美国作为缔约国的 1958 年《领海和毗连区公约》的规定稍作修整转化而来的,尽管 1958 年《领海和毗连区公约》的缔约国数量较少,但通过长期且艰难的谈判、最终以协商一致的方式达成的 1982 年《公约》如今为国际社会所广泛接受,并且被一致地普遍适用于各缔约国和非缔约国,则意味着 1982 年《公约》的内容反映了大多数国家的国际法观点。[9] 因此,无论是客观上的国家实践因素,还是主观上的法律确信因素,国际习惯法规则的形成所必需的两个因素都得到了满足,故美国接受《公约》中与航行自由相关的规范性条款为习惯国际法,[10] 从而进一步认为"航行自由计划"所反映出的美国的海洋权利主张与《公约》和习惯国际法规则的规定是一致的。

然而,早在《公约》制定过程当中,大多数发展中国家就已经否定了美国的上述观点:77 国集团主张《公约》中与航行自由相关的条款更多的是对新的国际法规则的制定,而非对习惯国际法的编纂;[11] 大会副主席许通美大使亦表示,《公约》并不是对习惯国际法或国际惯例的编纂。[12]

此外,国际社会上并没有明确的定论,《公约》中亦没有明文指出究竟《公约》中的哪些条款属于习惯国际法的范畴,因而谨慎识别其中的习惯国际法条

---

〔9〕 See Thomas A. Jr. Clingan, "Freedom of Navigation in a Post-UNCLOS Ⅲ Environment", *Law and Contemporary Problems* 46 (1983), pp. 120 – 121.

〔10〕 See John Norton Moore, "Navigational Freedom: The Most Critical Common Heritage", *International Law Studies Series US Naval War College* 93 (2017), p. 260.

〔11〕 当时的 77 国集团已由大约 120 个发展中国家构成。See Myron H. Nordquist (ed.), *United Nations Convention on the Law of the Sea* 1982: *A Commentary*, Volume I, Martinus Nijhoff Publishers, 1985, pp. 81 – 82.

〔12〕 See Tommy T. B. Koh, "A Constitution for the Ocean", in United Nations, *The Law of the Sea: Official Text of the United Nations Convention on the Law of the Sea with Annexes and Index*, New York, United Nations, 1983, pp. XXXIV–XXXV.

款也是颇有难度的。[13] 根据美国国务院法务顾问办公室发布的《美国国际法实践汇编》(Digest of United States Practice in International Law),美国认为《公约》中所反映的习惯国际法规则主要包括但不限于:直线基线的适用情形;12海里领海;领海无害通过制度;24海里毗连区;沿海国对毗连区的管辖权仅限于海关、财政、移民、卫生四个特定事项而不包括安全利益;沿海国在专属经济区内对海洋科学研究活动等事项具有管辖权;沿海国应当适当顾及其他国家在专属经济区内的权利和义务;所有国家在专属经济区内享有航行自由等与海洋传统利用相关的权利;海峡过境通行制度;与群岛相关的规定;群岛海道通行制度等。[14] 其中有不少规则所涉及的具体的海洋法问题在国际社会中至今仍然存在争议,例如,军舰进入领海是否须经事先授权、专属经济区内航行和飞越自由的界限、专属经济区内的军事活动和测量活动是否需要获得沿海国的事先批准、海洋科学研究活动的范围等。由于《公约》是缔约国妥协达成的"一揽子"协议,不允许国家做出一般保留,从而导致《公约》制定过程中颇具争议的事项都以模糊条款的形式被编纂入《公约》文本当中,《公约》对许多与航行自由相关的问题的规定或留有空白地带,或含糊其辞,相关概念的定义也不明晰,发达海洋大国与发展中沿海国家对此各执一词、分歧较大,并无普遍接受的定论。国际社会对此尚且没有一致、统一的国家实践,就提出存在相关习惯国际法规则,这种观点又如何站得住脚?[15]

综上可见,美国所认定的《公约》中反映的习惯国际法规则,实则是美国单方面解读《公约》模糊条款的结果,并非国际社会上唯一的、准确的解读,然而美国作为非缔约国,却就此认定与其对条款解释不一致的沿海国家的海洋权利主张违反《公约》或习惯国际法的规定、限制了美国及其他国家的航行自由权利,进而在这些沿海国的相关海域开展"航行自由行动"。因此,美国"航行自由计

[13] 参见牟文富:《美国在〈联合国海洋法公约〉之外塑造海洋秩序的战略》,载《中国海洋法学评论》2014年第2期。

[14] See U. S. Department of State, "Digest of United States Practice in International Law 1989 - 1990", *supra note* 4, pp. 441 - 473.

[15] 参见贾兵兵:《国际公法:和平时期的解释与适用》,清华大学出版社2015年版,第34页。

划"缺乏充分的国际法依据,其实施损害了遭受挑战的沿海国的国家安全和海洋权益,亦对《公约》框架下的国际海洋法秩序造成了一定的冲击。

2. 理论依据:"扩张性海洋权利主张"

在《公约》和习惯国际法的基础之上,美国创设了所谓的"扩张性海洋权利主张"理论,为其"航行自由行动"提供了所谓的理论依据。

在美国国防部发布的关于"航行自由计划"情况说明书中,"扩张性海洋权利主张"被定义为:"沿海国所提出的与国际海洋法不相符的海洋区域或管辖权的主张。如果不对这些主张进行挑战,将会侵犯国际法赋予所有国家的利用海洋和空域的权利和自由。"〔16〕换言之,即是指沿海国对海洋区域提出的不符合《公约》的有关主权、主权权利和管辖权的主张。〔17〕

在 1982 年里根政府颁布的第 72 号《国家安全决定指令》(National Security Decision Directives 72)当中,美国首次罗列了其所认定的沿海国"扩张性海洋权利主张"的主要类型:一是美国否认的历史性水域主张;二是过度的直线基线主张;三是过度的领海主张;四是对领海使用的非法限制主张;五是对领海之外的海域主张管辖权;六是过度的群岛主张。〔18〕 在各类型项下,还分别列有更为具体的"扩张性海洋权利主张"事项。此后,随着国家实践的不断发展,美国所认定的沿海国"扩张性海洋权利主张"的类型不断地增加,其内容亦在不断地丰富、充实,体现了一定的复杂性。

虽然美国的"扩张性海洋权利主张"理论中存在的部分解读具有一定的合理性,譬如美国认为超过 12 海里的领海宽度主张不符合海洋法的规定,而这种领海主张在当今国际法上确实缺乏合理性,但是其中不少对沿海国的扩张性海洋权利的认定都是美国单方面解读《公约》条款的结果,这既不是国际社会普遍接受的观点,更不是学界的定论。具体分歧将在下一节展开详细论述。故"航行自由计划"的理论依据也是存在缺陷的。

---

〔16〕 U. S. Department of Defense,"DOD FON Program Fact Sheet", *supra* note 2.

〔17〕 参见前引 6,J. Ashley Roach and Robert W. Smith 书,第 17 页。

〔18〕 See The White House,"National Security Decision Directives 72", https://fas.org/irp/offdocs/nsdd/nsdd-72.pdf, October 11, 2018.

二、对美国“航行自由行动”的质疑

自美国“航行自由计划”实施以来,中国一直是该计划年度报告中挑战名单上的常客。自2007年起,美国更是每年都在中国的相关海域实施所谓的“航行自由行动”。根据美国国防部发布的历年“航行自由计划”年度报告,美国长期以来挑战我国的所谓“扩张性海洋权利主张”主要有:外国军舰在领海内无害通过需经事先许可、国内法将外国实体在专属经济区内的测量活动定为犯罪、对专属经济区上空空域的管辖、过度的直线基线。〔19〕 2013年,中国宣布设立东海防空识别区,因而于2014财年报告中,美国随即认定“对无意进入中国领空但行经防空识别区的外国飞行器进行限制”为我国的“扩张性海洋权利主张”。近三年,在所谓“南海仲裁案”的背景之下,美国以南海航行自由为借端,转而在南海集中且频繁地执行“航行自由行动”,试图介入南海争端。随后美国又于最新的2017财年报告中再增一项对中国海洋权利的挑战事项:对不能产生领海的海洋地物主张领海。

可见,美国长期以来挑战中国的“扩张性海洋权利主张”所涉及的关于航行自由的分歧,与普遍存在于海洋强国和沿海国之间的海洋权益分歧基本上是重合的。纵观“航行自由计划”历年年度报告中所列明的中国“扩张性海洋权利主张”,多年来中美在南海海域关于航行自由权利的分歧,主要集中于军舰在领海的无害通过问题、专属经济区内的航行和飞越自由问题以及大陆国家远洋群岛适用直线基线的问题。故本节将就上述三个主要争议点,从中美双方立场、国家实践等角度,对美国所谓的“扩张性海洋权利主张”理论以及以该理论为基础而开展的“航行自由行动”实践中存在的法律缺陷予以分析。

(一)对美国“航行自由行动”理论基础的质疑

1. 领海内的“扩张性海洋权利主张”:军舰的无害通过

与领海相关的沿海国“扩张性海洋权利主张”是美国“航行自由计划”实施以来一直都重点关注的领域之一。根据美国国防部公布1991年以来的“航行自由计划”年度报告显示,限制军舰在领海内无害通过的问题是“航行自由计划”挑战频次最高的事项。在进入21世纪之前,沿海国的过度领海宽度主张也

〔19〕 See U. S. Department of Defense, “1991 - 2017 Annual Freedom of Navigation Reports”, http://policy. defense. gov/OUSDP-Offices/FON/, October 11, 2018.

是“航行自由计划”的重点挑战对象之一。此外，对于一些国家限制核动力船舶、装载核物质等有毒有害危险物质的船舶在领海内无害通过的主张，美国亦认为其不符合海洋法规则，并对之提出挑战。[20]

外国军舰在领海内无害通过需经事先许可是美国自上世纪末以来挑战中国频次最高的“扩张性海洋权利主张”事项。在近三年频繁的南海“航行自由行动”中，美国更是反复对该事项进行挑战。[21]

关于军舰的领海无害通过权，美国认为，依据《公约》第 17 条的规定，所有国家的船舶在他国领海内都享有无害通过的权利是海洋法的基本原则之一。[22] 1988 年，美国在第 5928 号总统令中重申其对于领海无害通过的立场，主张根据《公约》的相关条款，所有国家的船舶在美国领海内均享有无害通过权。[23] 1989 年，美国在其与苏联共同签署的《关于领海无害通过的国际法规则的联合解释》中进一步详细声明：不论其货物、装备或推进方法如何，包括军舰在内的所有船舶根据国际法都享有领海的无害通过权，无需事先通知或核准。美国参议院对外关系委员会亦在报告中指出，《公约》并未授权沿海国将军舰的领海无害通过权置于需要事先通知或获得批准的地位。[24] 依据《公约》第 21 条和第

[20] See U. S. Department of Defense, “1991 – 2017 Annual FON Reports”, *supra* note 19.

[21] 参见中华人民共和国外交部网站：《2015 年 10 月 27 日外交部发言人陆慷就美国拉森号军舰进入中国南沙群岛有关岛礁邻近海域答记者问》，载 https://www.fmprc.gov.cn/web/fyrbt_673021/t1309393.shtml；《2016 年 2 月 1 日外交部发言人陆慷主持例行记者会》，载 https://www.fmprc.gov.cn/web/fyrbt_673021/t1336958.shtml；《2016 年 5 月 10 日外交部发言人陆慷主持例行记者会》，载 https://www.fmprc.gov.cn/web/fyrbt_673021/jzhsl_673025/t1361960.shtml；《2018 年 1 月 20 日外交部发言人陆慷答记者问》，载 https://www.fmprc.gov.cn/web/fyrbt_673021/dhdw_673027/t1527156.shtml，最后访问日期：2018 年 10 月 11 日。

[22] See U. S. Department of State, “Limits in the Seas No. 112”, *supra* note 3, pp. 53 – 54.

[23] Ronald Reagan, “Presidential Proclamation No. 5928”, http://www.un.org/Depts/los/LEGISLATIONANDTREATIES/PDFFILES/USA_1988_Proclamation.pdf, October 11, 2018.

[24] See U. S. Senate, 110th Congress 1st Session, Committee on Foreign Relations, “Executive Report on the Law of the Sea Convention 110 – 9”, p. 20, https://www.gpo.gov/fdsys/pkg/CRPT-110erpt9/pdf/CRPT-110erpt9.pdf, October 11, 2018.

24 条的规定,虽然沿海国可出于环境保护、资源保护、航行安全等目的制定法律和规章对外国船舶的无害通过设定一定的限制,但这种限制必须是合理且必要的,并且不具有否认或损害无害通过权的实际影响。[25] 加之《公约》第 19 条第 2 款对非无害通过做出了穷尽式列举,其中亦并无涉及军舰的领海无害通过问题。故美国认为,要求军舰进入领海需事先通知或经沿海国许可的主张属于"扩张性海洋权利主张",与《公约》的规定不符,因而对相关国家的"扩张性海洋权利主张"实施"航行自由计划"进行挑战。[26]

然而,军舰在领海内是否享有与商船完全相同的无害通过权,是长期以来争论不休的一个问题。各国从其自身的利益出发往往采取不同的立场,学者的观点也不尽相同。

在第三次联合国海洋法会议期间,各国就此问题展开了激烈的争论:苏丹、罗马尼亚等国反对军舰在领海内享有无害通过权;埃及、马耳他、芬兰、瑞典等国要求军舰通过领海前事先通知;中国、伊朗等国主张军舰通过领海前应获得沿海国的许可;美国、英国、苏联等国则声明军舰在领海内享有无害通过权且无需事先通知或获得批准。[27] 加蓬以及包括中国在内的 28 国更是分别向大会提出了修正案,要求在《公约》第 21 条第 1 款中增加"安全"一词,以明确赋予沿海国制定有关军舰通过领海的法律和规章的权利。该提案在全体会议上获得 46 个国家的支持,而 30 多个国家表示反对。[28] 为避免会议出现分裂,提案国响应大会主席的呼吁不再坚持将提案付诸表决,但主席亦同时声明:"这并不妨碍沿海国依据《公约》第 19 条和第 25 条的规定采取措施维护其安全利益的权利"。[29] 最终大会依旧未能就此问题达成一致协议,致使《公约》对该事项并无

---

〔25〕 参见前引 6,J. Ashley Roach and Robert W. Smith 书,p. 224。

〔26〕 针对该项海洋权利主张,美国先后在阿尔巴尼亚、阿根廷、巴西、埃及、印度、马来西亚、菲律宾等 30 个国家的相关海域开展了"航行自由行动"。整理自前引 6,J. Ashley Roach and Robert W. Smith 书,pp. 250 – 251。

〔27〕 参见金永明:《论领海无害通过制度》,载《国际法研究》2016 年第 2 期。

〔28〕 参见高健军:《中国与国际海洋法——纪念〈联合国海洋法公约〉生效 10 周年》,海洋出版社 2004 年版,第 48 页。

〔29〕 Tommy T. B. Koh,"The Territorial Sea, Contiguous Zone, Straits and Archipelagoes under the 1982 Convention on the Law of the Sea",*Malaya Law Review* 29 (1987),pp. 172 – 173.

明确的规定,从而导致在实践中对《公约》条款的解释和适用存在分歧。

此外,有关军舰无害通过领海的问题在国际社会上也不存在广泛和一致的实践,因而相关的习惯国际法规则也并未形成。一方面,在 1982 年签署和批准《公约》之时,就有 30 个国家就领海无害通过问题发表声明,其中有 26 个国家要求对军舰以及携有危险或有毒物质的船舶的无害通过权进行限制,而另有 4 个国家主张一切船舶享有无害通过权。[30] 另一方面,根据美国国务院法律顾问的统计,如今仍有超过 40 个国家通过国内立法要求外国军舰进入领海需要事先通知或获得批准。[31]

学界对于军舰无害通过的问题也始终没有定论,不同学者观点各异。早在 17 世纪,德国法学家普芬多夫(Pufendorf)就对军舰在领海内的无害通过持否定态度,他认为在未经沿海国许可确保没有任何有害行为的前提之下让军舰进入领海是危险的行为。20 世纪初,英国学者霍尔(William E. Hall)指出外国商船所享有的无害通过权并不延伸至外国军舰,国家有权拒绝外国军舰进入其领海。此外,法国学者吉德尔(Gilbert Gidel)、前国际法院法官杰赛普(Philip C. Jessup)也持有类似的观点。而德国学者尤利乌斯(Julius Hastscheck)则认为,允许外国军舰在其领海内无害通过是沿海国的一项基本义务。[32]

中国在此问题上立场一贯,并通过国内立法明确。1958 年《中华人民共和国关于领海的声明》规定:"一切外国飞机和军用船舶,未经中华人民共和国政府的许可,不得进入中国的领海和领海上空。"1992 年《中华人民共和国领海及毗连区法》规定"外国非军用船舶,享有依法无害通过中华人民共和国领海的权利",但"外国军舰通过中国领海,须经中华人民共和国政府批准。"

《公约》中并没有明文规定军舰的无害通过权。由于第 17 条"无害通过权"被置于"适用于所有船舶的规则"分节之中,因而有学者将此解读为军舰固然属于"船舶",[33] 从而军舰在领海内享有与商船相同的无害通过权。然而,这种解

---

〔30〕 参见前引 28,高健军书,第 53 ~ 54 页。

〔31〕 如阿根廷、巴西、丹麦、芬兰、埃及、印度、韩国、菲律宾等国。参见前引 6,J. Ashley Roach and Robert W. Smith 书,pp. 250 – 251。

〔32〕 See Keyuan Zou, " Innocent Passage for Warships: The Chinese Doctrine and Practice", *Ocean Development & International Law* 29 (1998), pp. 197, 203 and 218.

〔33〕 参见前引 32,Keyuan Zou 文,p. 198。

读并不是唯一的,对此还可以有另一种完全不同的解释,即解释为仅指商船,因为军舰的性质不同于一般商船,因此如果公约有给予军舰相同的无害通过权的意思则应明确规定。[34]

即使是在第一种解读之下,沿海国要求采取事先通知或获得批准等预防措施与军舰在领海内享有无害通过权并不矛盾,其目的是保证通过的无害,而非否定或损害军舰的无害通过权。[35] 此外,联系《公约》序言中规定的和平利用海洋的宗旨以及《公约》的相关条款,《公约》也是允许沿海国采取这些预防措施对军舰的无害通过予以适当限制的,例如:在第19条所列举的非无害通过事项中,进行武力威胁或使用武力、以武器进行操练或演习、在船上起落或接载飞机、在船上发射、降落或接载军事装置等事项通常都是与军舰密切相关的;第25条规定沿海国可在其领海内采取必要的步骤以防止非无害的通过,区别于商船,一国军舰通过他国领海的权利并不是世界一般利益所要求的,这种特权只有利于该个别国家,而常常有害于第三国,有时也对其通过的水域的所属国构成威胁,因而军舰不能与商船按照同样的理由享有无害通过权,[36] 因此,基于军舰本身具有威胁性的特殊性质,其通过本身就会对沿海国的良好秩序与和平安全造成影响,因而可以认为对军舰无害通过予以适度限制涵盖在"必要的步骤"当中;第30条亦规定军舰应当遵守沿海国关于通过领海的法律和规章,否则沿海国可要求该军舰立即离开领海。而且在《公约》谈判制定过程中,大会主席亦在声明中提及国家保有维护其安全利益的权利。

因此,中国的相关立法与实践符合国际法,美国认为军舰的领海无害通过权受到事先通知或获得批准的限制即构成"扩张性海洋权利主张",违反《公约》的规定,仅仅只是美国自身在该问题上的立场而已。故美国将中国要求"军舰无害通过领海需要事先获批"的主张定性为违反海洋法之规定的观点是错误的。

2. 专属经济区内的"扩张性海洋权利主张":航行及飞越自由

纵观美国"航行自由计划"的年度报告,美国在专属经济区内挑战的沿海国

---

[34] 参见前引28,高健军书,第49页。

[35] See Budislav Vukas, "The New Law of the Sea and Navigation: A View from the Mediterranean", in Budislav Vukas, *The Law Of The Sea: Selected Writings*, Leiden/Boston, Martinus Nijhoff Publishers, 2004, p. 141.

[36] 参见周鲠生:《国际法》,商务印书馆1976年版,第370页。

的“扩张性海洋权利主张”的类型主要有:对外国军舰在专属经济区内的军事活动进行限制、对外国军舰在专属经济区内的测量活动进行限制、对专属经济区的上空进行管辖、外国军舰进入专属经济区需要事先通知或获得批准等。近十年来,美国越发关注沿海国在专属经济区内与测量活动、军事活动相关的“扩张性海洋权利主张”,并增加了对这些事项的挑战频次。[37]

对应南海海域,美国再三执行“航行自由行动”,对中国将外国实体在专属经济区内开展测量活动定性为犯罪的主张进行挑战,其中较为轰动的军事宣示行动即是2009年的“无暇号”摩擦事件。

虽然美国在南海海域挑战的主要是中国关于限制测量活动的主张,但其开展的主要是军事测量活动,而军事测量活动既涉及专属经济区内测量活动的问题,也涉及专属经济区内军事活动的问题。下文将对这两个问题分别进行探讨,并分析得出无论是测量活动还是军事活动都并非可以无限制地在沿海国专属经济区内开展,美国将中国在专属经济区内的海洋权利主张定性为是对《公约》的违反,这种观点依旧是错误的。

(1)专属经济区内的航行及飞越自由之界限

在详细探讨专属经济区内的测量活动和军事活动的问题之前,首先要解决的是对专属经济区内航行和飞越自由的界定问题。

1983年《美国海洋政策声明》指出,所有国家在专属经济区内享有与资源无关的公海权利和自由,包括航行和飞越自由。[38] 尔后,美国提出将世界海域划分为“国家水域”(national waters)和“国际水域”(international waters)两部分。前者包括内水、领海和群岛水域,其受到沿海国领土主权的管辖,仅为国际社会保留一定的航行权;而后者则包括毗连区、专属经济区及公海,所有国家在该区域内均享有与公海航行和飞越自由相一致的海洋权利。[39] 换言之,美国将专属经济区的航行和飞越自由等同于公海的航行和飞越自由,这种航行和飞越

〔37〕 See U. S. Department of Defense, “1991 – 2017 Annual FON Reports”, *supra* note 19.

〔38〕 See Ronald Reagan, “Statement on United States Oceans Policy”, *supra* note 5.

〔39〕 See U. S. Department of the Navy, *The Commander's Handbook on the Law of Naval Operation* (2007), pp. 1 – 7 and 1 – 9, http://www.jag.navy.mil/documents/NWP_1 – 14M_Commanders_Handbook.pdf, October 11, 2018.

自由还包括测量活动、军事活动等其他可在公海开展的活动,在专属经济区内开展这些活动不受沿海国的限制。

中国在此问题上通过国内立法明确:在遵守国际法和我国相关法律法规的前提之下,他国在我国专属经济区内均享有航行和飞越自由。[40] 根据我国相关法律法规的规定,在专属经济区内开展测量活动需事先获得批准。[41] 我国的官方声明亦多次明确表态反对外国未经允许在中国专属经济区内采取任何军事行动。[42] 简言之,中国认为测量活动、军事活动等可在公海开展的活动并不属于专属经济区航行和飞越自由的范围,从而专属经济区的航行和飞越自由并不等同于公海的航行和飞越自由。

根据《公约》第58条的规定,所有国家在专属经济区内均享有第87条所指的航行和飞越自由。《公约》并没有对船舶和飞机的种类加以限定,因此从理论上看,各国包括军用船舶和飞机在内的所有船舶和飞机在专属经济区内均可自由航行和飞越。[43]

然而,《公约》所认可的专属经济区航行和飞越自由是受到沿海国在专属经济区内的主权权利和管辖权限制的航行和飞越自由,并非与公海航行和飞越自由相等同。根据"陆地支配海洋"的原则,沿海国对海域的管辖控制自基线向海洋一侧逐步递减。公海中的航行自由尚且受到适用于和平目的、适当顾及其他国家行使公海自由的利益的限制,同时所有船旗国及其船舶还都承担着防止、减少和控制海洋污染、保护和保全海洋环境、安全航行和遵守海上交通规则等国际义务,[44] 专属经济区内的航行自由则受到有关国际法规则的更多限制,这主要体现在各国在专属经济区内行使航行和飞越自由权利时应当适当顾及沿

---

〔40〕《中华人民共和国专属经济区和大陆架法》(1998年通过)第11条。

〔41〕《中华人民共和国测绘法》(1992年通过)第8条;《中华人民共和国专属经济区和大陆架法》(1998年通过)第9条;《中华人民共和国涉外海洋科学研究管理规定》(1996年通过)第4条。

〔42〕例如:《2010年11月26日外交部发言人洪磊答记者问》,载https://www.fmprc.gov.cn/web/fyrbt_673021/dhdw_673027/t772435.shtml,最后访问日期:2018年10月11日。

〔43〕参见张海文主编:《〈联合国海洋法公约〉释义集》,海洋出版社2004年版,第108页以下。

〔44〕《公约》第87条第2款、第88条、第94条和第192条。

海国的权利和义务，遵守沿海国依照《公约》和其他国际法规则制定的法律和规章。[45] 虽然沿海国在专属经济区内行使权利时也承担着“适当顾及其他国家的权利和义务”的责任，[46]但由于沿海国的权利是“主权的”，因而它是全面且优于一般权利的。[47] 也就是说，当其他国家的航行和飞越自由权利与沿海国在专属经济区行使主权权利和管辖权发生冲突时，后者一般居于优先地位，其他国家在沿海国的专属经济区内行使航行和飞越自由权利不得干扰沿海国依《公约》行使主权权利和管辖权。[48] 因而在专属经济区内，各国的航行和飞越自由是被承认的，但它与公海的航行和飞越自由并非完全等同。

因此，中国的海洋权利主张并未违反《公约》的规定。与此相对应，美国认定包括中国在内的一些沿海国家限制外国军舰在其专属经济区内进行可在公海中开展的测量活动、军事活动的规定属于“扩张性海洋权利主张”[49]的观点是错误的。

(2)专属经济区内的测量活动

《公约》第56条规定沿海国对专属经济区内的海洋科学研究活动具有管辖权，但《公约》并未明确测量活动是否属于海洋科学研究的范畴，也未明晰“海洋科学研究”“测量活动”“调查活动”等相近概念的定义。

美国倾向于从狭义的角度解释海洋科学研究活动，明确地将其与水文测量、军事测量等其他海洋数据测量收集活动区别开来。它认为，测量活动泛指为航行安全而获取信息绘制航海图，[50]而海洋科学研究侧重于拓展海洋环境的科学知识，[51]从而测量活动不属于海洋科学研究活动的范畴，而是属于与公海

[45] 《公约》第58条第3款。

[46] 《公约》第56条第2款。

[47] 参见前引28，高健军书，第69页。

[48] 参见邵津：《专属经济区和大陆架的军事利用的法律问题》，载中国国际法学会主办：《中国国际法年刊(1985)》，中国对外翻译出版社1985年版，第193页。

[49] 参见前引6，J. Ashley Roach and Robert W. Smith书，p. 377。

[50] 参见前引6，J. Ashley Roach and Robert W. Smith书，p. 416。

[51] See George K. Walker (ed.), *Definition for the Law of the Sea: Terms Not Defined by the* 1982 *Convention*, Leiden, Martinus Nijhoff Publishers, 2012, p. 241.

自由相关的“海洋其他国际合法用途”的一部分。[52] 而且《公约》文本在用语上亦对研究(research)和测量(survey)活动、海洋科学研究和水文测量分别单独提及,[53]例如,第19条第2款阐明外国船舶在领海内进行无害通过时不得“进行研究或测量活动”。据此,美国认为《公约》已明确区分研究活动和测量活动是两个不同的概念,[54]因而沿海国不得规制领海之外其他国家的测量活动,后者开展此类活动也无需事先通知沿海国。[55]

然而,在国家实践当中,不少沿海国家认为,测量活动应当受到沿海国的管辖。如前所述,中国认为测量活动属于海洋科学研究的一部分,外方于我国专属经济区内进行测量活动应经过我国政府批准授权;此外,澳大利亚和加拿大等国亦要求在其专属经济区内进行测量活动之前应当征求其许可;[56]印度尼西亚则要求外国在其专属经济区内开展包含测量活动在内的海洋科学研究活动必须在尊重印度尼西亚利益的基础上进行。[57]

针对美国的主张,首先,关于《公约》诸如第19条第2款文本用语的解释在学界上并无定论,美国的解读并非唯一,甚至存在较之更为合理的解读,即研究活动和测量活动应被同等地对待,专属经济区内的测量活动亦同研究活动一样只能在沿海国许可的情况下进行。[58] 具体而言,这些用语都是置于限制外国船

---

〔52〕 See U. S. Senate, 110th Congress 1st Session, *supra* note 24, p. 13.

〔53〕 《公约》第19条、第40条、第54条的用语为“研究和测量活动”,第21条的用语为“海洋科学研究或水文测量”。

〔54〕 See Raul (Pete) Pedrozo, “Preserving Navigational Rights and Freedoms: The Right to Conduct Military Activities in China's Exclusive Economic Zone”, *Chinese Journal of International Law* 9 (2010), p. 11.

〔55〕 参见前引6, J. Ashley Roach and Robert W. Smith书, p. 29; 前引39, U. S. Department of the Navy文件, pp. 2-9; 前引51, George K. Walker书, p. 244。

〔56〕 See Sam Bateman, “Hydrographic Surveying in the EEZ: Differences and Overlaps with Marine Scientific Research”, *Marine Policy* 29 (2005), p. 170.

〔57〕 参见薛桂芳、张珊:《澳大利亚海事识别制度初探》,载《中国海洋大学学报》2007年第5期。

〔58〕 See Keyuan Zou, “Navigational rights and marine scientific research: a further clarification?”, in Shicun Wu and Keyuan Zou, eds., *Securing the Safety of Navigation in East Asia: Legal and Political Dimensions*, 1st Edition, Chandos Publishing, 2013, p. 84.

舶通过领海、国际海峡、群岛水域时开展研究活动的条款之下的，也就是说，将两个术语分别单独使用，更多体现的是起草者为了给受到禁止或需要沿海国授权的研究活动类型提供"一揽子"措辞的意图，而不是为了单独建立一项不受沿海国管辖控制的测量活动制度。[59] 其次，这些测量活动在实践中通常由军用船舶实施，军事测量活动在性质上难以排除其具有为军事目的所用的威胁性特点，[60]因而其实施在一定程度上会对沿海国的国家安全构成威胁，存在抵触《公约》和平利用海洋宗旨的可能性。此外，随着科学技术的发展、先进海洋技术设备的应用，从收集海洋资料的类型和潜在用途的角度来看，如今已很难准确区分海洋科学研究、测量活动和海洋数据收集，[61]实际上它们在一定程度上是重合的。一方面，测量活动与海洋科学研究活动通常使用相同的船舶和设备，[62]单从外观上看，并不容易区分船舶究竟是在进行海洋科学研究活动还是测量活动；另一方面，若不将测量活动纳入海洋科学研究的范畴，那么任何形式的海洋科学研究活动都可能在测量活动的伪装下肆意展开而不受沿海国管辖，如此一来不仅会导致《公约》中的海洋科学研究制度的瓦解，而且还存在他国在沿海国不知情的情况下将所获取的资料信息用于非科研领域的风险，从而侵害沿海国对海洋科学研究的管辖权利，损害沿海国的国家安全和利益。

因此，将专属经济区内进行的测量活动置于沿海国的管辖之下非但不违反海洋法的规定，而且具有一定的合理性。

(3)专属经济区内的军事活动

如前所述，美国认为专属经济区内诸如发射或接载军事装置、开展军事侦

---

〔59〕 See Sam Bateman, "A Response to Pedrozo: The Wider Utility of Hydrographic Surveys", *Chinese Journal of International Law* 10 (2011), p. 179.

〔60〕 See Zhiguo Gao, "China and the Law of the Sea", in Myron H. Nordquist, Tommy Thong Bee Koh and John Norton Moore, eds., *Freedom of Seas, Passage Rights and the* 1982 *Law of the Sea Convention*, Leiden, Martinus Nijhoff Publishers, 2009, p. 289.

〔61〕 See Haiwen Zhang, "Is it safeguarding the Freedom of Navigation or maritime hegemony of the United States? —Comments on Raul (Pete) Pedrozo's Article on Military Activities in the EEZ", *Chinese Journal of International Law* 9 (2010), p. 36.

〔62〕 See Desmond Ball, "Intelligence collection operations and EEZs: the implication of new technology", *Marine Policy* 28 (2004), pp. 73–76.

察、军事操练、军事演习等军事活动被包含在《公约》第58条所规定的海洋的“其他国际合法用途”之中。[63] 另有美国学者认为,较之《公约》中规制领海的部分有明确的条款描述不符合“无害通过”的行为,禁止领海内的军事活动,规制专属经济区活动的条款中却没有任何明确的类似禁令,这意味着《公约》的起草者未曾想要同样地在专属经济区内限制军事活动。[64] 换言之,他国在沿海国专属经济区内可以同在公海上一样自由地开展军事活动,不受沿海国的管辖。

然而,大多数发展中国家持相反的观点。例如,巴西主张在未经沿海国同意和授权的情况下,其他国家不得在沿海国家的专属经济区内进行军事操练或演习;佛得角主张在经得沿海国书面同意之前,其他国家在专属经济区享有的自由不包括譬如武装演习等任何非和平的用途。[65] 在第三次联合国海洋法会议上,中国代表提出“在专属经济区、大陆架和其他国家管辖海域,沿海国有权管制外国军事活动和军事设施”。[66] 此外,在签署或批准《公约》时,印度、泰国、孟加拉国、马来西亚、伊朗、巴基斯坦、乌拉圭等国亦声明《公约》并未授权其他国家在沿海国专属经济区内进行军事演习等军事活动。[67]

虽然《公约》并未确切地肯定或否定他国在沿海国专属经济区内开展军事活动,但是首先,《公约》明确了各国在专属经济区内行使权利和履行义务时,应适当顾及沿海国的权利和义务,并遵守沿海国的相关法律和规章。军事活动天然潜在的威胁属性或多或少地会对沿海国的领土完整、良好秩序、和平安全等方面造成影响,因而其开展必然需要顾及沿海国的权益。其次,如前所述,沿海国的权利基于其主权性,使其在与其他权利发生冲突时全面优于一般权利。他

---

〔63〕 See U. S. Senate, 108th Congress 2nd Session, Committee on Foreign Relations, “Executive Report on the Law of the Sea Convention 108 – 10”, pp. 17 – 18, https://www.gpo.gov/fdsys/pkg/CRPT – 108erpt10/pdf/CRPT – 108erpt10.pdf, October 11, 2018.

〔64〕 See James W. Houck and Nicole M. Anderson, “The United States, China, and Freedom of Navigation in the South China Sea”, *Washington University Global Studies Law Review* 13 (2014), pp. 443 – 444.

〔65〕 参见[斐济]萨切雅·南丹、沙泰·罗森主编:《1982年〈联合国海洋法公约〉评注》(第2卷),吕文正、毛彬译,海洋出版社2014年版,第513页。

〔66〕 参见前引28,高健军书,第71页。

〔67〕 参见前引6,J. Ashley Roach and Robert W. Smith 书,pp. 28 and 379 – 391。

国在沿海国专属经济区内开展军事活动时必然也会对沿海国的资源勘探、开发和保护以及海洋环境的保护造成干扰。可见,专属经济区内的军事活动实则且理应是受沿海国管辖的。

此外,由来自亚太地区国家的高级官员和专家学者制定的《专属经济区航行和飞越指南》亦指出,他国在沿海国专属经济区内开展军事活动是有所限制的。具体而言,在他国的专属经济区内开展军事活动的外国船舶和飞机有义务只将海洋用于和平目的,不得进行武力威胁或使用武力,避免挑衅行为,同时还应当适当顾及包括沿海国在内的其他国家利用海洋的权利,遵守国际法规定的其他义务。[68] 不过应当明确的是,虽然《公约》未给"和平目的"以明确定义,但和平也并非完全等同于非军事化,为和平目的所进行的军事活动也是符合《联合国宪章》和《公约》规定的。例如,根据联合国决议并经索马里政府的同意,自2008年起中国等国派出军舰于索马里海域开展护航军事行动,保护该区域内本国船舶的安全。这些军事行动虽然也涉及于他国管辖海域内航行和开展军事活动等问题,但因其符合《公约》的相关规定及和平利用海洋的宗旨,因此获得国际社会的认可。

总而言之,沿海国对他国在专属经济区内开展军事活动的行为加以限制并不违反海洋法的规定。相反,美国认定沿海国对专属经济区内的军事活动加以限制的规定违反《公约》以及其所持的"其他国家可以恣意地在沿海国专属经济区进行军事活动"的观点与前文阐述都是背道而驰的。

3. 基线的"扩张性海洋权利主张":大陆国家远洋群岛直线基线的适用

根据美国历年的"航行自由计划"年度报告,自20世纪末以来,与基线相关的沿海国"扩张性海洋权利主张"始终是"航行自由计划"高频率挑战的事项之一。我国西沙群岛的直线基线亦是美国"航行自由行动"自2007年起连年数次挑战的对象。我国在西沙群岛划定的直线基线涉及大陆国家远洋群岛适用直线基线的问题,可是关于这一问题,《公约》留有法律空白。

中国于1996年公布了《中华人民共和国政府关于中华人民共和国领海基线的声明》,其中明确直线基线适用于西沙群岛,因而从国家实践的层面表明了

---

[68] See EEZ Group 21, "Guidelines for Navigation and Overflight in the Exclusive Economic Zone", p. 9, https://nippon. zaidan. info/seikabutsu/2005/00816/pdf/0001. pdf, October 11,2018.

我国支持大陆国家远洋群岛适用直线基线的立场。

然而,美国始终反对大陆国家在其远洋群岛适用直线基线。美国认为,根据《公约》第7条的规定,直线基线仅适用于"海岸线极为曲折"或"紧邻海岸有一系列岛屿"的情形,而西沙群岛的地理情况并不符合适用直线基线的标准。加之《公约》明确规定群岛基线仅适用于群岛国,故西沙群岛的直线基线亦无法通过群岛基线制度做出合理的解释。[69] 因此,美国认为我国沿西沙群岛周围划定直线基线的海洋权利主张违反《公约》规定,属于"扩张性海洋权利主张"。

虽然《公约》中对于直线基线是否能够适用于大陆国家远洋群岛的问题并未作出规定,但可以明确的是,《公约》只是对适用直线基线方法的客观地理条件作出了限制,并没有对适用直线基线方法的具体地理范围作出限制。[70] 因而只要符合客观地理条件,大陆国家即可将直线基线适用于远洋群岛。而我国西沙群岛破碎的海岸以及岛屿众多的地理特征则说明了其有资格适用直线基线。

而且在实践当中,不少大陆国家都为其远洋群岛设立直线基线。早在《公约》制定之前,丹麦、厄瓜多尔就已为其远洋群岛设立了直线基线;在《公约》通过之后,葡萄牙、西班牙、印度、挪威、法国、英国等许多拥有远洋群岛的国家亦相继通过立法为其远洋群岛划定直线基线。对于上述国家的实践,国际社会基本都是采取默许的态度,一些大陆国家以其远洋群岛的直线基线为基础提交的外大陆架界线方案亦没有遭到其他国家的反对,更有一些国家通过与上述国家签订双边协议的方式从侧面反映了其承认远洋群岛适用直线基线的立场。[71] 因此可以认为,大陆国家在远洋群岛适用直线基线的做法越来越为国际社会所包容,有发展成为习惯国际法规则的趋势。

此外,针对美国依据《公约》第7条和第47条而否定西沙群岛直线基线的观点,有学者指出适用于远洋群岛的直线基线是区别于传统的直线基线和群岛

---

〔69〕 See U. S. Department of State, Bureau of Ocean and International Environmental and Scientific Affairs, "Limits in the Seas No. 117 Straight Baseline Claim: China", pp. 3 and 8, https://www.state.gov/documents/organization/57692.pdf, October 11, 2018.

〔70〕 参见前引43,张海文书,第89页。

〔71〕 参见卜凌嘉、黄靖文:《大陆国家在其远洋群岛适用直线基线问题》,载《中山大学法律评论》2013年第2期。

直线基线的一项独特的基线制度,[72]因而简单地援引《公约》条款并不能够准确且合理地解释我国西沙群岛直线基线的合法性。

(二)对美国南海"航行自由行动"实践的质疑

通过上述分析可见,美国"航行自由行动"的所谓理论依据"扩张性海洋权利主张"是存在缺陷的,而以此为基础而开展的"航行自由行动"的合法性亦有待商榷。

如前所述,美国开展"航行自由行动"的原因之一是试图通过国家实践对《公约》中模糊条款的解读以及海洋法的发展产生影响,防止因自身不积极做出抗议而产生默认他国"扩张性海洋权利主张"的法律效果。然而,国家实践的形式多样,例如外交行为、与国际组织或政府间会议通过的决议有关的行为、与条约有关的行为、行政行为、立法、国内法院判决等。[73]因此,采取行动宣示的方式并不是唯一的,而且采取这种方式极易造成意外事故和冲突,造成局势紧张,破坏地区的稳定,对于没有能力开展行动宣示的小国也是一种损害。[74]根据国际法院在"北海大陆架案"中所表达的观点,外交声明对于展现国家立场、维护国家权利已经足够。[75]当存在非暴力的方法维护国家权利、解决争端时,国家仍然采取具有对抗性质的行为,那么这种行为则可能涉及权利的滥用。[76]

在实践当中,美国"航行自由行动"实则在一定程度上对海洋环境的和平与安全造成了威胁,其实施与国家主权原则、禁止进行武力威胁或使用武力原则以及和平解决国际争端原则等国际法原则也并不完全一致。一方面,以南海"航行自由行动"为例,美国通过"航行自由行动"介入南海争端,依据所谓的"南海仲裁案"实体裁决,多次驶入我国南海美济礁领海执行"航行自由行动"。

---

[72] 参见张华:《中国洋中群岛适用直线基线的合法性:国际习惯法的视角》,载《外交评论》(外交学院学报)2014 年第 2 期。

[73] See International Law Commission, "Report on the work of the sixty-eighth session", p. 77, http://legal.un.org/ilc/reports/2016/english/chp5.pdf, October 11, 2018.

[74] 参见前引 6, J. Ashley Roach and Robert W. Smith 书, pp. 250-251。

[75] See North Sea Continental Shelf, Judgement, I. C. J. Reports 1969, paras. 32-33.

[76] 参见前引 6, William J. Aceves 文, p. 323。

而菲律宾提请仲裁的事项实质上涉及的是南海部分岛礁的领土主权问题,[77]美国仍以南海航行自由为托辞,试图涉足南海事务,这实际上是与以国家间互相尊重主权和领土完整为主要内容的国家主权原则不相一致的。另一方面,美国开展"航行自由行动"无不是派出军舰和军机进行有目的的军事行动,[78]在未经沿海国许可的情况下进入他国管辖的海域及其上空空域,并因此导致在沿海国邻近海域发生多起事故。例如,20世纪80年代,美国多次派出军舰在锡德拉湾执行"航行自由行动",挑战利比亚关于历史性海湾的"扩张性海洋权利主张",并因此与利比亚发生了数起冲突;1988年美国派出驱逐舰和导弹巡洋舰在黑海针对苏联要求外国军舰通过领海需要事先获得许可的"扩张性海洋权利主张"执行"航行自由行动"之时,因不顾苏联的警告未离开领海而导致双方军舰发生碰撞事故。此外,在南海海域,亦因美国多次无视我国的国家安全和海洋权益,屡次开展"航行自由行动"而导致摩擦事件频发:2001年美国派出侦察机未经许可于海南岛附近海域上空侦查,最终导致于我国专属经济区上空发生了震惊全球的中美撞机事件;2009年美国未获中国批准即派出美军潜艇监测船"无暇号"于南海海域开展军事测量活动,并因此导致冲突发生等。这与禁止进行武力威胁或使用武力原则以及和平解决国际争端原则亦存在出入。而根据《维也纳条约法公约》(以下简称《条约法公约》)第18条的规定,美国虽然没有批准《公约》,但亦是《公约》的签署国,因此,在美国没有正式表明其不欲成为《公约》缔约国的意思之前,它有义务不滥用权利而做出妨碍《公约》宗旨和和平利用海洋目的的行动。[79] 因此美国"航行自由行动"的合法性是存疑的。

---

〔77〕 参见中华人民共和国外交部:《中华人民共和国政府关于菲律宾共和国所提南海仲裁案管辖权问题的立场文件》,载 http://www.fmprc.gov.cn/web/ziliao_674904/tytj_674911/zcwj_674915/t1217143.shtml,最后访问日期:2018年10月11日。

〔78〕 See Ryan Santicola, "Legal Imperative: Deconstructing Acquiescence in Freedom of Navigation Operations", *National Security Law Journal* 5 (2016), p. 66.

〔79〕 参见管建强:《美国无权擅自在中国专属经济区从事"军事测量"——评"中美南海摩擦事件"》,载《法学》2009年第4期。

三、因应美国“航行自由计划”之对策

(一)中国的应对之策

随着国际局势的变化,美国不断地丰富其“扩张性海洋权利主张”理论、演变其“航行自由行动”的挑战事项。面对美国“航行自由计划”对我国日益频繁的挑战以及对南海海域海洋权利主张挑战事项的不断更新发展,中国应当积极进行对策研究,探寻现时有效的策略,以维护我国的国家安全和海洋权利。具体建议如下:

第一,对于关乎中国利益、与国际法不相符的“航行自由行动”,中国应当继续积极提出抗议,在维护我国领土主权和海洋权益的同时,防止因沉默而被视为是对相关海洋权利主张和行为的默认。抗议是国际法上具有法律意义的国家单方行为。通常而言,当国家不对其他国家对之有法律影响的行为进行抗议时,将被视为是对该行为的默认,即认为这种行为是正当的。〔80〕 因此,面对美国针对中国开展的“航行自由行动”,中国应当采取适当的行动表示抗议。一方面,对于美国打着“航行自由”的旗号多次派遣军舰擅自闯入我国管辖海域的挑衅行为,中国应采取程度相当的抗议行动进行识别查证和警告驱离,并予以适度的反击,以此捍卫和维护我国的领土主权和国家安全。另一方面,针对美国通过外交途径公开指责中国的海洋权利主张不符合《公约》或缺乏国际法依据的行为,中国应及时进行外交抗议以维护我国的海洋权益。但面对那些未能向国际社会提供明确的事实和法律依据证明中国的主张或行为违反国际法的不负责任的指控,中国可以尝试转变应对思路,在对方履行其法律义务、证明其指控的“正确性”及“合法性”之前,中国可不必急于辩解或证明自己所拥有的证据和国际法依据。〔81〕

第二,中国应加强国内海洋立法以及相关国际法理论研究,为自身的海洋政策、海洋权利主张以及海洋执法提供法理依据。在当今中国建设海洋强国的

〔80〕 参见[英]马尔科姆·N.肖:《国际法》(第6版),白桂梅、高健军等译,北京大学出版社2011年版,第71页。

〔81〕 参见张海文:《〈联合国海洋法公约〉与中国》,五洲传播出版社2014年版,第38页以下。

背景之下,完善我国海洋法律体系是必由之路。尽管我国在国内立法和海洋法实践层面一直保持着活跃的形象,相继颁布了《领海及毗连区法》《专属经济区和大陆架法》等一系列法律法规,《公约》中的许多条款也已被转化为国内法,但我国的海洋法律体系仍不完备。相较于美国等海洋大国,我国的海洋立法数量较少,调整对象亦相对局限。因此,中国可从维护国家海洋权益及《公约》和平利用海洋宗旨的角度出发,在坚持《公约》宗旨和目的的前提之下、在切实保护外国船舶合法的航行自由的同时,对《公约》中条款规定不太明确的相关海洋法问题以及海洋法发展领域的前沿问题做出进一步完善与细化。以专属经济区内的海洋科学研究为例,中国虽已制定《专属经济区和大陆架法》《涉外海洋科学研究管理规定》等法律法规对外国实体于我国开展海洋科学研究活动进行规制,但对于海洋科学研究的定义、种类、范围以及它与测量活动、调查活动等近似概念的区别均未做出规定,因此我国应通过修改相关的法律法规,对这些问题制定相关细则。再如,2016年美国于南海海域投放无人水下潜航器,开展测量活动,但我国并无相关法律法规对无人潜航器在我国海域的权利义务予以规制,因而我国可以考虑通过立法对未来可能出现的海洋执法问题加以防范。如此不仅有利于充分体现和维护我国的海洋权益,为自身的海洋主张提供法律依据,同时也有利于增强海洋执法强度,充分利用和保护我国管辖控制的海域。

第三,中国亦可通过自身的国家实践强化符合国际法与《公约》精神的海洋权利主张。《公约》被誉为当今世界的"海洋宪章",如何解释和适用其中的条款对海洋法规则的形成和发展具有重要意义。如前文所述,《公约》作为一个"一揽子交易",对军舰的无害通过、专属经济区制度等问题均未做出明确规定,其中存在许多模糊条款,不同国家对其作出不同的解释,相关的习惯国际法规则也并未形成。依据《条约法公约》第31条第3款,国家实践被认为与条约的解释相关。对条约的解释,除依上下文、参考条约的目的、宗旨及通常意义外,还应当考虑此后各当事国在适用条约时对条约解释的实践。因此,对于《公约》中颇具争议性的领域,目前尚存在充分的国家实践发展空间,中国亦可通过国家实践,把握对相关条款的解释和适用、习惯国际法规则的形成和发展发挥关键作用的机遇。[82] 因而中国可以考虑通过政策宣示和发布白皮书等形式,明确

〔82〕 前引13,牟文富文,第212页。

对相关海洋法问题的立场和态度,这既有利于从根源上消除他国诋毁我国的证据,[83]也有利于向国际社会表明中国的海洋权利主张和立场。此外,中国亦可以选择积极推动与其他国家的外交来往,促进交流对话,尤其是邻国以及与中国具有共同利益和相同立场的国家,推动各国就相关的海洋法问题共同缔结条约或达成协定,以此来强化对《公约》的解释,推动国家实践的统一,并对外国船舶危害沿海国安全的行为予以限制。

(二)国际社会应完善《公约》有关规定以防止航行自由权的滥用

1. 美国"航行自由计划"暴露出《公约》的缺陷

通过前文分析,追根溯源,美国南海"航行自由行动"所反映出的中美两国的争议,在法律上实则体现为海洋强国与发展中沿海国家对《公约》的解释和适用的不同而引起的冲突。因此,美国的"航行自由计划"从侧面暴露出《公约》的不完善之处:《公约》对于历史性权利、历史性海湾、历史性水域、大陆远洋群岛的基线划定等众多具有争议的重要海洋法问题留下了法律空白;对于无害通过、专属经济区航行和飞越自由、海洋科学研究活动等关键海洋法问题虽有规定,但却语焉不详,没有明确"和平目的""适当顾及""国际合法用途"等重要概念的含义及其范围界限。这些未作规定的事项或规定含糊其辞的条款引发了国际社会的诸多争议,其中以军舰领海无害通过问题与专属经济区航行和飞越自由问题最为突出,这亦即是美国"航行自由行动"在全球范围内挑战最为频繁的沿海国"扩张性海洋权利主张"的事项,也是中美两国关于航行自由涉及的海洋法问题的主要争议点所在。

2. 关于完善《公约》有关规定的思考

《公约》作为一个需要平衡各国法律利益的外交博弈的产物,注定了其中必定存在言之不详的条款,以给予各利益方根据自己的需要解读和适用《公约》的空间。然而,随着时代的发展,海洋秩序亦在不断更新,在实践中《公约》模糊条款所引起的争议问题日益突显。加之如英国、澳大利亚等拥有强大海军实力的发达海洋国家亦开始效仿美国,开展类似的"航行自由行动",宣示所谓的"航行自由"。[84] 因此,若能

---

〔83〕 参见冯梁、杜博:《对南海航行自由与安全稳定问题的理性认识》,载《学海》2016年第1期。

〔84〕 See Dale Stephens, "The Legal Efficacy of Freedom of Navigation Assertions", *International Law Studies US Naval War College* 80 (2006), p. 242.

有效促进国际社会对相关争议性海洋法问题达成共识,使《公约》中的模糊条款得以澄清和完善,即可在很大程度上遏制美国"航行自由行动"日趋常态化的开展。故从长远的角度来看,《公约》的有关规定亟待完善,以防止《公约》所维护的航行自由权利为海洋强国所滥用,损害沿海国的国家安全和海洋权益。

然而修改《公约》有一定的现实障碍。由于当今国家实践对《公约》模糊条款的解读和适用分歧较大,笼络足够数量的缔约国支持修正《公约》有极大的困难,因而难以满足《公约》第312条规定的启动修正程序的条件。而且即便修正会议有可能召开,也必将历经漫长的谈判协商过程,最终修正提案能否通过表决也是难以预测的。

除修改《公约》之外,完善《公约》还可通过其他途径完成。例如,《公约》中存在部分条款指明缔约国可以视情况所需,通过与邻国合作或制定区域协定的方式,在不违反《公约》目的和宗旨的前提之下对《公约》条款的内容加以完善。[85] 因而国家间可以通过外交途径,缔结双边或多边的区域协定或国际协定来对《公约》未做规定的事项加以调整,或者对《公约》规定不明的事项以协定的形式巩固和促进国家实践的统一。这不仅有利于推动相关习惯国际法的发展,而且还可以在日后有条件召开缔约国会议对《公约》进行修改之时提供修正参考文本。

再如,有学者指出,可以参照联合国的实践,通过对《联合国宪章》的条款进行扩大解释以达到对条款进行事实上的修改的形式,对《公约》的模糊条款进行扩大解释来做出修正。[86] 2001年《公约》缔约国会议对附件中规定的沿海国提交200海里以外大陆架划界案的期限进行解释修改的决定,即是扩大解释《公约》规定并对之做出修改的典型范例之一。另外,2008年安理会也曾做出决议,在索马里政府同意的前提之下,授权外国军队在其领海内打击海盗,这也可视为是对《公约》第101条中海盗行为只发生在公海的狭隘定义进行了扩大解释。[87]

---

[85] 例如《公约》第69条、第98条等。

[86] 参见杨泽伟:《〈联合国海洋法公约〉的主要缺陷及其完善》,载《法学评论》2012年第5期。

[87] 参见孔令杰:《〈联合国海洋法公约〉的完善》,载《中国海洋法学评论》2010年第1期。

此外，积极推动聚集各国专家学者召开专题研讨会，就颇具争议的海洋法问题进行磋商研讨，对于完善《公约》的未定事项及模糊条款亦有一定的积极影响。例如，在2002年至2005年期间，由来自中国、美国、俄罗斯、澳大利亚、日本、韩国、印度、印度尼西亚、菲律宾、越南等亚太地区国家的高级官员和专家学者就专属经济区内易引发争议的相关海洋法问题召开了一系列会议进行研讨，并于2005年制定了《专属经济区航行和飞越指南》。[88] 虽然该指南对各国并不具有普遍拘束力，但它对于澄清《公约》中语焉不详的权利义务规定、加深各国对专属经济区涉及的海洋法问题的理解、为相关争议行为提供一些基本准则、促进国际社会共识的达成均创造了良好的条件。

四、结　　语

综上所述，美国"航行自由计划"自其出台以来，就缺乏充分的国际法依据。实际上，美国是以其单方面解读《公约》的结果而非国际社会的普遍共识来认定其他沿海国家的海洋权利主张不符合《公约》和习惯国际法的规定，进而在相关海域开展"航行自由行动"，挑战这些沿海国家所谓的"扩张性海洋权利主张"，对沿海国的国家安全与海洋秩序造成了一定程度的负面影响。

如今，美国更是将"航行自由计划"的挑战中心转移至中国，以维护南海航行自由为借口，频繁地派遣军舰在南海海域进行所谓的"航行自由行动"，对我国的"扩张性海洋权利主张"进行挑战，威胁或危害我国在南海地区的国家安全和合法权益。对此，我国除了应继续不断地积极抗议，同时还应加强有关国际法理论研究，完善现有海洋法律法规体系，进一步做好法理斗争工作。此外，中美两国在美国南海"航行自由行动"上的意见分歧和博弈，在法律上实则体现为沿海国家和海洋大国对《公约》中模糊条款所做出的不同解读和适用，因而中国应积极推动国际社会完善美国"航行自由计划"所涉《公约》的规定，堵住《公约》规定的有关漏洞，以从源头遏制美国滥用航行自由权来实施所谓的"航行自由行动"。

（责任编辑：林思勤）

---

〔88〕 参见邹立刚：《〈专属经济区航行和飞越指南〉述评》，载《福建警察学院学报》2013年第3期。

确认仲裁裁决的外国判决的承认与执行法律问题分析

林　峰*

摘要：

确认仲裁裁决的判决有其特性，表现在辅助性、规避《纽约公约》、规避执行法院审查等方面。相关国家在承认与执行这类判决时依据的基础，包括平行权利、合并以及执行判决不能被执行等理论，但各有不足。既判力原则是判决承认与执行的重要理论基础。基于优先管辖权与次级管辖权的划分，具有优先管辖权的仲裁地法院作出的确认仲裁裁决的判决通常具有既判力，非仲裁地作出的则不一定。此外，既判力的内容之冲突应同时依原判决作出国和执行地国法律判断。最后，仅在债务人提出实体抗辩之时，法院才应考察仲裁裁决的既判力。实践中，除了本国的判决承认与执行制度外，法院应重点关注判决作出地、判决形式以及当事人的请求等内容。

关键词：

确认仲裁裁决的外国判决；外国判决承认与执行；既判力原则；优先管辖权

当仲裁庭作出一项仲裁裁决之后，当事人并非高枕无忧。仲裁裁决债权人还面临着仲裁裁决能否完全获得执行的问题。一方面，基于仲裁"民间性"的特点，作为一种私权的结果，仲裁裁决还受到司法的监督。然而，不同国家，司法监督的模式不一，方式也有所不同。其中，司法监督的方式一般包括撤销、确认和不予执行。就确认而言，有些国家设有该制度，有些则无，如中国、法国。另一方面，为了促进仲裁裁决的执行，多数国家都加入了《承认及执行外国仲裁裁决公约》（以下简称《纽约公约》）。据此，为了使债务得到履行，经仲裁后，债权

* 林峰，武汉大学法学院2016级硕士研究生。

人可采取多种方式,既可依《纽约公约》在他国寻求承认与执行仲裁裁决,也可以在某一国法院通过司法程序确认仲裁裁决并获得确认判决,而后持该确认判决在他国执行。[1] 在《纽约公约》的背景之下,仲裁裁决在全球范围内的流通相对比较顺畅。因而,相较于前一种承认与执行方式而言,后一种方式并不多见。但债权人仍可能选择此种"迂回"战略。原因在于:

一是有些国家法律为仲裁裁决规定了确认程序,依债权人请求,法院会作出一个确认性的判决,确认仲裁裁决的效力,如美国和法国。二是有些国家申请承认与执行外国判决的时效远远长于申请承认与执行仲裁裁决的时效。这些国家关于确认仲裁裁决的外国判决的承认与执行的法律制度比较宽松,当仲裁裁决在一国不能获得完全的履行而需要在多国获得承认与执行之时,判决承认与执行的优势便显现出来。三是仲裁裁决的承认与执行,并不当然比判决承认与执行更为容易,很多国家都有判决承认与执行的双边协定,这类双边协定规定的审查内容与《纽约公约》规定的内容相似,甚至更为宽松。另外,虽然判决承认与执行的审查内容与仲裁裁决审查的内容有很多相似之处,但二者也存在差异,当一个国家对同一法律争议具有不同看法之时,当事人可以利用确认之诉规避仲裁裁决审查中的不利,从而寻求判决的承认与执行,本文第一部分将举例解释这一点。

针对确认仲裁裁决的外国判决,学界的争论主要在于此种判决的效力。原因在于,各国国内法和相关国际条约(如《纽约公约》)均没有对此类判决的承认与执行问题直接规定,此类外国判决的性质难以确定,究竟是依据仲裁裁决的承认与执行制度处理,还是适用外国判决相关制度,抑或二者同时适用存在疑问。此外,如下文所述,确认仲裁裁决的外国判决可能会造成对现有国际公约的规避,特别是《纽约公约》。因此,这一问题构成了国内和国际法制的漏洞。

---

〔1〕《纽约公约》虽然废除了《日内瓦公约》的"双重许可"制度,但是并未规定当事人不得主动利用该制度。因此,在具有仲裁裁决确认制度的国家中,当事人可以请求当地法院确认其仲裁裁决。需要注意的是,大多数国家都建立了仲裁裁决的撤销制度,若仲裁裁决债务人提起仲裁裁决撤销之诉,且仲裁地法院拒绝撤销仲裁裁决,根据既判力原则,仲裁地法院的拒绝行为也可能被解读为一种确认。See Seetransport Wiking Trader v. Navimpex Cent Naval,29 F. 3D 79 (1994).

就性质而言,确认仲裁裁决的判决与撤销仲裁裁决的判决本质相同,二者均为法院对仲裁裁决的司法审查结果,只是结果的内容完全相反。因此,在处理这两种判决的效力之时,法院可采取基本一致的思路。两种判决不同的地方在于:当一国法院作出撤销判决之后,仲裁裁决的债权人通常只能通过原仲裁裁决来寻求执行,而债务人则可依赖于撤销判决来阻止胜诉方。因此,于执行地法院而言,争议焦点在于原仲裁裁决与撤销仲裁裁决的判决之间的效力冲突,这是非此即彼的矛盾,对当事人的权益影响非常大,可能直接决定了当事人权益能否实现。法院此时不仅需要解决国际法律秩序的冲突,还要衡量当事人之间的利益冲突。而仲裁裁决被确认后,胜诉方在寻求执行之时可选择原仲裁裁决或之后的确认判决。此时法院事实上并不面临前述不同法律文件之间的效力冲突问题,法院需要思考的问题在于如何看待之后的确认判决,也即国际法律秩序的问题。此时法院的处理结果对于当事人的权益影响并不是很大。因为即使该确认判决不被认可,债权人也可依原来的仲裁裁决来维护自己的利益。因此,尽管撤销判决与确认判决的性质具有一致性,但因各自内容不同,对当事人利益的影响程度不一,法院应当衡量的因素也不同,理论研究自然也不应完全等同对待,而需要分别观察。

针对仲裁裁决被撤销的情形,国内研究重点在于仲裁裁决被撤销后的承认与执行问题,关注点在于原仲裁裁决本身,但较少讨论外国撤销判决的承认与执行问题,而事实上这是原仲裁裁决能否被承认与执行的先决问题。〔2〕此外,现有的研究并未能提出一套逻辑严密的制度,未能就撤销或确认仲裁裁决的判决的承认与执行问题,为法院在现行法制下提供可行的解决方案。基于确认仲裁裁决的判决与撤销仲裁裁决的判决具有一致性,本文认为,通过解决确认仲

〔2〕国内学者的研究主要集中在硕士毕业论文领域,包括张圆:《〈纽约公约〉下已撤销外国商事仲裁裁决的承认与执行》,复旦大学2012年硕士学位论文;裴蓉清:《论被撤销的国际商事仲裁裁决及其承认与执行》,华东政法大学2012年硕士学位论文;陈辉:《已撤销仲裁裁决在〈纽约公约〉下的承认与执行研究》,华东政法大学2015年硕士学位论文。而期刊文章则主要参见傅攀峰:《未竟的争鸣:被撤销的国际商事仲裁裁决的承认与执行》,载《现代法学》2017年第1期。以上文章均就被撤销的国际商事仲裁裁决的承认与执行进行制度与价值分析,对撤销判决本身的分析较少,也没有就法院应当如何处理不同法律文件(原仲裁裁决与后续的撤销判决)之间的法律冲突提出完备的处理措施。

裁裁决的判决的承认与执行问题,或许能够为解决撤销仲裁裁决的判决的承认与执行问题提供借鉴,从而更好地解决已被撤销的仲裁裁决的承认与执行问题。同样地,从更宏观的角度来看,确认仲裁裁决的判决的承认与执行问题的解决,也能为仲裁裁决以及法院判决在跨境流通中产生的效力冲突提供一定思考。但尚未有国内学者关注过这一问题,或者从确认判决的角度来思考不同法律文件的效力秩序。

相反,国外对该问题的研究则不断丰富。相关文献主要研究美国的司法实践,并对现有理论进行概括,如"平行权利"理论和合并理论。另外,尽管现在我国法院尚未遇到此类问题,但我国与世界的联系越来越紧密,法院面对确认仲裁裁决的外国判决的承认与执行问题的可能性越来越高,而我国法律并未规定如何处理此问题。综上所述,本文研究的问题具有学术价值和实践意义。

基于此,本文试图结合《纽约公约》下仲裁裁决承认与执行制度和各国判决承认与执行制度,通过对此类判决的特性、现行主要理论及相关国家的实践,结合承认与执行中的基础理论,对确认仲裁裁决的外国判决的承认与执行涉及的问题进行研究,并提出破解之道。

一、确认仲裁裁决的外国判决的特殊性

针对确认仲裁裁决的外国判决,各国争议最核心的问题在于如何协调现有仲裁裁决和判决的承认与执行制度的适用,从而决定判决和仲裁裁决何者应被承认与执行。该问题又根源于各国法律制度的差异。正是因为无论是跨国仲裁裁决还是外国判决均没有完全统一的承认与执行制度,才导致两种制度在面对确认仲裁裁决的外国判决时,有时会难以共存。要解决这一问题,首先需要明确确认仲裁裁决的外国判决的特性,也即其与一般的外国判决的差异,以及承认与执行此类判决可能会带来的问题。

(一)辅助性

纵观外国判决的承认与执行制度,虽然各国原则上并不审查外国判决的实体部分,但大多要求判决具有实体内容,并且是终局性的。但本质上,确认仲裁裁决是司法监督程序的结果,是辅助性的(ancillary),其一般仅包括仲裁的有效

性与该裁决的效力如何两项内容。[3] 这是需要区别对待此类判决的根本原因。正是这种辅助性,使法院在处理此类判决之时,不能把此类判决完全等同于一般判决。这种辅助性带来的另一问题就是此类判决一般不具有实体内容。

《纽约公约》并未规定国家在确认仲裁裁决时的程序。因此,确认仲裁裁决的程序适用的是各国国内法。各国法关于仲裁裁决的确认形式各不一致。法国采取的是执行令(enforcement order 或者是 *exequatur*)。[4] 而且拒绝撤销的命令也自动具有执行效力,无需再申请执行令。[5] 荷兰采取的是执行令状(writ of execution),可以由法院院长签发。[6] 英国一般采取法院命令的形式(order)。[7] 中国虽然并未确立仲裁裁决确认制度,但针对类似的撤销制度采用的是裁定。大陆法系国家确认仲裁裁决的判决大多不涉及当事人有关的权利义务,而只是单纯地宣告所涉仲裁裁决的效力;普通法系国家的判决则有可能会另行明确债务人需承担的债务,从而可能具有实体内容。[8] 总体来说,此类判决的内容主要为程序性内容,大多不具有实体内容,不具有可执行的客体。因此,从这一角度来看,这类判决并不完全符合外国判决承认与执行的条件,存在不被承认与执行的风险。

---

[3] See Maxi Scherer, "Effects of Foreign Judgments Relating to International Arbitral Awards: Is the 'Judgment Route' the Wrong Road?", *Journal of International Dispute Settlement* 43, 2013, pp. 605-606.

[4] 参见法国新《仲裁法》第1487条(Decree No 2011-48 of 13 January 2011)。

[5] See Guido Carducci, "The Arbitration Reform in France: Domestic and International Arbitration Law", 28 (1) *Arbitration International* 28 (1), 2012, p. 146.

[6] See Solitron Devices, Inc. v. Island Territory of Curacao, D. C. 356 F. Supp. 1, 10 (1973); Ocean Warehousing B. V. v. Baron Metals and Alloy, 157 F. Supp. 2d 245 (S. D. N. Y. 2001).

[7] See 1996 Arbitration Act section 66 and 67(3). 美国也是采取命令的形式。See 9 U. S. C § 9(2006).

[8] See Linda J. Silberman & Scherer Maxi, "Forum Shopping and Post-Award Judgments", New York University Public Law and Theory Working Papers, http://lsr.nellco.org/nyu_plltwp/447, May 20, 2017. 是否有实体内容取决于法官是否在判决中写明债务人的责任,而这完全视法官心情而定。如果因为这种单纯的文字差异,多一句话或者少一句话,就使得确认仲裁裁决的判决面临完全不同的命运似乎并不公平。

(二)规避性

依据国际法一般理论,缔约国均需承担执行《纽约公约》和促进仲裁裁决流通的义务。但是,若各国均承认与执行确认仲裁裁决的外国判决,那么《纽约公约》将被架空,不再有适用的余地。因为在一些判决承认与执行较为宽松的国家,承认与执行外国判决可能比承认与执行仲裁裁决更为有利。[9] 这会促使当事人选择这种"迂回"战略。

具体来说,一般情况下,对仲裁裁决的司法审查主要由仲裁地法院进行。而对于仲裁地来说,在其国内作出的仲裁裁决可能被识别为内国裁决,仲裁地法院对该仲裁裁决的审查(包括确认)不适用《纽约公约》,[10] 而适用内国法律。之后,在承认与执行的阶段,债权人寻求的是确认仲裁裁决的外国判决的承认与执行,而非仲裁裁决,执行地法院可能认为《纽约公约》仅调整仲裁裁决的承认与执行,不适用于确认仲裁裁决的外国判决的承认与执行。因此,《纽约公约》也无法得到适用,从而完全被架空。

当然,这种间接使仲裁裁决获得承认与执行的方式本身并不一定违背《纽约公约》追求的目标,甚至还可能促进该目标的实现。[11] 但是,从目前收集的资料来看,并不是所有国家均认可这种方式。[12]

(三)不稳定性

各国判决承认与执行制度差异大,加剧了此类判决承认与执行的不确定

[9] 如美国,外国仲裁裁决适用联邦法,申请仲裁裁决的时效只有3年;外国判决承认与执行适用州法,有的州规定的判决承认时效则超过10年。

[10] 《纽约公约》第1条第1款规定:仲裁裁决,因自然人或法人间之争议而产生且在申请承认及执行地所在国以外之国家领土内作成者,其承认及执行适用本公约。本公约对于仲裁裁决经声请承认及执行地所在国认为非内国裁决者,亦适用之。

[11] 《纽约公约》第7条第1款规定:本公约之规定不影响缔约国间所订关于承认及执行仲裁裁决之多边或双边协定之效力,亦不剥夺任何利害关系人可依援引裁决地所在国之法律或条约所认许之方式,在其许可范围内,援用仲裁裁决之任何权利。

[12] 目前,仅收集到美国、英国、澳大利亚、印度、以色列、瑞士、法国等国家确实予以承认这类判决的效力。而其他国家,诸如德国,采取完全废除"双重许可"(*double exequatur*)制度的态度,则不认可此种制度。主要拉丁国家则根据"执行令不可执行"原则(*exequatur sur exequatur ne vaut*)拒绝承认与执行确认仲裁裁决的外国判决,这与德国的态度类似。

性,使得当事人的权益更加处于不确定的状态。特别是在申请承认与执行外国判决和仲裁裁决时效不同的国家,比如美国,《纽约公约》被规避的情况很容易发生。根据《美国联邦仲裁法》(Federal Arbitration Act)的规定,外国仲裁裁决在美国申请承认与执行的期限为3年。[13] 而外国判决的承认与执行因为适用的是州法,各州并无统一规定,有的州期限长达十几年。这就可能导致当事人在美国更愿意寻求承认与执行其获得的确认仲裁裁决的判决,或者同时寻求确认仲裁裁决的判决和该仲裁裁决的承认与执行,仲裁败诉方无法预计债权人会在何地寻求承认与执行,其权益处于极其不稳定的状态。这也是有些国家拒绝承认与执行此类判决的理由之一。[14]

(四)侵犯性

从国际条约和各国国内法来看,判决和仲裁裁决的承认与执行中的审查范围也大体相同,无非是管辖权、程序违法、公共政策等因素。[15] 但是,一方面,因为《纽约公约》本身并未对其条文中一些有争议的关键名词进行解释,而把解释权留给了各成员国;另一方面,外国判决的承认与执行尚未形成统一的制度,即使存在区域性的或者有全球性的草案,这些条约或条约草案不可避免地存在与《纽约公约》一样的条文解释问题。这也就意味着,事实上仲裁裁决与判决的在承认与执行过程中的审查结果,很大程度上是取决于各国国内法的。但各国国内法差异较大,其各自审查结果也很可能不一致。

此外,《纽约公约》列明的拒绝理由总共可以分为两类。第一类是规定应依据非执行地国法判断的,包括当事人的行为能力、仲裁协议的效力、仲裁庭的组成和仲裁程序以及撤销仲裁裁决。[16] 第二类是未规定法律适用或规定应适用执行地国法的,包括仲裁的送达程序、仲裁的范围、争议事项的可仲裁性以及公

---

〔13〕 See 9 U. S. C § 207(2006).

〔14〕 如德国,参见本文第二部分对德国的实践分析。

〔15〕 See Talia Einhorn, "The Recognition and Enforcement of Foreign Judgments on Arbitral Awards", *Yearbook of Private International Law* 20, 2010, p. 59.

〔16〕 根据《纽约公约》第5条第1款的规定,当事人的行为能力适用其人身法,仲裁协议适用当事人选择的法或在当事人未选择时适用仲裁地国法,仲裁庭的组成和仲裁程序依据当事人的约定或未约定时适用仲裁地国法,撤销仲裁裁决依据仲裁地国法或者仲裁准据法国法。

共政策。

第一类因法律适用较为统一,结果产生争议的可能性较小,但是也并非绝对,因为执行地国法院在适用外国法时,并不能保证外国法适用的结果与其来源国完全一致。例如,关于仲裁协议对第三人的效力,各国的法律规定或司法实践就可能不同。[17] 若一国法律对此并无明文规定,且没有统一的司法实践,而仲裁机构认为第三人应受该仲裁协议约束,并对第三人作出了不利判决。同时仲裁地法院也持相同意见并确认了该仲裁裁决。但是,执行地法院在适用该国法律则可能采取不一样的态度,可能严格解释合同相对性原则,认为第三人不应受仲裁协议约束,因此根据《纽约公约》第 5 条第 1 款第 1 项,不予承认执行该仲裁裁决。但是,因为仲裁胜诉方寻求的是确认该仲裁裁决的判决的承认与执行,在无其他理由的情况下,执行地法院不得援引《纽约公约》拒绝认可该判决。这便间接地违反了执行地国法律。

第二类理由因其无统一的准据法,主要根据执行地国法律进行判断,这会导致各国针对同一情形作出不同的法律评价。最典型的例子就是公共政策保留,多数国家都把公共政策同时作为仲裁裁决和判决承认与执行的审查理由。基于前述仲裁协议对第三人效力的同一逻辑,不难得出,执行地国很可能不得不承认确认仲裁裁决的外国判决,而该被确认的仲裁裁决却违反了执行地国的公共政策。

最后,针对判决和仲裁裁决的承认与执行,国际通行的原则是形式审查,只有在例外情况下才进行实体审查。而如前所述,确认判决的主要内容也为程序性的,通常无实体内容可审查。所以,若把确认仲裁裁决的外国判决等同于一般性的外国判决,则会导致执行地法院无法根据其内国法对原仲裁裁决进行审查,甚至有可能间接地剥夺内国法院的审查权,而执行地法院的审查结果可能与确认地法院的审查结果并不一致。据此,在债权人直接寻求确认仲裁裁决的承认与执行时,执行地法院无法对原仲裁裁决进行充分审查,可能会导致本国权益受到侵害。

基于上述分析,本文认为,执行地法院有必要对此类判决进行特殊审查,不应将其与一般判决等同对待。本文接下来将结合各国实践进行总结,分析确认

〔17〕 See Tyler B. Robinson,"The Recognition and Enforcement of Foreign Judgments in the United States",*The American Review of International Arbitration* 24 (1),2013,p. 66.

仲裁裁决的外国判决的理论基础,提出该类判决承认与执行的合理模型。

二、“一刀切”——现有理论及其实践

就笔者收集到的资料而言,大多数国家的立法中都未明确应如何处理确认仲裁裁决的外国判决的承认与执行问题。从相关的司法实践来看,不同国家有其不同的做法,也各有其不同理论支持。

(一)“平行权利”理论(Parallel Entitlement)

目前大多数普通法系国家均采此理论。“平行权利”理论,也被称为“双重执行”(double enforceability),是指外国法院作出确认仲裁裁决的判决之后,仲裁裁决债权人可以选择寻求原仲裁裁决的承认与执行,也可以寻求该外国判决的承认与执行,或者同时申请二者,二者均有可能被承认与执行。采这一理论的国家主要有美国、英国、澳大利亚、印度、以色列等主要英美法系国家。[18] 其中以美国和英国为代表,下文简要介绍之。

1. 美国

美国的外国仲裁裁决与外国判决承认与执行分别适用不同的法律。目前,外国仲裁裁决的承认与执行适用的是统一的联邦法,而外国判决的承认与执行则属于各州的管辖范围。为了统一外国判决的承认与执行制度,美国制定了1962年和2005年《统一外国金钱判决承认与执行法》,二者目前在美国均有效,并分别在不同的州实施。前者未规定确认仲裁裁决的判决能否予以承认与执行。后者则在评论部分对此明确。[19] 但理论界对其效力存有争议。

但与学界的争议不同,从第 起此类案件Island Territory of Curacao案[20],一直到最近的Congo案[21],美国司法界的态度基本是把确认仲裁裁决的外国判决与一般性的外国判决等同看待,适用相同的审查标准。从美国的司法实践

[18] See *supra* note 8.

[19] See Uniform Foreign Country Money Judgments Recognition Act § 2 cmt. 3 (2005).

[20] Island Territory of Curacao v. Solitron Devices, Inc., 489 F. 2d 1313 (2d Cir. 1973).

[21] Commissions Import Export S. A. v. Republic of the Congo, 757 F. 3d 321 (2014).

中可以看出,美国法院对于此类判决的审查要求较为宽松。无论是执行令(writ of execution)、[22]判决[23]还是非仲裁地的执行判决,[24]在美国均不被排除在其承认与执行制度中的外国判决的范围之外,只要符合一般条件,都能得到认可。

另外,基于外国判决和仲裁裁决在联邦法和州法层面的二分,债务人提出的重要抗辩理由就是《联邦仲裁法》优先于(preempt)州法的适用,认为确认仲裁裁决的外国判决应适用联邦法,应当适用《纽约公约》,不予承认与执行。[25]但此抗辩理由基本未被法院支持。[26] 美国法院认为《纽约公约》与各州的判决承认与执行制度完全分离,相互不受影响,从而把确认仲裁裁决的外国判决排除在《纽约公约》适用范围外。[27] 因此,在判决承认与执行的领域,联邦法并无优先适用性,确认仲裁裁决的外国判决的承认与执行完全依据各州法进行。

2. 英国

英国法院的做法与美国的做法基本相同。虽然欧盟范围内的系列判决承认与执行公约,如《洛迦诺公约》和《布鲁塞尔条例》均把仲裁裁决排除在外,且这一排除范围还扩展至与仲裁裁决有关的法院判决,其中就包括了确认仲裁裁

---

〔22〕 See Island Territory of Curacao v. Solitron Devices, Inc. ,489 F. 2d 1313 (2d Cir. 1973).

〔23〕 See Ocean Warehousing B. V. v. Baron Metals & Alloys, Inc. 157 F. Supp. 2d 245 (S. D. N. Y. 2001).

〔24〕 See Commissions Import Export S. A. v. Republic of the Congo, 757 F. 3d 321 (2014).

〔25〕 《联邦仲裁法》(Federal Arbitration Act)区别对待国内仲裁裁决和外国仲裁裁决,其中第二部分把《纽约公约》并入其中,适用于外国仲裁裁决在美国的承认与执行。

〔26〕 联邦法优先适用(preemption)这一理论源于美国宪法对州权和联邦权力的协调,当州法与联邦法冲突时,联邦法优先。据此,在Congo案的一审中,哥伦比亚地区法院认为联邦在仲裁裁决承认执行领域具有程序统一和终局性的目标,承认与执行这类判决会违反这些目标,因此联邦法具有优先性,应当适用《联邦仲裁法》,根据其申请承认与执行的3年时效,该确认仲裁裁决的外国判决不能获得承认与执行。See Commissions Import Export S. A. v. Republic of the Congo, 916 F. Supp. 2d 48 (2013). 但该观点被联邦第二巡回法院推翻。

〔27〕 See Island Territory of Curacao v. Solitron Devices, Inc. ,489 F. 2d 1313 at [1319].

决的判决,但英国的国内法依旧很可能会承认与执行此类判决。[28] 同时,与美国不同的是,外国法院在简易程序中作出的执行令(enforcement order)和执行书(*exequatur*)不能获得许可,因为此类执行令仅仅只是宣告仲裁裁决可以在法院地执行,并未确定某项债务。[29] 但这类判决在英国同样会产生一定的影响,也可能产生禁反言的效力。[30]

(二)合并理论(Merger)

就本文而言,合并理论是指仲裁裁决被确认后,即并入该确认判决,此时仅确认仲裁裁决的判决可以被执行,而原仲裁裁决不能被承认与执行,也即当事人被禁止(bar)申请承认与执行仲裁裁决。[31] 但是,这一理论通常适用于国内判决,至于国外判决则适用非合并理论(non-merger),也即适用上文中的"平行权利"。因此大多数国家均不采此理论,特别是普通法系国家。相关国家的案例较少,且均已年代久远,同时这些国家基本上已经推翻了合并理论,普遍采取"平行权利"的路径。[32] 事实上,就本文讨论的问题而言,这个理论似乎已经不再可行,因为大多数国家均是《纽约公约》的缔约国,其有义务执行其他缔约国的仲裁裁决,而且仲裁裁决被外国判决确认并不是《纽约公约》规定的拒绝仲裁裁决承认与执行的理由。

(三)执行令不能被执行(*exequatur sur exequatur ne vaut*)

针对确认仲裁裁决的外国判决,德国采取了与上述两种理论完全不一致的做法。在一项德国联邦最高法院的判决中,法院认为,美国加州法院作出的确

[28] See Lawrence Collins (eds.), *Dicey, Morris and Collins on The Conflict of Laws*, 14th ed., London, Sweet & Maxwell, 2006, p. 775.

[29] Jonathan Hill, "The Significance of Foreign Judgments Relating to an Arbitral Award in the Context of an Application to Enforce the Award in England", *Journal of Private International Law* 8(2), 2012, p. 179.

[30] 英国的判决禁反言原则并不完全局限于针对实体问题作出的判决。See Desert Sun Loan Corporation v. Hill [1996] 2 All ER 847.

[31] See Editors, "Foreign Judgments Based on Foreign Arbitral Awards: The Applicability of Res Judicata", *University of Pennsylvania . Law Review* 124, 1975, pp. 234 - 235.

[32] Ibid.

认仲裁裁决的判决在德国不能被承认与执行,当事人只能寻求仲裁裁决的承认与执行。[33] 事实上,德国以前的做法是:理论上采取合并路径,但实践中却采纳"平行权利"理论。德国最高法院推翻先例的理由包括以下几个:(1)执行第三国判决的判决在德国不能得到执行,这一理论同样适用于仲裁裁决,否则会规避《纽约公约》在德国的适用;(2)债权人不应获得两次相互独立的机会去启动承认与执行程序,债务人也不应面临双重危险;(3)承认确认仲裁裁决的外国判决将会违反高等区域法院对仲裁裁决承认与执行的专属管辖权,因为外国判决的承认与执行由地方法院管辖。采取同样做法的还有西班牙、塞尔维亚等国。[34]

据此,德国彻底废除了双重认可制度(*double exequatur*),而仅允许仲裁裁决获得承认与执行,确认仲裁裁决的外国判决不能获得承认与执行。这一做法正好与大陆法系判决理论中的"执行令不能被执行"(*exequatur sur exequatur ne vaut*)相吻合。该理论认为,当事人只能请求原始判决的承认与执行,针对原始判决作出的确认或执行命令不具有域外效力。[35] 执行性判决(*exequatur* judgment)不能被执行是众多国家的法律原则,包括大陆法系和英美法系。因此,此类判决在这些国家中,基于与德国最高法院相似的理由,存在无法执行的可能。

确认仲裁裁决的外国判决本身具有双重性质——仲裁裁决和判决,本质上附属于仲裁裁决,也正是因为这种特性,才有必要对其进行特别讨论。这种特性背后反映的是外国法院判决的既判力和保护债务人的利益二者的冲突。前述三种理论在解决这一冲突时均存在问题。首先,"平行权利"理论过于尊重外国判决的既判力,不关注此类判决的附属特性,从而导致极易出现本文第一部分提出的问题。其次,以德国为代表的"执行令不能被执行"理论则过于关注债务人权利的稳定,而对此类外国法院判决熟视无睹,完全不尊重外国判决的效力。合并理论因其目前不具有实践价值,本文不做过多讨论。基于此,本文以下部分试图结合优先管辖权和既判力理论提出合理的解决路径。

---

〔33〕 BGH, decision of July 2, 2009, File No. IX ZR 152/06.

〔34〕 See *supra* note 3, p. 616.

〔35〕 See *supra* note 15, pp. 56 - 57.

三、"分步走"——优先管辖权下的既判力理论

如前所述,大陆法系国家和普通法系国家的传统理论及实践未充分考虑确认仲裁裁决之判决的双重性质,而对此种判决采取"一刀切"的态度,导致无法在尊重外国判决以及保护债务人利益二者间实现平衡。为此,本文提出,在处理此类确认判决的承认与执行问题之时,应当采取"分步走"的策略:

第一,根据优先与次级管辖权的划分,确定不同国家或地区法院对仲裁裁决进行司法审查的权力层级;

第二,根据既判力理论及其法律适用的实践,分别依据不同国家或地区法院对仲裁裁决进行司法审查的不同权力层级,确定确认仲裁裁决的外国判决的既判力范围;

第三,根据当事人的诉讼请求或抗辩,法院决定进行形式或实体审查。

(一)司法审查的权力层级

根据国际公法的一般原则,各国主权平等,其衍生而出的司法审查权理应也互相平等,并无先后之分。但在涉及一项仲裁裁决或其确认判决在不同国家寻求承认与执行之时,基于对他国司法主权的尊重,后审查的国家应当尊重先审查国家的审查结果。这便可能导致国家审查一项判决或仲裁裁决的先后顺序不同,而对应地享有不同的审查权力。就国际商事仲裁而言,"仲裁地"以及"裁决所依据法律的国家"法院通常对仲裁裁决享有较为完全的司法审查权。国际上通行的理论是,一般来说,只有仲裁裁决的作出地才有权对其进行司法监督,也即只有其作出地法院才有权撤销、确认仲裁裁决,其他国家只有承认和执行的权力,其他国家即使撤销或者确认了仲裁裁决,也不一定能得到他国的认可。[36]

1.《纽约公约》的规定

《纽约公约》并未对仲裁裁决的司法审查作出完备的规定。但根据《纽约公约》第5条第1款第5项的规定,"仲裁地"和"裁决所依据法律的国家"作出的撤销仲裁裁决可以使得该仲裁裁决无法获得执行。其中,后者的"所依据法律"

---

〔36〕 See *supra* note 17, p. 67;参见王芳:《英国承认与执行外国仲裁裁决制度研究》,中国政法大学出版社2012年版,第51页;参见王政:《论仲裁地及其法律意义》,外交学院2015年硕士学位论文,第14页。

一般解释为仲裁程序法(*lex arbitri*)。[37] 而仲裁程序法大多都是仲裁地的立法。[38] 也就是说,从《纽约公约》的用语可以推断出,“仲裁地”和“裁决所依据法律的国家”可以对仲裁裁决进行司法监督,至少可以撤销仲裁裁决。至于仲裁地进行的其他方式的监督,以及其他国家进行的司法监督,其域外效力应当取决于各国国内法。虽然有学者认为仲裁应去本地化(delocalization),应由当事人自由决定由何国对其仲裁裁决进行审查,但是这种观点过于理想化,只存在于理论中。[39]

2. 优先管辖权与次级管辖权的划分

划分优先与次级管辖权的理论首先在美国 TermoRio 案中确立。[40] 该案确立的原则是具有优先管辖权的国家(primary jurisdiction)可以撤销其国内仲裁裁决,而次级管辖权国家(secondary jurisdiction)则要尊重这种撤销裁决,特殊情况例外。通常来说,仲裁地和仲裁所依据法律所属国是具有优先管辖权的国家。[41] 据此,美国还把这一原则扩展至认为具有优先管辖权的国家能根据其国内法对仲裁裁决进行监督,撤销、修改或者确认。[42] 而次级管辖权的国家则仅能根据《纽约公约》的规定承认或拒绝承认仲裁裁决。[43]

---

〔37〕 也有国家把“under the law”解释为实体法,也即仲裁准据法国有权对仲裁裁决进行监督,如印度。但目前,印度最高法院也推翻了这一解读,从而确立了只有仲裁地和仲裁程序法地才有权撤销仲裁裁决这一规则。See Bharat Aluminium Co. (Balco) v. Kaiser Aluminium Technical Servies, Civil Appeal No. 7019 of 2005, 6 September 2012.

〔38〕 See Gary B. Born, *International Arbitration: Law and Practice*, 1st ed., Alphen aan den Rijn, Kluwer Law International, 2012, § 6.02.

〔39〕 See Blackaby Nigel et al., *Redfern and Hunter on International Arbitration*, 15th ed., Oxford, Oxford University Press, 2015, pp. 577 – 578.

〔40〕 See TermoRio v. Electrificadoria Dela Atlantico, 421 F. Supp. 2d 87 (D. D. C. 2006).

〔41〕 前引 2,陈辉文,第 24 页。

〔42〕 See Gulf Petro Trading Co. v. Nigerian Nat'l Petroleum Corp., 512 F. 3d 742, 747 (5th Cir. 2008).

〔43〕 See Burton S. DeWitt, “A Judgment Without Merits: The Recognition and Enforcement of Foreign Judgments Confirming Recognizing or Enforcing Arbitral Awards”, *Texas International Law Journal* 50(3), 2015, p. 513.

从上述论述可以得出,“仲裁地”和“裁决所依据法律的国家”对其仲裁裁决具有比较完整的司法审查权,其行使监督权的行为也很有可能得到其他国家的支持。虽然《纽约公约》只规定了撤销仲裁的管辖权,相关国家的实践也更多地集中在撤销仲裁裁决上,但是,应当认为,仲裁裁决的确认行为与撤销行为本身性质是相同的,都是法院的一种司法审查行为。同时,如前所述,有些国家并未规定确认仲裁裁决的制度,撤销仲裁裁决的行为即具有确认的效力,从这一角度来看,仲裁裁决的确认和撤销是一体两面的。基于此,笔者认为,确认仲裁裁决的权力也应当仅由“仲裁地”和“裁决所依据法律的国家”所享有。这些国家对仲裁裁决的确认具有优先管辖权。

(二)外国法院判决的效力层级

外国判决承认与执行的理论基础众多,其中一项重要的理论基础即是既判力(*res judicata*)。[44] 本文着重关注这一理论的原因在于,本文所涉问题通常涉及多个法律文书,这些法律文书生效时间先后不同,存在效力冲突,既判力原则可解决该冲突。根据既判力原则,当有关案件经过有管辖权的外国法院审理之后,该外国法院作出终局性的判决,内国法院基于当事人的请求,不再另行审理而应径直承认与执行该外国法院的判决,其价值取向在于不允许当事人就同一案件提出无休止的重复诉讼。[45]

既判力是民事诉讼判决效力的一种,这一概念源于罗马法中的“一案不二讼”和“既决案件”原则。大陆法系认为,判决确定后可以产生既判力、形成力以及执行力。其中既判力,是指“判决一旦获得确定,其就诉讼中出现的实体性主张,就成为规范双方当事人间民事法律权利义务关系的法定依据,双方当事人均不得就统一实体性事项再行诉讼或提出不同的主张,法院也不得就统一实体事项再次以诉的形式受理或作出不同的判断。”[46] 英美法系并未形成大陆法系国家的完备判决效力概念和理论体系,但其也形成了一些相对应的民事判决效力制度。

1. 英美法系民事判决既判力制度

英美法系判决效力制度有两个基本原则:一是既判事项原则(*res judicata*),

〔44〕 参见何其生:《比较法视野下的国际民事诉讼》,高等教育出版社2015年版,第317页。

〔45〕 参见钱锋:《外国法院民商事判决承认与执行研究》,中国民主法制出版社2010年版,第18页以下。

〔46〕 丁宝同:《民事判决既判力研究》,法律出版社2012年版,第34页以下。

二是间接禁反言原则(collateral estoppel)。后经美国《判决重述》(Restatement of Judgment)第2版修改,把二者分别称为"请求排除"(claim preclusion)和"争点排除"(issue preclusion),并统称为"排除效力"(preclusion)。[47] 但在美国司法实践中,大多数情况下"*res judicata*"是指广义的既判力,包括了前述两项排除内容。[48]

"请求排除"与"争点排除"最核心的区别在于,前者是禁止诉因(cause of action)完全相同的诉讼的二次诉讼,其构成要件有三:当事人相同,诉因相同以及已经针对实体做出判决;后者则禁止已经经过审理的事项(issue)再次被审理,对于诉因是否相同在所不问。[49]

2. 大陆法系与英美法系民事判决既判力制度之差异

第一,判决形式。不同国家关于何种判决具有既判力有不同的规定和实践。英美法系的既判力制度并未直接排除某类判决,而是仅规定既判力的构成要件,由法官结合具体案件来确定某种形式的判决是否具有既判力。法国民事诉讼法规定中间判决、简易程序判决和凭一方当事人申请作出的裁决对案件的实质不具有既判力。[50] 而德国则规定实质的既判力适用于程序法上的裁决,在管辖权问题上,中间判决具有既判力。[51] 同样地,在承认与执行领域,有些也不认可执行令的承认与执行,一项仅确认仲裁裁决可执行的命令难以得到承认与执行,如法国和英国。[52]

第二,客观范围。既判力的客观范围解决的是民事判决文书中哪部分具有既判力。通常来说,一份民事判决书包括技术性事项(通常包括法院信息、诉讼时间等)、当事人主张的案件事实、判决理由(我国民事判决的"本院认为"部分)以及判决结果。大陆法系通常认为仅判决结果部分具有既判力,判决理由

〔47〕 前引46,丁宝同书,第8页。

〔48〕 参见胡军辉:《美国民事既判力研究》,北京师范大学出版社2015年版,第3页。

〔49〕 See *supra* note 43, pp. 508 – 511.

〔50〕 参见沈达明:《比较民事诉讼法初论》,对外经济贸易出版社2015年版,第139页。

〔51〕 前引50,沈达明书,第169页。

〔52〕 See Dominique T. Hascher, "Recognition and Enforcement of Arbitration Awards and the Brussels Convention", *Arbitration International* 12(3), 1996, pp. 238 – 239.

仅在特殊情况才具有既判力。[53] 英美法系的既判力理论并无此限制。这便造成了同一份民事判决的审理事项在不同国家,面临着不同的效力待遇。

此外,除了上述主要区别,大陆法系既判力制度一般不包括"争点排除",而且各国关于既判力的效力内容为何也不尽相同。[54]

3. 既判力冲突及其解决

如前所述,既判力制度可被用于解决不同国家法院法律文件的效力冲突。但是,既判力制度本身在不同国家之间仍存冲突,因此必须先解决此种冲突。只有该冲突得到解决后,既判力制度才能被用于确定不同国家法律文件的效力冲突。本文认为,既判力的审查本质上属于司法审查的范畴,其也遵循前述司法审查权力的层级划分。也即通过司法审查权力高的法院作出的裁决具有优先的既判力,应当得到其他国家遵守。以下详述之。

通常来说,既判力冲突有两种表现形式:第一种冲突是指针对同一事项,不同判决之间的效力冲突;第二种冲突是指同一项判决的既判力之内容、范围等相互冲突。

第一种冲突表现在针对同一事项,不同国家作出了效力相互冲突的判决,这些不同判决的既判力之间便存在矛盾。这一矛盾背后主要是不同国家之间的司法权力冲突。本文涉及的确认仲裁裁决之判决可能引发的冲突即属于此种情形。因此,这一冲突可以通过前述司法审查权的权力层级中确定的原则解决。故而,若确认仲裁裁决的判决由仲裁地作出,该确认判决享有优先效力,任何其他第三国作出的确认或撤销仲裁裁决之判决均不得抵消仲裁地确认判决的效力。在不考虑其他因素的情况下,执行地法院应当优先认可仲裁地作出的确认判决。同样,若仲裁地针对仲裁裁决作出撤销判决,则该撤销判决一般也应享有优先效力,任何其他第三国的确认或撤销判决均不得推翻仲裁地撤销判决的效力。

---

[53] 如根据法国民事诉讼法,为解释主文,可使用理由来确定主文意思;按照判例,凡是理由构成主文的必要支持时,与主文不可分开,既判力就包括理由在内。前引50,沈达明书,第532页。

[54] 如法国《民事诉讼法》规定民事判决构成既判力必须满足三个要素:当事人、标的、诉讼原因相同。这非常接近英美法系下的"请求排除",但也仅限于此,并没有"争点排除"的规定。前引50,沈达明书,第532~534页。另外,关于既判力的效力,德国认为,既判力仅具有诉讼法上的效力,通常不具有证据上的效力。前引50,沈达明书,第167页。

就第二种冲突而言，因各国法律制度的差异，在同一项判决既判力的内容上，国家间可能会产生法律冲突。但在确定外国法院判决的既判力内容之时，只存在一项判决，只涉及判决债权人权利内容的多少，而并不涉及不同法院的权力冲突。此时执行地法院应当基于同等原则，使本国国民与外国人获得一致的法律保护，而不应依司法审查的权力层级来确定既判力的大小。如前所述，大陆法系国家允许的既判力的客观范围就要比英美法系的窄。因此，若当事人在大陆法系国家获得一项终局判决，而后在英美法系国家寻求承认与执行，相比在原判决作出国，根据执行地法律，该判决在执行地可能会获得更多的既判力，这是为执行地国所不能接受的。[55] 在外国判决的承认与执行领域，无论是采取债务说，还是既得权说，债务或既得权的来源依据均是原审国法律，其范围也不能超出原审国法律规定的范围。因此，英美法系国家大多同时适用原判决作出国法律和执行地法律来确认外国判决的既判力范围。[56] 本文赞同此种做法。

（三）仲裁裁决的既判力

一般认为，从当前各国立法和司法实践来看，仲裁裁决具有既判力，其既判力与民事判决的既判力并无明显差异。[57] 仲裁裁决确定后，对后来的仲裁活动产生既判力，但其并不当然对后来的诉讼活动产生既判力。也就是说，法院仍然享有审查仲裁裁决的权力，仲裁裁决本身所具有的既判力并不能阻止法院对其进行确认或者撤销。在法院对其确认之后，该仲裁裁决即具有完全的既判力。因此，后续确认仲裁裁决的判决的承认与执行也会受其影响。

仲裁裁决因其具有实体内容，其既判力与确认仲裁裁决的判决的既判力是不一致的。仲裁裁决的既判力在于约束后续法院或者仲裁庭的重复审理实体事项的行为。确认仲裁裁决的判决通常不具有实体内容，主要内容是确认仲裁有效性和仲裁裁决的效力。但也并非绝对，若法院在确认程序中针对败诉方提出的实体抗辩也进行了审理，则此类判决在实体内容上也可产生既判力，是对原仲裁裁决既判力的补充。

因此在确认仲裁裁决的外国判决的承认与执行阶段，基于当事人主义的原

---

〔55〕 See Robert C. Casad, "Issue Preclusion and Foreign Country Judgments: Whose Law?", *Iowa Law Review* 70, 1984, pp. 75 – 76.

〔56〕 See *supra* note 43, p. 504.

〔57〕 参见邓辉辉：《民事诉讼既判力理论研究》，中国政法大学出版社 2014 年版，第 140 页。

则,若债务人提出实体抗辩,执行地法院需同时考虑仲裁裁决和确认判决的既判力;否则,执行地法院仅需审查确认判决的效力。仅需审查确认仲裁裁决的判决的效力的原因在于:一是无实体争议,没必要也不应当审查实体内容;二是法院在确认仲裁裁决的过程中,通常也会对管辖权、仲裁程序等因素进行审查,这些因素中很多与判决承认与执行阶段需要考察的因素相一致;三是原仲裁裁决通常不会对这些因素进行审查,即使进行审查也不具有终局性,法院有最终决定权,因此在程序内容方面,后续的确认判决既判力要比原仲裁裁决的既判力范围更广。故而,债务人未提出实体性抗辩之时,基于债权人的请求,审查确认仲裁裁决的外国判决的效力即足够。

四、结　　论

从上述理论及实践的分析可以发现,无论是采取“平行权利”路径的国家,还是只承认确认仲裁裁决的判决的国家,法院在推理论证过程中均未考虑此类判决的来源地和判决的形式,对既判力的关注程度也轻重不一。这使这些“一刀切”的方式均难以平衡外国法院判决的既判力和保护债务人的利益。[58]

为了更好地解决此矛盾,本文认为应采取优先管辖权下的既判力理论来解决此问题。结合上述“分步走”的理论分析,可以得出,法院在面对确认仲裁裁决的外国判决之时,需要分别考虑以下因素:

1. 作出确认仲裁裁决之判决的法院地。若法院地位于仲裁地,则该法院具有优先管辖权,通常该确认仲裁裁决的外国判决具有既判力。若法院地为第三国,则其确认仲裁裁决的效力应考虑:第一,仲裁地是否已发布撤销判决,若有,则第三国法院的确认仲裁裁决行为可能无法被认可;第二,若存有其他国家的撤销判决,则由执行法院地根据其国内法进行审查,此时第三国法院的撤销判决和确认仲裁裁决的判决均可能被认为不具有既判力。

---

[58] 特别是美国,不论此类判决来自何地,法院均予以认可。美国《联邦仲裁法》还规定了外国仲裁裁决的确认制度,这便使当事人几乎可以把任何仲裁裁决变成美国的国内判决,从而在美国获得承认执行。而且,美国法院在承认与执行外国判决之时,几乎不考虑判决的形式。此外,结合美国法院还享有长臂管辖权,有权签发跨境交付令。这些制度虽然使得判决在美国相对较容易得到执行,也可能会导致债务人的利益处于非常不稳定之中。

2. 确认仲裁裁决的判决的既判力。执行地法院应结合作出该判决的法院地国法认定判决的既判力范围，包括具有既判力的判决文书类型、既判力的客观范围等。根据原判决地国法，认定此类判决的全部或部分具有既判力之后，执行地国法院还应结合其本国的法律对该判决的既判力进行审查。

3. 债务人的抗辩。若债务人提出实体性抗辩，执行地法院应当综合考虑原仲裁裁决和后续的确认判决所审理的事实。若当事人未提出，执行地法院仅需考虑第1、2项因素。

基于其与仲裁裁决紧密相关的特点，确认仲裁裁决的外国判决的承认与执行制度理应与一般的外国判决承认与执行制度有所区别。虽然确认仲裁裁决的外国判决的承认与执行问题早已在相关国家出现，但这些国家的司法机关并未对此予以足够重视，甚至忽略了确认仲裁裁决的外国判决的特殊性质。基于对既判力理论和仲裁地优先管辖权的分析，本文认为法院在面对确认仲裁裁决的外国判决的承认与执行问题时，需要考虑此类判决的作出地、判决的形式与当事人的抗辩请求，共同结合原判决作出国的既判力制度和执行地国的既判力制度与判决的承认与执行制度，来判断此类判决是否可以获得承认与执行。

目前，中国与世界的联系越来越紧密，法院面对确认仲裁裁决的外国判决的承认与执行问题的可能性越来越高。但是，正如大多数国家一样，我国法律未明文规定此类判决的承认与执行问题。此外，我国民事判决的既判力制度也并没有真正的建立。但是，作为一种间接执行仲裁裁决的方式，我国法院未来很有可能会面对此类问题。法院在面对此类判决之时，应当立足我国的外国仲裁裁决和外国判决的承认与执行法律制度，结合既判力的理念和司法实践，通过考察此类判决的形式、既判力的范围和当事人请求等因素，合理地解决此类判决的承认与执行问题。

（责任编辑：吴劲文）

《中山大学青年法律评论》稿约

一、简　介

《中山大学青年法律评论》是由中山大学法学院学生独立运作、由法律出版社公开发行的法学学术性出版物，创立于2017年，一年两卷。本评论致力于为青年法学人搭建一个学术成果的交流平台，活跃学术研究氛围，开阔研究视野。

二、征稿对象及范围

1. 本评论面向国内外知名院校学生征稿。

2. 本评论奉行一切从学术出发的宗旨，对来稿不限主题和体裁。来稿篇幅以1万～1.5万字为宜，最长不超过2万字。

3. 本评论尤其欢迎细致的制度分析和案例研究，也欢迎优质的翻译稿件，不接受无问题意识的空泛议论或简单介绍，也不接受无深度的表面化评论。

4. 若为翻译稿，请译者投稿时附上原文及作者授权证明。

5. 本评论欢迎专稿专投，反对一稿多发。

三、格式体例

1. 来稿请在正文前加列“目次”、“摘要”和“关键词”，无需英文标题和英文摘要。“摘要”为稿件核心观点的凝练，字数不超过300字。关键词不超过5个。

2. 来稿须符合学术规范，注释体例参照《法学研究》。注释是否符合本评论体例不影响稿件评价，但注释是否符合学术规范将影响稿件采用。

四、评审规则

为公正选稿,本评论实行匿名三审制。为加快稿件处理速度,本评论实行快速审稿和审稿意见及时反馈制度。自投稿起一个月内未获任何通知,请作者主动联系编辑部,以免遗漏或耽误稿件。

五、投稿方式

1. 本评论工作邮箱:sysuyouthlaw@163.com。来稿请勿发送包括主编在内的任何工作人员。

2. 投稿请以 Word 文档形式以附件发送。Word 文档标题只须填写论文题目,无须填写作者信息,Word 正文内亦无须包含任何作者个人信息,保证编辑匿名审稿。

3. 作者个人信息以及论文题目请在邮件正文中列明,建议投稿邮件标题格式为"投稿+作者姓名+论文题目",方便编辑部准确回复邮件。

六、特别提醒

本评论不以任何形式向投稿者收取审稿费、版面费等费用,也从未授权任何机构或个人代理投稿事宜。所有投稿事宜仅在工作邮箱处理。未尽事宜,请直接与本评论编辑部工作邮箱联系。

(更多信息可关注本评论微信"SYSU 青年法律评论",微信号为 sysuyouthlaw,或查阅中山大学法学院官网 http://law.sysu.edu.cn/)

《中山大学青年法律评论》编辑部

2019 年 7 月

图书在版编目(CIP)数据

中山大学青年法律评论. 第4卷 /《中山大学青年法律评论》编辑部组编 ; 巢志雄主编. -- 北京 : 法律出版社, 2019
ISBN 978-7-5197-3687-3

Ⅰ. ①中… Ⅱ. ①中… ②巢… Ⅲ. ①法律-文集 Ⅳ. ①D9-53

中国版本图书馆CIP数据核字(2019)第151102号

中山大学青年法律评论(第4卷)
ZHONGSHAN DAXUE QINGNIAN FALÜ PINGLUN (DI 4 JUAN)

《中山大学青年法律评论》编辑部 组编
巢志雄 主编
彭箫剑 执行主编

责任编辑 王 珊
装帧设计 臧晓飞

出版 法律出版社
总发行 中国法律图书有限公司
经销 新华书店
印刷 北京虎彩文化传播有限公司
责任校对 郭艳萍
责任印制 陶 松

编辑统筹 学术·对外出版分社
开本 710毫米×1000毫米 1/16
印张 21.5
字数 344千
版本 2019年10月第1版
印次 2019年10月第1次印刷

法律出版社/北京市丰台区莲花池西里7号(100073)
网址/www.lawpress.com.cn
投稿邮箱/info@lawpress.com.cn
举报维权邮箱/jbwq@lawpress.com.cn
销售热线/400-660-8393
咨询电话/010-63939796

中国法律图书有限公司/北京市丰台区莲花池西里7号(100073)
全国各地中法图分、子公司销售电话:
统一销售客服/400-660-8393/6393
第一法律书店/010-83938432/8433　西安分公司/029-85330678　重庆分公司/023-67453036
上海分公司/021-62071639/1636　深圳分公司/0755-83072995

书号:ISBN 978-7-5197-3687-3
定价:88.00元